Anarchy and the Kingdom of God

I0085890

ORTHODOX CHRISTIANITY AND CONTEMPORARY THOUGHT

Aristotle Papanikolau and Ashley M. Purpura, series editors

This series consists of books that seek to bring Orthodox Christianity into an engagement with contemporary forms of thought. Its goal is to promote (1) historical studies in Orthodox Christianity that are interdisciplinary, employ a variety of methods, and speak to contemporary issues; and (2) constructive theological arguments in conversation with patristic sources and that focus on contemporary questions ranging from the traditional theological and philosophical themes of God and human identity to cultural, political, economic, and ethical concerns. The books in the series explore both the relevancy of Orthodox Christianity to contemporary challenges and the impact of contemporary modes of thought on Orthodox self-understandings.

ANARCHY AND THE KINGDOM OF GOD

From Eschatology to Orthodox Political Theology and Back

DAVOR DŽALTO

FORDHAM UNIVERSITY PRESS
New York • 2021

Copyright © 2021 Davor Džalto

All rights reserved. No part of this publication may be reproduced, stored in a retrieval system, or transmitted in any form or by any means—electronic, mechanical, photocopy, recording, or any other—except for brief quotations in printed reviews, without the prior permission of the publisher.

Fordham University Press has no responsibility for the persistence or accuracy of URLs for external or third-party Internet websites referred to in this publication and does not guarantee that any content on such websites is, or will remain, accurate or appropriate.

Fordham University Press also publishes its books in a variety of electronic formats. Some content that appears in print may not be available in electronic books.

Visit us online at www.fordhampress.com.

Library of Congress Cataloging-in-Publication Data

Names: Džalto, Davor, 1980– author.
Title: Anarchy and the kingdom of God : from eschatology to orthodox
   political theology and back / Davor Džalto.
Description: First edition. | New York : Fordham University Press, [2021] |
   Series: Orthodox Christianity and contemporary thought | Includes
   bibliographical references and index.
Identifiers: LCCN 2021014278 | ISBN 9780823294381 (hardback) | ISBN
   9780823294398 (paperback) | ISBN 9780823294404 (epub)
Subjects: LCSH: Christianity and politics—Orthodox Eastern Church. |
   Liberty—Religious aspects—Orthodox Eastern Church.
Classification: LCC BX342.9.P64 D93 2021 | DDC 261.7—dc23
LC record available at https://lccn.loc.gov/2021014278
Printed in the United States of America

23 22 21   5 4 3 2 1

First edition

Dedicated to all those who suffer from injustice, oppression,
and the oppressors of this world.
—D. Dž.

CONTENTS

ANARCHY AND THE KINGDOM OF GOD

INTRODUCTION

When love is not self-seeking,
When you love somebody without any logic—that is true love.
That is also true freedom. That is why I am a Christian.

—Patriarch Pavle of Serbia

The main purpose of this book is to discuss the socio-political sphere from a theological point of view.

To that end, first part of the book discusses traditional Orthodox Christian theological approaches to the socio-political sphere (and some of their Western counterparts). The second part offers a theological articulation of the socio-political sphere based on some of the central aspects of the Orthodox Christian faith.

It is the primary assertion of this book that some kind of "anarchist" approach to the sphere of the political is the only approach that is consistent with the basic presuppositions of Orthodox Christian theology. However, this book acknowledges that, from an Orthodox Christian perspective, no social or political order (or lack thereof) will ever be able to represent an "ideal" form of interhuman relations, since, from the Christian point of view, the only "ideal" form of human existence is the Kingdom of God as an eschatological reality. This (fully manifested) Kingdom cannot be established within the boundaries of the world we live in and in the historical process as we know it. In history, we can only have a glimpse of it, as "in a mirror, darkly."

The issue of Orthodox political theology is situated here within the broader context of (Orthodox) Christian ontology and anthropology, as a backdrop for theological reflection upon the socio-political sphere—hence the subtitle: "From Eschatology to Orthodox Political Theology and Back." What this approach implies is that eschatology *is* Christian *ontology* (although a "deontologized" "ontology"), and the eschaton the criterion of *truth*.

1

The eschaton is both "place" and "time" (understood outside their ordinary meanings) where *true* (and, in this sense, also the "last") *things* appear. The eschatological mode of existence is, therefore, the manifestation of the *truthfulness* of all particular beings.

The history of (Orthodox) Christian reflections upon the political is complex and, more often than not, inconsistent and even paradoxical. Over the past two millennia, many Christian authors and church representatives have addressed social and political issues in a variety of ways. From the early days of Christianity to contemporary times, a whole range of not only different but even mutually exclusive positions have been taken by Christian authors about the function, meaning, and value of particular socio-political institutions and the socio-political sphere as a whole. Disagreements exist not only as to the desirable character of Orthodox political theology, but also as to the very need for such theology. Some argue, for instance, that it is necessary to formulate theological positions (whatever those positions may be) vis-à-vis the political, while others would deny the very need for a more elaborate Orthodox Christian theology of the political, or even the possibility of such theology.

The fact that there are conflicting and even mutually exclusive approaches to the socio-political sphere reflects, in my view, a more basic feature of the whole enterprise. It seems that there is something problematic about the theological articulation of the socio-political sphere at a very fundamental level. As will become apparent in the following chapters, I assume, in my own theological approach to the sphere of the political, that there is a profound tension between, on the one side, Christian faith and the Church,[1] and, on the other side, the sphere of the political. By the "sphere of the political," I mean here primarily the sphere of the institutional exercise of power, which produces, perpetuates or changes the socio-political "order" (e.g., through the "legal use of force," as it were, within the traditional state competences). However, other factors and institutions also belong to the "sphere of the political"—in fact, all of those, formal or informal, power agents, including those entities that have assumed many roles and competences that were traditionally reserved for the state (such as international military or business organizations, for instance).

The final basic presumption from which I depart in my analysis of the socio-political sphere is that the Church and Christian theology have a responsibility to articulate the position and meaning of this sphere, not for the sake of creating a separate ("Christian") social or political program, let alone another ideology, but for the sake of *living* Christian faith in concrete historical, cultural, and social contexts.

The book, therefore, aims more specifically at (1) revisiting the dominant and traditional (Orthodox) approaches to the sphere of the political; (2) deconstructing them from the point of view of some of the basic elements of the Orthodox Christian faith; and (3) advancing an alternative Orthodox theological approach to the socio-political, which would be consistent with Orthodox Christian ontology and anthropology; and on that basis (4) reflecting upon the ways and the extent to which such an approach can be applied in concrete social and political contexts, when dealing with many practical issues.

The relationship between Christianity and the realm of the socio-political seems to be a deep one. This is not only because many Christians feel it necessary to try to articulate certain social, political, and ethical issues from the point of view of their faith and teachings of the church and particular church authorities; in fact, the very theological language that early Christian authors employed (including in the books of the New Testament) makes use of the political and even military vocabulary. One comes across the concepts of "king," "kingdom," "master," "rule," "armor," "shield," "law," and so forth, not only in the contexts where specifically political or military issues are addressed, but also in the context of the exegesis of basic theological (faith-related) issues. This marks the beginning of a long history of *politicized* theological language and political theologies that would often confuse the realm of God and His "Kingdom" with the realm of political leaders ("Caesars") and their power.

The need to somehow understand the social and historical contexts in which Christians lived, and the need to relate those contexts to their broader eschatological and existential concerns, gave birth to many theologies that used theological vocabulary to rationalize and justify the socio-political reality around them.

Already in the first centuries of the Christian era, some authors offered a rationale according to which the empire (at that time still predominantly polytheistic) acquired a certain metaphysical significance, becoming an important, if not indispensable, element in the general scheme of salvation. From this time on, the temptation of merging these two spheres—the sphere of Christian faith (with its focus on eschatological reality, as a different mode of existence) and the socio-political sphere (with its focus on power, control, and domination as its inherent elements)—or even substituting one with the other, remains one of the greatest challenges for all political theologies. This has, as a result, given birth to the series of political theologies that function as useful political ideologies or, sometimes, even as propaganda instruments.

It is this confusion and the insistence of many Christian (including Orthodox Christian) authors in rationalizing and justifying power structures that form the primary reasons for writing this book. It seems important to me to draw attention to the imminent danger of such theological discourses, to deconstruct the mechanisms of rationalization and justification of power systems that theologians have traditionally been employing, and to show why these mechanisms, and the theologies based on them, are not compatible with some of the basic aspects of Orthodox Christian faith.

Another temptation, which this book tries to avoid, is a radical separation between the "world" and the "Church," or turning the Church (and Christian faith) into some kind of parallel reality that forms a world unto itself, disentangled from the rest of creation, its beauties and its suffering. "Being in the world" but "not of the world," for the purpose of changing the world, enabling it to conform to its eschatological face, is, in my view, one of the best ways to think of the mission of the Church.

With this book I also want to affirm an "anarchist" theological approach as, in my view, the only approach to the socio-political sphere that is consistent (to the extent that a *Christian* political philosophy can be consistent) with the basic aspects of the Christian faith and its focus on a new mode of existence. It is important to note at the very beginning that, in spite of many similarities, a "theological anarchist" approach to the sphere of the political is in some basic aspects different from nontheological anarchist philosophies. "Christian anarchism," in my view, should never lose sight of the Kingdom of God and should never make the socio-political institutions and processes the only or the central focus. In this, Orthodox Christian "anarchist" political theology should be understood more as a critical position vis-à-vis various power agents rather than as an attempt to construct coherent and/or normative theoretical models or offer practical solutions that would be universally applicable. The focus here is on the human person rather than on the affirmation of apersonal socio-political models and institutions. From this particular perspective, which is elaborated upon later on, the roots of power structures and oppression that manifest themselves in history are not in the political but in the existential realm. Therefore, "anarchism" of Orthodox Christian political theology is just a consequential application, in the sphere of the socio-political, of broader (Orthodox) Christian metaphysical concerns.

In my analysis, I will refer to various authors and tendencies in the Orthodox tradition (which I, broadly and somewhat provocatively, call "proto-anarchist") who have understood the socio-political sphere in a way that is different from the theological (and political-philosophical) mainstream. These authors and particular phenomena from Christian history are used to demonstrate the existence and continuity of ideas and practices from the earliest period of Christianity—the kind of ideas and practices that I find comparable, close, or, sometimes, virtually identical to the "anarchist" approach as I understand it. This alternative reading of the tradition of Orthodox Christian political theology may help us grasp a different understanding of what an *authentic* Orthodox Christian approach to the socio-political sphere can look like.

It is my conviction that at the very heart of (Orthodox) Christian faith lies nothing other than the trust and hope that freedom and love constitute the foundations of the *real* eschatological existence. This will be the central leitmotif throughout this study. Freedom, love, and creativity represent, in my view, the "building blocks" of Orthodox Christian anthropology, which is the reason why this anthropology is at odds with the logic of "this world." The reader should be ready to embrace this tension and to accept the paradoxical position of Christian faith within the boundaries of "this world." Those who expect simple answers or recipes for what is "right" and what is "wrong," or how to build a harmonious, rational, and efficient sociopolitical whole—or a coherent and comforting (theological) narrative about that *clockwork orange* world—will certainly be disappointed. I suggest they stop reading this book immediately and take Morpheus's blue pill. This book is for those who are ready to see what's behind both of those pills, but who want, ultimately, to reject them both and instead (to paraphrase Slavoj Žižek) take a "third" (or fourth) pill.

ANARCHISM AND (ORTHODOX) CHRISTIANITY: AN (UN)NATURAL ALLIANCE?

The Kingdom of God is anarchy.

—Nikolai Berdyaev

Anarchism and Christianity (especially Orthodox Christianity) represent in the eyes of many two very different and even opposite sets of teachings and practices. "Is it not clear," some may ask, "that Christianity, like many other religions, affirms existing social and state institutions, defends a hierarchically organized society, and advocates certain (oppressive) ethical norms, while promoting a supreme deity that people should be afraid of?" "In contrast to that," they may continue, "is it not clear that anarchism stands for exactly the opposite ideas and values, such as dismantling the state apparatus, a 'horizontal' organization of society, and opposition to all authority and power imposed from 'above'?" "Is it not the case," they may still insist, "that the phrase 'without god or master' has been the dominant motto of anarchists since the late nineteenth century?" "Having all of this in mind," they may conclude, "how can there be a meaningful alliance between anarchism and Christianity, let alone 'Orthodox Christian anarchism'?" This is likely to be heard as part of the dominant, public perception of both Christianity and anarchism. However, as with all dominant, generally accepted (public) perceptions, it is likely to be wrong on multiple levels.

The concept of "anarchism" shares the (unfortunate) destiny of many other concepts from the political vocabulary. Just like "democracy," "liberalism," "capitalism," or "communism," "anarchism" has been used (and misused) in a variety of ways. As a result, it is first necessary to define what is meant by the word "anarchism."

The first hurdle (which is also its greatest advantage) is that anarchism has never been a unified, organized movement, or a coherent teaching. The second, even bigger difficulty is that the concept has been used both in a derogatory sense (by its opponents) and affirmatively (by its proponents). Many understand this concept as a synonym for "chaos": For example, advocates of various social "orders" that affirm some kind of hierarchy and subordination are eager to interpret "anarchy" as "chaos." As a result, this is how the word has sometimes been interpreted.[1] This is, of course, not how the "classical" anarchist authors, such as William Godwin (1756–1836), Pierre-Joseph Proudhon (1809–65) or Peter Kropotkin (1842–1921), understood the concept. *Anarchy*, Proudhon would argue, should be identified with *order*,[2] but a different kind of order.

However, it is not only the political opponents, usually on the "right," who have had issues with anarchism. The nineteenth century split on the "left," between Karl Marx and Michael Bakunin, was, at its core, also a split between the affirmation of the "statist left" and the "libertarian" (or anarchist) left. Bakunin correctly perceived that merely substituting one ruling class with another one would not lead to a free and more equal society.[3] Over the course of the last decades of the nineteenth and early decades of the twentieth century, anarchists were perceived as a danger to the dominant systems of power, both in the West and in the Soviet Union, and were treated with exemplary brutality.[4] As a result, both the (mainstream) "right" and the (mainstream) "left" have contributed to the defamation of anarchism over the course of the twentieth century.

Yet another difficulty with the term "anarchism" lies with the many violent groups, whose actions are closer to terrorism than to any constructive expression of political goals, that are labeled (by others, or sometimes even themselves) as "anarchists." This is also not a new phenomenon. Already in the nineteenth century, Octave Mirbeau wrote that there are those who call themselves "anarchists" although their acts are such that "a mortal enemy of anarchism could not have done better."[5] This continues to be true in many areas of social and political life. However, despite all these obstacles, I do not want to dismiss the concept of anarchism for a "milder" concept (such as "democratic socialism," for instance) simply to please the ears of those who subscribe to the dominant ideological discourse, which has shifted so far to the (corporate-led) "right" that even the word "socialism" has become in many countries too radical to be heard in the mainstream media (let alone among policymakers) in a positive context. I think that the concept of anarchism should be reaffirmed in opposition to the ideological blackmail that comes from many different directions, ranging from the standard business-ideology accusations against everything that has a humane dimension to it, to the so-called "leftist" proponents of the oppressive ideology of political correctness that cultivate a similar hatred for any real, meaningful, and free interaction among human beings.

My understanding of anarchism as a political philosophy follows some of the main principles that can be derived based on what most of the anarchist "schools" have shared over the past two centuries or so. Noam Chomsky summarized these core principles in the following description of anarchism as a *tendency*, something

> that is suspicious and skeptical of domination, authority, and hierarchy. It seeks structures of hierarchy and domination in human life over the whole range, extending from, say, patriarchal families to, say, imperial systems, and it asks whether those systems are justified. . . . Their authority is not self-justifying. . . . And, as I understand it, anarchy is just that tendency. It takes different forms at different times.[6]

Following this understanding of anarchism, I use the term to describe the *tendency* (not a fixed, coherent, or universally applicable set of teachings or practices) that we can find in various historical periods that is critical of power structures and the exercise of power and authority, and that seeks to dismantle those structures whenever their existence cannot be justified, and to resist the illegitimate exercise of power across the whole range of social networks. To again quote from Chomsky:

> At every stage of history our concern must be to dismantle those forms of authority and oppression that survive from an era when they might have been justified in terms of the need for security or survival or economic development, but that now contribute to—rather than alleviate—material and cultural deficit. If so, there will be no doctrine of social change fixed for the present and future, not even, necessarily, a specific and unchanging concept of the goals towards which social change should tend.[7]

One can note that such a definition of "anarchism" is a "negative" one—it says more about what anarchism and anarchists are against rather than what they *positively* propose for organizing a society (locally and globally) on anarchist principles. I side with this understanding of anarchism precisely because of its "incompleteness" or "open-endedness."

Many anarchists, of course, do offer more elaborate proposals for what an "ideal" anarchist society might look like. Anarchy can be described, for instance, as "a form of political organization in which (1) all members may participate directly in the collective and the deliberative decision-making process, through which (2) they seek consensus."[8] Some would advocate dismantling of state structures as either a necessary step or the chief goal, which brings about a classless commune with direct and communal decision-making.[9] Others advance social models that are opposite to the socialist/communal anarchy, in which there should be a high degree of mutual support, cooperation, and solidarity (although this is a minority or even marginal position), proposing instead an "egotistic" version of anarchy, where everyone affirms their individual freedoms alone, cooperating with others only when necessary and when mutually beneficial.[10]

Describing anarchism (especially "theological anarchism," which is explained in more detail later on) as a tendency, with certain ideas and values at its core, but without ready-made solutions and fixed models (whether they be syndicalist, communal, or something else), reveals a precaution in order to avoid turning a political philosophy that advances freedom, human creativity, and dignity into yet another ideology with a coercive potential once it comes up with a certain abstract ("ideal") model that should then automatically be applied, irrespectively of social complexities and cultural differences in each given context. For instance, it has been shown that the elimination of traditional institutional power structures (e.g., states) does not necessarily or automatically lead to a society where there is no oppression or exercise of authority. Old-fashioned power structures can easily be replaced by new ones, and formal institutions can easily be substituted by informal power networks.[11] That means that if we are serious about the affirmation of human freedom against all types of oppression, we should not target only one or certain types of power structures, but, as a matter of principle, all types of domination and oppression, no matter what form they may historically take. Focusing only on one type of power structures, even if those power structures are the most visible or most troubling in the present time, may lead to their dismantling in the future, but that does not mean that new forms of oppression and domination (maybe even more harmful to human freedom and dignity) will not appear, to which those who are too preoccupied with fixed "enemies" or fixed ("ideal") models for alternative social organization will be blind.

Another reason why I chose the *via negativa* approach in saying what anarchism means for me, especially in the context discussed in this book, is that I see it as the best way in which an Orthodox Christian approach to the political sphere can be conceptually expressed. Let me explore this point more closely.

As it will become clear from the analysis presented later on, I think that the Orthodox Christian vision of the human being leads to a negative attitude toward any affirmation of violence and oppression, whether that violence and oppression (as manifestations of power) come from institutions, other human beings or, for that matter, our own being. The consequence of this is that some kind of *anarchism* is the only consistent expression of Orthodox political theology. However, unlike in many anarchist schools that propose concrete theories for how to achieve an "ideal" anarchist society (or even only a *better* one) and how to order it, an Orthodox theological approach to the sphere of the socio-political needs to refuse to offer such an account. This is an important distinction between anarchism as a (non-Christian, secular) political philosophy and "anarchism" as Orthodox political theology. The former has the privilege of reflecting upon and proposing conceptually coherent, appealing, practical, and even "ideal" social models; it can even promote certain forms of political organization as the best possible ones, believing that in such and such system, human freedom will finally be affirmed to the highest possible degree, and oppression erased or reduced to the absolute minimum. The latter, however, is primarily concerned with the Kingdom of God as eschatological reality, which renders (for the reasons explained later in this study) the entire political sphere—no matter what form—as problematic in principle. The strictly theological foundations of the (theological) argument on the socio-political sphere prevents Christians from apprising any form of government as "good" or "just" per se, let alone "ideal."

One should also make here a clear distinction between principles on the one side, and strategies and tactics on the other. Although the basic principles of a Christian theological approach to the political (Orthodox Christian "anarchism") outlined here are different from secular anarchist engagements with the sphere of the political (in that the latter does not take into account the eschaton and therefore does not need to reject the possibility, even if only as a theoretical speculation, of establishing a free and just society within the confines of history, which would be, for instance, in full accordance with human nature), at the level of actual strategies/tactics these two can be similar. The major difference between many of the (secular) anarchist political philosophies and a Christian theological approach to the political is the difference in goals and priorities. For the majority of anarchists as well as other (secular) political thinkers, the goal of a political philosophy and the practice based on or led by that philosophy is the ordering of a society, providing of security, stability, etc. In contrast to that, a Christian "anarchist," looking upon the socio-political from a theological perspective, is primarily interested in the new mode of existence, and the communion with God and the rest of creatures in the eschatological reality of the Kingdom of God. Social and political structures as such do not have, from this perspective, any real meaning or significance per se. They are a "necessary evil," which may be changed but can never be turned into something immanently *good* or *just*, something that would satisfy Christian eschatological maximalism. However, this does not mean that both a Christian and a (secular) anarchist cannot act in the same or similar fashion in concrete situations, responding to concrete socio-political challenges while, at the same time, continuing to practice their different (metaphysical) orientations. By deconstructing power structures, showing care for other human beings, being compassionate, affirming human freedom, helping the poor and needy, taking care of the environment, etc., one can practice one's *belief* that human social and biological existence is all that there is to human existence, the ultimate horizon of being, or, on the contrary, one can practice one's belief that human existence is rooted in the eschaton, and that the way we relate to other human beings in history (and society) tells something about who we are, eschatologically speaking.

From what has been said so far, one can also conclude that my theological approach to the socio-political sphere is different from some *religious* or *Christian* anarchist political philosophies/theologies. Many theologians (of different denominations) have been starting from some Christian ideas or Biblical texts in order to formulate a vision of society that would, in history, bring about a *Christian society*, based on freedom and justice.[12] My approach differs from these in that I do not think that such "Christian" (let alone "perfect Christian") societies are possible within the boundaries of "this world." In that, my argument is closer to Jacques Ellul's. For the reasons that have to do with our very existence—upon which political structures rest—the (Orthodox) Christian understanding of "justice" and "ideal" interhuman relationships is eschatologically rooted. From this perspective, freedom and love, as well as justice, as ontological categories, can never fully materialize in history. This means that within the boundaries of "this world," one will always need to deal with power dynamics, various exercises of authority and domination. The forms may change—hence the need for criticizing them in principle, and developing concrete strategies in each period to cope with them. However, Christians should never mistake the goals, concerns, and structures that belong to "this world" with the real goal of Christian life—new creation and communion with God and the entirety of creation.

The concept of "justifiable" (or "legitimate") exercise of power, mentioned above in the context of determining the meaning of the concept of anarchism, still requires some clarification. Although one should always be skeptical when it comes to the exercise of authority and violence, and one should especially be careful when violence comes from social institutions claiming that what they do is "legal" and (therefore) "good" (thus, by default, assuming also the legitimacy of their actions), my position is that, in certain cases, acts of authority and even some violent acts can be justified on pragmatic grounds, and on the grounds of respect for another human being, his/her freedom and dignity. For instance, if you suddenly grab someone's hand and pull that person toward you, it is undoubtedly a violent act. However, it can be legitimized and justified if that act was an act that prevented an accident, in which a car might have hit that person. This act can be justified on the grounds that it saved the life and well-being of an individual. However, it still remains, essentially, a violent act, an exercise of power. Similarly, I perceive preventing someone from committing a murder or an act of torture, even if that act of prevention includes an act of violence, as another justifiable and legitimate exercise of power. Stopping, individually or collectively, that person from what they are doing or clearly intend to do would most probably include violence, an exercise of authority, but can be justified in those concrete cases on the basis of the protection of lives and well-being of other human beings. The point of both of these examples is that the exercise of power and authority is never self-evident, and should never be taken for granted. It should rather always be questioned, especially since we ordinarily deal with much more complex exercises of power and authority than the simple models I have used here. Sometimes the legitimacy of those acts can be demonstrated, based on the values of human freedom, life, dignity, and well-being; however, even then, these exercises of authority and power should be kept to the absolute minimum, should be questioned, and should take into account not only the well-being of those we try to protect, but also the well-being and dignity of those against whom the exercises of power is employed. In most of the cases, however, the legitimacy cannot be demonstrated, meaning that in these situations the exercises of power and power structures as such should be dismantled. However, even when these exercises of power and authority are justifiable (in the above-mentioned situations and contexts) they still should not be taken, from a Christian perspective, as something *good* and *just*, in themselves, but rather as the necessary evil that our existence in history compels us to do. "Justice" of this world, and the "well-being" in the world we live in, are not the same, often not even similar, and sometimes are even opposite to the Christian understanding of justice, or the "good" of eschatological existence. Confusing the two, or giving (legal, social-political) "justice" a theological affirmation, has been, historically, one of the greatest sources of oppression.

This means that the concept of "anarchism" can be understood in a couple of interrelated and yet distinct ways.

The first one is the concept of "anarchy/anarchism" used to denote concrete anarchist schools and/or political philosophies, such as "classical" anarchist authors and contemporary approaches that build directly on them. In this case, one can, as an anarchist, advocate various models of social organization (e.g., anarcho-communism) as those toward which one or all societies on this planet should strive for. An antistatist position for instance can be advocated in this context as the minimal requirement for someone to be an anarchist (of a certain kind).

The second meaning of "anarchism" (as a tendency) follows the logic that can be derived (abstracted) from various "classical" anarchist schools in their approaches to advocating various models and concrete strategies as to how to come to a more just, equal, and humane society. In this sense "anarchism" means a tendency (following the definition provided above) that is critical of every exercise of power, no matter what form. It seeks to detect them, critically examine them, and dismantle them whenever their legitimacy cannot be shown. One who defines him/herself as an anarchist in this sense can rely, in concrete situations, on the same or similar models as anarchists from the first category—but as a concrete strategy one uses under concrete circumstances, not as the ultimate goal. Taking this approach, one in principle does not argue for a specific, *best* or *universal*

model of organizing an "anarchist society," but focuses instead on challenging, both in theory and in practice, concrete cases of oppression and
power structures in order to reduce the amount of oppression, change the
(oppressive) power dynamics, and arrive at a more just and free social order. The focus on freedom and the critical stance toward power structures
and the exercise of authority as the guiding principles has led, historically,
many anarchists to targeting specifically the most oppressive institutions
and phenomena of their time, such as the state, economic inequality, and
exploitation in the name of more communitarian ways of organizing human
society.

Finally, in the third case we deal with a "theological anarchism," which
implies both a critical approach to power structures and oppression, as well
as an eschatological orientation. This skepticism toward power structures
and oppression (both concrete manifestations of power and oppression
and in principle) comes as a result of Christian belief in human freedom,
love, and creativity primarily as existential realities, which are then also
manifested, to various degrees, in social and political realms. This means
that a "theological anarchist," at the level of concrete strategies in concrete situations, can employ some of the non-Christian anarchist models
or actions aimed at the transformation of local or global polities into
more just, humane, and free communities. However, a Christian should
never confuse any concrete social organization, theoretical model, or practical strategy with the Kingdom of God as eschatological reality, or glorify it. Looking from a metahistorical perspective, "theological anarchism"
is skeptical toward the socio-political sphere as such, as this sphere is the
result of our existence in history and in "this world," the existence that
needs to be transfigured to conform to the logic of free eschatological
existence.

I also want to say something about why anarchist thinking (and acting) is
still very much relevant and needed. (By *anarchist* thinking and acting
I do not mean now specifically a Christian "theological anarchism" with
its metaphysical/eschatological concerns, but anarchism as a as a tendency
manifested both in political philosophy and political practice—which is
captured in the second meaning of the term explained above.)

From the previous description of anarchism, one can easily see what is
problematic about anarchism in every given historical period, and why this
tendency (although it can be very broad and inclusive) has not managed

to establish itself as the mainstream. Anarchism is supposed to challenge power structures and dominant ideological narratives in each society, and since oppressive power structures of various kinds (from patriarchal families, autocracies, and oligarchies to modern plutocracies, corporate dictatorships, "liberal" totalitarianism, or oppressive dominant ethical systems) remain the dominant factors shaping the socio-political reality, authentic anarchism remains an opponent to all repressive power agents and narratives, representing an alternative strategy of dealing with the social and political issues. The value and strength of anarchism as a tendency is that it does not simply prescribe ready-made solutions and definite answers, but points to the values and principles that should be implemented differently in different places and at different times.

Many criticize anarchism as a utopian philosophy that may inspire young people before they become *serious* and realize what the "real world" looks like. Taking the world "seriously" and "responsibly" should, in this logic, result in finding one's place within the existing (power) structures in each given social context, then conforming to those structures, absorbing the dominant ideology that rationalizes both them and one's place within them.

To this kind of criticism (which comes from a very conservative perspective, although many who exercise it would certainly describe themselves as "liberals") one may reply that such an ideological position is, in fact, very irresponsible and ethically highly problematic. The same logic could have been employed (and has been employed) in defending slavery (both ancient and modern), subordination of women, racism, nationalism (even Nazism), exploitation of the workforce or any other type of socio-political "normality" in a given society and historical period, which has come as a reflection of the dominant power structures and their ideological narratives. Attempts to question these "normalities," expose them as *insanities*, and contribute to their deconstruction should not be called "childish" but should rather be acknowledged as attempts that affirm human dignity and freedom against various types of oppression and illegitimate exercise of power. Such attempts have, in fact, won many important historical battles in making our societies more decent places to live in. As a tendency that questions power structures, seeking to deconstruct (i.e., expose and dismantle) them and eliminate their exercise of power and domination, anarchism is a vital tendency in human history, which targets one of the most persistent and most problematic phenomena in human history—the quest for power and domination. As such, the anarchist critique has to be taken into consideration if we do not want to live in savagery, where the rules are defined by the one with a longer stick (or by higher figures in a bank account, as its modern equivalent).

There is also another type of criticism against anarchism in the contemporary world, a criticism that structurally is not very different from the previous one. If anarchism is primarily about freedom, justice, and, consequently, a more democratic society, why do we need anarchism in a situation in which we already have (at least in the "Western" or "free" world) advanced democracies that are gradually perfecting our freedoms and rights? Are we not already on the "right track," with "liberal democracy" gradually defeating authoritarian tendencies, bringing the light of political freedom, justice, and democracy to almost all of the "dark corners" of the world?

There are many reasons to doubt such a fundamentally confused picture, which simply solidifies the existing social order and the power of those who already have it. This is done based on the claim (sometimes implicitly assumed) that what we have now is the best possible track that, although it may not be perfect, or one-hundred-percent realized in practice, leads to a better future, at least more than any other (uncertain) track could possibly offer. This argument resembles the old Soviet rationale for (their interpretation of) communism as maybe not yet one-hundred-percent perfect or fully achieved, but as a tendency that was certainly on the right track toward the promised future communist paradise. Both of these claims represent fundamentalist ideological positions. Let us, however, take a closer look at these claims.

The very idea that "liberal democracy" represents the utmost, the best if not yet perfect, form of social organization, and that there is a continuous evolution (at least in the "Western world") toward this form of government, turns out to be an effective ideological tool that, quite predictably, diminishes the development of a more democratic social organization. In its well-known form—Fukuyama's famous doctrine of "the end of history"—this idea reveals itself as an eloquently phrased ideological narrative that (conceptually) paved the way for the new phase of neoliberal (and anti-democratic) expansion at the end of the Cold War.

First of all, the very concept of liberal democracy and the way this concept is normally used nowadays is highly problematic. It is mostly used simply as a label to distinguish "us" and "our" ("Western," i.e., EU/US) policies and socio-economic models (that are superior by definition) from "them" and "their" ("authoritarian," "antidemocratic," and "retrograde") systems and values. This position is normally held even when those very policies and models that "we" practice, both domestically and internationally, are remarkably antiliberal and antidemocratic. By usurping the concepts of liberalism and democracy as a way of legitimizing the political system in the "West," the political and financial elites secure their privileges and the position of power. That this position of power is illegitimate and often extremely antidemocratic and even authoritarian can be seen from the scale of private-corporate interests—not those of the general population—being promoted and defended by the political establishment and the mainstream political parties, both on the "left" and on the "right." These privileges range from the monopoly or highly privileged market positions that many corporations have (together with the public money that, directly or indirectly, ends up in private pockets) to the scale and intensity of the media propaganda that is being employed to convince people that the corrupt political system and the rising inequality is exactly what democracy is supposed to look like. That is why today the "liberal democracy" phrase normally sounds more like a propaganda slogan advanced on behalf of highly corrupt and dysfunctional socio-political systems than a meaningful concept with a certain degree of descriptive power.

Moreover, contrary to the (essentially Hegelian) progressivist paradigm that has dominated the history of modernity, societies do not follow a linear path of development or progression. One and the same society can (and actually often does) progress in some areas while stagnating or regressing in others. For instance, certain ideals, values, and standards that have been achieved in the past can be diminished in other periods, which is precisely the kind of regression that many Western societies have been experiencing over the past decades. Once understood as the self-evident achievements of the human civilization (through, primarily, popular struggle), many of the human rights and freedoms, such as freedom of thought and speech, affordable education and healthcare for all citizens, social security, a high level of workers' rights, and so forth, have been dramatically diminished over the last couple of decades in the West. Fear, persecutions of those we do not like or whose ideas we do not agree with, the opening and maintaining of concentration camps and torture chambers (such as those of Guantanamo), and a perverted judicial system in which money and the dominant prejudices (often created by the mainstream media) matter more than justice and evidence, are among the "blessings" that characterize many *posttruth* "liberal democracies" nowadays. Many developed industrial societies are becoming societies of growing inequality, with a small, spectacularly rich and privileged oligarchy and a growing population of temporarily employed, unemployed, or even permanently unemployable citizens.[13]

This is to say that most of those societies are becoming increasingly remote from the ideals of transparent democracy, freedom, or justice. Imperfect democracies are becoming replaced by plutocracies. The "dedemocratization" process goes hand in hand with the rise of multinational corporations as the key economic and political factors on a global stage. These corporations, in symbiosis with state power and driven by the ruthless logic of profit, do not only destroy societies but even, at this point, threaten the survival of organized human life on this planet. Their *business interests*—taken to be a self-evident justification for all monstrosities done to protect and advance private profits—contribute to the rising tensions in the world, such as the increasing threat of a nuclear war, environmental destruction, and the extinction of thousands of species. Major multinational corporations have become more powerful than many states, capable of using their financial power to control state authorities, political parties, legislation, and the decision-making process. This tendency has become a constitutive part of the economic-political processes both in "developed" and in "developing" countries (although to various degrees). The corporate world exercises a real and often decisive influence on social and political life that affects the entire population, ranging from the type of labor legislation that is being implemented, to the media and war industry, environmental issues, etc. Because of these corporate interests, and simultaneously under the pressure of powerful "liberal" and "democratic" states, many countries are driven into debt-slavery, in which the system is set up in such a way that national wealth and resources are being sucked out of these countries and the population is turned into a precarious slave-labor force. Despite their enormous impact on the entire social sphere (and even the natural environment), corporate strategic plans, decision-making, and the election of companies' senior management remains completely beyond the reach of democratic control. In other words, the corporate sector has a real power over the lives of most citizens, but these citizens have almost no (legal) power over the international corporate world (which is the reason why this unofficial source of political power is often labeled as a "corporate dictatorship"[14]). Due to enormous wealth, often far surpassing the wealth of entire nations,[15] and frequent support from state structures, the corporate sector became very difficult to fight through the existing institutions of the system, such as old-fashioned national courts.

This is one point in which anarchy as a tendency may differ from some of the classical anarchist views of the state. Although traditionally the major source of power and authority, state power, while still very strong, becomes increasingly diminished by the private (corporate) dictatorships, and is sometimes turned into an office of those dictatorships. This is the reason why, in my view, the target of the anarchist critique in each given historical period should be the illegitimate, harmful power structures— including, but never limited to only the state, which is sometimes itself playing second fiddle to more dominant power structures. State structures, if democratized and used for the benefit of the population, can in fact be quite useful in fighting the power of unaccountable and undemocratic power structures, such as international corporate capital. This does not mean, of course, that state structures should be affirmed as such, only that, follow- ing the anarchist affirmation of human freedom, justice, and equality, one should not make certain positions (such as a traditional anarchist anti- state perspective) an abstract dogma that is blindly followed. One should (re)act in a real (and ever-changing) context, fighting what, in each given historical period and in each given society, is the greatest threat to human freedom and dignity.

At the end of this "why anarchism" chapter, I want to add yet another reason for affirming an anarchist approach, especially in the context of Christian political theology. In many countries with some kind of demo- cratic tradition and Western-style political organization, we witness the rise of right-wing (sometimes ultra-right) political options that use Christian- ity as an ideological pretext for their policies. They often advance concepts such as "Christian nation" or (in Europe) "Christian Europe," in contrast to the perceived threat coming from the "others" (i.e., Muslims, immigrants, etc.). This is, of course, the type of political manipulation that is very well known to any student of the history of political ideas, especially in the West. This requires a renewed effort in exposing the manipulatory and coercive nature of such narratives, demonstrating that such "Christian" politics have nothing to do with any meaningful form of Christianity, and that they, in fact, contradict Christianity in a variety of ways.

Orthodox Christian "anarchism" is based on the assumption that freedom is a fundamental constituent of the human being, that human beings have inalienable dignity and that each person represents an absolute value, making each one of us unique and uniquely precious from an eschatological point of view. That means that human beings should never be used for any other end (apart from the *apophatic end* of being human), no matter how noble or good that end may seem. That also means that the basis for questioning the legitimacy of power structures from an Orthodox perspective can be found in the belief in human freedom, both as an ontic truth and something that should be affirmed (although it can never be fully achieved) in the course of history. Here we come across the first paradox that characterizes "Orthodox Christian anarchism": the tension between the Christian understanding of freedom as an existential and eschatological reality and the particular manifestations of freedom in the world we live in, including human freedom in the socio-political realm.

From the point of view of Orthodox Christian theology, human freedom (in its eschatological and ontological meaning) *is* the basis of human existence. That means that a *being* is not meant first to exist and then to have the opportunity to be free (e.g., choose what and how to do), but that the very existence should be identical with freedom. The prototype of such an existence is found in the (incomprehensible) existence of the Triune God.

However, it is clear that such freedom is not something that can be achieved within the boundaries of the world we live in. This *metaphysical freedom* can fully be manifested only at the end of the world (history) as we know it. Within the boundaries of "this world," individual beings are determined by many factors, limited and confined in a variety of ways. These limitations are clearly discernable in human biological and socio-political dimensions of existence.

While advocating a maximization of human freedom as the maximization of opportunities for each human being to develop their creative potential, anarchism acknowledges the need for that freedom to be limited by the freedom of others. The principle that the boundary of my freedom is the freedom of others should be taken as a leading principle, although, of course, it has different manifestations and implementations in different social and historical contexts. This very tangible freedom that can be achieved within the boundaries of "this world" remains the guiding principle in the anarchist critique of authority, power structures, and the illegitimate exercise of violence.[16] In Orthodox "theological anarchism," this "limitation" is, actually, an opportunity. "Others," understood properly, and their freedom, do not necessarily pose a limitation on one's own freedom; rather, the presence of others affirms one's freedom, one's creative potential. Without communion with others, our freedom and our creative potentials cannot be realized.

Mainstream Orthodox Christianity, as it will become clear from the following chapters, has cultivated a certain understanding of the political sphere, which affirms a hierarchically organized society, with a vertical distribution of power, for a very long time. When viewed from this perspective, the idea that anarchism (in the above-described sense) is the only consequential Orthodox political theology might seem simply absurd.

However, it is not only mainstream Orthodox political theology that finds this alliance problematic or even impossible. The antichurch or antireligion position seems to be one of the very core principles that many anarchists have traditionally affirmed. Some of the most prominent authors in the history of anarchist thinking made anarchism almost a natural enemy of religion and Christianity. Already Proudhon claimed that *God was evil*.[17] We find probably the best example of a bitterly antichurch and antireligious anarchist in Michael Bakunin (1814–76).[18]

Looking from this perspective, one could assume that the gap between anarchism and Christianity, and especially anarchism and Orthodox Christianity, is unbridgeable. However, even Bakunin's passionate opposition to religion is understandable when one takes a closer look at the context of his critique. The oppression of the state apparatus (such as in the Russian czarist system or West European monarchies), supported by the ecclesial structures and solidified by an ideological narrative reliant upon specific interpretations of Christianity (affirming politically profitable concepts of obedience to power systems, traditionalism, skepticism to critical inquiry, etc.) was such that many honest and serious Christians could have shared Bakunin's frustration. Popular versions of Christianity (intertwined with mainstream ideological narratives), especially when combined with oppressive political structures, can and, in reality, often do result in narratives and policies that, under the pretext of "Christianity," affirm exactly the opposite views, values, and ideas of those that can be considered *authentically* Christian. This is the reason why, in the words of one of the most prominent contemporary Orthodox theologians, "Atheism sprang out of the very heart of the Church."[19] The church power structures that Bakunin criticized did function in a very oppressive and, we can add, anti-Christian way. In this sense, the values that are at the very core of Bakunin's critique (including even the concept of rebellion, as long as it is nonviolent), although formally antireligious, appear, in fact, as something that Christians can and, I think, should be very sympathetic to under the same or similar circumstances.

In addition to this, one should also bear in mind that Bakunin belongs to the age of positivism, a time when human freedom was sought in the rejection of all "irrationalities," when authority, obedience, and ignorance were taken by many as the most profound characteristics of all religions and religious systems. Due to the social context out of which Bakunin came, his rebellion against the state and religious authorities and his attack on faith in the name of freedom, science, and rationality appear in a different light.

All of this is, however, hardly a critique of Christianity. In fact, had Bakunin had an interest in the Christian tradition and the patience to explore theology much more closely, he might have appreciated some of the values and ideas from the Christian tradition—values and ideas that are very compatible with the main elements of his own argument, such as the love of freedom. Given the historical context and the way in which the ecclesiastical structures functioned in the late Russian Empire, the rebellion against them was a meaningful position that both nonbelieving anarchists and believing Orthodox Christians could take. One should always keep in mind that most of the historical manifestations of Christianity have rarely been helpful in an individual's attempt to embrace and understand Christianity. If undertaking an honest pursuit of freedom, while looking, at the same time, at the historical and institutional manifestations of Christianity, one can easily end up in atheism—and this has often been the case. However, to reject Christianity because of oppressive church and political power structures—structures that sharply deviate from Christianity—seems to me to be as sensible as rejecting *leftist* ideas because there was Stalin and there were the Bolsheviks. It is the same paradoxical logic that is at work when people reject democracy as such because some Western countries, under the slogan of "bringing democracy," launch offensive military campaigns to occupy other countries and exploit their energy resources. In all of these cases, particular ideas are rejected because of something that is, in reality, opposite to the original intent of the ideas.

If one wants to take the anarchist critique seriously, one needs to take into account the distinction between, on the one hand, the institutional church, which often functions as another power agent in this world, and, on the other hand, the eschatologically oriented Church and Christianity, which is based on freedom and love. This distinction is vital for the story of an "anarchist" Orthodox political theology, the story this book aspires to tell.

PART I

(Un)Orthodox Political Theologies

Histories

THE SYMPHONIA DOCTRINE:
INTRODUCTION

The history of the church is a history of art,
wars, conflict and the persecution of dissidents,
and to find in the history of Christianity
the true history of the Church with a capital "c,"
is an art form and it is not an easy task.

—Alexander V. Men

One concept dominates the history of Orthodox Christian thinking about the socio-political sphere: the concept of the so-called *Byzantine Symphony* (hereafter *symphonia*). This concept implies a "harmony"— close and even organic ties—between the state and the church, between state authorities (i.e., emperors) and church representatives (i.e., patriarchs of Constantinople). This "harmony" was meant to contribute to the well-being of the empire and the well-being of the Roman people (*populus*), satisfying both their "material" and "spiritual" needs. The model thus affirms the imperial office and strengthens, at the same time, the political and institutional role of the episcopate within the state.

The interesting thing about the phrase "Byzantine Symphony" is that both concepts, "Byzantium" and "Byzantine Symphony," represent later inventions that were applied to the state and its political ideals (symphonia) after the actual state had already ceased to exist.[1]

Nevertheless, many Orthodox Christians still consider the symphonia doctrine the most authoritative, if not the only *authentic* expression of Orthodox Christian political theology. Even many contemporary authors who admit that symphonia cannot be realized in the modern world, or that it cannot be realized at all, still hold it as a noble ideal and refer to it with certain nostalgia.[2]

As soon as one starts to think about the history of Orthodox Christian political theology, several issues arise that need to be clarified at the outset in order to avoid, or at least to minimize, later confusions.

First of all, particular concepts and theories found in historiography, meant to define "ideal" church-state relations (such as the symphonia concept) have been changing over the course of history. It may seem, from a modern (Western) perspective, that there was only one symphonia model of the church-state relations throughout the more-than-a-millennium-long history of the New Roman (Byzantine) Empire. However, as will become clear in the following chapters, there was never only one "ideal" model of church-state relations, only one symphonia. Instead, there have been many different models and ideas about the "proper" place of the state and the church in the "grand scheme" of history and salvation that have been collectively, and somewhat simplistically, named "symphonia." The concrete models of church-state relations have depended on the historical circumstances in which they were developed. Thus, the concept of symphonia appears as a highly dubious one, which is normally used in a vague, general sense to imply the (pre)supposed harmony between the church and the state. When this abstract, normative concept is used in a descriptive sense, it embraces many different, more specific models that have been developed. I will return to these nuances later in this chapter.

Excurse I

"ROMAN," "EASTERN," "BYZANTINE," OR "GREEK" EMPIRE?

An explanation is needed at this point as to the concept of the "Byzantine" Empire and its derivatives, such as "Byzantium" or "Byzantine" (or, in German, "Byzanz" and "byzantinisch"). I use this concept reluctantly, as I find it highly problematic for a couple of reasons. The first is the obvious one: the fact that the concept (although not the term) was invented and promoted by early modern scholarship after the political entity that this concept was meant to describe had already disappeared from the historical stage. As it is generally known, this concept was not used within the political entity that now bears its name to describe the state/empire. The inhabitants of this empire called themselves "Romans" (Greek: Ῥωμαῖοι; Latin: *Romani*), and their state the "Roman Empire" (Greek: Βασιλεία τῶν Ῥωμαίων; Latin: *Imperium Romanum*), "Roman Republic" (Greek: Πολιτεῖα τῶν Ῥωμαίων; Latin: *Res Publica Romana*) or just "Romania" (Greek: Ῥωμανία).

There is, however, another reason why this concept should be revisited. This reason has to do with the ideological baggage that the term "Byzantine" has traditionally carried, influencing the way in which many social and political phenomena that characterized this empire have been interpreted. One of the purposes of the concept (and that is how it is still used in many German sources) was to delegitimize the Eastern Empire as a continuation of the (classical) Roman Empire (which it was), and to, consequently, legitimize the *translatio imperii* to the German-dominated West, several centuries after the abdication of the last "legitimate" Western Roman emperor. This period between "the fall" of the empire in the West (476) and the advent of the "Holy Roman Empire" (Latin: *Sacrum Imperium Romanum*) is normally interpreted as the period of *transition*, during which the (late) "Roman Empire" in the East became medieval, Greek-dominated "Byzantium." Although the general approach of scholarly literature in interpreting the character, procedures, and culture of the Eastern empire has changed significantly over the course of the twentieth century, it is still not uncommon to find scholarly texts that repeat some of those stereotypes and prejudices (see Canning 2003, 1–15). It seems that the term "Byzantine" still obscures many important features of the empire that continued to be "classical (Roman)," much more than distinctly *medieval*, well into the history of this state.

Another dimension of the problem is that no one can say *when* this "Byzantium" came into existence as an entity distinct from the "Roman Empire." The reason is not the lack of documents but rather the artificial nature of the very attempt to separate the "Roman Empire" proper from the "Byzantine" ("not quite Roman") Empire. What should be taken as the basis for this demanding ideological project? Is it the foundation of the new imperial capital on the Bosporus? Or the abdication of the last emperor in the "West" (meaning Italy)? Is it the post-Justinian period? Or the time of Heraclius? Maybe the time of the Macedonian dynasty? The obvious problem is sometimes resolved by introducing a couple of steps that bridge the empire of "late antiquity" (still "Roman," but already somewhat *deficient* in its too "Eastern" character), and the predominantly Greek-speaking empire of the "late Byzantine" period, during which the (Greek) "East" was becoming more and more alienated from the (Latin, Germanic) "West."

In actual reality, there was no discontinuity between the "East" and the "classical" Roman times. The earliest meaningful date that can be taken as the end of the empire that drew its identity from the ancient *Res Publica* is the fall of Constantinople under the Crusaders in 1204. However, already Georgije Ostrogorski refers to this problem when he claims that a new, culturally distinct "Byzantine" identity had emerged during the reign of Heraclius (610–41), when the ancient *Roman* (predominantly Latin) empire had slowly begun to change into the medieval *Byzantine* (predominantly "Greek") state (see Ostrogorski 1998, 122). Ostrogorski lists many changes that had taken place in the seventh century that had contributed to a different administrative organization of the empire, changed cultural/ethnic landscape, etc.

The change was quite real, and one should not minimize it. However, the problem is that there never was a "transubstantiation" of the Roman into some other empire, but rather constant changes (of a greater or lesser significance) *within* the political entity that continued to exist based on the "classical" Roman political heritage. There is no doubt that the empire, with Constantinople as its capital, was very different in the thirteenth century compared to the empire, with the same capital, in the fifth century. However, the same is true of the ancient Roman empire in various periods of its history. The social and political landscape in the time of Augustus was very different from the one under Diocletian or Constantine. Even if we take the change under Heraclius (together with all the other elements that transformed the religious, cultural, and economic life of the empire in the previous centuries) as decisive, it is unclear why this emerging "medieval" state should be called "Byzantium," which implies a clear discontinuity with the Roman cultural and historical context out of which it, gradually, grew. Is the fact that this state, in the course of its history, became predominantly "Greek" (although this word meant something else for the "Byzantine" *Romans*) sufficient to treat it as a separate political entity, let alone to *alienate* it from its (archaic and classical) Roman heritage?

Of course, part of the problem is that the very concept of "state" as a concrete political phenomenon with a distinct "identity," whose existence simply stretches over a long period of time, is fictional. In any state, the actual people, territories, social, and cultural circumstances change all the time. Calling present-day Great Britain basically the same entity as the Kingdom of Great Britain of two hundred years ago would also be problematic if one is interested in concrete social realities. The same is true of most of the concepts that supposedly describe the existence of particular products of human culture over a long period of time. And yet, we use the concepts such as "Russian," "Persian" or "Roman" Empire partly because they allow us to discuss particular political entities and processes in a more efficient way, and partly because these concepts indicate the existence of certain continuities, in spite of many (sometimes dramatic) changes. If acceptance of dynamic growth is true of other cases, it should also be true of the "Roman Empire": a political entity that went through many significant changes, from the "classical" times of the "Republic" (which, let us not forget, also relied on the concept of *imperium*), via the "Principate" and "Dominate" through to the "Tetrarchy" and the "Vasileia."

One criterion that many would affirm as decisive and, for example, the reason why the France of 2017 and the France of the end of the eighteenth century (or, maybe, even before) are both political entities called "France" would be language. This, so the argument goes, cannot be applied to the "Greek" empire in the East since it, at one point, stopped using Latin as the language of its administration, and, the argument continues, a Roman empire without Latin is the same as France without the French language. What this logic overlooks is that our focus on language as a distinct criterion in defining political entities is the result of the Romanticist obsession with (one, codified, "proper") language and its almost (secular) mystical role in the process of (modern) nation-building. One (national) language as the common denominator of one (national) state and one national identity (which then stretches back in time as far as possible) is a typically modern construct that cannot be applied to earlier times, at least not without the use of many parentheses. (In addition to this, this logic is also oblivious of the fact that it was not uncommon to use a different language at modern European courts from the languages spoken by the majority of the population.)

To conclude: If we recognize, on the one hand, the need to point to the changing character of this empire that had Constantinople as its capital, and that, definitively, collapsed in 1453 (bearing in mind that this change was a long, gradual, and multifaceted process), and, on the other hand, the need to also acknowledge the undeniable administrative, cultural, and legal continuities that connected the empire of, say, the Macedonian dynasty with pre-fourth-century Roman traditions, the question remains: What shall we call this political entity? Given the fact that there were important changes over such a long period of time, such as the spread of Christianity, or the gradual Hellenization of the empire (which was a process that, actually, had started much earlier, and was increased with the spread of the Roman state over the eastern, Greek-dominated parts of the Mediterranean), it would be, indeed, deficient to call it simply the "Roman state" or "Roman Empire." I object to the word "Byzantine" as a highly ideologically charged concept that in my view creates more problems than it solves. However, the term has gained such prominence that it is, by now, used to characterize entire disciplines, thus making it difficult to simply reject it.

Several alternative names—such as the "Roman Empire of the East," or the "New Roman Empire" (to reflect the reality of the new capital, "New Rome")—would, perhaps, more correctly describe the historical and political reality of this empire, both in terms of its continuities and changes.

As the general acceptance of any of these alternative names is unlikely to happen any time soon, I will use in this study both the term "Byzantine" and "New/Eastern Roman" Empire interchangeably, to refer to the state that had Constantinople as its capital but that, at the same time, continued to cultivate "Roman" ideas in many aspects of its political life until much later in its history. Using both of these terms can help deconstruct the ideological baggage and stereotypes implicit in the concept of "Byzantium" and shift the perception of that state more toward its Roman history and the continuity of some of the typically Roman institutions and ideas.

An additional problem is that the "ideal" models of church-state relations that theologians and clergymen, as well as political leaders, were developing, have rarely coincided with actual practice. Many of these theoretical/theological accounts instead served as political propaganda or state ideology. The purpose of these narratives was to advocate, contextualize, and rationalize the power dynamics in the empire. Instead of a "harmonious" cooperation between the political and ecclesial authorities, the history of the New Roman Empire was in reality full of antagonisms and violence—emperors were regularly using their power to force the patriarchs to concur and accept their will or, in cases where this strategy was not working, to remove them and appoint new, more obedient patriarchs. There were, however, different episodes as well, when the church and its leaders managed to impose their views, forcing the emperors to comply. At times, individual ecclesiastical leaders would become so influential that they would, practically, rule the empire. In times of crisis accompanied by weak political figures, the patriarchs would even advance the Western, papacy-inspired ideas that ecclesial power should be above political power. This ever-changing reality of both social and political life and church-state power dynamics influenced the character of the political theologies that were produced in particular periods.

This shows that the "real" history of the church-state relations in the New Roman Empire, the history beyond rhetoric, conceptualizations, and church/state propaganda, was in fact complex and dynamic. It embraced a variety of ideas and practices, depending both on particular theological and political idea(l)s, as well as on the political pressures of the day, both inside and outside the empire.

The result is that the concept of symphonia can refer to various types of Orthodox Christian political "ideals." Symphonia appears thus both as an ideal to which the concrete socio-political-ecclesial realities should aspire and as a description of the (supposed) reality of coexistence of the ecclesial and political domains. Of course, one can also find these two meanings of symphonia confused when one refers to the church-state relations as both "ideal" and "real" (in the sense that the God-inspired "ideal" was given shape and body in the concrete political and historical context). This means that one must constantly mind the gap between what actually *was* (or *is*) and what (from a theological perspective) *should (have) be(en)*, both at the level of theory and in actual practice. This raises the question of whether particular teachings and practices should have a normative character, and how to decide what has a "canonical" status and what has just been a distortion of "authentic" tradition. One can also wonder if there are any general (theological) criteria that can be used to judge various Orthodox political theologies and various socio-political realities in various historical periods? These questions are very important since Orthodox Christian political theology has only recently begun to critically and systematically assess its own tradition. Therefore I will return to these questions more than once in the course of my analysis, evaluating particular teachings and practices on the basis of what seems to me an *authentic* Orthodox Christian position, a position that can also be grounded in the tradition.

The attempts of Christian theologians, clergymen, as well as political leaders, to justify and defend the state (empire), its head (emperor, king), and the exercise of political power by employing Christian theology has a long history. In this respect, Orthodox Christianity is not fundamentally different from other Christian denominations, nor is Christian history fundamentally different from the general tendency we can observe in other major religious traditions.[3] Religious narratives and practices have commonly been used to construct, articulate, and justify political ideological narratives and the exercise of power of the ruling elites. What is, however, different in the context of Christianity and, in particular, Orthodox Christianity, is that one cannot affirm state ideologies and the exercise of political power—which necessarily involves some types of violence and oppression—without giving up on some of the very fundamental elements of Christian faith. This is precisely what, in my view, has been going on in the manifold expressions of the mainstream narratives of Christian political theologies, greatly distorting Christian faith for the sake of constructing useful and "normalizing" political narratives.

The symphonia doctrine is in this sense paradigmatic, since it shows how some distinctly non-Christian political ideas decisively influenced Christian political philosophy and how this philosophy then continued to evolve (often as official state ideology), being modified in various historical periods to embrace the needs of those in power, as well as the expectations of their subjects.

Early Christianity: Who's Conducting "Symphonia"?

C hristianity and political power have had an ambiguous relationship since the very beginning. Instead of one unified "Christian" political philosophy, one can notice two different, and even opposite, tendencies in the history of Christian theological reflections upon the political sphere. One (mainstream) tendency is open to embracing, justifying, and rationalizing the political power and power structures (e.g., states). The other, less prominent and often quite marginal, is skeptical, critical, and even openly opposed to the political power and its institutions.

The symphonia doctrine clearly belongs to the first tendency. In this chapter, I will briefly analyze the theologies from the earliest period of Christianity (prior to the fourth century AD) that laid the foundations for the later theologies that we characterize as "symphonia."

Christianity evolved in the context of the Roman Empire. It is, therefore, no wonder that the first attempts to construct politico-theological narratives that would reconcile Christianity and the sphere of the political were profoundly informed by the character of ancient Roman political philosophy and the Roman type of government. In fact, one can even claim that the origins of (Christian) symphonia lie mostly in ancient Roman political theology.

An attempt to articulate the Christian relationship to the (Roman) state is already visible in what are probably the earliest surviving written documents of Christianity—the epistles of Paul. Already in the Epistle to the Romans, we find very elaborate instructions to the church in Rome as to how to relate to the state and state authorities, including on the issue of paying taxes:

> Let everyone be subject to the governing authorities, for there is no authority except that which God has established. The authorities that exist have been established by God. Consequently, whoever rebels against the authority is rebelling against what God has instituted, and those who do so will bring judgment on themselves. For rulers hold no terror for those who do right, but for those who do wrong. Do you want to be free from fear of the one in authority? Then do what is right and you will be commended. For the one in authority is God's servant for your good. But if you do wrong, be afraid, for rulers do not bear the sword for no reason. They are God's servants, agents of wrath to bring punishment on the wrongdoer. Therefore, it is necessary to submit to the authorities, not only because of possible punishment but also as a matter of conscience. This is also why you pay taxes, for the authorities are God's servants, who give their full time to governing. Give to everyone what you owe them: If you owe taxes, pay taxes; if revenue, then revenue; if respect, then respect; if honor, then honor. (Romans 13:1–7)[1]

The tone is more than conciliatory; the epistle offers a justification of political leadership and authority both on pragmatic, ethical, and, so to say, metaphysical grounds, linking the power of the political leaders with God's providence. This attitude is echoed in Titus, and in First Timothy[2] we find the apostle's famous call to Christians to "pray for kings":

> Remind the people to be subject to rulers and authorities, to be obedient, to be ready to do whatever is good. (Titus 3:1)

> I urge, then, first of all, that petitions, prayers, intercession and thanksgiving be made for all people—for kings and all those in authority, that we may live peaceful and quiet lives in all godliness and holiness. (1 Timothy 2:1–2)

The submissive tone vis-à-vis the political power that we find in these epistles is even more explicit in the First Epistle of Peter, which can be read as a theological justification of not only imperial and state power in general, but also as a justification of the social status quo, in which the power structures are affirmed, not necessarily as *good*, but as part of a bigger "grand design":

Submit yourselves for the Lord's sake to every human authority: whether to the emperor, as the supreme authority, or to governors, who are sent by him to punish those who do wrong and to commend those who do right. For it is God's will that by doing good you should silence the ignorant talk of foolish people. Live as free people, but do not use your freedom as a cover-up for evil; live as God's slaves. Show proper respect to everyone, love the family of believers, fear God, honor the emperor. Slaves, in reverent fear of God submit yourselves to your masters, not only to those who are good and considerate, but also to those who are harsh. (1 Peter 2:13–18)

This kind of political theology[3] laid the foundation for the dominant type of Christian political theologies—those that would perceive the head of the state, and political authorities in general, as those who rule "by the mercy of God." The model has been used ever since as the foundation of a *conservative* Christian approach to the socio-political sphere. Based on the above quotations, one can understand the political authorities and their exercise of power either as being "blessed by God" (being, therefore, an expression of God's will) or as the rule "allowed by God," meaning that, although maybe not good, ideal, or in accordance with God's will, the government can still be "used" by God for certain purposes (not necessarily clear or intelligible).

"Giving honor" to emperors is a concept that would be echoed by many later Christian writers. An interesting case is found in the second-century letter *To Autolycus* by Theophilus of Antioch, which repeats the widely accepted motif of *honoring the emperor*, and *praying for him*:

Accordingly, I will pay honor to the emperor not by worshipping him but by praying for him. I worship the God who is the real and true God, since I know that the emperor was made by him. You will say to me, "Why do you not worship the emperor?" Because he was made not to be worshipped but to be honored with legitimate honor. He is not God but a man appointed by God, not to be worshipped but to judge justly.[4]

This additional explanation might have come as a comment upon the broader tendency in the political theology of the ancient Roman Empire at this time, a tendency that would insist on the divine attributes of emperors. The change from the policy of keeping the Roman pantheon free from deified human beings (which seems to be the case in the "classical" Republican times) to the policy of "all emperors are gods" was a slow process that mirrored the changes in the political organization of the Roman state and, probably, its well-advanced Hellenization. Deification of (Roman) generals/political leaders, which had started in the late Republic, became a tradition by the time of Domitian (♔ AD 81–96), in parallel with the deteriorating power of the senate. This means that the call we find in many early Christian authors to "honor" the emperor and the governing authorities could also be interpreted as taking the (pragmatic) *via media*, which would allow Christians to survive within the empire, without directly challenging state authorities, but refraining, at the same time, from acknowledging the emperor's divine attributes. Interpreted this way, Theophilus's position (as well as those of some later authors such as Origen or Lactantius) could be understood as a way of stripping the emperor and the state of their sacred (pagan) prerogatives, imposing in that way serious limitations on their dominion (still very radical measured by comparative standards).

Whatever the initial impetus for this kind of political theology, "praying" for those in power and "submission to authorities" has remained one of the most persistent elements in the Christian articulation of the sociopolitical sphere, from early visions of autocracy as the "God-given" form of government, to modern right-wing Christian statist and nationalist discourses.

Praying for those in power also entered the liturgical tradition. Though most often rationalized as part of offering "petitions, prayers, intercession and thanksgiving . . . for all people" (1 Timothy 2:1), the political implications of the explicit mention of state leaders and even armed forces in the liturgical petitions (which is still practiced in many local Orthodox churches) has clear political implications. Mentioning "kings," "presidents," and/or (our) "armed forces," immediately after offering prayers for the church and church leaders, clearly transmits the message of conceptual proximity of the state authorities to God or, at least, to the church. The context in which these prayers appear (prayers that are, incidentally, not prayers for their repentance or the forgiveness of their sins) places the national political leaderships and armed forces in a theologically affirmative context, turning the church into a machine for the production of political ideology and state propaganda.[5]

Another influential early Christian text—*First Letter of Clement to the Corinthians*—is also illustrative in regard to this tendency among many Christian authors to try to "make friends" with the emperors and the empire. Traditionally ascribed to Clement, late first-century bishop of Rome, the letter comes from the very heart of the empire, being written, most probably, around the time of Emperor Domitian, when the Roman state was definitely departing from many of its old Republican institutions and procedures. The central topics of the letter are *peace* and *order* (the very same concepts that, let us remind ourselves, figure as central motifs in the official Roman state propaganda since the time of Augustus). In this context, the author also deals with the issue of authority and obedience. The author calls for peace and order both in the world and among Christians (and, concretely, in the church of Corinth). In it, Clement preaches that the way to establish and preserve peace and order is through obedience to the governing authorities. Universal "harmony and peace" are preserved by obedience to God, just as political order and harmony within the church are preserved by obedience to the relevant authorities:

> Give harmony and peace both to us and to all those who inhabit the earth, just as you gave it to our ancestors when they called upon you in a holy way, in faith and truth; and allow us to be obedient to your all powerful and all virtuous name, and to those who rule and lead us here on earth. You have given them, O Master, the authority to rule through your magnificent and indescribable power, that we may both recognize the glory and honor you have given them and subject ourselves to them, resisting nothing that conforms to your will. Give to them, O Lord, health, peace, harmony, and stability, so that without faltering they may administer the rule that you have given to them.[6]

The basic logic here (which would continue to be extremely important for the later justifications of hierarchically organized political structures) rests upon the ancient understanding of the world as *kosmos* (κόσμος). The whole world is imagined as an essentially harmonious, ordered place. This order is administered by God as the supreme authority. The order and harmony of the universe are reflected in the socio-political order, which is administered by political authorities. To live in a harmonious, orderly manner—in other words, to live a *good life*—one needs to obey this order and, thus, in a daily context, must also obey the authorities that (by the will and mercy of the universal administrator—God) take care of the public order.

Clement of Alexandria (ca. 150–ca. 215) gives a more subtle account of political power. He does not question rule and authority ("kingship") as such, but does differentiate between various types of "kingship," from the Divine kingship to the kingship that operates "at the prompting of passion," which he considers to be the worst kind. The order envisioned here is clearly one of descent: The ideal rule is the one of God, with all types of kingship on earth inferior to this one, but these earthly kingships can be differentiated among themselves based on how perverted they are in ethical terms.[7]

In a Platonic manner (also reflecting a more widely held position among early Christian authors that Plato was influenced by Moses,[8] enabling them to "domesticate" Plato for their own purposes), Clement explains that the goal "of all politics . . . as of all law-governed life, is contemplation." "A well-conducted polity" he claims, "is a necessity of life; but philosophy is the best and highest aim."[9] This is how the earthly sphere, including the sphere of governance, customs, and laws, is integrated into the universal order, with specifications as to how to distinguish between better and worse forms of government.

Another figure whose work has had an everlasting impact on Christian theology is Origen (ca. 185–ca. 254). He also articulates a generally positive stance toward political power. In *Against Celsus* (*Contra Celsum*), Origen's political theology affirms the autocratic principle:

> "Let there be one ruler, one king" I agree, yet not "him to whom the son of crafty Kronos [Saturn—D.Dž] gave the power," but the one whose power was given by him who "appoints and changes kings and from time to time raises up a useful man on the earth" (Dan. 2:21, Sir. 10:4).[10]

Origen also articulates a conciliatory attitude toward the empire, yet he is careful not to support all aspects of the political rule—such as military campaigns—or Christian engagement in those activities. Even when he explains how Christians are useful to the emperor and the empire, he links this loyalty to the "righteousness" of the emperor and the just cause.[11] Origen thus phrased an argument that would, in various forms, be used by the church in the coming centuries to link the support to political leaders to their morality and piety (and use real or alleged deviation from these as the reason to criticize them).

On the other hand, Tertullian (ca. 160–ca. 225), another major author from the same period, approaches the sphere of the political in a remarkably enthusiastic way. Although well aware of the persecution of Christians, in *To Scapula* (*Ad Scapulam*) Tertullian nevertheless articulates a political theology that would portray Christians as strong supporters of the state and the emperor:

> A Christian is enemy to none, least of all to the Emperor of Rome, whom he knows to be appointed by his God, and so cannot but love and honour; and whose well-being moreover, he must needs desire, with that of the empire over which he reigns so long as the world shall stand—for so long as that shall Rome continue. To the emperor, therefore, we render such reverential homage as is lawful for us and good for him; regarding him as the human being next to God who from God has received all his power, and is less than God alone. And this will be according to his own desires. For thus—as less only than the true God—he is greater than all besides. Thus he is greater than the very gods themselves, even they, too, being subject to him. We therefore sacrifice for the emperor's safety, but to our God and his, and after the manner God has enjoined, in simple prayer. For God, Creator of the universe, has no need of odors or of blood. These things are the food of devils. But we not only reject those wicked spirits: we overcome them; we daily hold them up to contempt; we exorcise them from their victims, as multitudes can testify. So all the more we pray for the imperial well-being, as those who seek it at the hands of Him who is able to bestow it.[12]

And, in his *Apology*:

> For we call upon God for the safety of the Emperor . . . the Scripture says expressly and clearly, "Pray for kings, and princes, and powers, that all may be peace for you." . . . There is another and a greater need for us to pray for the Emperor, and, indeed, for the whole estate of the empire, and the interests of Rome. For we know that the great upheaval which hangs over the whole earth, and the very end of all things, threatening terrible woes, is only delayed by the respite granted to the Roman empire.[13]

Tertullian's argumentation as expressed in these works represents the model for later Christian affirmations of the imperial office, autocracy, and various forms of statism. Tertullian here captures the idea that there is something providential about the (Roman) empire, that it plays an important (maybe even indispensable) part in the history of salvation. The idea that "the great upheaval which hangs over the whole earth, and the very end of all things, threatening terrible woes, is only delayed by the respite granted to the Roman empire" would be taken up in many (pseudo)theological discourses that would affirm the Roman empire (and its successors) and autocracy. This would be matched with the famous quote from 2 Thessalonians 2:7, and the "one who restrains" the powers of evil ("the mystery of lawlessness") would be interpreted as the imperial office itself. Thus, the Roman emperor, especially the Christian (Roman) emperor (czar), would be charged with heavy metaphysical as well as political responsibilities. In this sense, Tertullian's account represents one of the most elaborate political theologies in defense of the imperial power in the pre-Constantine period.

However, in spite of the predominantly affirmative or conciliatory position toward the political power, state, and emperor, the early Christian period, prior to the "Constantinian revolution," was far from being uniform. As we will see later on, one can also find, parallel to this "conservative" and "statist" attitude, positions that were much more skeptical and even (proto) "anarchist" in their theological articulation of the political.

DIVUS CONSTANTINUS AND COURT
THEOLOGY IN THE EASTERN EMPIRE

The major change in the social status of Christianity came in the fourth century with the appearance of Constantine the Great on the political stage of the Roman Empire. The new era was not only marked by the abolition of persecutions, but also by considerable advantages that Christians and, especially, church leaders started to enjoy. The bishops began to be treated as state officials, and the ties between the church and the state became institutionalized. This would provide the institutional basis for the articulation of "symphonic" doctrines in the later phases of the development of the church-state relations.

At the beginning of the fourth century, Lactantius (ca. 250–ca. 325), an author and later political advisor, was the one who came to lay the ground for a new type of "Christian-Roman" political theology. Although his approach to the socio-political sphere contains many elements that can be read as *anarchist* in spirit (as we will see in Part II), his *Institutes* project required a political theology that would not further antagonize the already hostile Roman government under Diocletian (♔ 284–305). The heart of the *Institutes* project was to build an eloquent argument that could convince Romans that "only a state that worshiped the Supreme God could embody true justice."[1] As a result, he aspired to demonstrate that "Christian conceptions of rule, law, and theology were actually closer to those of the early Roman Empire, so returning to the old constitution would allow all people to exercise their citizenship without impediment."[2]

Arguing against the Tetrarchy, Lactantius also provides the future proponents of "Christian autocracy" with the "one God, one emperor"

Zeus Enthroned. (Based on a medieval book illumination from Saint Panteleimon monastery on Mount Athos, depicting Zeus as a Byzantine Emperor, with small Dionysius.)

formula, which was grounded in a well-developed theological framework. Following Elizabeth D. Digeser:

> Lactantius suggests that if there is indeed one God, then the most stable regime is led by one person. By saying repeatedly that "one must rule the world [*mundus*]" . . . he reinforces the idea that Rome should have one emperor, since the Latin *mundus* can mean both "universe" and the "earthly world." Like most Romans, Lactantius believed that Rome ruled the world . . . or at least the only part of the world that mattered.[3]

He does not merely advocate for the Christian-type of monotheism within the Roman system of the Dominate; he also argues in favor of a change in the perception of the emperor and the meaning of the imperial office. In Lactantius's political theology, the emperor is stripped of his divine attributes and the specific religious cults dedicated to the Caesar. A new interpretation of the (Augustan-type) Principate is emerging here, but this time in a monotheistic context, which Lactantius was advocating as part of the policy of "going back to the (imagined) roots" of the Roman state and religion:

> The poets clearly understood that justice was absent from human affairs. The explanation they devised was that it took offense at the viciousness of human life and withdrew to the heavens. To instruct us, then, in what living justly means—for poets customarily adopt indirect means of pedagogy—they give illustrations from the age of Saturn, the Golden Age, and describe the condition of human society while justice still had dealings on the earth. This should not be taken for poetic fiction, but as simple truth.
>
> During the reign of Saturn the cults of the gods were not established, for his descendants had not yet been elevated to the status of divinity. It was God that was worshiped. Correspondingly, there were no disputes, no hostilities or wars.[4]

The ultimate ill-fate of (evil) Rome, which persecutes Christians, can be prevented if Rome turns to its original (and true) religion—the monotheism of the ancient days—that is to say, to the only true (Christian) God:

> God can be worshiped under Saturn, that is, under the revived Augustan principate—a regime that would be the true mirror of heaven and bring a new golden age.[5]

Lactantius lived long enough to see some of his ideas and hopes put into practice.

The three major events from the first half of the fourth century that would have an everlasting impact on the character of later political theologies (especially in what would become the *Orthodox* tradition, as opposed to the *Roman Catholic* one), were all sponsored by Emperor Constantine. The first one is the Edict of Milan (313), which granted freedom to Christianity, ordering also the restitution of confiscated church property. The second one is the organization of the first "universal" (ecumenical) council in Nicaea (325), which showed the growing significance of Christian doctrines for politics, as well as the level of *partnership* established between the state and the church. The third one is the foundation of the new capital, Constantinople-New Rome (dedicated in 330). Apart from strategic reasons (and the recognition of the fact that the eastern provinces had gained more importance than the western ones), this change also bore potentially a strong symbolic message—the new "Christian" capital was established, to replace the declining old "pagan" Rome.

The "Constantinian revolution" consisted not only of the fact that Constantine the Great granted freedom to the church and Christianity, but also in the privileged position that the church and Christianity acquired within the Roman society in the course of his reign. Constantine was the first emperor who was openly (and generously) supportive of the church and who was, it seems genuinely, interested in ecclesial matters.[6] His reign marks the moment when "the state . . . became an interested party in everything that concerned the church and was often called upon to use its machinery for maintenance of ecclesiastical peace and unity."[7]

The exact reasoning behind Constantine's policies of tolerance and support of Christianity remains a matter of dispute.[8] What, however, seems clear is that the empire and ecclesial authorities were entering a partnership (although, from the perspective of the available instruments of power, an imbalanced one) that would help both of them spread their fields of influence.[9] Christian authors from the fourth century onward tended to exaggerate the *Christian* elements in Constantine's polices at the expense of the *traditional* Roman ones, or to interpret "real" *Romanness* as, essentially, *Christian*. This was possible not only because, from this time on, the Roman and the (state-ideological) Christian would be increasingly confused, up to the point of producing one unified *Roman-Christian* political ideology, but also because of the proximity of influential figures such as Lactantius, Eusebius of Nicomedia, and Eusebius of Caesarea to the imperial court.

There is, however, another more complex issue that official Christian ideological narratives have tended to obscure—the fact that Constantine was a *Roman emperor*, with everything that that office implied. As an emperor, he held the title of *pontifex maximus* ex officio, and so did his successors (up until Gratian's rule and his rejection of the title in 379).[10] This title remained a symbol of the imperial Roman religious-political ideas that acquired new, Christian robes. Later on, Roman bishops would frequently use this title as part of papal ideology.[11] This practice serves as another indication of the longevity of ancient Roman imperial (which meant both *religious* and *political*) aspirations. The process that started as an attempt to pacify the empire and promote Christianity as, potentially, a very useful partner of the state, was entering, at this point, a new phase, during which one can talk about the gradual formation of "symphonic" doctrines (although without using this wording) as an attempt to closely relate both Christian teaching and the official state ideology, the church, and the state institutions. An impressive, and some would claim even decisive, contribution to this end was given by Eusebius, bishop of Caesarea, the chief ideologist of Constantine's time.

Eusebius (ca. 260–ca. 340) develops a political theology in which direct parallels between heavenly and earthly "kings" are established, even more explicitly (and some might claim more problematically) than in Lactantius. For Eusebius, there is a direct parallel between Christian revelation, the heavenly domain, and the course of political history. Here we find a detailed and very clearly articulated (Christian) "imperial theology," which uses theological vocabulary to explain and justify the establishment of the Roman Empire as the *universal* and the only *legitimate* empire. One universal empire is part of God's providence, and part of bringing peace to the world:

> The manifold forms of government, the tyrannies and republics, the siege of cities and devastation of countries caused thereby, were now no more, and one God was proclaimed to all mankind. At the same time one universal power, the Roman empire, arose and flourished, while the enduring and implacable hatred of nation against nation was now removed; and as the knowledge of one God and one way of religion and salvation, even the doctrine of Christ, was made known to all mankind; so at the self-same period the entire dominion of the Roman empire being vested in a single sovereign, profound peace reigned

throughout the world. And thus by the express appointment of the same God, two roots of blessing, the Roman empire and the doctrine of Christian piety, sprang up together for the benefit of men.... Meantime the Roman empire, the causes of multiplied governments being thus removed, effected an easy conquest of those which yet remained, its object being to unite all nations in one harmonious whole, an object in great measure already secured and destined to be still more perfectly attained, even to the final conquest of the ends of the habitable world, by means of the salutary doctrine and through the aid of that divine power which facilitates and soothes its way.[12]

Eusebius's argument would remain relevant for many later imperial projects, including those of the modern period and even today, when imperial ambitions and the intent to dominate the entire world (or as much of it as possible) are defended based on the idea of bringing *peace, stability,* and *prosperity* to the world. The goal, in other words, is "one harmonious whole" as a political project that is about to be achieved in history. In this political theology, God appears as the "King of everything," while Constantine acts as the universal king on earth. The emperor becomes an "image" of God, and, by analogy, the empire becomes an image of the Kingdom of God. This image theory would prove very influential over the course of the following centuries through various theories of monarchy based, supposedly, on the (pseudo) Christian worldview:

This is he who holds a supreme dominion over this whole world, who is over and in all things and pervades all things visible and invisible, the Word of God. From whom and by whom our divinely favoured emperor, receiving as it were a transcript of the divine sovereignty, directs in imitation of God himself the administration of this world's affairs.... Lastly, invested as he is with a semblance (*eikōn*) of heavenly sovereignty (*basileia*), he directs his gaze above, and frames his earthly government according to the pattern of that divine original, feeling strength in its conformity to the monarchy of God.[13]

In this kind of *imagining* of the heavenly sphere, Eusebius goes so far as to make parallels between God and His Son (Christ) and Constantine and his son (Crispus):

Wherefore, Constantine, the protector of the good, combining his hatred of wickedness with love of goodness, went forth with his son Crispus, the most benevolent Caesar, to extend a saving arm to all those perishing. Both, therefore, the father and son, having God the universal King and his Son our Savior, as their leaders and aids, drawing up on the army on all sides against the enemies of God, bore away an easy victory. . . . But the mighty and victorious Constantine, adorned with every virtue of religion, with his most pious son, Crispus Caesar, resembling in all things his father, recovered the East as his own, and thus restored the Roman Empire to its ancient state of one unified body. They extended their peaceful sway around the world, from the rising sun, to the opposite regions, to the north and the south, even to the last borders of the declining day.[14]

Eusebius is to be credited (or blamed) for supplying the "Christian" emperor with certain attributes that would make the emperor appear almost a super-human, endowed by superior powers.[15] Traces of such an image of the emperor, formulated as part of a panegyric, propaganda-type of political theology, would survive well into the period of modernity—it can be found, for instance, in the way in which the aura of the Russian autocrats would be understood.

Through this image theory, the emperor effectively replaces Christ as the "king" of Christians (in history). This allowed the socio-political sphere—the *oecumene*—to become sacralized ("Christianized") on ancient Roman (imperial) premises. In Eusebius's "Christian" imperial ideology, the goal of the "Christian emperor" and his government is to be a "safeguard of the power of Rome and of the empire of the world," while the cross becomes an imperial symbol.[16]

Eusebius's conception makes it possible for Constantine to even assume a special position within the church, as a "universal bishop" (i.e., *universal supervisor*, "overseer"—*episkopos*), able to convoke church councils.[17] Eusebius gives him the role of, one is tempted to say, a "secular bishop," who oversees not only those who are outside the church, but also "all his subjects" (which includes the church) to ensure they all lead a "godly life":

> Hence it is not surprising that on one occasion, when entertaining bishops to dinner, he let slip the remark that he was perhaps himself a bishop too, using some such words as these in our hearing: "You are bishops of those within the Church, but I am perhaps a bishop appointed by God over those outside." In accordance with this saying, he exercised a bishop's supervision over all his subjects, and pressed them all, as far as lay in his power, to lead the godly life.[18]

In the early phase of the formation of the symphonia doctrine, the emperor would (ideally) unite both the political and ecclesial roles as the supreme "bishop" who is also the emperor.[19]

The empire thus becomes "the providential instrument of salvation," as Gilbert Dagron puts it,[20] and this topic would, from this time on, be reiterated countless times in the narratives about Christian empires, both in the East and in the West. The idea, as we have seen, was not new. In the second century, Melito of Sardis (died ca. 180) spoke of the appearance of Christianity in reference to Augustus's rule and the establishment of the age of peace and prosperity in Rome.[21] Building on this history, Eusebius gives this idea the most elaborate ideological expression to date: Since the Son of God comes to the earth when the *universal* empire is established, the political realm—the imperium—becomes included in the "grand scheme" of salvation, into the universal, cosmic history, in which the birth of Christ is a landmark. *Pax Romana*—given shape and body through *Pax Augustea*—becomes also *Pax Christiana*, and *Pax Christiana* becomes manifested as *Pax Constantiniana*. The peace of Christ becomes imperial "peace," monopoly of the Roman state.

The *Romanness* of the newly emerging "Christian" political theology deserves a few more lines. As already noted, Constantine's role as the emperor gave him both political and priestly prerogatives. This is why assuming the role of a "universal bishop" (even if only as a rhetorical figure) aligned with his title of pontifex maximus.

The tension between the priestly roles and the high state offices (so prominent in some Christian understandings of the church, priesthood, and their relationship with the state, explored in Part II) was not part of the ancient Roman mindset. The sphere of the political actually *was* the religious sphere, and the purpose of the religious sphere was primarily to ensure the well-being of the city of Rome and the (ever-expanding) Roman state. In this sense, ideologists like Eusebius were making a pragmatic move and, contrary to the advice given in the Gospel (Luke 5:37–38), they were using the *old wineskins for the new wine*. The tension between Christian faith and political power, so vivid both in the Gospels and in Revelation, for example, was also abandoned in the mainstream political theologies under Constantine. Dagron gives an example of how specifically (Christian) religious issues in the time of Constantine were dealt with in a typically "Roman manner":

Worship and the faith being an affair of state, the Donatist crisis and its consequences were sorted out "in the Roman manner," by bishops to whom the emperor delegated the powers of *iudices*, or by councils which the emperor summoned and which he might attend, but at which he did not vote, just as he summoned the senate and might attend its meetings without taking part in the voting. This was the logic of Constantine; it was also that of the Church, as long as "orthodoxy" and the emperor were on the same side.[22]

In other words, Constantine and his ideologists were appropriating the old Roman understanding of the religious-political *sphere*, and Eusebius was giving it an eloquent rhetorical expression. Religion was a public and political affair, and religious institutions and practices were also parts of the Res Publica Romana in the true meaning of the word. Religious practices were practices of the public and state interest, reflecting the time of Augustus, in which the entire religious (gods-related) sphere became unified under the supreme political leader, who also became the supreme religious authority for the first time in the Roman state (or at least after the period of the so-called *monarchy*). At this time, the political-religious authority became concentrated in the figure of the Princeps. The time of Augustus—a time of stability, prosperity, and the "universal" peace—was also *favorable* time, the time of mercy of the (Roman) gods. The gates of the temple of Janus were closed, relating thus, symbolically, the rule of Augustus with the paradigmatic time of Saturn.[23] In other words, even the idea that, in the time of Augustus, heaven and earth met and merged, was a Roman idea, part of the Roman religious-political ideology, which is paralleled in the Christian dogma of the Incarnation. Augustus became not only an emperor, but a new Romulus, a descendent of Mars, a political ruler of Divine origin.

Following this typically Roman logic, outlined above, it is not surprising that some early Christian authors perceived the age of Augustus as *kairos*, the time when political changes within the Roman Empire enabled the crucial events of religious (Christian) history: the annunciation of the Kingdom of God that is "at hand" (see Matthew 3:2; Mark 1:15).

The residues of the ancient Roman and Old Testament models, as well as the early Christian tradition (including Eusebius's accounts) would continue to inspire Christian writers and would eventually lead to fully developed symphonic doctrines.

Because of the different social and political situations that the Eastern and Western parts of the Roman Empire were facing in late antiquity (fourth to sixth century), political theology began to develop in somewhat divergent ways. Faced with the irregular and weakened presence of the imperial power over the Italian peninsula from the fifth century onwards (ranging from full control over some regions, and a symbolic presence in other parts, to a complete absence), the papacy gradually advanced its claims for the universal ecclesial and then, assuming the prerogatives of the imperial office, also supreme political authority. In the eastern part of the empire, the church and Christianity were incorporated into the Roman state structures and state ideology. This is to say that the mainstream political theologies both in the East and in the West evolved as variations of the Roman imperial aspirations—one with the Roman pope as the "universal emperor," the other with the "Christianized" Roman emperor.

One important stage in the development of symphonia (and in the development of the institutional ties between the state and the church) was also the introduction of the ritual of imperial coronation performed by the bishop/patriarch of Constantinople. This ritual was initially merely an addition to the traditional Roman ritual of raising the newly elected emperor on a shield, and the acclamation by the people and the senate. It seems that the first emperor crowned with the participation of the patriarch was Leo I (♔ 457–74).[24] In contrast to Western theocratic models, where crowning was usually central to the legitimization of ascension to kingly/imperial office, the "Christian coronation" in the East, in the presence of (or performed by) the patriarch, was initially only a supplement to the ancient Roman legitimation practices. Especially in the early period, the (pseudo) liturgical coronation was not considered the key element of the process, nor was it crucial for legitimizing the election of the emperor.[25] Only gradually would Roman "republican" ideological elements lose pace with the medieval "theocratic" elements, and the coronations by the patriarch would acquire the importance of the (pseudo) liturgical services, becoming themselves a sign of approval/legitimization.[26] However, from the point of view of the protagonists of the symphonic model, coronation was certainly an important symbol—it gave the symphonia a visible expression, allowing the subjects of the church and the state to *see* God's approval coming down upon the emperor, and to take part in this cosmic legitimization of the political power.

Parallel to these developments, another idea was advanced—the idea of (Christian) hierarchy as a cosmological principle, which could, then, also be applied to the ecclesial and the political realm. This idea has played a central role in the history of both medieval and modern political theologies, and has profoundly influenced Christian ecclesiology as well as the prevailing models of morality.

The church administration was well developed even before the Constantinian revolution. The more informal Christian gatherings and eschatology-inspired communities, which must have, at least up to a point, characterized the earliest times of Christianity, gradually became much more developed and structured. Church, as an organization with an elaborate administrative network, took part in many aspects of the daily lives of its followers—from worship to humanitarian activities and funerary practices. Even before the fourth century, the bishops of the major church centers were influential figures, and those local churches were accumulating significant financial resources. As the church acquired a privileged status, its administrative network started to become much more explicitly organized according to the Roman model. Bishops, once "overseers" of the community and its liturgical offerings, became powerful political subjects, acquiring the dignity of high state officials with an important role in the state apparatus. Bishops of the most important dioceses were elevated first to the status of metropolitans and archbishops and then to popes and patriarchs (what had been informal designations for the elders, "fathers," became in the end the highest formal ecclesiastical titles). The power and status of the "lower" hierarchy increased as well. Presbyters and deacons, once "assistants" in the liturgical service, started to play the role of the leaders of local parish communities (acting on behalf of the local bishop). The ecclesial organization was thus slowly growing into its medieval form, in which it mirrored the state and the social (feudal) organization.

This institutional growth and the vertical distribution of power within the church organization was supported and justified by the theory of hierarchy as a universal order. We find a very developed example of this theory/theology of hierarchy and order in the *Corpus Areopagiticum* (late fifth or early sixth century). The author of the *Hierarchies*, Pseudo-Dionysius Areopagite, develops a theology of both heavenly hierarchy (over which God himself presides) and the ecclesial hierarchy (which is supposed to mirror the heavenly one). The hierarchy does not simply imply different offices but rather a pyramidal structure in which the lower orders are subordinated to the higher ones. This appears as an indispensable part of the very fabric of the world: Hierarchy is a "divine and holy order," which all beings aspire to reach.[27]

The elaborate heavenly hierarchy, which includes angelic orders, topped by God Almighty, mirrors the Neoplatonic logic of the metaphysical organization of reality, in which the movement along one, vertical path—from the One to the most distant (alienated from the One) parts of the world and vice versa—constitutes the only possible corridor along which existence, meaning, the good, and the beautiful are organized. Moving upward signifies moving toward the greater beauty and good, moving away from the upper levels inevitably leads to lower stages of not just importance, but also beauty.

Hierarchy described this way, as both a metaphysical structure and the logic governing the organization of the church, finds its parallel in the socio-political organization of the empire. The "Christian empire" had to be modeled in such a way that it (theoretically) resembled the metaphysical hierarchical principles. Because of this, all individuals and groups should, thus, have a clearly determined position within the social and political hierarchy, which is crowned by the emperor.

Only this vertical, strictly hierarchical distribution of power was a (conceptual) guarantee of the order of (and within) both the universe and the political community. This way, tension between the metaphysical and political realms was eliminated. Consequently, anyone questioning such a *reasonable*, harmonious, natural, and God-given order would also be disturbing this "Christian" variation of the ancient idea of kosmos, producing thus disorder and chaos. As a result, the equation *the enemy of the dominant (cosmic) order = the enemy of God = the enemy of the state* would remain the dominant logic for the justification of the ecclesial and political power structures in the West for centuries to come (later also supporting the business power structure, and continuing to be influential even in its secularized forms).

The idea that the Roman Empire is the only legitimate empire, and that the emperor of Constantinople is the only legitimate ruler of the entire (Christian) world, would be vivid in the consciousness of the "Christianized Romans" ("Byzantines") throughout their history. From time to time, this idea would be used as a practical political program—for example, in the attempts to restore the "legitimate" presence of the Roman Empire on all of its historical territories. The most successful emperor in this respect was Justinian (⚜ 527–65). True (Orthodox) faith appears by now as an indispensable element of the empire, securing its order and stability. Consequently, the protection and advancement of the faith falls directly under the jurisdiction of the emperor.

The understanding that the church and Christian faith should ensure the well-being of the empire, while the empire (and the emperor) should protect the true faith and the church, is at the very heart of Justinian's account of ideal church-state relations. It was Justinian, the restorer of the *universal* Roman Empire, who gave the classical expression to the doctrine which would later be named symphonia, in the preface to his *Sixth Novel*:

> The priesthood and the Empire are the two greatest gifts which God, in His infinite clemency, has bestowed upon mortals; the former has reference to Divine matters, the latter presides over and directs human affairs, and both, proceeding from the same principle, adorn the life of mankind; hence nothing should be such a source of care to the emperors as the honor of the priests who constantly pray to God for their salvation. For if the priesthood is everywhere free from blame, and the Empire full of confidence in God is administered equitably and judiciously, general good will result, and whatever is beneficial will be bestowed upon the human race. Therefore We have the greatest solicitude for the observance of the divine rules and the preservation of the honor of the priesthood, which, if they are maintained, will result in the greatest advantages that can be conferred upon us by God, as well as in the confirmation of those which We already enjoy, and whatever We have not yet obtained We shall hereafter acquire. For all things terminate happily where the beginning is proper and agreeable to God. We think that this will take place if the sacred rules of the Church, which the just, praiseworthy, and adorable Apostles, the inspectors and ministers of the Word of God, and the Holy Fathers have explained and preserved for Us, are obeyed.[28]

And, in the *Seventh Novel* (Chapter 2):

> . . . since the priesthood and the Empire differ greatly from one another, as sacred things do from those which are common and public, and the abundance enjoyed by the churches is continually derived from the munificence of the Emperors. Hence, where compensation is given by either party, neither can legally be blamed by anyone.[29]

Justinian understands the *spiritual* ("Divine matters," "holy things") and the *political* ("human affairs," "public things") as two spheres that should work together for the general well-being. Consequently, the priesthood, in charge of the "holy things," and the empire, in charge of the "public things," are two branches of Divine-human reality. Both of them, after all, proceed from the "same principle."

Justinian also clearly explains the duties that the state has toward the church and vice versa. The emperor has the duty to observe the "divine rules" and "preserve the honor of the priesthood." The imperial office is also there to ensure that the "holy churches always receive their abundance and their status." This will lead to stability and prosperity, for if the above list is observed, it will result in the "greatest advantages that can be conferred upon us by God."

The symbolic expression of this symphony was the newly (re)built church of "Holy Wisdom" (Hagia Sophia) in Constantinople, which very well illustrates the ideas as well as the practical tensions that characterized the church-state relations. As a church, it was the seat of the patriarch of Constantinople who became de facto the spiritual leader of the "Orthodox" (within the boundaries of the empire at least). However, it was also part of the imperial court complex, where church-state rituals were staged, in this way signifying the integration of both the "spiritual" and "earthly" governments. The church becomes thus the visible expression of symphonia, unifying the liturgical performances with imperial ceremonies.

The tradition of comparing Christian leaders to the Old Testament kings also played an important part in the time of Justinian, just as it would later play an important role in the West during the Middle Ages. Upon the completion of the Hagia Sophia church, Justinian allegedly exclaimed, "Solomon, I have outdone you!"[30] As William Desmond notes, he "might well have boasted that he had outdone Moses also, when he organized the systematization of 1,400 years of Roman law, into two 'tablets'—the *Codex Constituionum* and *Digest*."[31]

These political theologies that were advocating a type of symphonic model were doing so in an attempt to make use of Old Testament imagery to solidify the concept of "Christian emperors" and "Christian empire." That means that, in addition to ancient Roman religious-political ideas, and the new socio-political reality that came about in the fourth century, the new "Christian" political theology in the "Christian" Roman Empire (as well as in medieval political theory in the West) was also informed by Old Testament political theology. And many Old Testament stories were readily waiting to be used in the construction of this new political ideology:

> From Constantine's time onwards the custom of calling the emperor the "New David" and the "New Solomon" and comparing him to Melchizedek and Moses started to emerge. In this way the Byzan-

tine emperor gained the reputation of being the successor of the kings of the Old Testament. . . . In court ceremonies and acclamations, Byzantine emperors were often compared to Moses, David, Solomon, and Constantine.[32]

A comparison between emperors and the Old Testament kings was even included in the prayers of the patriarch during the coronation ceremony:

> You who, through the intermediary of your prophet Samuel, chose your servant David and, by unction, made him king or your people Israel, hear also today our supplication, look down from your holy dwelling on high on we who are unworthy, deign to anoint with the oil of gladness your faithful servant, a man it has pleased you to establish as emperor over the holy nation which you have made your own by the blood of your only Son.[33]

Emperors were in charge of leading the "new Israel" and the entire Christian oecumene, which should, ideally, embrace the entire world. Interestingly, and paradoxically enough, the Old Testament examples have remained the main source of inspiration among those who advocate for "Christian" and, specifically, "Orthodox" autocracy/monarchy up to the present day.[34] The idea that the king (emperor) is an image of Christ, as well as the successor to the Old Testament kings, whose supreme duty is to take care of the chosen "people of God" (their tribe or other ethnic group, which is identified with the "New Israel") became commonplace, both in the Eastern Roman Empire and in Western European monarchies.[35]

Just as the Old Testament political leaders had been in charge of leading the "chosen nation" (Israel), looking after its well-being and its faith to God and the Law, the emperors of New Rome were seen as leaders of the "new Israel," as those who were in charge of looking after Christians and the newly baptized "chosen people," securing its well-being and also taking care of the true faith. The analogy with the Old Testament rulers served as a form of legitimation both for the Roman emperors in the East and the medieval kings in the West, with both Justinian and, later, Charlemagne, assuming the symbolism of Old Testament chief, as "new Davids," "new Solomons," or "new Moseses."[36]

Symphonia, in its classical Justinian form, however, was not the result, as many authors have fantasized in the past, of a dark, mystical, *Byzantine* theocratic caesaropapism. It was rather a consequential development of the

Roman understanding of the role of religious institutions vis-à-vis the state, now reinterpreted in the new "Christian" ideological context. The church was a state institution, similar to the ancient Roman pontifical colleges that were integrated into the state system, even though they enjoyed autonomy within their particular field of expertise (and in some sense "differed greatly" from one another). This had two consequences: The state of the Roman *populus* continued to be (pseudo) "sacred" in its character, while the emperors continued to supervise the religious sphere, similar to the role state authorities had been playing since classical "republican" times. The state, personified in the imperial office, continued with its aspirations to exercise authority over the highest church dignitaries, subordinating them to the emperor, as the head of the political pyramid. Justinian, as Ostrogorski puts it, although a Christian, remained Roman.[37] The idea of the religious sphere (sphere of faith) being completely autonomous from the political one was not part of this symphonic worldview.[38]

Only later would some church circles (primarily the monks, often supported by the pope) push for a greater autonomy of the ecclesiastical sphere (present in Justinian), advancing the idea of a (hoped for) harmonious coexistence between two distinct spheres, in which everyone maintains their autonomy in things that are specific to them, without being, necessarily, subordinated one to the other. This advancement of political theology, advocating more autonomy for the church, coincided with times of aggressive imposition of particular theological views by the emperors: Some emperors openly supported various "heretical" positions (e.g., monothelitism, iconoclasm), mostly as tools in the realization of political goals. Faced with pressure from the emperors to accept, tolerate, or promote these views, the church (or some parts of the church) would often stand up to the imperial office, claiming its autonomous sphere of competence.

One such example was the critique of the imperial involvement in strictly theological disputes that was advanced by Maximus the Confessor (ca. 580–662). He advocated for a considerable independence of the church from the state.[39] However, even Maximus's critique does not seek for a separation of the church and state, but rather for the church's autonomy in the domain of religious matters.[40] This means that we are faced here with another version of symphonia (also known as *synallelia*)—not the one of subordination or absorption within one ecclesial-political whole, but one of cooperation between two spheres and two institutions, in which both of them retain autonomy in the matters specific to them.[41]

Excurse II

SYMPHONIA AND SYNALLELIA

At this point, and for the purposes of later analysis, two distinct meanings of symphonia should be noted. These two meanings can produce a conceptual tension, present in the articulations of various forms of church-state relations, which has often been translated into practical tensions and conflicts between the state and the church. Following one (the synallelia) conception, the church and state are two distinct, yet complementary spheres. Each of these spheres—the *sacerdotium* and the *imperium*—preserves its autonomy and competences while contributing to the overall well-being of the whole.[42] In contrast, when following the symphonia interpretation, there is an organic unity, a symbiosis, between the church and the state, between theological concepts and political ideology, without separation or strictly or clearly defined boundaries.

This distinction, however, which we can find in the technical literature, seems to me very abstract. Except purely conceptually, it is very difficult to specify where symphonia, described this way, begins and where synallelia ends, and vice versa. The analysis that follows will show that instead of one symphonia and one synallelia we actually operate, both conceptually and practically, with a variety of *degrees of proximity* between the church and the state. On the one conceptual pole is a complete separation of the church from the state, up to the point of hostility (unknown in the mainstream premodern discourses, and also rare in practice even in modern "secular" societies); on the other pole is a complete immersion of the church in the state or the state in the church, with the emperor or the pope/patriarch on the top of this unified socio-political whole. Most of the time, the church-state relationship in the East, in reality, fell somewhere in the middle of this spectrum. For this reason, instead of using separate names to distinguish various degrees of proximity of the church to the state, and vice versa, I will use only the concept of symphonia as a collective term that refers to a variety of possible ways in which the church and the state were "harmonized" (or called on to enter a "harmonious" partnership).

In the political theology advanced during the iconoclastic period we find an affirmation of the symphonic model according to which the church and the state are intimately connected, working together for the well-being of both the state and the church. The case of iconoclasm shows the extent to which the emperors were willing and capable of intervening into church matters and doctrines, while, at the same time, demonstrating the willingness of segments of the church (primarily the monks) to oppose those policies and try to limit their power.

The political theology of Emperor Leo III (♔ 717–41) can be perceived as an advancement in the direction already traced by Constantine the Great. In Leo III's version of symphonia, the highest ecclesial and political roles tended to merge, with the emperor on top of the unified social and ecclesial whole. Leo III perceived himself as a priest ex officio. A famous correspondence between the emperor and Pope Gregory II suggests that the emperor called himself "emperor and priest,"[43] assuming thus the ecclesiastical role, at the moment when the papacy was making decisive steps toward the assumption of a stronger and more independent position. It is not surprising, then, that this led to a significant alienation between the papacy and the eastern empire,[44] which put Rome and Constantinople on two tracks that would lead to further alienation and, eventually, a formal split.

At the same time, the iconophiles tried to counter the aggressive policies of the iconoclastic emperors by advocating a different understanding of symphonia, one that would recognize the autonomous domains of the church and the state, opposing the exercise of the imperial power in the realm of matters specific to the church/theology. It is noteworthy, however, that the iconophiles, in their words and actions, were not per se questioning the imperial power; instead, the call was to exercise imperial power within the political domain, leaving the church to attend to its own business. This same logic is affirmed by Pope Gregory II who tried to delineate the business of the emperor/state and that of the priest/church.[45] The patriarch of Constantinople, Germanus, mentioned by Gregory II in his letter (ca. 726 or later), also took a similar position, protesting the iconoclastic imperial policies on the grounds that only an (ecumenical) council could declare the (true) faith.[46] This conception of symphonia would imply cooperation, mutual recognition, and respect, but would also insist that harmony should be sought by minding the boundaries of each other's domain: The empire and the emperor should not exceed the limits of their power, and the church should respect the empire and its power as long as it does not interfere with the doctrinal matters. Or, in the famous words of John of Damascus:

> We submit to you, O Emperor, in the matters of this life, taxes, revenues, commercial dues, in which our concerns are entrusted to you. For the ecclesiastical constitution we have pastors who speak to us the word and represent the ecclesiastical ordinance. We do not remove ancient boundaries, set in place by our fathers, but we hold fast to the traditions, as we have received them. For if we begin to remove even a tiny part of the structure of the Church, in a short time the whole edifice will be destroyed.[47]

The iconoclastic dispute was important not only because certain theological and church circles stood up against political interference, but also because, at the same time, they formulated a proto-secular understanding of the church-state relations, without radically departing from the symphonia tradition.

The iconoclastic crisis and the further political complications significantly deteriorated the strength and authority of the imperial office. The Macedonian dynasty (867–1056) invested a lot of effort in the consolidation of the empire and reestablishing the prestige of the imperial office. One document, a law book, from this period, *Epanagoge* (*Eisagoge*) (ca. 866), is particularly important for understanding church-state relations and the symphonia doctrine in the post-iconoclastic era. In the part concerning the church, the document aspires to (re)formulate the delicate balance of ecclesial and political powers. The church-state organism is supposed to represent an ideal unity, presided over by both the emperor and the patriarch, who were supposed to "take care of the well-being of humanity, in a perfect harmony."[48] The emperor was responsible for taking care of all material things, and the patriarch for the spiritual well-being of the subjects. This is all the more interesting given the "absolutist" tendencies of the Macedonian dynasty. It shows that the church won an important battle in the previous period, and that even the absolutist, unifying policies of the Macedonian emperors (such as the marginalization of ancient institutions, like the senate) could not revoke the level of church autonomy that had been established. The emperor consolidates the power in his hands (lowering the significance of the aristocracy and also of the senate) and rules by the mercy and providence of God, as His chosen one. However, the emperor's power is limited in matters of the church—the emperor is expected to protect the church, but not to rule over it, especially not in cases of doctrinal issues.[49]

The rise of the influence of the church and the patriarchal office—and, consequently, the rise of the corresponding theologies—culminates in the political theology of Patriarch Michael Cerularius (☗ 1043–59). In this form of symphonia, we find the Eastern version of the Roman papal ideology.[50] Although the existence and legitimacy of the two spheres is, of course, acknowledged and rhetorically affirmed, the argument is that the church and the patriarch should rise above the imperial power.[51] This theory comes as a reflection of the patriarch's personal influence, as well as a reflection of the context, as this was the time during which the official split between the church of Constantinople and the church of Rome took place (1054).

An important concept, which shows both the complexity of symphonia and the extent to which the political power was intertwined with the ecclesial, was the concept of *epistemonarches*. This word, when applied to the emperors, can be generally understood as a special, quasi-ecclesial prerogative of the emperor, in line with Constantine's concept of a "universal bishop." In one reading, epistemonarches could mean that the emperor was "the secular arm of the Church," which would correspond to the "oath later sworn by the sovereigns at the time of their coronation,"[52] to be defenders of the church and faith. On the other hand, though, the same concept can instead be understood as a special prerogative of the emperors, which implies their "sanctity" (which might be derived from unction, as Dagron proposes[53]) and which also enables the emperor to have certain competences *over* the church. Job Iasites's *Response* illustrates the understanding of the role of the emperor in the late Byzantine period:

> This role of *epistemonarches* is given to him [emperor—D.Dž.] because he is recognized as pious and most Christian: it is his duty, therefore, to repay to his mother the Church the cost of his education, to protect her and support her with great gratitude in exchange not only for the milk she gave him, the basic initiation in piety, but for the bread he has eaten, that of piety, in full initiation into the dogmas, the manly nourishment.[54]

Under the pressure of the deteriorating political circumstances that the Eastern Empire was experiencing, we find yet another expression of the symphonia doctrine in the twelfth century. In his letter to Pope Innocent

II (in 1141), appealing to the pope for his support in the attempts to reestablish the unified Roman empire, Emperor John II elaborates on the theory of "two swords" that should be in harmony. According to the emperor,
the political sword should be reserved for the emperor, and the spiritual
one for the pope.[55] This would (re)create the ideal unity of Christian
oecumene—one political rule and one church, within one Roman empire.
This political theology is compatible with the main elements of the "two
swords" theory that we find in the West in the medieval period.[56]

We also find a late variation of the symphonia doctrine—one that follows some aspects of the epistemonarches logic—in Emperor Theodore II
Laskaris's attempts to reestablish the empire, which had collapsed under
the Crusaders. Emperor Theodore II of Nicea thought of himself as the
supreme authority not only in political, but also in church, matters. He
was open to the union with the church of Rome, but only if his voice would
be decisive in all of the critical issues, for both of the churches.[57]

Two more examples from the late Byzantine period are worth mentioning, as they further demonstrate the range of possible interpretations of the
symphonia doctrine that can be found within the Eastern Roman political
theology. The symphonic models that dominated in this period reflected the
decline of the political power of the empire. Patriarch Athanasius (⚜ 1289–
93, 1303–9), to a much greater extent than in the traditional symphonia
models, affirms the authority of the church, following the model provided by
the papal claims to (political) power. As John Meyendorff puts it:

> Athanasius also demanded from the emperor a strict adherence to
> the faith and ethics of Orthodoxy, and obedience to the Church.
> Upon returning to the patriarchate in September 1303, he had [Em-
> peror—D.Dž.] Andronicus sign a promise "not only to keep the
> Church fully independent and free . . . , but also to practice towards
> Her a servant's obedience, and to submit to Her every just and God-
> pleasing demand."[58]

At a moment when the imperial office was getting weaker and the empire
was shrinking, the universalist aspirations of the patriarchs of Constantinople—in themselves a mirror image of the universalist claims of the Roman emperors—become advanced. Directly involved with the church
administration in Russia, the patriarchs of Constantinople used the opportunity to affirm their role as a "universal" authority, affirmations that
were, as Meyendorff puts it, "practically indistinguishable from the most

authoritarian pronouncements by Roman popes."[59] In a letter to the princes of Russia, Patriarch Philotheos (♔ 1353–54, 1364–76) wrote:

> Since God has appointed Our Humility as leader . . . of all Christians found anywhere in the inhabited earth, as solicitor and guardian of their souls, all of them depend on me . . . the father and teacher of them all. . . . Our Humility chooses the best among men, the most eminent in virtue, establishes and ordains them as pastors, teachers and high-priests, and sends them to the ends of the universe.[60]

Philotheos was not an isolated case. Patriarch Anthony IV (♔ 1388–90, 1391–97) also affirmed his leadership over "all Christians of the universe," and reminded Grand Prince Basil that the patriarch is "the vicar of Christ . . . and sits on the very throne of the Master."[61]

During the last chapter of Byzantine history, when the empire—reduced to Constantinople and its neighboring territory—was already a Turkish vassal, even Russia turned its back on the Roman emperor. Grand Duke Vasily I (♔1389–95, 1412–25) ordered the church in Russia to no longer mention the emperor of Constantinople in the liturgical services, claiming that, "We have the church but we don't have the emperor."[62] This provoked the famous response from Patriarch Anthony, which in many ways articulates the version of Orthodox political theology that has remained vivid in the imagination of many ecclesial, theological, and political circles in the Orthodox world, to this day:

> With sorrow I also learn of some words spoken by Your Nobility about my Mightiest and Holy Autocrat and Emperor. It is said that you do not allow the Metropolitan to mention in the diptychs the Holy Name of the Emperor—a thing which has never been possible before—and you say: "We have the Church, but we have no Emperor nor wish to know him." This is by no means good. . . . If, with the will of God, the pagans have surrounded the possessions and the land of the Emperor, yet up to this day the Emperor has the same coronation from the Church according to the same ritual and with the same prayers; he is anointed with great consecrated oil and elected Emperor and Autocrat of the Romans, i.e., of all Christians. If the Great Emperor, the Lord and Master of the Universe, invested with such power, has been reduced to such straits, what might not other local rulers and small princes endure? . . . Thus, it is by no means good, My Son, if you say

COURT THEOLOGY IN THE EASTERN EMPIRE 65

that "We have the Church, not the Emperor." It is impossible to Christians to have the Church, but not to have the Emperor.[63]

The patriarch reaffirms the idea that there can be only one emperor—and that all the others are illegitimate, taking the title against "nature and law," through "tyranny and violence."[64]

The Eastern Roman political theology, thus, evolved significantly: What was once primarily an imperial Roman ideology dressed up in Christian robes became the doctrine of union and even organic symbiosis between the church, Christianity, and the state that the church leaders advocated on the eve of the dissolution of the empire. Symphonic doctrines, developed and rejuvenated throughout the history of the New Roman Empire, would continue their life even in the post-(Eastern) Roman times. The aspirations of the new, rising Slavic state would take over symphonia and develop new variations of this political theology that suited the new time and the new environment.

Looking at some of the most important episodes in the history of the symphonia doctrine, we can see that the concept of symphonia should in fact be understood as a set of various types of church-state relations that were, contrary to Steven Runciman's observation, complicated not only in practice but also in theory.[65] On the one pole was the concept according to which the emperor was on the top of the (social-political) pyramid, with certain (quasi) ecclesial functions—and the power to dethrone even the highest church dignitaries, if not to his liking. On the opposite pole stood the strong role of the patriarch, a conception in which his office even acquires certain state prerogatives and he rises in his power (in theory) even above the emperor. Between these poles lie the "moderate" symphonic models in which the two spheres are in a delicate balance of power, each preserving its own field of competence and authority—delineations that are often difficult to specify and maintain in practice.

All these variations that we find in the long history of the Christianized Roman Empire (fourth to fifteenth century) testify to the difficulty that the ideologists had when trying to harmonize very incoherent ideas, such as the Roman imperial ideology and the Christian faith, the Kingdom of Caesar and the Kingdom of God.

The symphonia doctrine, in its various forms, was in reality always a theoretical/theological rationalization of the power dynamics (and power aspirations) between the church (i.e., the dominant parties within the church and the patriarch of Constantinople) and the empire, personified in the emperor. As the above examples have shown, the weakening of the power of the imperial office (due to, for instance, the incapability of emperors, lack of military or economic success, loss of moral integrity, etc.) could easily lead, in the presence of capable and ambitious patriarchs, to the strengthening of the ecclesial power—which would, in turn, redefine the (desired) meaning of symphonia for that particular era.

Despite the attempt to give it a sacred halo, symphonia remains primarily a political ideology, affirmed both by the state and ecclesial authorities for their own benefit, under the pretext of the preservation (or reestablishment) of the "ideal" and "sacred" order.

Powerful states need powerful ideologies. The (Eastern) Roman Empire was certainly such a state, and, one could claim, an entire civilization. Symphonic doctrines were expressions of a powerful ideology, giving theological significance and justification to the political sphere and the power structures. The strength and vitality of symphonia, in its numerous interpretations, can be seen in the everlasting effect it has had on the character of socio-political thought within the Orthodox Christian context. We find variations of these doctrines in the post-Byzantine times in the Orthodox monarchic discourse, most prominently in Imperial Russia.

Conducting "Symphonia" in Russian Lands

That the Byzantine culture had a major, some would even claim decisive, impact on the formation of the medieval Russian cultural and religious identity is a well-known thesis.[1] The early Russian state—the Kievan Rus'[2]—was undoubtedly under the strong influence of Constantinople. Although not without mutual hostilities and wars, the Kievan state had, from the very beginning, strong economic and cultural ties with its southern neighbor.

The crucial moment in bringing Russia into the cultural and religious orbit of the New Roman Empire can be found in the conversion of Russia's Great Princess Olga and Grand Prince Vladimir (ca. 958–1015) to the "Greek" type of Christianity. Russia thus came under the influence of the southern empire, with Constantinople now as its church/spiritual center, and would remain part of the "Byzantine commonwealth"[3] until the fall of Constantinople. The empire from the Bosporus was skilled and eager enough to use the "soft power" of the church and the mostly Greek metropolitans heading the church in Russian lands to advance its presence and influence over the territories of its northern neighbor.

All of this, however, should not obscure the fact that the foundations upon which Russia was built were significantly different from those of the (New) Roman Empire. The Roman heritage and Roman state institutions were absent from the traditionally Russian territories. Instead of Roman legislation, institutions, and developed urban infrastructure, the medieval Russian state grew as a federation of tribes led by their tribal leaders. In such a context, a unified faith of what then was the "civilized" and developed world—namely, the Christian states and, foremost, the (New) Roman Empire—became a very important factor in achieving cohesion within the Russian state.[4]

Several explanations have been proposed as to why Grand Prince Vladimir decided to convert to "Greek" Orthodoxy, as opposed to the "Latin" type of Christianity (though mainstream Christianity was still officially unified at the time of the Christianization of the Slavic tribes). Following Boris Rauschenbach, one can point to two main factors:

> First, unlike the Western Church, the Orthodox Church was not a political force independent of the Emperor. The Church did not have its own military forces (unlike the papacy), and it was quite impossible to imagine Constantinople as the scene of battles of the sort taking between the armies of popes and kings in the west of Europe. Vladimir, whose aim was to unite territories and create a country, needed a church that would be obedient to his will (in political matters), rather than another disruptive force in the state.
>
> Secondly, Rus's neighbor was Orthodox Bulgaria, which had been converted approximately 100 years earlier. Bulgaria already had church service books in the Bulgarian language, and, at that time, the ancient Bulgarian and Russian languages were so similar that, unlike the Greek books, Bulgarian books did not need to be translated, just copied. What is more, the Bulgarian clergy could easily, without interpreters, preach the new religion and conduct church services in Rus'.[5]

In addition to the above, the well-organized, centralized administration of the Christian church was unknown to paganism. This (institutional) factor, following Rauschenbach, played "a markedly positive role in the country's history."[6]

The prestige of Grand Prince Vladimir and his state was established by his marriage with Princess Anna of Constantinople, sister of Emperor Basil II (♔ 976–1025). Though a marriage between the emperor's sister and a "barbaric" leader would otherwise have been unthinkable, Basil II was forced into this political move by the growing power of his northern neighbor. And it was, indeed, until then, an unprecedented move in the history of the empire. The marriage secured the court of Vladimir the "rank of the foremost royal houses of Europe,"[7] and the title "Emperor of the Russians," as Basil called him.[8]

Thus, the Orthodox faith and the institutional church organization quickly became an important element of Russia's dominant socio-political ideology. The growth of the young state under Vladimir and his son Yaroslav (ca. 978–1054) was paralleled in the growth of Orthodoxy manifested in, among other things, the lively construction of church buildings.

However, the complex social and political circumstances out of which the young Russian state grew were reflected in the complex character of its ideology. Unsurprisingly, this gave birth to yet another variation of the symphonia doctrine, shaped to satisfy the needs of the new environment.[9]

The basic ideological issue, which left an important mark on the character of the church-state ideology in both the Kievan and in the young Muscovite state, was the tension between the need to promote the prestige and political authority of the Kievan princes and, at the same time, the necessity of recognizing the supreme authority of the one (and only possible) universal emperor, residing in Constantinople. This issue was also mirrored in the ecclesial organization, where the primates of the church of Russia were mostly Greek metropolitans appointed by the patriarch of Constantinople. In other words, symphonia, which had already proved to be difficult enough to conceptually justify in the Roman Empire, was experiencing another challenge in the Russian context: How could symphonia be "planted" into a new political reality, given the fact that it was designed to fit the ideology of one, universal ("Christian") Roman Empire, led by one emperor, whose "spiritual" needs are administered by (one) patriarch?

By accepting, in theory, the primacy of the empire and the emperor, the ideologists of the Kievan state were trying to articulate a doctrine that would make the Russian state virtually equal to, if not even "better" and "more legitimate" than, the Roman/Byzantine Empire. This was clearly the case in the *Sermon on Law and Grace* by Metropolitan Hilarion (ca. 1050), who, following the New Testament logic of the primacy of grace over the law, and the primacy of the "new" over the "old," exalts Christianized Russia over the pagan and Jewish religions. The *Sermon* also combines the (Old Testament) motifs of the "chosen" political rulers, whose rule is included within the broader narrative of the universal history of salvation, stretching all the way from ancient Israel up to the Kievan state. Because of this, Vladimir (who adopted "Vasilij"—Basil—as his Christian name out of respect for Emperor Basil II) and his deeds are compared both to those of Constantine the Great and those of King David:

O you likeness of the great Constantine: of like wisdom, of like love for Christ, with like honour for his servants! With the blessed fathers of the Council of Nicaea, he set down the law for the people; and you, with our new fathers—the bishops—in frequent assembly and utmost humility took counsel on how to establish the law for these people new in their knowledge of God. He among the Hellenes and the Romans made the kingdom subject to God. And you, O blessed Vasilij, did likewise in Rus', so that now, both for us as for them, Christ is called king. . . . Your devotion is well witnessed and faithfully proved by Georgij, your son . . . for he finished your unfinished works, as Solomon finished David's.[10]

Let us not forget that these arguments were developed in the context of Vladimir's decision to upgrade the bishopric of Kiev to the rank of metropolitan seat, and to make Hilarion—a court chaplain—the metropolitan, done without the consent of the patriarch of Constantinople. Metropolitan Hilarion explained that

Prince Vladimir . . . had adopted Christianity of his own accord, free will and virtue and on his own initiative; the people of Rus' were fully entitled to organize their own Church as they saw fit.[11]

The argument here is an interesting one; it introduces the concept of the popular sovereignty (of the "people"), as a rhetorical figure of speech, of course. And, yet, the assertion that the *people* (premodern and modern "nations") have the right to organize "their" own churches would become the key argument in the claims for local church autocephaly in the ages to come—up to the present day.

The adoption of the New Roman canon law (*The Syntagma in Fourteen Titles*) also served practical purposes (for the organization and *modernization* of the state and society), but also ideological ones—modeling the church-state relations "on the basis of the vital *symphonia* of powers that would ensure *taxis*: i.e., order and peace."[12]

One project, whose purpose was to symbolically express the aspirations of the new political center to compare itself to Constantinople and assume (although in an adjusted form) the latter's ideology, was the building of the St. Sophia's Cathedral in Kiev. This project, executed under Yaroslav, conceptually, though not necessarily formally, imitated the "mother church" of Hagia Sophia from Constantinople.[13] The project was also a physical expression of the political theology expressed in Hilarion's *Sermon*. Apart from building the central cathedral, in the image of and maybe even to rival the one in Constantinople, other parallels with the symphonia ideology can be read from this project. Just as Old Testament imagery was once used for Justinian, the same imagery was now being used in the case of Yaroslav, appearing as a "new Solomon" in Hilarion's *Sermon*.

This Old Testament imagery shows the reliance, from a very early period, on the Old Testament in the construction of the Russian political and, eventually, imperial ideology. There is, of course, nothing specifically Russian or Orthodox about this; as has already been pointed out, this was commonplace among virtually all of the medieval and early modern "Christian" monarchical discourses, both in continental Europe and in England.[14]

It was only following Yaroslav's death, in the period of crisis and wars among competing principalities, that the political significance of the institutional church would become apparent. In this period, it was the church that "counteracted feudal fragmentation by opposing internal struggles between princes."[15] This was an early episode in the history of Slavic Orthodoxy in which the church, in the absence of a strong, central political authority, would assume a political role.

The church also played an important, and maybe even decisive, role in the later promotion of one political center over others. In the fourteenth century, Moscow became the seat of the metropolitan, who had moved his seat from Vladimir, the previous ecclesial and political center. This, in turn, gave the prince of Moscow a strategic advantage over the other princes. Thus the head of the (new) state and the head of the church were residing in the same place, mirroring again the symphonic ideal.

It is no surprise then that the structure of the religious-political ideas found in the Byzantine empire were also adopted in Russia, where it was further advanced to reflect the new reality of Russian ethnic, political, and cultural life. As a result, the symphonic ideal remained relevant and active throughout the history of the Russian state, from the time of Kievan Rus' to the end of the Russian Empire in 1917. However, this model was modified more than once in the course of this turbulent history, again reflecting changing political realities.

Similarly, and probably even more so than in the Byzantine empire, the official versions of Orthodox Christianity and Orthodox Christian political theologies in Russia continued to serve the state and, primarily, autocracy, recognizing the latter as the only legitimate and divinely inspired form of government. However, political theology served an international, as well as a domestic, purpose for the Russian state. With the rise of Muscovite Russia in the 1320s, under Prince Ivan I, more elaborate political theologies were constructed to articulate Russia as the strongest "Orthodox" state. This project became especially critical in the final decades of the Byzantine history, when all that was left of the former power of Constantinople was its symbolic meaning and long-standing prestige.

The Russian church and state would rise as the stronghold of Orthodoxy in the aftermath of the Council of Florence in 1439. The former empire on the Bosporus—reduced by this time mostly to the city of Constantinople—was desperately looking for help and for support from the papacy. As had been the case before, the papacy was hoping to resolve the split between the churches of Constantinople and Rome to its advantage. Formally, the Council of Florence brought the union, which was never implemented. Under pressure from the emperor, the leaders of the church of Constantinople signed the treaty, hoping, in vain, to receive political and military aid. This acquiescence was viewed, and used, in Russia as a sign of the departure of Constantinople from the true faith, quite similar to the earlier departure of Rome from Orthodoxy and the sacred tradition. Metropolitan Isidore (♗ 1437–41), who represented the church of Russia at the Council of Florence, and who signed the union with Rome, was deposed, excommunicated, and imprisoned upon his return to Russia, and a new metropolitan was appointed independently of Constantinople. The Russians interpreted the union of Florence as the betrayal of Orthodoxy by the patriarchate of Constantinople. This meant, by implication, that the "Orthodox capital" that still held the true faith—Moscow— also became the true (legitimate) imperial capital.

The definite fall of the New Roman Empire happened during the lifetime of Ivan III (1440–1505). After the fall of Constantinople in 1453 and the liberation of the Russian lands from Mongol rule in 1480, Ivan assumed the title of czar (царь, i.e., emperor/Caesar), which, at the symbolic level, implied the full transfer of imperial power from the only legitimate (Orthodox) Roman Empire to the new empire and the new stronghold of Orthodoxy—Russia.

It is this political shift that generated the formulation of the theory of Moscow (and Russia) as the "Third Rome," a topic of extensive discussion within the academic literature. In its classical form, this idea was formulated by Monk Filofei (Philotheos) of Pskov in letters to Princes Ivan III (♔1462–1505) and Vasilij III (♔ 1505–33) of Moscow, and Munechin, Vasilij's representative. The famous passage in which the topic of the "Third Rome" was given classical expression—and, literarily, a very powerful one—is from Filofei's letter to Munechin:

> I would like to say a few words about the existing Orthodox empire of our most illustrious, exalted ruler. He is the only emperor on all the earth over the Christians, the governor of the holy, divine throne of the holy, ecumenical, apostolic church which in place of the churches of Rome and Constantinople is in the city of Moscow, protected by God, in the holy and glorious Uspenskij Church of the most pure Mother of God. It alone shines over all the earth more radiantly than the sun. For know well, those who love Christ and those who love God, that all Christian empires will perish and give way to the one kingdom of our ruler, in accord with the books of the prophet, which is the Russian empire (*rosejskoe carstvo*). For two Romes have fallen, but the third stands, and there will never be a fourth.[16]

The basic idea is the one of *translatio imperii*; just as Constantinople inherited dignity and (legitimate) authority from the classical (first) Rome, the new imperial center—Moscow—inherits prestige and authority from "New Rome." Of course, the idea was not invented in sixteenth-century Russia but was, instead, a widespread theme in the political theologies of the Middle Ages.[17] Other princely centers in Russia also claimed their ranks as "new Romes," comparing their own leaders to Old Testament kings as a way of legitimization. The city of Tver, for example, was also "the center of the world," with its ruler, Prince Boris, as the "new Jacob . . . new Joseph . . . new Moses . . . new David, the equal of Solomon, a second Constantine."[18] Boris was also compared to the emperors Tiberius, Augustus, and Justinian.[19]

Translatio imperii, in the case of Muscovite Russia, was linked with another idea that directly impacted the further development of symphonia— the transfer of the supreme ecclesial authority. The *Story of the White Miter* (1490), written by Dimitrij Gerasimov and originally developed in Novgorod, was appropriated by Moscow. Here we find the idea that after the fall of Constantinople, Novgorod (another ecclesial center, headed by an archbishop) became the new center of Orthodoxy. The story is reminiscent of the so-called *The Donation of Constantine*. Similar to *The Donation*, the *Story of the White Miter* repeats the motif of the special gift that Emperor Constantine gave to the pope (and, by extension, to the papacy or the church as a whole).[20] However, instead of lands and political authority over the "West," the *Story of the White Miter* focuses on the ecclesial authority, symbolized by the white episcopal miter that was, supposedly, given to the pope when Constantine moved the capital to Constantinople. Once Rome departed from the true faith, so the logic goes, the supreme ecclesial authority, with the white miter as its symbol, was transferred to Constantinople. Before the fall of Constantinople, the patriarch received a vision of its destiny and, as he was ordered, sent the miter to Archbishop Vasilij of Novgorod. "There it was put in the Sophia Cathedral as a sign that Novgorod had become the guardian of Christian orthodoxy."[21]

What is important to notice in this story is that, unlike in the Roman tradition, the concept of legitimacy is not primarily related to legality, institutions, and procedures (even fake ones), but instead depends on "true faith." The loss or distortion of true faith (Orthodoxy) in itself delegitimizes both the political and the ecclesial authority.

Filofei's story and the *Story of the White Miter* allow us to formulate the "Third Rome" doctrine in yet another way: The fate of the imperial capital and the spiritual ("true faith") capital are indivisible; the capital of true faith travels together with the imperial capital and vice versa. As such, this logic manifests itself as another expression of symphonia. Faithfulness to true faith is a prerequisite for the very existence of the legitimate imperial center, to enable the (one and only) legitimate imperial center to also be the center of Orthodoxy. This logic continued to be present in the imagination of many Orthodox believers until the modern time.

The practice of referring to "original" Rome, as a means of legitimizing Moscow as the new imperial center, can be found in the "Third Rome" political theology. The family tree of the grand princes of Moscow was extended so that it now went back to Augustus himself.[22]

The "first Rome" motif, however, did not play a major role in the development of the Russian political theology in this period. The topic of the "first Rome" (with both its ancient and Christian heritage) would wait for the time of Peter the Great to become utilized as another element in the construction of the new (modern) empire.

The breadth of their political aspirations, united with the *translatio* narratives, and solidified by the variations of symphonia, gave enormous symbolic weight and prestige to the Russian rulers. An articulation of an "official" political theology regarding the place and role of the ruler came in 1551, with the Hundred Chapters (*Stoglav*) Council. In its decisions, the council referred to Justinian's *Novella* as the foundation of the Russian-type of church-state relations. Although the council glorified the "sacred autocracy," there was an attempt to find a balance between the church and the state within the discussions of the Council: The czar urged the bishops to oppose him if he transgressed God's commandments. Metropolitan Macarius promised opposition to the czar if pressed by the czar to act against divine law.[23]

The theological basis for this council and the *translatio* of the imperial title ("czar") to the Russian rulers was provided by Joseph Volotsky (1439/40–1515). Volotsky advocated a form of a political theocracy, accentuating the role of the emperor as a defender of Orthodoxy against all heresies.[24] Calling emperor Vasilij III "czar" and "*Vladyka*," he appropriated the word "Vladyka"—meaning "ruler" in a broad sense, but also used in Slavonic specifically for "bishop"—for the political context. This resembles a Constantinian-type of political theology, in which the emperor appears also as a "bishop."

Metropolitan Macarius (⚜ 1542–63), mentioned above, played an important role in the creation of the imperial political theology in the sixteenth century. During the coronation of Ivan IV (1547), Macarius, like Volotsky, called the ruler "czar," which was "reserved earlier for Christ, Biblical kings and the mightiest secular rulers known to the Muscovites, the Byzantine emperor and the Mongol khan."[25] In this way, conceptual continuity was established between the emperors of the Second Rome and Ivan IV.[26]

The elevation of the metropolitan to the rank of patriarch was the next logical step, even though it came relatively late in the history of the church in Russia—in 1589—more than a hundred years after the fall of Constantinople. In large part because much of the survival of the church, at this time, depended largely on finances from Russia, Patriarch of Constantinople Jeremiah II was pressed to elevate the rank of the metropolis of Moscow to that of the patriarchate. He consecrated Metropolitan Job of Moscow as patriarch, and the other traditional patriarchal sees, financially dependent upon Russia, approved this. Here, again, the same "Rome" motif figured as an important idea in the elevation process; the patriarch referred to the Russian Empire as "third Rome."[27]

The "Third Rome" doctrine is instructive as to the difference between the "Christian" character of the Russian Empire, as its ideologists and political theologians envisioned it, and the "Romanness" of the Christianized Roman Empire. In addition to the promotion of the new imperial center, Filofei's narrative also has a strong eschatological element to it, something that did not play an important role in the context of the Roman Empire, either classical or "Christian." Filofei suggests that the end of history is approaching and that Russia, through both its church and its state apparatus (the emperor), has an important role to play in the cosmic drama that the world is about to go through. He asserts that Russia will become indispensable in the "end things" that will take place before the establishment of the universal and ever-lasting Kingdom of God. This idea would continue to excite various later Orthodox believers, priests, and political theologians, not only in Russia but in other Slavic countries as well. In this construct, the Russian Orthodox emperor becomes thus the "eschatological emperor,"[28] the emperor of all Orthodox Christians, inside and outside of Russia, their protector and defender. In view of this "Russian messianism" and the *eschatological urge* (also very political in its character), one can even claim that the Bolshevik-type of messianism is a late, secular appropriation of this political theology.[29]

However, in spite of all its attractiveness and the powerful imagery it uses, the idea of the "Third Rome" was popular in rather limited circles in the sixteenth century, and it practically played no role in later Russian history until its revitalization in the nineteenth century. It has been argued that the idea had no significant impact on the official state policies in this interim period, contrary to what was held in the West for a very long period. As Will van den Bercken points out:

> No expansionist or messianic aims lay behind the doctrine of the third Rome. The Orthodox tsars never engaged in a war against the Latin world for their faith; they never made attempts to recapture Constantinople. The idea of the last Rome, of being the last Christian empire, was an eschatological notion: Russia had to preserve its rich store of faith in purity in the last phase before the end of the world, which had begun in 1492, or the year 7000 according to the Byzantine reckoning.[30]

"Third Rome" thus appears, in its original context, primarily as a rhetorical instrument useful for constructing political theologies—probably designed to flatter the rulers or to make the church and its representatives look good in the eyes of the emperors. However, the "Third Rome" narrative would become much more popular and influential in the nineteenth century with Russian Romanticism. The rediscovery of the "Third Rome" discourse in the latter period seems to have played an important role in the application of the meaning, significance and popularity of the concept retroactively, projecting the aspirations, interests, and fascination of its modern interpreters onto the past.[31] This, of course, does not exclude the possibility that those individuals who composed the texts elaborating upon the doctrine genuinely believed in such a providential course of history and in the continuity of the church-state prerogatives stretching back to Constantinople and even, in some cases, to the classical Roman heritage.

Another concept seems to have been much more influential in the history of Muscovite Russia—the idea of Moscow as the "New Jerusalem." As we have already seen, the Old Testament imagery played an important role from the very beginning in contextualizing Russian (Christian) rulers within the broader, universal "sacred" history. Of course, Old Testament, ancient Roman, early Christian, or "Roman Christian" motifs are by no means mutually exclusive or contradictory in this kind of ideological project: The papal ideology of the Renaissance period, for example, had no problem relating the stories of Romulus, Augustus, and Greek mythological heroes to the Christian martyrs, Apostle Peter, and the papacy.

The idea of the New Jerusalem was also not a Russian invention. Russians,

> like early medieval Western Emperors, imagined themselves as part of a historical process stretching from the creation of the world to the apocalypse, and were certainly aware of the prestige and importance of Rome as part of this divinely guided process. Yet the evidence overwhelmingly indicates that the Bible in general, and the Old Testament in particular, loomed far larger in the historical imagination of Muscovites than did any image of Rome. This correction in turn implies a common Christian ideological heritage shared by both Russia and Western Europe instead of an exotic Russian ideology which drove the Russian state in peculiar (and largely undesirable) directions.[32]

In such a perception—which, again, was probably much more ideological imagery than a widely and strongly held belief—there was no contradiction between the ideas of Rome and Jerusalem, as both of them had to be incorporated into the universal narrative, of which Moscow and Russia became indispensable parts.

The concepts of the "New Jerusalem" and/or the "New Israel," emptied of their eschatological and liturgical meaning, played an important role in the formulation of Russian imperial political theology, just as they had previously played an important role in Byzantine or in medieval Western monarchical discourses. As a result, the prestige and authority of Moscow and Muscovite Russia were constructed based on the idea that the Russian state represented the (re)embodiment of the Old Testament kingdom of David and Solomon. The rulers of this reincarnated state were, as already mentioned, the "New Davids," "New Solomons," or "New Moseses," and the people subjected to them, the "New Israel."

These motifs found their place in the coronation ceremony for Ivan IV, during which, in the prayers lifted up for the emperor, the metropolitan explicitly mentioned Israel, Samuel, and David.[33] This tells us something about the character of symphonic ideas in Muscovite Russia. An attentive listener recognizes in the imagery of Samuel and David their contemporary Russian counterparts: Metropolitan Macarius and Ivan IV. It is also possible to read a subtler message—one about the aspiration of the church and metropolitans to secure a special position within the ecclesial-political order, as those who mediate (and ultimately decide on) the coronation/appointment of the ruler. In other words, this utilization of the Old Testament stories advances the message that God, who acts through His prophets/priests, also appoints, through them, the (legitimate) kings. Equally important, lest anyone forget: The same God, acting again through His prophets/priests, can revoke His blessing if the ruler sins against Him.

This method opens the door for a theocratic interpretation of symphonia, in which the church (and its representatives) acts as the indispensable ingredient of the socio-political reality—the church even more important/authoritative than the ruler. In this narrative, God's presence and will among the "chosen nation" is secured through His prophets and priests (which become especially important if/when the appointed kings depart from the path of the Lord). This idea would continue to inspire Russian political theologians in the centuries to come.

The construction of the Kremlin—the crown jewel of the new imperial center—is a telling example of the larger-scale project underway, a project that made use of the Old Testament images and history of the ancient Israelites. This construction started in the fifteenth century and would continue throughout the sixteenth. This very heart of the Russian state (designed by Italian architects) was the "New Zion" and "New Jerusalem" built for the "New Israel," the new "people of God."[34] In accordance with its ideological program, the decorative program of the "Golden Palace" of the Kremlin compares Moses, Gideon, and Joshua and his conquest of the Promised Land with Prince Vladimir and the history of Russia. More significantly yet, Boris Godunov (♔ 1598–1605) planned to

> Build a new church in the Kremlin that would eclipse all others in richness of decoration as well as in size, a church meant to be modeled both on Solomon's temple in ancient Jerusalem (it was referred to as the "holy of holies") and on the Church of the Holy Sepulcher in contemporary Jerusalem.[35]

Patriarch Nikon (♔ 1652–66) also repeats these same themes: His designs for the New Jerusalem monastery on the Istra River near Moscow also contained a reconstruction of the Holy Sepulcher Church within "New Jerusalem" (although not without strong criticism[36]). Nikon is also known for his political engagement and aspirations to "put the authority of the church above that of the state,"[37] which eventually led to his deposition.

There was, however, another manifestation of symphonic tendencies in Russian lands, exceptional in that they did not follow autocratic or imperial models, much less the dynastic principle of Western kingdoms but, on the contrary, were a reflection of a *republican* and (premodern) *democratic* organization. Such is the case of "Lord Novgorod the Great," as its citizens called it, known also in literature as "Novgorod Republic," "Novgorod Democracy" and the "Republic of St Sophia."[38]

The Novgorod Republic existed from the twelfth century until it was finally conquered by Moscow in 1471. The very description as well as the assessment of the political system, its successes and failures, has historically depended on the ideological perspective from which individual authors were writing, and the political agendas they had—it was dismissed as dysfunctional and chaotic when centralized autocratic rule was supposed to be affirmed; it was uncritically idealized and romanticized as a premodern social paradise by the opponents of autocracy; and it was revived also in modern times as a proof of the presence of republican and democratic tendencies in the tradition of Russia that were not only older than most of their Western counterparts, but also much more advanced, covering a much larger territory.

Based on the available sources, it seems that Novgorod state represents an important chapter in the history of political organization, especially in the context of Orthodox Christianity:

> The burgess, the responsible citizen, who possesses a stake in the Republic, and who deliberates, votes, and fights for its freedom and greatness, is constantly in evidence. . . . Every rank, power, and interest in Novgorod rests upon the sovereign people. As no dynasty can establish itself permanently, still less any aristocracy of western type, the Republic preserves with peculiar purity the ancient democratic ideas and institutions. Down to the Muscovite conquest, the city is more powerful than any of its lords, officials, or classes. The great popular assembly, comparable to that of Athens in power, is supremely characteristic of Novgorod among Russian states. The *Veche* invites a new prince, and arraigns, imprisons, or expels him when it pleases.[39]

Having many parallels in the institutions of both the Athenian democracy and the Roman republic,[40] Novgorod's popular assembly is not only the supreme social-political decision-making body, which elects and removes public officials, but it also elects religious leaders—archbishops:

> The Archbishops, usually chosen by the Prince and citizens—but needing confirmation by the "Metropolitan of all Russia" at Kiev, Vladimir, or Moscow—ultimately depend on popular favour. Thus in 1211 Mitrofan is exiled, "bearing this gladly, like John Chrysostom," and after eight years is recalled by the same popular voice. . . . Within the limits of the sacred lot, and of Orthodox feeling, it [popular assembly, *Veche*—D.Dž.] elects, as it can depose, the *Vladykas* or Archbishops.[41]

It is for this reason that the Novgorod system is sometimes called a theocratic (or "half-theocratic") democracy.[42] The cathedral of St Sophia was a common place where the popular assembly would meet. In parallel to the Roman interest in the religious sphere as a vital component of the political, the citizens of Novgorod were very much interested in the preservation and defense of the *true* (and *pure*) faith, which occasionally led into what we would call nowadays acts of religious intolerance.[43] The importance of Novgorod is that it allowed for a symphonic model that is closest to the ancient Roman republican understanding of the integration of the religious and the socio-political, on top of which is neither one supreme political figure (emperor) nor one supreme religious figure (bishop/patriarch), but rather the republic itself, as a *people* (citizens) in their articulated political presence, who are expressed through the popular assembly. Depending on the angle from which we look at this political phenomenon, and how much significance we give to particular aspects of the religious-political life of the Novgorod state, it can be an example of an alternative (democratic/republican) symphonic model, which would be an inspiration for modern nation/ethnicity-based interpretations of "ideal" political systems from an Orthodox point of view, or as an example of a more "anarchic" form of social organization within the Orthodox tradition.

Given the position, status, and historical influence of the church in Muscovite Russia, and the absence of the tradition of Roman sources of legitimization (such as the Roman army, people, or the Senate), the appointment of the political leaders by the "will and mercy of God," using the imagery of the Old Testament, was the narrative promoted as the chief source of legitimization. This, naturally, gave Orthodoxy (as a new form of political ideology) and the church an extremely important place in the socio-political sphere.

There was also another important aspect of the Old Testament imagery exploited by the dominant political theology in Russia—one that would leave an everlasting trace and remain at the heart of the dominant Orthodox political theologies in the modern period. Unlike the New Testament concept of the (new) "chosen people," essentially meaning the Church (as a liturgical assembly of all the faithful), the Old Testament concept of the "chosen nation" implies a concrete ethnic and political entity, a certain *nation* (*narod*) with a particular mission in the world. This is why the Old Testament understanding of the "chosen people" has been tirelessly exploited over the past two millennia by numerous Christian theologians aspiring to identify specific socio-political collectives (tribes, ethnicities, nations) as analogous to the Old Testament "Israel." Because of the numerous attempts to apply this Old Testament concept to the present, the concept of "New Israel" or the "new chosen nation" has come to play quite a prominent role in political and religious discourse since the fourth century, implying that a specific "Christian(ized) nation," as an ethnic and political entity, replaces the ancient Israel in its historical mission. Such an understanding of the "New Israel" concept is exactly the opposite of what is implied by "chosen people" or "holy nation" in the New Testament,[44] but this complexity was irrelevant for those with an interest in designating their own nation/ethnicity as the "new chosen nation."

This explains why Old Testament imagery was very suitable for the dominant type of church-state ideologies in general and, in this case, for Muscovite Russia in particular. This "New Israel," as a specific tribal/ethnic/ national entity with a special role in the whole history of salvation, became the image of what the (unified) Russians were supposed to become. Through this lens, this ethnic group becomes God's people, who will enjoy his support as long as they and their leaders remain faithful to Him.

Here one can notice an important difference when one compares the Russian context (once the territories were unified under an autocratic rule) and the context of the New Roman Empire. As a multiethnic and multicultural empire (at least until much later in its history), the empire of New Rome could not create an ideological mirror image of the Old Testament Israel based on a specific ethnic identity and common "founding fathers" (whose, blood-related descendants constitute the "chosen nation"). Instead, it relied upon its *Romanness*, together with its "Christian" character, to form the basis for that kind of "New Israel" imagery. The "people," both as the subjects and the source of legitimization of the imperial office, were "Roman Christians" (or "Christianized Romans"), unified under the protection and care of one (Roman) emperor and one church. "Roman Christians" (that would, eventually, become "Orthodox Greeks") thus became the successors of the Old Testament "Israel," as well as of the classical Roman *populus*. The "multicultural" character of the Christian Roman Empire (until late in its history) was, formally speaking, somewhat closer to the New Testament idea of the new "chosen people" in its universalism. The difficulty, however, was that the ecclesial/eschatological concept of "chosen people/New Israel" was also here "kidnapped" from its original (eschatological and liturgical) context and was identified with political phenomena belonging to "this world." And a side effect was that this "kidnapping" of the idea of the "new chosen people" obscured (as it always does) the immediacy of the eschatological expectations that are attached to it in the New Testament tradition.

The image of a particular "Orthodox nation" (e.g., the Russians, Serbs, Greeks, etc.) as an ecclesial-political collective standing in a specific relationship with God would become the dominant idea and one of the cornerstones in the formation of modern nation-based (Orthodox) political theologies. Each Orthodox nation, understood this way, is supposed to be governed by an Orthodox king/emperor, and to be "spiritually" united through the local church, administered by a metropolitan, archbishop, or patriarch.[45] This logic would be incorporated into modern "Orthodox monarchy" theories, but it can also be found in nation/ethnicity-based "Orthodox democracies."[46] *Local churches*, meant to be territorially organized units enabling all of the faithful to celebrate the Eucharist together (irrespective of their ethnic, racial, or national identities) and in communion with all other local churches, would effectively (and regrettably) become "national churches" in the course of modernity. In such a context, the priests, monks, or charismatic (lay) individuals often become the "prophets," assuming upon themselves the role of God-appointed tribunes whose duty is to warn, instruct, and protect the nation.[47]

The religious-political motifs discussed above, from the rich arsenal of political theology in czarist Russia, speak also to the broader topic of "Holy Russia," which requires at least a brief comment. The "Holy Russia" discourse is connected to the idea of the (sacred) "Orthodox monarchy" (although it cannot be reduced to it). It remains influential in Orthodox political theologies through present time. Symphonic elements can still be recognized in these discourses in their aspirations to offer accounts that advocate the union of the church, the *people*, the *land*, and/or the *state* (*zemlja* and *gosudarstvo*). This union often becomes mystical: something that cannot necessarily be sorted out in institutional or legal terms, or fully realized within the course of history.

The mystical sources of the Russian state and its mission in the world are somewhat different from the "sacred" character of the (New) Roman Empire. What acquires importance in the Russian context is the *national* dimension, i.e., the ethnicity-based character of the (Christianized) *Slavs*, out of which the state structures, their ideology and their (metaphysical) mission in the world grow.[48]

Church-state relations in Russia entered a new phase during the reign of Peter the Great. This new phase would also mark a new type of modern, and one could claim *secularized*, symphonia, in which the modern absolutist state becomes dominant, aspiring to control the church or, at least, to limit its influence.

Following the death of Patriarch Adrian (in 1700), Peter the Great (♔ 1696–1725) prevented the appointment of Adrian's successor, leaving the post vacant for two decades. As part of his modernization project, the emperor issued *Spiritual Regulation* (1721), which abolished the patriarchate altogether, instead instituting the collective body—the Holy Synod—to govern the church. Although traditionally interpreted as just a state office, with the decisive influence of the chief procurator (and, through the Office of the Procurator, the emperor himself), G. L. Freeze convincingly demonstrates that the situation, in practice, was different. The Synod enjoyed significant autonomy in ecclesiastical matters, primarily as a result of the opposition of the members of the Synod (the bishops) to the secular intrusion into strictly church business. One could, in fact, speak of a specific revival of the earlier symphonic model, in which the state was supposed to take care of the "worldly" needs of its subjects, and the "'ecclesiastical'—literally, the 'spiritual' (*dukhovnaia*)—college was to satisfy the spiritual needs of the Orthodox population."[49] Freeze also points to the significance of particular personalities that occupied both the offices of the procurator and the Holy Synod, which arguably mattered more than the formal regulations. This became apparent under Chief Procurator Protasov in the 1840s, who established an "unprecedented influence over church affairs," which then became "the prototype for the usual—and greatly exaggerated assessment of the chief procurator's authority."[50] It is also important to note that local dioceses enjoyed virtually complete autonomy in their daily operations, where the oversight of the church business depended on the local bishops. Nevertheless, the state—following the contemporary paradigms of the "enlightened" Western (absolutist) monarchies—aspired to oversee and control the ecclesial businesses when and where it was important for the state.

Peter the Great also abandoned Moscow and the New Jerusalem symbolism. As a grandiose modernizing project, he would build a new imperial capital—Saint Petersburg. This project, although not primarily religious in its aspirations and symbolism, still combined ancient motifs with those of Christian Rome. The city was named after Peter the Apostle (not Apostle Andrew, the traditional protector of Russia), and parallels to ancient Rome can be seen in the "two bronze knights" with Peter's equestrian statue in St. Petersburg, a reference to the famous statue of Marcus Aurelius decorating the Campidoglio square.[51]

During this time, the main ideologist-theologian, Feofan Prokopovich (1681–1736), contributed to the mainstream political theology by reaffirming monarchy and absolutism as a divine institution.[52] In his view, the superiority of the state over the church becomes a distinctly "Orthodox" feature, as opposed to the heretical "papist" approach that sees the state subordinated to the church and its primates. Prokopovich's support for Peter and his reforms was somewhat paradoxical, though: Peter's modernization plans were largely a reflection of the Enlightenment and modernizing aspirations, but Prokopovich himself held anti-Enlightenment and anti-(secular) modernizing positions, which reflected the contemporary Protestant models (that he presented as distinctly "Orthodox"). Among the victims of the modernizing (also "Westernizing") projects of this time were also earlier, anti-autocratic and popular-democratic tendencies from the history of Russian lands.

Attempts to subordinate the church to the state would continue throughout the eighteenth century. Aspirations of Russian rulers to be, de facto, the heads of the church would explicitly be expressed by Catherine the Great (♕ 1762–96), who called herself *chef de l'église*.[53] It was Czar Paul (♕ 1796–1801) who would bring this process to the logical end, assuming the title of the "head of the church."[54] This tendency was strongly opposed only by Czar Alexander I (♕ 1801–25), who rejected the veneration of the rulers as blasphemous. Paradoxically enough, the idea that many Orthodox would later hold to be the traditional Orthodox model—in which the monarch and the state have a preeminent position both in society and in the church—in fact came to imperial Russia by mirroring contemporary Western European (primarily Protestant) models.

Finally, the reign of Nicholas I (♕ 1825–55) is of particular interest in the history of the idea of Russian autocracy. During this time, the official motto of the state (coined by Sergei Uvarov) was "Orthodoxy, Autocracy, and Nationality (Nationhood)."[55] It can be understood as the peak of the Romanticist political theology based on earlier symphonic models, reinterpreted for the sake of Russia's nineteenth-century national and imperial aspirations. This version of state ideology implied a harmonious unity between the "holy trinity" of the modern Russian Empire: the state, personified in the figure of the autocrat, the nation, and the dominant/official religion. The "Russian" type of czarist ideology, in its symbiosis with the church, would remain in the imagination of many, both inside and outside the Orthodox world, as the ideal (and for many the only possible) form of Orthodox "symphonic" political theology and political organization.

Parallel to the tendencies to further advance absolutism, nineteenth-century political theology would also see new pushes for the revival of the more traditional variations of symphonia, in which the church enjoys autonomy in the ecclesial ("spiritual") sphere. Metropolitan Philaret (☦ 1821–67) was one of the prominent church figures who argued against a complete subordination of the church to the state. His political theology recognized the importance and even the necessity of the empire and autocracy, yet grounded the independence and authority of the church precisely in the idea that the czar's rule is sanctioned by the church, becoming legitimate only through the anointing which only the church can perform. This resembles many Western medieval political ideas. This formula implies that the empire (personified by the emperor and his coronation) bows its head before the church (personified by the priesthood), promising its obedience and faithfulness to the church and the Orthodox faith. Philaret's symphonic model implies that the church must remain independent from the state, and, since the church's only real ruler is Christ Himself, priests are forbidden from taking public (political) duties as state officials (which had already been expressed in the Sixth Canon of the Holy Apostles).

By refusing to recognize any metaphysical significance of the state or its function in the structure of salvation, Philaret could have been on the path to construct an alternative theological approach to the sphere of the political, asserting that, although not in a mutual conflict, church and state should remain in their distinct autonomous spheres and should not intervene in each other's competences. Unlike many of his predecessors, Philaret does not see the origin of the state in some sacred prototype (e.g., the Kingdom of God), but in natural categories, such as family. Although this insight could have led Philaret to outline a stronger contrast between the socio-political and the ecclesial (with its origin in the Kingdom of God and the not-of-flesh-and-blood reality), he instead tried to reconcile the two by affirming autocracy as being "naturally" derived from the patriarchal family model, and as something that should be in harmony with the Heavenly Monarchy, led by God. Although potentially very subversive, Philaret's political theology concludes with a more or less conventional affirmation of the emperor's office.

Variations of the symphonic ideal continued to inspire theologians, even in the new social and political environments that the nineteenth and twentieth centuries brought. To illustrate the persistence of the idea, its traces are found even in the opus of Sergei Bulgakov (1871–1944),[56] one of the most complex and most influential modern Orthodox theologians. It seems that for a brief period of time, after his disappointment with the Second

Duma (1907), a czarist-based symphonia resonated with him, although in a novel form. As Rowan Williams puts it,

> He describes in his autobiographical notes how, in the wake of the traumatic experience of the Duma, he abandoned his former republicanism and developed an intense devotion to the ideal of monarchy— indeed, to the person of the tsar. He was, he says, fully aware of the corruption of the tsarist system and of the personal weakness and suicidal incompetence of Nicholas II; but he was at the same time struck by a sense of the tsar as carrying the cross for his people, of the tsar not as the presiding authority in a police state but as the symbolic focus of Russia in all its pain and confusion. . . .
>
> Without the sacramental anchorage of political power in the Christian monarch, democracy was simply the perpetuation of the competing self-interest that had paralysed the Duma. . . .
>
> He believes it is important to underline the sense he had of royal authority as, so to speak, cruciform . . . what Bulgakov finds morally and spiritually compelling in the image of royal authority (and the reality of the monarchy in the Russia of 1907 and the years following) could almost be characterized as its anti-heroic quality: Nicholas II is not the doer of great deeds, the self-conscious savior of the nation, but someone bearing what is laid on him, like the monk bearing the duty or the penance imposed by a superior.[57]

THE MODERN NATION, ETHNICITY, AND STATE-BASED POLITICAL THEOLOGIES

T ogether with the political theologies affirming "Orthodox monarchy," the period of modernity has also seen the development of political theologies focusing primarily on ethnicity and/or nation and the affirmation of the nation-state.

The ideas of modern nations and nation-states are, to a large extent, in collision with the ideas of (pre-modern) aristocracy, monarchy, autocracy, and their—supposedly—sacred character. However, the concept of sacredness does not disappear in ("secular") modernity as the political models shift. Instead, the "national body" (both in "conservative" and "liberal" ideological orientations) begins to be understood as possessing the quality of (secular) *sacredness*, which, consequently, gives the state the quality of (secularized) *political sacredness*. The concept of "political sacredness" is thus detached from the monarchy/autocracy and the king or emperor, and transferred to the modern nation and nation states.[1] Because of this, modern (formally "secular") states and their rulers do not require an additional source of legitimization, although they often employ traditional churches (and their political theologies) to promote and solidify the social-political cohesion, dominant ideology, and the order of power.

In many modern nation- and/or state-inspired political theologies, including Orthodox ones, we find narratives in which the national/ethnic whole appears as the pseudo-ecclesial entity, which seeks to reconcile symphonic ideals with the modern, secular religious understanding of nations and nation states (not excluding monarchic or autocratic rule).[2]

88

In contrast to the Roman Empire, whose ideology (and corresponding political theologies) was not primarily based on an *ethnic* identity (given its multiethnic character), but rather on a state-based political theology, personified in the office of the emperor, the situation changed with the spread of Christianity to the "barbaric" tribes. With this development, Christianity encountered, on a much larger scale than it was before, specific ethnic, tribal identities. A clear majority of the people within these communities shared a common language, culture, blood-ties (conceptually speaking at least), and, also, religion. This premodern, Christianized ethnic/national identity was then appropriated in the period of the formation of modern nations/states, becoming the basis for both the modern understanding of what counts as "Orthodox people" (or "Orthodox nation") and the popular understanding of church autocephaly, not as an administrative territorial organization of the local church (irrespective of the ethnic, national, racial, or other identities of the local believers), but as a national question of supreme importance, the final step in the creation of modern "Orthodox" nations.[3]

The formation of modern nation-states in the territories where Orthodoxy was the dominant and traditional faith gave birth to modern interpretations of symphonia that primarily served the purpose of creating national cohesion. Many of the territories in which Orthodoxy had been the dominant faith in medieval times were occupied by the Ottoman Empire in the early modern period. Close ties between the national/ethnic identity and religion were forged by the millet system of the Ottoman Empire, which recognized religious institutions as political subjects in charge of their "population" (believers). This allowed for a certain level of autonomy of minority non-Muslim religious groups, but also contributed to the promotion of religious identity as a central feature for the identification of people's collective identity in a certain territory. Speaking the same language, and following a certain rite, became the basis for the formation of a political identity of non-Muslim groups within the empire. Thus, in the territories where the Orthodox population of, say, Serbian- or Bulgarian-speaking people lived, their specific (non-Muslim and non-Turkish) identity was produced as a combination of ethnic/national, linguistic, and religious (Orthodox) identities.

The nineteenth century saw liberation movements in many of the territories inhabited by the Orthodox population, and, in each, the population's religious identity became an indispensable part of its modern national

identity. This gave rise to the unfortunate situation in which the Orthodox world still finds itself, with the jurisdictions of local (autocephalous or
autonomous) churches mostly coinciding with national borders (or, where
new, specific national identities would be formed in distinction from, or
even opposition to, the already existing national-Orthodox identity and
its corresponding church organization; claims for the formation of new autocephalous churches would be advanced). Later, with the migration of
people from these national collectives (e.g., Serbs, Romanians . . .) to the
West, where there was no previous presence of the infrastructure of the
Orthodox church, those local autocephalous churches would start establishing their church networks to serve the national "diaspora." Thus, autocephalous churches became not only a way to territorially organize church
administration, but primarily a matter of the utmost national and political importance, up to the point that one often hears that a local church is
a national institution of utmost importance. This created the very unorthodox, and yet very popular, perception that the Orthodox Church consists of local "national churches." It seems to be of little use repeating that
the concept of a "national church" is oxymoronic and even heretical from
the perspective of Orthodox theology, as the phrase continues to be used
both inside and outside the "Orthodox countries."

The scale of this problem was already recognized in the nineteenth
century, which resulted in the famous 1872 condemnation of nationalism
(or *ethnophyletism*) as a heresy by the local council of the church of Constantinople (motivated by the defense of its own interests, to be sure).

One should, of course, note that such developments, resulting in "national" or "state churches," were by no means uniquely "Orthodox." Similar widely spread adaptations of Christianity for the purpose of national/
state ideologies are visible across the Protestant world, where "national
churches" and their theology played a decisive role in the formation of
modern national identities in these countries (while state churches still
continue to exist in some of them). We find a similar development (although more paradoxical) in the Roman Catholic world as well, where in
spite of the centralized church administration the "Roman Catholic identity" was an important ingredient in the formation of modern national
identities. What made Orthodoxy particularly prone to strong identification
with national ideologies was the fact that there was no unity on the administrative level (which, in this respect, made it similar to some Protestant
communities). There was a unity in faith, but not in terms of institution.

Thus, church authorities and church organization in each local "nation" became equivalent to the (national) state authorities and state organization. In addition to that, local languages have been affirmed in Orthodoxy throughout its history, which also contributed to the development of local ethnic/national identities in connection to the local church organization even in the pre-modern period (which makes the nation-religion-state dynamics in these countries, in the modern period, somewhat different from those in the West). This, inevitably, left its mark on the character of the dominant type of Orthodox political theologies in the period of modernity.

Yet, in spite of the significant changes in all of the local Orthodox contexts over the course of modernity, symphonic doctrines remained relevant and influential concepts. Political theologies that aspired to account for the modern nation or ethnicity, still sought for a "harmony" between the religious/ecclesial and socio-political spheres. In the absence of the "Christian" state authorities (e.g., due to the Ottoman rule, or under Bolshevism), the church takes upon itself the duty of preservation of the national identity and culture as one of the national institutions until there is a recovery of national/state institutions that can carry that task on.

An interesting phenomenon in this context is Russian *Narodnichestvo*. Although it can be considered as an offspring of Romanticism, it was very different from modern nationalism, or nation (and nation-state) building. To a certain extent, the concepts of Narodnichestvo and nation were even opposite. As Nikolai Berdyaev (1874–1948) notes, "Russian *narodniks* of all shades believed that among the people was preserved the secret of true life, a secret concealed from the governing cultured classes."[4] Narodnichestvo was, thus, not primarily interested in individual liberties, but rather in the *people* (as a more primordial social reality compared to the "nation") and the land/soil on which people live and work in order to survive. As a result, there was an intrinsic rural, anticapitalist, and even antimodernizing mentality among the narodniks. Berdyaev holds Narodnichestvo to be immanently socialist in its worldview, and the general context out of which anarchism grew:

> One of the chief supports of *narodnik* socialism was the fact that the Roman conception of property was always alien to the Russian people. The absolute nature of private property was always denied.[5]

In his view, Narodnichestvo inspired two different streams of thought, leading in two different directions: the nonreligious (and often antireligious) wing, which would become openly (and "classically") anarchist (of Bakunin's type, for instance), and the religious wing, the Slavophiles.[6]

The Slavophiles were among the most influential nineteenth-century intellectual movements in Russia. In their search for an organic wholeness of society, the Slavophiles can be seen as a manifestation of Romanticism, and more specifically as under the influence of German Romanticism. They sought to unite Orthodoxy and the "national (folk) spirit" and to *liberate* the Russian people and Russian Orthodoxy from their Western influences. However, in reality, this was not a single movement but rather a diverse set of ideas—sometimes even mutually exclusive—that revolved around various understandings of the mission and importance of the Slavic or Russian-Slavic people.[7]

Although they differ in their understanding of the dominion of the czars, or the place and role of the church in the social and the political realm, the core of Slavophile ideas was formulated by authors such as Mikhail Pogodin (1800–75), Aleksey Khomyakov (1804–60), Ivan Kireyevsky (1806–56), Konstantin Aksakov (1817–60), Nikolay Danilevsky (1822–85), and Konstantin Leontiev (1831–91).[8] These thinkers advocate varying "organic" models, in which society exists as a harmonious unity of the "people" and Orthodoxy. The "people" (or *narod*, or "nation" in its etymological meaning) does not appear primarily in the sense of a political collective that forms a state, but is rather a Romanticist, ahistorical concept that is supposed to describe the people's premodern (primarily rural) way of life, supposedly organic and innocent prior to contamination by the processes of modernization.

Khomyakov perceived the West as a society that had not successfully responded to the issue of human freedom, having chosen either "unity without freedom" or "freedom without unity," as expressed in the type and structure of the Western (Roman Catholic and Protestant) churches.[9] Instead of atomized, individualized citizens living in a "society" (based on alienation and private ownership), the Slavophiles proposed "community" (or *obščina*—a commune), in which there is no alienation but a harmonious communal life, in which Orthodoxy plays a vital role as the "soul" of the people. Symphonia was thus not sought in the (institutional) harmony between the state and the church, but rather in more abstract harmony of the "soul" of the nation and national cohesion.

This is why the Slavophile ideas could be, at one level, related to the premodern *democratic* tendencies in Russian lands, and for the same reason they often clashed with the Russian imperial ideology. The time of Nicholas I was a time of continuous aspirations to *modernize* and "Westernize" Russia, building on the tradition of Peter the Great. But, in their advocacy of freedom and the organic and natural ties uniting the Slavs in a brotherly kind of community and in their attempt to restrict the power of the czars and affirm the *sobornost* as the main principle of Orthodoxy, both Khomyakov's and Kireyevsky's versions of Slavophile political theology exhibit some elements of anarchism.

On the contrary, the "state nationalists" perceived "Orthodoxy, autocracy, and nationality" as inseparable—with this "holy trinity" (surviving as a slogan even today) as the official motto during the reign of Nicolas I. Given the diversity among the Slavophiles, some philosophical overlap did occur. The "holy trinity" principle was also attractive to the Pan-Slavists, such as Ivan Aksakov (1823–86) and Nikolai J. Danilevsky (1822–85), who, contrary to the rest of mainstream Slavophiles, promoted statism and the imperialist policies of Russia across the Slavic Orthodox world.

Offering yet another perspective and standing in contrast to Khomyakov's "church democracy," Leontiev, a later Slavophile, defended organized church structures, hierarchically organized society, despotism, and the splendor of both the church and the state, best represented by the Byzantine Empire. For Leontiev, it was precisely Byzantine times and the social organization that should serve as the inspiration for Russia and the Slavic people.[10]

Finally, no matter how brief, any overview of nineteenth-century intellectual and religious streams of thought in Russia, must include the figure of Vladimir Solovyov (1853–1900). Although his name is strongly associated with Sophiology, Solovyov can also be considered a follower of the early Slavophiles, primarily of Khomyakov. The concept of *sobornost* is central to Solovyov's religious philosophy. Although it is first of all a religious-metaphysical concept, *sobornost* also carries social and political implications. Solovyov saw the unique position of the Orthodox church in its rejection of legalistic systems of authority (which he links primarily with Roman Catholicism) and individualism (which is typical of Protestantism). This makes the Orthodox church capable of affirming the "sophianic humanity" and establishing a "free theocracy" that would be an organic expression of the universal Christian communion, embracing both the church and the state.[11]

These Slavophile ideas resonated to quite a significant degree in other "Orthodox countries" both in the nineteenth and in the twentieth centuries.

Variations of the Slavophile political theologies, together with Romanticist reinterpretations of symphonia (merged with modern nation-building), remain influential in the Orthodox world up to this day. The dominant political theologies (often affirmed by the institutional church) in Russia, Greece, Serbia, Bulgaria, and other "Orthodox countries," have been exploiting primarily this kind of symphonia (and not the "original," Eastern Roman variations) in their attempts to make sense of the sociopolitical reality.

The nation- and ethnicity-based Orthodox political theologies have survived the collapse of "Orthodox monarchies" and continued to exist in the twentieth and twenty-first centuries as a strong opposition to "godless" communist regimes that, in one way or another, affected most of those countries with Orthodoxy as the dominant and traditional faith. These political theologies would also remain the foundations for contemporary "Orthodox nationalisms" and a variety of right-wing political movements and ideas representing themselves as "Orthodox" or traditional(istic). For such nation/ethnicity-based political theology, it is not only the godless communism—now habitually blamed for all evils of the twentieth century— but also the godless "West" that poses a threat to the national (and *Orthodox*) identity, to the survival of the "soul" of the nation and to the traditional way of life. In such a discourse, the "West" plays a role similar to the one that "Russia" (or the "East") plays in the imagination of the West—a constant threat, the source of evil, and yet it is also the source of never-ending, almost erotic fascination.

A good illustration of this post-monarchy, nation- and ethnicity-based political theology is offered by the theology of Justin Popović (1894–1979). His version of the Orthodox (Serbian) national symphonia continues to inspire the theological as well as popular and political imagination of many Serbs, and translates even into the programs of some political parties. A prolific author, often inconsistent or unclear in his claims, Popović's theology is difficult to analyze, especially within a very brief account. However, his political theology (although he does not use this concept, and would probably oppose its usage) is exemplified in his concept of *Svetosavlje*. In the preface to his book *Svetosavlje kao filosofija života* (Svetosavlje as a Philosophy of Life), in 1953, Bishop Nikolaj Velimirović, Popović's friend and collaborator, gave the classical definition of Svetosavlje as "Orthodox Christianity of the Serbian style and experience."[12] The word "Svetosavlje" is derived from the name of the first Serbian archbishop of the autocephalous church—St. Sava (Serbian: *sveti Sava*). Popović explains how this "philoso-phy" should be applied to various domains, including cultural and social life: "We want a society that represents and is, in itself, one organism, one body, and members of that society are (its) organic parts."[13] He claims that both society and individual human beings have the same aim—to make God present in each person and to "incarnate" Him in the society.[14] Al-though Popović does not give any precise description of how this society is supposed to function, it is certain that it should exist in a *harmonious* (symphonic) manner, maybe even as some kind of theocracy. He, for ex-ample, claims that, according to the Svetosavlje philosophy, everything, including the human being, society, people (nation), and the state "have to conform to the Church as an eternal ideal, but the Church must not, under any condition, conform to them or, even less, to be their slave."[15] He also defines the Church as both "a Divine-human organism" and "a Divine-human organization."[16] In the same chapter Popović identifies the New Testament concept of the "holy people" or "God's people" (1 Petr 2:9–10; 1.15–16) with the concrete political, national and ethnic collective—the Serbian people:

> The goal of the people as a whole is the same as the goal of an indi-vidual: to incarnate the Evangelical justice, love, holiness in one's self, to become a "holy nation" (1 Peter 2:9–10; 1 Peter 1:15–16); the "people of God" which, with its whole history, proclaims God's values and virtues.[17]

Similar discourse continues to develop Atanasije Jevtić (1938–2021), one of the students and spiritual children of Popović. Jevtić speaks of the "Or-thodox identity" of the Serbian people, of the "Christianization of the people's being and life," and also of the Serbian commitment to the "spiri-tual values" that became an "integral part of the people's soul" very early in its history.[18]

Some episodes from the national past certainly had an impact on the character of modern political theologies in Serbian territories. We can find a symphonic model in the Serbian medieval kingdom not only in the sense that the autocephalous church was closely related to the state, but also in some other, more specific elements: The first king and the first archbishop (of the autocephalous church) were brothers; almost all of the rulers of the Nemanjić dynasty were canonized as saints; and finally, in addition to being generous patrons of extensive monastery and church construction activities, there was a tradition among the rulers of resigning their post as kings toward the end of their lives and withdrawing to a monastery.

Montenegro represents another interesting case, as the territory that resisted the Turkish conquest much longer and much more successfully than most of the other parts of the Balkans (primarily because it was difficult to access it and even more difficult to maintain efficient control), preserving various degrees of independence during the modern period. For centuries, it was an ecclesiastical principality, a church metropolis ruled by Vladykas—bishops who were also performing the role of secular rulers. In the beginning, bishop-princes were elected (including the election at popular assemblies), then the office became hereditary. Because Orthodox bishops are monks, the throne was passed from uncles to nephews.

Ethnicity/nation/folk-based political theologies, usually relying on a (post)Romantic idealization of an "innocent," often village-oriented, premodern "real Orthodoxy" and an (innocent, traditional) people and their political expressions, bear the elements of a "theocratic democracy," which exhibits sometimes also anarchic elements. This is the reason why premodern examples of social organizations that were not based on monarchy/autocracy (such as the Novgorod Republic) could be a source of inspiration as well as of uncritical idealizations.

This, however, does not mean that the idea of autocracy or monarchy has disappeared from modern Orthodox political theologies, after the Orthodox kingdoms and their dynasties ceased to exist. The "Orthodox monarchy" (also "Sacred autocracy") discourse continues to be present in the contemporary Orthodox world. Approaches range from the more articulate theological arguments to the popular and theologically ill-articulated narratives defending monarchy simply by reiterating its position within the imaginary national/ethnic tradition, in each given local context. In Russia, this discourse was further strengthened with the canonization of Czar Nicholas II Romanov and his family in 2000.

Among the most vocal contemporary proponents of "Orthodox autocracy" (in the literature available in English) are Michael Azkoul and Vladimir Moss. Azkoul holds that the "sacred monarchy" is the only possible political form consistent with Orthodoxy. According to his arguments, the monarchy and the empire "imitate" the Incarnation.[19] Vladimir Moss is the author of numerous texts on a variety of subjects, including the topic of "Orthodox autocracy." Some of his works on this topic include *The Rise and Fall of the Russian Autocracy* and *A Monarchist Theology of Politics*.[20]

Contemporary "Orthodox autocracy" discourses often rely on some of the motifs related to the imperial rule that go back to the early Christian authors mentioned before, combined with the motifs from modern history. An example of such a discourse (which has a certain following in the Orthodox world, but outside of academic theological circles) articulates Yuri Vorobievsky (Юрий Ю. Воробьёвский), an Orthodox author, in his *The Path to the Apocalypse*. There we find a contemporary interpretation of the idea that the "one who restrains" the powers of evil (Thessalonians 2:7) is the (Orthodox) czar. Since there can only be one czar (just as there can only be one true faith), it was the Russian czars who were restraining the powers of evil, until Nicholas II Romanov abdicated. Leaving the imperial throne empty signified the beginning of the apocalyptic time resulting in the imminent arrival of the antichrist. On the same day, however, on which Nicholas II abdicated, an icon of Virgin Mary miraculously appeared in a village church, with imperial insignias. This signifies that the Mother of God took upon herself the prerogatives and (most important) functions of the imperial power, becoming thus the one who restrains the powers of evil—and that is the reason why the antichrist still has not appeared.[21]

Sometimes it is difficult to clearly differentiate between the "Orthodox monarchy/autocracy" discourse narrowly taken—relying upon the classical or modern variations of symphonia—and the more fluid traditionalist (in their author's claims, at least), patriotic, and imperial discourses offered by contemporary "Orthodox" political thought. As an example, Aleksandr Dugin (b. 1962), relying on some ideas from Ivan Ilyin's political philosophy, articulates a philosophy of geopolitics (also called "Neo-Eurasianism" and "Fourth Political Theory")[22] in which Russia has a central and unique role to play. The primary focuses of his critique are the "post-liberalism," "globalization," "post-modernity," and "the end of history" philosophies. He calls for a return to and reaffirmation of "tradition" (defined as "religion, hierarchy, the family") and "theology." Although his political philosophy has been characterized as "neo-pagan," he calls Putin a "czar," implying that there is a need both for a "strongman" to lead the country and for Orthodoxy to offer an ideological contextualization of the political.[23]

Interesting developments in this regard can be seen in contemporary (popular) Orthodox political theologies in the West (primarily in the US). Following the predominant right (and far right) public and political discourses (which in an almost fundamentalist manner affirm the "values" of nationalism and militarism), one can find Orthodox believers, authors, and clergymen formulating their political theologies in a way that is remarkably similar to traditional Orthodox (statist) political theologies, but adjusted to conform to their own social and political context. In the aftermath of the September 11, 2001, terrorist attacks, we find the cases when Orthodox clergy prayed "that the Lord our God may bring us speedily to victory," asking the Lord to "rise up to help us, and grant our Armed Forces in Your name to be victorious,"[24] while some authors construct extremely militaristic political theologies that not only justify wars, but also understand wars as a "virtue."[25] Many other theologians, both on the "right" and on the "left," adopt essentially the same position, only express it in much more delicate ways. In such cases the earlier imperial logic is adjusted for the purposes of the new (geo)political environment, but it remains consistent— just as the Roman Empire (eventually "Christianized") was supposed to rule the world, and the church prayed for it, so the empire of our times (the US) should exercise its hegemony, and the church should serve it (hoping that the present-day empire will also, eventually, become "Orthodox").

The Orthodox Christian tradition has presented us with a rich treasure of various theologies, and practical arrangements, articulating the meaning and purpose of the socio-political sphere within the broader theological concerns. Historically speaking, the church-state relations can be categorized in a series of models that show various degrees to which the state and church could be close to one another, alienated from one another, or integrated into one another:

> Church as the enemy of the state (the example of which would be the persecutions of the church under the Roman Empire or the Bolshevik regime);

> Church and state in an organic, harmonious unity, either as two expressions of one unified socio-political whole, or as two parts that are in a mutual harmony and understanding, thus producing a harmonious social sphere (many medieval and modern symphonic models would fall into this category);

> Cooperative autonomy, where each sphere preserves its autonomy and distinctiveness; however, they work together for the benefit

of each other and society as a whole (some symphonic models discussed above would fall into this category, as well as some modern secular models that do not radically distinguish between the religious and socio-political spheres);

Church subordinated to the state (evidenced in the aspirations of some Eastern Roman and Russian emperors, as well as in similar tendencies in the Protestant world);

Church as an above-state entity (where the state, or state rulers are subordinate, or supposed to be subordinate, to the church and/ or patriarch/pope, evidenced in in "papist" tendencies both in the West and in the East);

Church as state, which includes various types of "theocratic" forms of government, when church leaders and church organization effectively replace state leaders and state organization (e.g., papal states or ecclesiastical principalities);

Church and state as two distinct, separate, and/or antagonistic realities (present in some understandings of monasticism and Christian anarchist discourses).

This shows that the prevalent popular as well as scholarly perception of symphonia as a clear and coherent model and/or reality of church-state relations that represents *the* Orthodox understanding of the (ideal) character of church-state relations is deficient on multiple levels. There has never been one symphonia, either as a concept or a concrete practice. However, it is true that the majority of church-state models developed historically have been searching for various "harmonies" between the religious and the political sphere. The concept of symphonia can, thus, be used only in that very broad sense, as a concept that covers a variety of different ideas and practices aimed at articulating those relationships for the benefit of the church, state, or community as such. In this sense, symphonia also ceases to be sui generis "Orthodox" in any meaningful sense. As we saw, various types of symphonic models that can be found in the Orthodox world (including monarchic/republican, autocratic, democratic, imperial, or anarchic models) have their parallels outside of the Orthodox world as well. The period of modernity brought additional variation upon the topic. Some symphonic elements can be recognized even in the theologies focused on nation or ethnicity. We can recognize them in the attempts to integrate the socio-political, cultural, and the ecclesial/spiritual realms within one, harmonious "Orthodox-national" whole.

More importantly yet, the tradition of Orthodox Christian thinking about the relations between religion and politics, or church and state, as well as histories of those relations in concrete societies, is much more complex and cannot be reduced to symphonic models alone. Both actual events and theological thinking about the political in the Orthodox tradition demonstrate the presence of alternative political theologies (analyzed in Part II), that significantly, and sometimes even very sharply, depart from the dominant, symphonic models in understanding the political sphere or church-state relations.

Over the period of modernity, we have seen that those political theologies that cannot see any fundamental tensions or conflicts between the political and the Christian, between the state (or nation) and liturgy (eschatology) often end up serving the conservative and sometimes even reactionary ideological agendas in the modern period. In their logic, the harmony of the social and the political is primordial, natural, and logical, and any disturbance of such a harmoniously envisioned socio-political (and ecclesial-metaphysical) whole is a deviation and disturbance coming from the outside, from either the devil or a group of godless, wicked people who are against God, the church, "our" nation or culture. In the name of these (traditional religious or secular religious) values and concepts, devoted, pious believers are often ready to spill other people's blood, sacrificing them on the altar of the powerful idols—the nation and the state.

That said, another approach to the sphere of the political can also be found both in historical and in contemporary Orthodoxy. That is the "indifference" approach, claiming that Christianity (Orthodoxy) should primarily be focused on the "spiritual," and that theology as well as church representatives should refrain from entering into the political discourse or politics, regardless of the form of government or type of church-state relations. Though seemingly a very apolitical attitude, which sometimes can seem as an implicit affirmation of the status quo, the purpose of this position of a withdrawal from the explicit political discourse has often been not passivity or lack of interest for the world, but rather a protest against doing bad (political) theologies and bad politics in the name of the church or faith. And doing *bad* political theologies is what has, traditionally, constituted the mainstream of the political theology discourse.

Newer Approaches

O ver the last couple of decades, Orthodox theologians have started to look more carefully and systematically at modern phenomena such as parliamentary democracy, or pluralistic and secular society, and modern Western political philosophies, as phenomena that Orthodox political theology should somehow articulate and enter into a dialogue with. The results of these theological reflections have not been monolithic—in some cases we witness a very affirmative approach toward (Western-type) political institutions, the concepts of human rights, secular society, liberalism, etc., while, in others, many of these concepts are examined critically, and sometimes also rejected. These new approaches come as a result of several major changes in the Orthodox world that have occurred over the last hundred years:

A more significant presence of the "Orthodox diaspora" in Western countries, in which Orthodox Christians have been able to experience different forms of political and legal systems: An important moment in the formation of a more theologically vocal "Orthodox diaspora" was the Russian Revolution and the formation of the Bolshevik regime, which caused many Russians, including some of the leading thinkers, to emigrate to Western Europe and North America. The experience of different modes of social organization has gradually received its theological articulation.

The fall of the Berlin Wall and the collapse of the Soviet Union, which created a new socio-political situation in most of the countries with a majority Orthodox population: Theological responses to this change can be, very generally, divided into two categories: those that turned to traditionalism and/or some form of nationalism in search of a new conceptual/ideological framework, and those that opened the theological discourse toward the articulation and a more positive evaluation of modern (Western) political phenomena, such as democracy or pluralism.

Significant changes within the vocabulary and the focus of Orthodox theology: In spite of the widely held position that the *creative* age of Orthodox theological production ended with the time of the Seven Holy Ecumenical Councils (or no later than with the hesychastic controversy in the fourteenth century), the last hundred years or so have been the time of a renaissance of Orthodox Christian thinking (which can only be compared to the most creative periods of patristic theology), allowing for Orthodox theology to be "reinvented." Figures such as Sergei Bulgakov, Nikolai Berdyaev, Pavel Florensky, Nikolai Afanasiev, Paul Evdokimov, Vladimir Lossky, George Florovsky, Alexander Schmemann, all the way to Christos Yannaras, John Zizioulas, Andrew Louth, and Kallistos Ware, have made a tremendous impact on Orthodox theology and Christian thinking in general. The range of topics, the methodological approaches, and the strong eschatological element in some of them have enabled Orthodox theologians to start using a much more developed conceptual theological apparatus, able to address a variety of issues. This has made an impact on political theology as well. For instance, rather than repeating medieval or Romanticist postulates, it has become possible to think of the socio-political sphere based on renewed interest in eschatology, Eucharistic theology, and fresh readings of the Fathers.

One of the most prominent advocates of (Orthodox) "Christian democracy" and republicanism in the first part of the twentieth century is Georgy P. Fedotov (1886–1951). In the words of Mikhail Sergeev, Fedotov

saw the roots of democracy not in ancient Greece and Rome, but in the heritage of the Old Testament, which contains one of the most ancient critiques of monarchy. In his article "Foundations of Christian Democracy" Fedotov contrasts the charismatic authority of popular leaders described in the *Book of Judges* to the hereditary kingship defended in the *Book of Kings*.[1]

He based many of his concepts about Christian democracy on the analysis of the Novgorod Republic. He saw autocracy as a form of government that is alien to the Russian tradition. Unlike in the period of czarism, the power of Russian princes was limited by many factors, including public assemblies, boyars, and the church. In his view the Novgorod Republic represents "the most Russian" phenomenon of political organization.[2] Fedotov sees the political organization and ideology of the "Republic of St. Sophia" in parallel to the Old Testament theocratic (and anarchic) tendencies: It was Sophia (Mother of God), who was the supreme "ruler," while the sovereignty (in practical terms) was with the people, expressed through public assemblies. It was, in Fedotov's view, in these expressions of the "religious ideal of freedom in Orthodoxy" (suppressed over the centuries) where the "Orthodox supporters of democratic Russia" could find their inspiration.[3]

In addition to their broader metaphysical interests, some of the great Russian thinkers of the early and mid-twentieth century also made important steps toward a different kind of theological and religious-philosophical approach to the socio-political sphere. Two names stand out in this respect: Nikolai Berdyaev and Sergei Bulgakov. Both of them represent giants of Christian thought, and are indispensable in telling the story of Orthodox Christian political theology, particularly when it comes to the articulation of the socialist, communist, and anarchist ideas within it (which is why I will return to both of them in the second part of this book).

Bulgakov's articulation of democracy and secular society would receive a fresh evaluation in contemporary Orthodox political theology.[4] Both theological and political considerations of Bulgakov represent a complex endeavor. They reflect his own intellectual and spiritual growth, but also the rapidly changing socio-political context in which he lived. This is why some of his positions, when taken from different periods and in isolation from the issues he was responding to, may sound mutually incompatible, if not exclusive.

One such difficult place is Bulgakov's articulation of the modern ideas of secularity, democracy, or pluralism. On the one hand, it seems that he favored the ideas and values behind these political phenomena, as opposed to authoritarianism and the slavery of the people. And yet, it seems that he saw them as irreconcilable with the objective of transforming society into a sophianic reality, which would reflect the *Godmanhood* as the center of creation. In 1909, Bulgakov wrote: "The new personality of European humanity was, in this sense, born in the Reformation era, and this origin has left its mark: political freedom, liberty of conscience, human and civic rights were all proclaimed by the Reformation (at least in England)."[5] Yet, in 1932/33, he noted:

> Here we come up against the fundamental question of Christian life in our times: that of the "churching" of culture, as it is now expressed. . . . The simplest thing is to evade the question under the pretext of a distinction between what belongs to Caesar and what belongs to God (in the individual spirit). That has been the answer of Protestantism, which has put in train the secularization that is now suffocating the world. . . . The Church cannot be a party; it must be *the conscience of a society*, never using humility as an excuse for compromise or indifferentism. But it cannot go along with the secularist disintegration of social order; rather must its spiritual domination struggle towards victory *from within*. This was the ideal of a "free theocracy" found in the early Soloviev and the later Dostoevsky.[6]

Among the contemporary Orthodox Christian theologians whose theology is indebted to Bulgakov is Aristotle Papanikolaou (b. 1967). Papanikolaou's approach is complementary to Bulgakov's in two senses. Papanikolaou aspires to articulate the place and meaning of certain modern political phenomena such as democracy, liberalism, secularity, or pluralism, and to give a (positive) theological evaluation of the same. On the other hand, he also aspires to construct a political theology that would (while embracing the modern political concepts/phenomena mentioned above) be consistent with what he perceives as the "core axiom" of Orthodox Christianity— namely, "the principle of divine-human communion."[7] In this sense, when it comes to the political sphere, Papanikolaou gave himself the same task that Bulgakov was preoccupied with.

Alongside Papanikolaou, Pantelis Kalaitzidis (b. 1961) gave an important contribution in articulating alternative theological approaches to the socio-political sphere. Through his political theology, Kalaitzidis often reacts against the conservative, nationalistic, and right-wing tendencies in the Orthodox world—with a focus primarily on those in Greece. Similar to Papanikolaou's, Kalaitzidis's political theology aspires to be consistent with the fundamental elements of Orthodox theology while, at the same time, appreciating some aspects of the modern social and political phenomena and institutions, such as democracy, pluralism, or human rights.[8] Kalaitzidis strongly reacts against the ideologies that exploit the Orthodox Christian conceptual apparatus in order to defend or solidify national(istic) agendas or make the Church and faith into servants of state or national goals. His political theology also aspires to be consistent with the eschatological orientation of the Church.[9]

Although one can find many similarities between the approaches of these two theologians to the socio-political sphere, one can also notice some differences. Kalaitzidis is primarily focused on the issue of nationalism in its symbiosis with church structures, primarily in traditional Orthodox contexts (such as Greece). This critique and the realization that such traditionalist and even right-wing orientations cannot be reconciled with Orthodoxy and its understanding of the Church and liturgy make him embrace a more *leftist* approach (although he refuses the word "anarchist," probably because of the way this concept is being manipulated in the political sphere, not least in Greece).

Papanikolaou, on the other hand, reacts against right-wing tendencies both in the traditional Orthodox contexts and in the US, which makes him embrace "liberal democracy" as an optimal political system. It seems that Papanikolaou provides a theological justification/rationalization of "liberal democracy" out of the need to, first, respond to the "right-wing" political theologies that reject both any (meaningful) concept of "liberalism" as well as (parliamentary) democracy by offering different models that would be incompatible with the ("liberal") mainstream political discourse in the West, and second, avoid what he perceives as "political Nestorianism" (see below). It seems to me that one can theologically respond to both of these needs and concerns precisely by refusing to theologically appreciate or justify any specific socio-political system. My argument in the subsequent chapters responds, in part, precisely to this problem, and seeks to explain why only an "anarchist" position, which refuses to theologically affirm any political system as such, or recognize any metaphysical significance of political (power) structures (whether they are "liberal" or "conservative"), is consistent with some of the basic premises of Orthodox Christianity, including "the principle of divine-human communion."

Cyril Hovorun (b. 1974) is another prolific contemporary Orthodox theologian who has made a contribution to a variety of topics, such as ecclesiology, patristic theology, and ecumenical theology.[10] His interest in church-state relations, and in the presence of the church in the public sphere grew out of his interest in ecclesiology and contemporary political topics, and has become a focus of his more recent publications. With both his scholarly work and essays that are accessible to a more general audience, Hovorun has been addressing the issues of contemporary Orthodoxy in the political sphere and the relationships between the church and state in Russia and Ukraine, as well as the implications of traditional (symphonic) Orthodox political theologies on the contemporary social and political context.[11]

In the theology of Athanasios Papathanasiou (b. 1959) we find an approach to the political sphere that would be consistent with what I call "anarchist" tendencies in the history of Orthodox political theologies. Using the concepts such as "sacred anarchy," or referring to the Gospel and Resurrection as a "weak force" (vis-à-vis the political realm),[12] Papathanasiou addresses a number of crucial questions that need to be articulated in the socio-political realm (including economic issues). His articulation of an authentically Christian approach to the political realm, which he carefully differentiates from other political options, both on the "left" and on the "right," makes his political theology consistent with what I call "anarchist" tendencies in Orthodox Christian theology.

This makes Papathanasiou's approach to the political in some important respects similar to the approach of two contemporary Serbian priests and authors, Radovan Bigović (1956–2012) and Zoran Krstić (b. 1962). They are among those theologians who have tried to articulate an approach toward the socio-political sphere that would depart from the traditional symphonia models (and/or nation-based discourses) and engage in a dialogue with some of the typically modern (and Western) social and political ideas and institutions.[13] Both authors develop a theology that is critical of the traditionalistic (especially nationalistic and anti-West) theological discourses in the Orthodox world, as well as appreciative of many of the modern achievements in the socio-political realm. Both authors, however, are cautious not to uncritically celebrate or dogmatize any of the typically modern phenomena, drawing a clear distinction between the Church and Her approach to the world, and the social and political phenomena that have only relative significance. Krstić in particular is careful not to champion any model of political organization per se. In his view, there is a reason why Orthodox Christianity has never come up with a formal social teaching that would present a clearer (more defined) version for the socio-political whole: "Truth cannot be locked into a system, no matter how good that system may be."[14] This approach, and Krstić's insistence on the (essentially) apophatic character of Orthodox theology qua theology, are very compatible with the approach in this study and the theological argument presented in Part II.

Some of the contemporary Orthodox political theologies aspire to articulate the issues of human rights, the secular state, etc. in a way that would be consistent with—or at least not openly antagonistic toward—a more "traditionally Orthodox" understanding of the socio-political sphere. Important in this respect are two documents issued by the patriarchate of Moscow (the Holy Council of Bishops of the Russian Orthodox Church): *The Bases of the Social Concept of the Russian Orthodox Church* (2000), and *The Russian Orthodox Church's Basic Teaching on Human Dignity, Freedom and Rights* (2008).

The *Bases* is an elaborate document that aspires to articulate an Orthodox approach to a variety of social, political, and ethical issues. Relying on the Old Testament-type of arguments in defense of the nation, patriotism, state, dominant type of morality, etc., we learn from the document that "the Church unites in herself the universal with the national" (II. 2), that the patriotism of the Orthodox Christian "should be active" and that it is "manifested when he defends his fatherland against an enemy, works for the good of the motherland, cares for the good order of people's life through, among other things, participation in the affairs of government" (II. 3). The document even affirms the concepts of "National Churches" (II. 2) and "Orthodox nation."[15]

Of special interest is Chapter 3, which is dedicated to the relationships between the church and the state. The document recognizes that "the emergence of the temporal state should not be understood as a reality originally established by God" (III. 1). Probably reflecting on the experience of the Orthodox Church in Russia during the Soviet times, the authors are careful to point out that "Christians should avoid attempts to make it absolute and fail to recognize the limits of its purely earthly, temporal and transient value," while also asserting that "power itself has no right to make itself absolute by extending its limits up to complete autonomy from God and from the order of things established by Him. This can lead to the abuse of power and even to the deification of rulers" (III. 2).

Even though there is a long section dedicated to the traditional models of church-state relations and the "explicit ideal of church-state relations" (i.e., symphonia), the document recognizes the secular system as a reality of many modern states. It calls for cooperation between the church and the state in certain domains such as humanitarian activities, but it also affirms a clear distinction between the two. The document explicitly states that the church "should not assume the prerogatives of the state," and that the state "should not interfere in the life of the Church" (III. 3), and the faithful are also reminded that the "Church may request or urge the government to exercise power in particular cases" (III. 3) and that the "Church remains loyal to the state" (III. 5). This, in many ways a self-contradicting chapter, also allows for a possibility of a genuine "spiritual revival" of society (in the future), which would allow—as seems to be implied by the text—for a different (theocratic?) form of government that would depart from secular principles:

> Any change in the form of government to that more religiously rooted, introduced without spiritualising society itself, will inevitably degenerate into falsehood and hypocrisy and make this form weak and valueless in the eyes of the people. However, one cannot altogether exclude the possibility of such a spiritual revival of society as to make natural a religiously higher form of government. (III. 7)

In the second document, *The Russian Orthodox Church's Basic Teaching on Human Dignity, Freedom and Rights*—which by no means exhibits the highest levels of theological sophistication—we find an attempt to articulate "the human rights institution" from an Orthodox Christian perspective. Human rights are, generally, defended and affirmed, but throughout the document we find an accentuation of the limited scope of their application every time they contradict (or depart from) the "moral dimension of life."[16] The document also operates with obscure concepts such as "natural" and "traditional morality" (III. 3, 4). The most controversial part, however, is the one in which human rights are restricted when and if they contradict "love for one's homeland" (III. 4). The document authoritatively claims that the "love of a person for his family and other loved ones cannot but spread to his people and the country in which he lives" (III. 4) and concludes:

> From the point of view of the Orthodox Church the political and legal institution of human rights can promote the good goals of

protecting human dignity and contribute to the spiritual and ethical development of the personality. To make it possible the implementation of human rights should not come into conflict with God-established moral norms and traditional morality based on them. One's human rights cannot be set against the values and interests of one's homeland, community and family. The exercise of human rights should not be used to justify any encroachment on religious holy symbols [and] things, cultural values and the identity of a nation. Human rights cannot be used as a pretext for inflicting irretrievable damage on nature. (III. 5)

In 2020, a "Greek" (mostly Greek-American) response to the "Russian" documents was produced. *For the Life of the World: Toward a Social Ethos of the Orthodox Church* represents a clear departure from the documents of the Moscow Patriarchate in many ways, and one can even say that this "teaching" was written in opposition to them. It is clear that its authors were trying to be as comprehensive as possible in the scope of topics they address (e.g., the issues of social and political organization, human rights, climate change, sexuality, gender equality, etc.), and to offer a balanced view, which would be rooted in the tradition, and yet also embrace a variety of contemporary perspectives. While in some of its segments (and up to a point), the document does express particular claims that are similar to the positions this book argues for, one cannot overlook that, in other segments, the document affirms a particular order of power, with its ideological narratives that, implicitly, justify imperial aspirations.

In chapter II, §10, we are thus informed that "in many countries in the world today, civil order, freedom, human rights, and democracy are realities in which citizens may trust; and, to a very real degree, these societies accord persons the fundamental dignity of the liberty to seek and pursue the good ends they desire for themselves, their families, and their communities."[17] However, no evidence for such an ex cathedra claim is offered, and it is not even clear what would constitute evidence, since none of the concepts employed is clearly defined in the document. There is even less clarity about what constitutes the basis for the authors' claim that people "may trust" in the above-proclaimed "realities."

The lack of clarity and foundations for particular claims is compensated by the ideological function these claims perform. A careful reader should recognize that the ideological space in which all of those earthly blessings are manifested (regardless of whether they actually exist, or the degree to which they exist) is—"us." If the reader is not sophisticated enough to grasp the message immediately, the authors will instruct him/her to appreciate those "realities" as "a very rare blessing indeed," and warn him/her that it would be "irrational and uncharitable of Christians not to feel a genuine gratitude for the special democratic genius of the modern age."[18]

The way in which the issue of human rights is often approached—including the above-mentioned ecclesiastical documents—shows that it is primarily the "ideology of human rights," and not the issue of human rights per se, that is at stake most of the time when human rights are discussed. This is also how many critical positions voiced against "human rights" should be understood, not as an anti–human rights position, but as a critical position against what Eric Hobsbawm calls the "imperialism of human rights."[19] This also means that "anti–human rights" positions are often coupled with a broader "anti-West" or "anti-modernity" (i.e., anti-Enlightenment) discourse.

One instance of such positions we find in one of the most influential Orthodox thinkers over the past half a century—Christos Yannaras (b. 1935). Yannaras criticizes "human rights" not only as a phrase that exposes a certain hypocrisy in the way it is used in the contemporary political discourse in the West (insofar as they have been applied selectively, and used mostly as propaganda slogans),[20] he also criticizes the anthropological and metaphysical logics hidden behind the "human rights" concept. The logic of human rights appears in Yannaras (or, at least, in my reading of him) as an inferior type of thinking of interhuman relationships (within the political community) compared to both the (Orthodox) Christian ideal of interhuman relationships, and to the ancient (Greek) organization of the polity. In the latter two, there is something about the very thinking and experiencing of the human community that reveals (but also, in certain sense, constitutes) the *truth*, and that cannot be grasped by the concept of human rights, which already implies a certain fundamental alienation:

> Similar to the ancient Greek "assembly of the people," Greek citizens did not assemble primarily to discuss, judge and take decisions, but mainly to constitute, concretize and reveal the *city* (the *way* of life "according to the truth"); in the same way, Christians would not assemble primarily to pray, worship, and be catechized but mainly to constitute, concretize and reveal, in the Eucharistic dinner, the way of life "according to the truth," incorruptibility and immortality: not

the imitation of the secular "logic," but of the Trinitarian Society of Persons, the society which constitutes the true existence and life, because "He is Life" (1 John 4.16). Participants to this ecclesiastical event, even robbers, publicans, prostitutes, or sinners, do not need to establish individual rights. Being a participant and a member of the body of the Church means that one only exists in order to love and be loved—therefore, far from any expectation of self-protection through a legislation which would be "mandatory for all."[21]

It is important to note how, in spite of formal similarities between the two assemblies, Yannaras confuses the political and the liturgical-eschatological dimensions of these gatherings to the point where they become indistinguishable. Now, this is not to say that political gatherings of the local polity do not have a (quasi) liturgical or (quasi) sacred character, or that a liturgical service cannot have its political implications and, actually, be informed, when it comes to the actual performance, by social and political factors (e.g., social, political, military ranks of people). It seems, however, important to differentiate between their fundamental properties, and not to let many confusions that are at work in practice obscure their very different orientations—one toward "this world" (and the ordering of the political realm), the other toward the eschaton where its real roots are located. The personal and the liturgical, manifested through love, seem to be treated here in the same way as the constitution of a political community. Seeing eschatological dimensions in certain political phenomena bears an imminent danger of confusing the two (what we often find at the bottom of many political theologies). While Yannaras is very vocal when it comes to the critique of individualism in the West and the socio-political structures built on that individualism, he seems not particularly interested in power dynamics that are also at work in political structures of more "collectivist" (and non-Western, or premodern) polities—and they are also, arguably, rooted in the individualized mode of existence.

POLITICAL THEOLOGY AS IDEOLOGY:
A DECONSTRUCTION

The previous chapters have shown that, in most of the dominant Orthodox theological approaches to the political sphere, there is a tendency to use Orthodox theology as a political ideology. Orthodox theology has been employed to contextualize, justify, rationalize, and, when necessary, defend the dominant social and political order, so long as that order is not openly anti-Christian or anti-Orthodox (as in the cases of open persecutions of Christians). Social, state, and church hierarchies are, thus, also defended either explicitly ("for the King, and the Fatherland," "for the venerable cross and golden freedom") or implicitly by constructing theological narratives that would call for "patriotism" or affirm "our" social and political context and its values.

This means that the problem with most political theologies (Orthodox or not) is that they almost instinctively defend the dominant systems of power in which they operate, be it "conservative" or "liberal," "democratic," or autocratic. Theology there effectively functions as a political ideology, giving metaphysical significance to political institutions.

As will become clear from the next chapter, such approaches are, in my view, incompatible with the Christian faith, Christian understanding of the Kingdom of God, and the corresponding understanding of the political realities of "this world." It is precisely this incompatibility that was the most difficult part in constructing various symphonic models. This is also the reason why these models suffered, from the very beginning, from inconsistences, not to mention the practical tensions that accompanied church-state relations throughout the period of the (New) Roman Empire.

The problem with prevalent symphonic doctrines is not (only) that they have never been a reality; the problem with them is that they have never been (authentically) *Orthodox*.

Most of the variations of symphonia, viewed from this perspective, are thus less of theological and more of political doctrines. They have served the rulers or, more broadly, the ruling classes, offering an ontological justification to their power. For most of the time, symphonia also worked quite well for the institutional church, securing the prominent position of (official) Orthodoxy and the prominent public and political role and influence of the institutional church representatives.

If symphonia—cutting across various, more specific models of church-state relations—rests upon the idea that there should be a "harmony" between "spiritual" and "political" hierarchies, between the ecclesial and state regulations, between Christian teachings and the reality (and life) of the "Christian" state/empire, then one can raise a number of objections to it from a theological perspective.

As we have seen, there is nothing specifically Christian or Orthodox in this logic. In fact, medieval and modern symphonic models can be traced back to the Roman times,[1] when such *harmony* of the religious and political spheres effectively existed. In the imperial time, under Augustus, a new interpretation of symphonia occurred when the Princeps, contrary to the tradition of the "classical" republic, assumed both the supreme political/military and religious roles/titles. The same logic (just inverse in its path) exists in the papal ideology, with the pontifex maximus (the pope) assuming the political role as well, becoming thus de facto and de jure both the king and the (supreme) priest.

However, we must ask also whether or not the idea of "harmonizing" the spheres of faith and the church with the sphere of the political (or vice versa) is theologically acceptable and meaningful, and to what extent. Are these two spheres essentially *compatible*? Do their logics allow for their integration within one harmonious whole? Is it justifiable to see the Church and the political sphere (state) in comparison with the Divine and human natures, both of which should be united in analogy to Christ and His natures that are "without separation or confusion"?

My position is that the main purpose of this proposed *harmony* has been ideological. Symphonic theories functioned as a form of theological-political narrative, with the aim of either advocating for a certain (prestigious) position and role of the church and its officials within the state (and vice versa) or defending the already established power systems. As Part II shows, there are no serious theological reasons for advocating any of the symphonia models, and there are even fewer theological reasons for understanding the *symphonic unity* of the ecclesial and political in comparison with the logic of the Incarnation dogma.

A typically Roman element can be noticed in the mainstream history of Christian political theologies: The purpose of this harmony was to secure the stability and prosperity of the empire and humankind (since, *ideally*, all humankind should be embraced by one empire and one church). This should not be surprising, as the empire in the East, as we saw, continued to be *Roman*, although it became, formally, "Christian." This effectively led to theology functioning as the state ideology, and even, at times, to the new imperial cult, in which the emperor acquired (quasi) Divine attributes, becoming a special kind of "image of God."[2] Paradoxically enough, by confusing the competences of the Church and state, symphonic models cause, theologically speaking, more tension than they bring harmony.

The Eusebian idea that the empire (state) is the image of the Kingdom of God is one of the core issues here. In such a model, the state—not the Church—becomes the image of the Kingdom of God. The result of this logic is that the meaning and the role of the Church as the (only true) image of the Kingdom of God is diminished. Furthermore, the very need for the eschaton, for the future Kingdom of God, is obscured. The empire (state) replaces the eschatological Kingdom. Christian "image theory" is also transferred here from its proper, liturgical, context (with the bishop as the *image* of Christ in the liturgical performance, which is the *image* of the Kingdom of God) to the political one. The emperor becomes the image of Christ (as the universal ruler) and the empire becomes the image of the Kingdom of God. Since the "earthly" kingdom (empire) can be seen as the par excellence manifestation of the necessity of "this world" (as discussed in Part II), by turning this ("earthly") kingdom (state) into an image of the eschaton, this image becomes an idol, not an icon. It becomes an image of a diabolical (false) eschatology, which results in a secular eschatology—turning the "eschatological" kingdom into something of "this world," of the world that "lies in evil."

This Eusebian type of political theology not only confuses Christian concerns, values, and virtues with the exercise of political power (making the political power a virtue in itself) but it also turns the Christian Messiah into what He is not—an image (prototype) of an earthly ruler, another power agent. By claiming that the emperor imitates the "heavenly ruler," Eusebius and his followers secularized not only Christian eschatology but the Kingdom of God itself, turning the Christian understanding of faith into a political ideology. This has proved to be an extremely attractive intellectual construction, which survives into the present day.[3]

A variation of this Christian "secularism" can be found in later discourses, where the "people" or the "nation" substitutes for the Church and the liturgy, becoming the "New Israel." The temptation to take the Old Testament concept of "Israel" (which was to a significant extent—although never entirely—ethnically and politically determined) and to understand the concept of the "New Israel" along the same ethnic or tribal lines, was too strong to resist in most Christian political theologies, both medieval and modern. The Old Testament idea is based upon a theocratic model in which there is no distinction between ethnicity (tribal or national belonging) and faith. The chosen people are primarily those who are related by blood (descendants of the same patriarchs) and who have the same God (and who then follow the commandments of that God). However, the Christian concept of the "New Israel" is different. It refers primarily to the Church as a free communion of those who freely chose to belong to Her, not to any given socio-political community.

This is where most modern and contemporary nation- or state-centered Christian authors (from radical evangelicals in the US to nationalistic Roman Catholic and Orthodox authors) are profoundly mistaken. The immanent potential for political exploitation embedded in the "New Israel" concept (understood as referring to a tribal/ethnic/national community) is the reason why "right-wing" ideologies—if we take this to primarily denote ideologies that understand the social reality as an organic, unified "whole," based upon a coherent ethnic, national, or religious identity and tradition—are so inclined toward religion and what they perceive as Christianity. But this is precisely where Christianity cannot be used unless it is falsified. If there has ever been a religious system that is skeptical toward the necessity embedded in the phenomena such as family, ethnicity, nation, or state, it is Christianity. Christianity is incompatible with the logic of "this world," which is the reason why many Christians have been reluctant in defending this Christian radicalism. This is also why we have witnessed all sorts of compromises with "this world" as the most common manifestation of historical Christianity (although one has to admit that without compromises it would be difficult, and maybe even impossible for the Church and Christianity to perform their transformative role in the world).

Symphonic models are attractive for all those who are eager to read in them an image of the *Incarnation*. The logic is that just as God came down from Heaven and became one with the human being and the material reality (without separation and without confusion, following the dogma), there is also in the reality of "this world" a mirror image of the Incarnation—the symphonia, which unifies the "spiritual" (ecclesial) and the "worldly" (political), also without separation and (if and when possible) without confusion.

Using the Incarnation of God as the basis for developing a theology of the political-ecclesial (spiritual) whole represents, in my view, a very fundamental misunderstanding, or maybe even an intentional forgery of the whole idea of the Incarnation. The sphere of the political—and this will be the main thesis in Part II of this study—together with other power structures, belongs to those aspects of "this world" that do not have the potential of acquiring an everlasting existence. The realm of power, the exercise of power, is a par excellence manifestation of the existential logic that runs in exactly the opposite direction from the meaning and purpose of the Incarnation and Resurrection. Power structures—and that includes states—conform to the logic of "this world," which is, ultimately, the logic of death. Deifying those structures, or claiming that (as in the Incarnation analogy), they stand for "human nature," is nothing else but a rejection of Christian faith.

Another problematic aspect found in the prevailing type of Orthodox political ideologies is the appreciation of hierarchy as a vertical distribution of power. This is, again, not unique to institutional Orthodoxy/Christianity. The idea is linked to the understanding of god as a master who rules over his/her obedient subjects. Following the "as in heaven, so on earth" logic, kings became either representatives (*vicarii*) of this god, or images of the supreme cosmic ruler, whom all of their subjects must obey.

It is clear how and why some modern leftist (and, more often than not, atheist) critiques of religion in general can often be justified and can even, up to a point, be considered *Christian-like* in the main values they advocate (justice, equality, freedom, etc.). Religion all too often *does* function as an ideology whose purpose is to solidify the system of power and keep the people obedient. In this sense, the role of religion has been comparable to the role that modern-day ideologies (such as "free-market" or consumerist ideology, the ideology of "democracy" or even dogmatic *scientism*, which is, of course, very different from a serious scientific enterprise) perform in modern *secular* society.

It is, however, also clear that such a concept of god and hierarchy is not only different, but actually quite the opposite from the Christian understanding of God, who comes as a servant, who refuses to rule or to be a king, and who dies—and dies, let us not forget, as a *criminal*—for his *friends*.

In the absence of many useful New Testament sources, the concept of a hierarchically organized society and the corresponding distribution of power is generally rationalized in Christian political theology by references to Old Testament examples. This became commonplace in the Middle Ages and also in modern discourses on "Christian" and "Orthodox" monarchies. In actuality, however, evoking the image of the Old Testament kingship provides one of the strongest theological arguments against monarchy or hierarchically organized society.

When we go back to the Old Testament narrative about the establishment of monarchy in ancient Israel, we find an account that portrays it as a deficient form of government, as something that replaced the original (and more favorable) *anarchist* organization of society. In 1 Samuel we find the following narrative:

> So all the elders of Israel gathered together and came to Samuel at Ramah. They said to him, "You are old, and your sons do not follow your ways; now appoint a king to lead us, such as all the other nations have."
>
> But when they said, "Give us a king to lead us," this displeased Samuel; so he prayed to the Lord. And the Lord told him: "Listen to all that the people are saying to you; it is not you they have rejected, but they have rejected me as their king. As they have done from the day I brought them up out of Egypt until this day, forsaking me and serving other gods, so they are doing to you. Now listen to them; but warn them solemnly and let them know what the king who will reign over them will claim as his rights." (1 Samuel 8:4–9)

The appointment of the kings signifies the alienation of the chosen people from God. So, not only does the concept of "chosen nation" (Israel) and its leader ("king") have a significantly different meaning in the New Testament/

Church perspective, but even the Old Testament narrative about the establishment of a structured, monarchical state system depicts it as an evil, which comes as a result of an obscured eschatological awareness of ancient Israel. God warns them that abandoning the earlier (communal or *anarchist*) type of social organization will lead to enormous suffering of the people who will be subordinated to the newly established political power structures. What comes after the quotation given above is a long list of all the "blessings" that the people will "enjoy" as a result of this establishing of rigid power structures (in this case in the monarchical form):

> Samuel told all the words of the Lord to the people who were asking him for a king. He said, "This is what the king who will reign over you will claim as his rights: He will take your sons and make them serve with his chariots and horses, and they will run in front of his chariots. Some he will assign to be commanders of thousands and commanders of fifties, and others to plow his ground and reap his harvest, and still others to make weapons of war and equipment for his chariots. He will take your daughters to be perfumers and cooks and bakers. He will take the best of your fields and vineyards and olive groves and give them to his attendants. He will take a tenth of your grain and of your vintage and give it to his officials and attendants. Your male and female servants and the best of your cattle and donkeys he will take for his own use. He will take a tenth of your flocks, and you yourselves will become his slaves. When that day comes, you will cry out for relief from the king you have chosen, but the Lord will not answer you in that day."
>
> But the people refused to listen to Samuel. "No!" they said. "We want a king over us. Then we will be like all the other nations, with a king to lead us and to go out before us and fight our battles."
>
> When Samuel heard all that the people said, he repeated it before the Lord. The Lord answered, "Listen to them and give them a king." (1 Samuel 8:10–22)

Historically speaking, theologians, like intellectuals in general, have followed a fairly consistent pattern when it comes to the construction of political theologies. They have normally been constructing theological or secular religious narratives that offered a rationale for and a justification of the prevailing power system in which they lived. This often resulted not only in solidifying that power system—in making it appear a necessary and "God-given" order—but also in tragic consequences for all of those who were perceived as enemies of those systems. Little has changed in this respect even now.

We can see the same patterns not only in modern and contemporary theological discourses that affirm some form of autocracy or promote national or ethnic identities as something Christian per se; in those theological narratives that promote "democratic" or "liberal" values we find the same logic. In this sense, when we compare the contemporary church documents produced in the Russian and Greco-American cultural and political contexts, in spite of many differences, at the level of political narratives/messages they send, they actually follow a very similar logic. The subtext in both of them is the affirmation of a spirit of submission to the dominant ideological system in which the authors of these documents live, quite comparable to the authors of various "symphonic" models. The message, dressed up in more or less sophisticated rhetoric, is about the affirmation of "our" system, "our" way of thinking or doing things ("our way of life"), "our" mission in the world, etc., in order to convince the disbelievers ("them") that "our" system is the best, or at least better than what "they" have. It would be, however, unfair to accuse only theology of such ideological blind spots. The same features characterize dominant intellectual discourses in general. Instead of a critical discourse, as a dynamic and critical assessment of the ways in which we think of the world and the socio-political sphere, we normally deal with ideological ways of thinking based on simplistic (often binary) categories that are not examined but rather dogmatically applied. A variety of phenomena and all sorts of complexities are thus forced into rigid theoretical constructs that reflect and satisfy broader (social-political) ideological concerns. If this is the case, then simplistic theoretical models, both in political theologies and (secular) political philosophies, that divide political systems and types of government into clear-cut categories such as "democracies" vs. "autocracies" or "totalitarianism," "republics" vs. "monarchies," "liberal" vs. "conservative," "theocratic" vs. "secular," and so forth, need to be replaced by much more complex and nuanced conceptual instruments.

Especially in the times of conflict, the political collective ("we") easily becomes an idol, a god who requires "them" to be offered as sacrifices. Examples of this include the way intellectuals defend those in power and create useful ideological narratives, from defending the Christian Roman emperors (against the "barbarians") to defending today's political systems and modern empires.

Many local Orthodox churches nowadays practice the offering of prayers for state authorities and the armed forces during the liturgy. The context of these prayers, as indicated before, turns liturgical service into a stage for spreading political ideologies and championing national symbols and interests. The situation becomes all the more grotesque given the fact that some of these governments (represented by the office of the "president") and their armed forces are responsible for some of the worst atrocities in the contemporary world. Turning the liturgy into a kind of "secular religious" spectacle, in which it becomes the icon of the national "heaven" rather than the icon of the Kingdom of God, shows a remarkable lack of theological sensibility, perhaps even of the basic Christian conscience.

What can be learned from the long history of Orthodox Christian political theologies is that they have been predominantly based on the affirmation of various kinds of symphonic ideals. As already suggested, this model is problematic not because it has had many different (and sometimes mutually inconsistent) variations, and certainly not because it has not been, for most of the time, based on the actual reality of the church-state relationships, but because it goes against what an *authentic* Orthodox Christian theological stance toward the socio-political should look like.

However, in spite of the predominance of the power-affirmation discourses in Christian political theologies, alternative tendencies can also be found in the Christian tradition, the tendencies that exhibit many "(proto)anarchist" elements. Although marginal (and marginalized), it nevertheless includes the views and actions of some of the most authoritative Orthodox theological and ecclesial figures and movements. Part II begins with an outline of these alternative approaches to the socio-political realm. The reader should not be surprised to discover that some of the phenomena already described as "symphonic" can overlap to a certain extent with "proto-anarchist" tendencies. Depending on the context and the perspective from which certain phenomena are assessed, one and the same (formally speaking) concept, process or institution can perform both emancipatory and oppressive roles.

PART II

ANARCHY AND THE KINGDOM OF GOD

PROPHECIES

Ambrose of Milan with Emperor Theodosius. (Inspired by *Saint Ambrose Forbids Emperor Theodosius from Entering the Cathedral* by Andrei I. Ivanov.)

ALTERNATIVE AND "PROTO-ANARCHIST" POLITICAL THEOLOGIES

God does not ask of us virtue, moralism,
blind obedience, but a cry of assurance and
of love from the depth of our hell.

—*Paul Evdokimov*

Historically speaking, "anarchist" tendencies (in the sense defined at the beginning of this study) within Orthodox Christian theology have been a minority and even marginal phenomenon for most of time. Many would even claim that something like "anarchist" political ideas in the context of Orthodoxy are an oxymoron, which cannot exist in principle since some of the basic ideas, values, and intentions that we find in anarchism and Orthodoxy are mutually irreconcilable. There are many reasons for such perceptions.

Questioning, in principle, the authority of the state, the emperor, or the authority of the church structures and their exercise of (illegitimate) power has been historically perceived as disloyalty, treason, or heresy (or, probably, all of them). As we have already seen in the previous chapters, dominant versions of Orthodoxy have functioned as state ideologies for centuries. They have been perceived as the vital ingredient of national identities, so questioning any of the official "gods" (national or state ideology, political leaders, etc.) would have been perceived as unorthodox and heretical, if not even as madness.[1]

However, a closer look at the history of Orthodox political theologies and the positions that various authors have held toward the concepts of authority, domination, and exercise of power—both in the political realm and in the strictly ecclesial context—shows that the questioning of dominant power structures, based on the foundational elements of the Christian

123

faith, is not a recent invention. It is this questioning of oppressive power structures, on the grounds that they are illegitimate from a Christian perspective, together with the advocacy of equality and justice (including economic equality and justice), that I call the "proto-anarchist" tendencies within Orthodox political theology.[2]

It is clear from this that the concept of "proto-anarchism" can be employed only conditionally (which is the reason why I use it in quotation marks). It refers to various tendencies, not to a coherent category. It is sometimes difficult to draw a clear line of what should belong to it (even only as a tendency). One can roughly differentiate between those positions that do not follow any of the prevalent symphonic models, and those that in more specific terms advocate for the values and ideas that are compatible with the definition of anarchism as a tendency. In the first case, we come across positions that, for instance, aspire simply to separate the field of the church and faith-related issues from the sphere of politics and the state, for the sake of pointing to their different and even mutually irreconcilable natures and orientations. There are, however, more specific instances of resistance to the political sphere and political power, including open confrontations with them, as something contrary to the logic of Christianity and the Church. Both of these tendencies are included in this chapter as an illustration of the existence of alternative positions compared to the historically dominant models, some of which more specifically speak to the anarchist concerns and focuses as they are described in the beginning.

"Proto-anarchist" Orthodox political theologies can already be found in the earliest periods of Christianity, when Christians tried to articulate their (op)position to the Pax Romana.[3] The project of these Christians went in the opposite direction from the project of their sisters and brothers in faith who, as we saw, were trying to reconcile the Roman and Christian *peace*. In contrast to the attempts to harmonize these two spheres, which laid the foundations for the later symphonic aspirations, "proto-anarchist" political theologies perceived Pax Christiana as something fundamentally different from (and even the opposite of) Pax Romana. These tendencies serve as the basis on which I develop my own approach to Orthodox political theology.

The most significant document in this respect, from the early period, is the book of Revelation, which can be read as exposing a strong opposition to the Roman Empire. What is significant is that this kind of opposition is not

only an opposition to particular state policies: the empire as such is contextu-
alized as a metaphysical evil that stands in opposition to Christ and His
Kingdom. According to a broad consensus among scholars, many of the
vivid images of evil, wickedness, and opposition to God, such as the image of
the "great harlot" (Revelation 17) or "Babylon" (Revelation 14:8), can be interpreted as referring to Rome and the imperial rule. "At first or even second
glance," argues Steven D. Moore, "revelation would appear to be an anti-
imperial(istic) text that, in effect, announces the transfer of world-wide imperium from the Roman Emperor to the heavenly Emperor and his Son and
co-regent, the 'King of kings and Lord of lords.'"[4] The central point in these
interpretations (and a major obstacle too) is the question of the relationship
between the earthly kingdom of the emperors and the Heavenly Kingdom of
Christ. Moore captures this problem in the following way:

> Revelation's implicit claim, as commentators never tire of telling us,
> is that Roman imperial court ceremonial, together with the imperial
> court itself, are but pale imitations—diabolic imitations, indeed—
> of the heavenly throne room and the heavenly liturgy. But commen-
> tators also routinely note that the heavenly court and liturgy in
> Revelation are themselves modelled in no small part on the Roman
> imperial court and cult.[5]

This is an important point, since it explains both the "anti-imperial" (and,
understood more broadly, anti–political power) attitude and the appropriation of the imperial imagery in the characterization of the Divine rule
(the concept of the Kingdom of God being one of them). Moore is right in
pointing to the process of appropriation of the imagery typical of the imperial rule in Revelation's depiction of the dominion of God. This imagery would continue to play quite an important role in the history of
Christianity, during which the "rule of God" was imagined as structurally
similar to the "rule of Caesar," except more just (and "Christian"). This is
why the "Kingdom" phrase "Kingdom of God" should be understood in
this study, and in my argument, only metaphorically, as an indication of
the eschatological reality that is characterized by a new existence that does
not require any "rule" and does not follow the logic of any earthly social
organization.

In spite of this parallelism, the point about Revelation's opposition to
the dominion of Caesar holds. The Seventh Trumpet reveals that, in the
end, the "kingdom of the world" is overcome. It was no longer the realm

of earthly kings, but became the realm of the Lord: "The kingdom of the world [ἡ βασιλεία τοῦ κόσμου] has become the kingdom of our Lord and of his Messiah, and he will reign for ever and ever" (Revelation 11:15).

However, Revelation can be interpreted as a piece of "proto-anarchist" Christian political theology not only because it can be seen as a critique of an empire that was, in many ways, anti-Christian. It can also be interpreted as a contextualization of that empire as an image of political power in general, which is finally defeated only by the arrival of the eschaton. The Kingdom of God appears thus as a different kind of reality; the "rule of God" is given as an antidote against the political power. In this sense, the Kingdom of God should not be understood as another political system, different only in its "pro-Christian" character, as opposed to "anti-Christian" political systems. The Kingdom of God is rather a different kind of reality, which comes at the end of time as we know it.[6]

The "anti-imperial" (antistate or antipolitical rule) position that we can identify in Revelation might reflect an older Jewish tradition that had already been present when Christianity appeared. In the figure of John the Baptist, who might have been one of the Essenes, we find such a "proto-anarchist" and proto-(Christian) monastic figure.[7] As the Essenes used to practice, John lived in the desert, outside the cities (that is, the political and administrative centers). In his image, we find an image of a Christian monk who renounces "the world" not as the sphere of the material (vs. "spiritual") but as a certain logic of being, as a particular way of life based on domination of those in power, on pregiven family, ethnic, and other social identities and relationships, all of which reflect the fallen logic of necessity, and all of which are in contradiction with the logic of the Kingdom that "came near."

In addition to Revelation, which seems to portray political power in a radically negative way, several other places from the New Testament are often quoted in Christian anarchist literature as illustrative of the "anarchist" character of the early Christian community.[8] In episodes from Acts (15:1–35), it seems that the early Christian community was more "horizontally" organized, rather than a hierarchically organized institution with an autocratic "head" on its top. There were "elders" and apostles who had spiritual/moral authority, but the issues seem to have been discussed rather openly, and the conclusions were reached collectively, as one body: "Then the apostles and elders, with the whole church, decided" (Acts 15:22), "It seemed good to the Holy Spirit and to us" (Acts 15:28).

In addition to the New Testament, many early Christian authors also criticized political power, and it is notable that, sometimes in the opus of the same author, we can find both pro and con positions vis-à-vis political power and authority.

One case against political power—at least that of the Roman Empire—can be found in the theology of Justin the Martyr (ca. 100–ca. 165). In his famous letter to Emperor Antoninus Pius, Justin clearly separates the King-dom of God and the "human" kingdom as two different kinds of reality:

> And when you hear that we look for a kingdom, you uncritically sup-pose that we speak of a human one; whereas we speak of that with God. . . . For if we looked for a human kingdom, we would deny it, that we might not be slain; and we would try to escape detection, that we might obtain the things we look for. But since we do not have our hope on the present, we do not heed our executioners, since death is in any case the debt of nature.[9]

Justin not only separates the political ("human kingdom") from the realm of God, but implicitly links the political realm, and the logic that belongs to that realm, to (fallen) nature. Death comes as a natural result of the (fallen) nature of the (fallen) world, and this is why Christians seek the heavenly realm (the Kingdom of God) not simply as a different kind of "rule," but as a different kind of existence.

Justin's political position is thus grounded in his metaphysics. Elaine Pagels captured the point quite clearly:

> Justin answered that Christians had discovered a terrible secret: the powers behind the Roman magistrates—and, in particular, behind the emperors themselves—are not gods, but demons, active evil forces bent upon corrupting and destroying human beings, determined to blind people to the truth that there is only one God, creator of all, who made all humankind alike.[10]

More explicit "anarchist" elements can be found in the theologies of the next generation of early Christian thinkers. Clement of Alexandria clearly contrasts submission to God and submission to (any) other master. Fol-lowing Justin, Clement also sees the realm of the political as the realm dominated by demons, and the realm of God as the realm of freedom, which is negated by human submission to any authority ("master") other than God:

And I would ask you, if it does not appear to you monstrous, that you men who are God's handiwork, who have received your souls from Him, and belong wholly to God, should be subject to another master, and, what is more, serve the tyrant instead of the rightful King—the evil one instead of the good? For, in the name of truth, what man in his senses turns his back on good, and attaches himself to evil? What, then, is he who flees from God to consort with demons? Who, that may become a son of God, prefers to be in bondage?[11]

This is one of the most vocal patristic claims in defense of the fundamental *equality* of all people. This equality is grounded precisely in the human dignity coming from freedom that all human beings have as "icons of God." Consequently, their submission to any human or other authority, apart from God, is subjecting themselves to someone/something lower than the human being him/herself, which ultimately leads to idolatry. Clement's interpretation of human social realities (including religious idolatry) in view of God's supreme authority and human dignity before God and in this world remains one of the strongest Christian arguments in favor of some form of anarchy as an approach to the political.

Tertullian, who offered such an eloquent rationale for harmonizing the state power and the heavenly realm, was, at the same time, the creator of one of the strongest antistate positions in the history of "proto-anarchist" political theologies. The author of the famous "credo" dictum,[12] Tertullian tried to protect and affirm the radical character of Christianity vis-à-vis "this world." Unlike many other Christian authors, Tertullian rejects military service. Embracing the logic that "no one can serve two masters" (Matthew 6:24), Tertullian affirms the radicalism of the Christian message, bringing it to its logical conclusion by rejecting the state and the legitimacy of its authority. In his *Apology*, Tertullian claims:

We, however, whom all the flames of glory and dignity leave cold, have no need to combine; nothing is more foreign to us than the state (*res publica*). One state we know, of which all are citizens—the universe.[13]

A similar logic contrasting the heavenly "citizenship" to the earthly one can be found in the famous lines from the *Epistle to Diognetus* (after AD 150), discussing the Christian "being in the world." The Epistle presents the Christian condition in this world as a paradoxical one. Christians are described as foreigners in this world, those whose real "country" is in the heaven. They, however, do not make their separate cities, neither do they differ from other people by any formal characteristics:

> For Christians are no different from other people in terms of their country, language, or customs. Nowhere do they inhabit cities of their own, use a strange dialect, or live life out of the ordinary. They have not discovered this teaching of theirs through reflection or through the thought of meddlesome people, not do they set forth any human doctrine, as do some. They inhabit both Greek and barbarian cities, according to the lot assigned to each. And they show forth the character of their own citizenship in a marvelous and admittedly paradoxical way by following local customs in what they wear and what they eat and in the rest of their lives. They live in their respective countries, but only as resident aliens; they participate in all things as citizens, and they endure all things as foreigners. Every foreign territory is a homeland for them, every homeland foreign territory. . . . They are found in the flesh but do not live according to the flesh. They live on earth but participate in the life of heaven.[14]

Although expressing basically the same idea as Tertullian, the accent here is somewhat different. It is not so much about antagonizing the two realms (which, ultimately, results in the rejection of any metaphysical significance of the political institutions) as it is about recognizing that political and social institutions and identities do not have any immanent value or meaning for Christians (while recognizing that they are still part of our going through history, on our way to the Kingdom of God).

As one of the most important early Christian theologians, Irenaeus of Lyons (ca. 130–ca. 202) is another author who understood the political sphere as something linked to the fallen state of our historical existence. The fallen state makes us to look at other human beings as enemies, which then imposes the need to regulate interhuman relationships through laws. This logic is clearly expressed in Irenaeus's *Against Heresies* (Book V), where he states:

> For since man, by departing from God, reached such a pitch of bestiality as even to look upon his kinsman as his enemy, and engaged

without fear in every kind of disordered conduct, murder and ava-
rice, God imposed upon mankind the fear of man, as they did not
acknowledge the fear of God; in order that, being subjected to the
authority of men, and under the custody of their laws, they might
attain to some degree of justice, and exercise mutual forbearance
through dread of the sword suspended full in their view.[15]

Although Irenaeus does not share the view that the earthly government is
the work of the devil, he, nevertheless, sees it in negative terms, as a necessary evil rather than a value per se:

Earthly rule, therefore has been appointed by God for the benefit of
the nations (and not by the devil, who is never at rest at all, nay, who
does not love to see even nations conducting themselves after a quiet
manner), so that under the fear of it men may not eat each other up
like fishes; but that, by means of the establishment of laws, they may
keep down the great wickedness of the nations. And in this way they
are "God's ministers."[16]

Similar to the Book of Revelation, Irenaeus sees Christ as the one who
"shall destroy temporal kingdoms and introduce an eternal one."[17]

Among those early Christian authors who are not known for their per
se antagonistic positions toward the political sphere is Origen of Alexandria. As we have seen, Origen's theology was not antagonistic toward the
political sphere or the empire as such. He holds that kings are "appointed
by God," and contextualizes Christianity within the socio-historical context in such a way that their spiritual conduct becomes "effective . . . in
helping the emperors."[18] Origen, thus, could be accused of contributing to
the formulation of a "patriotic" Christian theology that does not perceive
Christians as "foreigners" in their countries, but rather as their loyal
citizens—actually, the most patriotic of all.[19] However, Origen was aware
of a certain tension between the socio-political sphere and "God's country." He differentiates and, up to a point, even contrasts the earthly countries and "God's country," which he identifies with the Church:

But we know of the existence in each city of another sort of country,
created by the Logos of God. . . . We do not accept those who love
power. But we put pressure on those who on account of their great
humility are reluctant hastily to take upon themselves the common
responsibility of the church of God. . . . Even if it is power over God's

country (I mean the Church) which is exercised by those who "hold office" well in the Church, we say that their rule is in accordance with God's prior authority, and they do not thereby "defile" the appointed "laws." If Christians do avoid these responsibilities, it is not with the motive of shirking the public services of life. But they keep themselves for a more divine and necessary service in the church of God for the sake of the salvation of men.[20]

In post-Constantinian times, one of the harshest critics of emperors and the exercise of political power was Athanasius of Alexandria (ca. 299–373). In his *History of the Arians*, Athanasius depicts Emperor Constantius II (⚓ 337–61) as "more bitter than Pilate,"[21] and compares him with Ahab, Belshazzar,[22] the Pharaohs,[23] Saul, and even the Antichrist.[24] However, in spite of such bitter characterizations of the emperor, it is clear that with his critique, Athanasius was not constructing a case against the legitimacy of political power or the imperial office per se, but rather against the policies of concrete emperors with whom he had many conflicts. Nevertheless, it shows the underlying logic behind Athanasius's attacks—the idea that the church and bishops are there to defend the faith, and that if emperors dare to do something unjust, something against the faith or the church, that the faithful, and primarily the church hierarchy, have the duty to stand up to them, and even subject them to harshest criticisms.

The same logic we find in another famous example of opposition to imperial power—in matters that concern faith and Church. It comes from Ambrose of Milan (ca. 340–97). We do not find here an elaborate or well-grounded opposition to political authority in principle. Instead, a case is constructed for a clear demarcation between the realm of the church and the political realm, and only implicitly, one may speculate, the political realm was perceived as something deficient in principle. As narrated in Theodoret's *The Ecclesiastical History* (V:17), Ambrose stood up to the emperor, condemned his crimes, and imposed spiritual sanctions on the emperor, prohibiting him to enter the church or participate in the liturgy until he repented. Ambrose's position as the superior one within the spiritual realm is also clear from his letter to Emperor Theodosius following the massacre of Thessaloniki.[25] He is even clearer in differentiating between the ecclesial and political spheres, and the competences of emperors and bishops, in his letter to Emperor Valentinian II.[26]

However, unlike Athanasius, Ambrose's critical position toward imperial power was not limited only to the concrete wrongdoings he was sanc-
tioning, or to concrete personalities. In fact, Ambrose constructs a much
more elaborate political theology in which the spheres of the political (belonging to the Caesar) and the ecclesial are separated. The realm of earthly
laws and taxation is in the domain of the Caesar; however, Ambrose is quick
to point out that emperors are not above the church, but, when baptized,
within the church, and therefore they must obey the bishops in ecclesial
matters:

> In the church I know only one image, and that is the image of the
> invisible God. . . . If the emperor wants tax, we do not refuse. The
> church's estates are taxed. If the emperor needs estates, he has
> the power to appropriate them, and not one of us stands in his way. The
> congregation's donations are more than enough for the poor; there is
> no reason for resentment about our estates. Let them sequestrate
> them, if the emperor pleases; I am not offering, but I do not refuse
> them. . . . Taxation is a matter for Caesar, that is beyond question;
> but the church is God's, and so it ought not to be given over to Cae-
> sar, because Caesar's sway cannot extend over the temple of God. . . .
> The emperor is within the church, not above it; the good emperor
> asks for the church's help, he does not refuse it.[27]

One of the chief anarchist concerns has been the care for the poor and
the deprivileged. This care for those marginalized and poor plays a
prominent role in the "proto-anarchist" theologies. Many early Christian authors—including Ambrose—show concern for the poor and made
this point an important aspect of the entire Christian enterprise. Some
of them were not just concerned about the poor, but went further to condemn wealth and its accumulation in principle, linking it directly to
fallen human nature. These authors were building on the New Testament
episodes in which loving acts of charity are praised, and money and wealth
are explicitly condemned as something standing in the way to God and
His Kingdom:

> So when you give to the needy, do not announce it with trumpets, as
> the hypocrites do in the synagogues and on the streets, to be hon-
> ored by others. Truly I tell you, they have received their reward in
> full. But when you give to the needy, do not let your left hand know

what your right hand is doing, so that your giving may be in secret. (Matthew 6:2–4)

Jesus answered, "If you want to be perfect, go, sell your possessions and give to the poor, and you will have treasure in heaven. Then come, follow me." When the young man heard this, he went away sad, because he had great wealth. Then Jesus said to his disciples, "Truly I tell you, it is hard for someone who is rich to enter the kingdom of heaven. Again I tell you, it is easier for a camel to go through the eye of a needle than for someone who is rich to enter the kingdom of God." (Matthew 19:21–24)

No one can serve two masters. Either you will hate the one and love the other, or you will be devoted to the one and despise the other. You cannot serve both God and money. (Luke 16:13)

Those who want to get rich fall into temptation and a trap and into many foolish and harmful desires that plunge people into ruin and destruction. For the love of money is a root of all kinds of evil. (1 Timothy 6:9–10)

Command those who are rich in this present world not to be arrogant nor to put their hope in wealth, which is so uncertain, but to put their hope in God, who richly provides us with everything for our enjoyment. Command them to do good, to be rich in good deeds, and to be generous and willing to share. (1 Timothy 6:17–18)

A strong preference for (material/financial) poverty here has its direct social implications. Early Christian authors (see below) developed these points, raising their voices against exploitation, concentration of wealth, and the oppression that comes with it. However, to read these passages only or primarily as a social program would be, from an Orthodox theological perspective, a mistake. Orthodox tradition has always seen in these lines something much more important. The issue of wealth and poverty is the issue of human freedom, of interhuman (personal) relationships, and because of that the issue of human identity as well. Leaving all wealth, which provides material security (in addition to power) demonstrates one's readiness to make the leap of faith, to enter into the realm of *insecurity* (when viewed from the perspective of "this world")—that is the realm of freedom. Accumulation of wealth is a symptom of one's existential anxiety and crisis, one's inability to live freely (which means relying primarily on God), not on material means. In addition to this, with material wealth and its expansion comes exploitation and oppression that, again, have their existential implications—they signify the inability to see in the poor our sisters and brothers, the icons of God. In order to accumulate, expend, and sustain huge amounts of wealth, one needs to relate to other human beings in an instrumental way, treating them as the means for satisfying our individual goals, not as personal beings. This is the case when other human beings cease to be icons of God, to which we relate with love, and become simply "workers" or "customers" that we relate to instrumentally, out of interest.

This was one dimension of poverty—when one freely chooses to abandon one's property or to embrace one's poverty as a means toward liberation. There is also another dimension of the poverty, when people live in extreme conditions out of necessity, without even elementary means to satisfy basic needs. There is a long tradition in Orthodox Christianity, which goes back to the Gospel, in which the poor and the needy, together with all those who are social outcasts (sometimes referred to as the "dirt" of society), are perceived as being closer to God than the privileged and the wealthier segments of the population.[28]

Following the Gospel's condemnation of wealth, Ambrose formulates a critique that even today sounds remarkably apt, as a general critique of capitalist (both premodern and modern) greed and the prospect of money standing between human beings, defining their relationships and corrupting human freedom, sense of love, and solidarity:

> What rich man does not daily set his heart on other people's goods?
> What millionaire is not engaged in tearing the poor man from his
> tiny holding and driving him empty-handed from the borders of his
> family allotment? . . . What rich man's heart is not fired by the prospect of acquiring his neighbor's property? . . . An Ahab is born every
> day, alas! and Ahab will never die in this age.[29]

The desire to gain wealth, which Ambrose holds to be in itself *mad* (see below), reflects a state of existence based on egotism, which is not (primarily) a moral transgression but the sign of separation from God, which Christ pointed to as something that prevents the rich from acquiring the Kingdom of God:

What is the attraction nature's bounty has for you? The world was created for all; but you, the few rich men, try to keep it for yourselves. Not only land, but the very sky, air, and sea are appropriated for the use of the rich minority. . . . The greedy man has no idea of "goods," except investments. . . . Riches are goods for whoever knows how to used them properly, but evils for whoever does not. . . . They are goods if you give them to the poor.[30]

The problem of wealth—again building on the Gospel's stories—is that it corrupts human freedom and turns the human being into a slave.[31] It obscures the fundamental *equality* of human beings (which does not reduce the diversity of their personal characteristics and talents) to which Ambrose points:

How far can you take this mad acquisitiveness, you rich? Will you make yourselves the only inhabitants of the earth? . . . The earth was created for all in common, rich and poor alike. . . . Nature knows no rich men, she makes us all poor at birth. . . . The narrow covering of turf is room enough for poor and rich alike. . . . It creates us all equals. . . . You are anointed, rich man, but you stink all the same.[32]

The Christian critique of the private accumulation of wealth—and the power that it brings—finds, in these paragraphs, an everlasting source of inspiration, which is perfectly applicable to the contemporary contexts of the corporate world. The predominant business ideology of today (driven by various [pseudo] theological narratives, as some would claim[33]), which advances profit-making as the goal in itself and an ultimate value, is mirrored in these words. Is it not what the corporate world precisely aspires to do nowadays, to privatize the "very sky, air, and sea" for the "use of the rich minority"? This very robbery is celebrated as a value, a reason to be proud of one's self, something that states and international institutions should unconditionally support. This ideology is *madness*, but there are nowadays very few of those in the ecclesiastical structures who would find it appropriate, let alone necessary, to tell the super wealthy that they "stink all the same."

Equality was also an important topic in Lactantius. His theology has already been discussed in regard to the construction of symphonia. However, one can also find in his writings many "anarchist" elements when it comes to his vision of the "ideal" social organization. Based on the ancient Roman authors, Lactantius presents a case for a type of human community, which is envisioned as, supposedly, the "original" form of human society—and with a striking resemblance to some of the modern anarchist discourses. Referencing Cicero, Ovid, and Virgil in his attempt to defend Christianity as something quite compatible with the *original Romanness* (as the original *Republican* element of the Roman polity), Lactantius speaks of a "classless" society as the primordial and ideal human society, one in which everything was shared equally:

> With justice present and prevailing, why would anyone worry about defending himself, there being no one to fear? or about harming someone else, there being nothing to gain? It is a feature reminiscent of our own religion that "they lived content upon a modest plot" . . . nor was it ". . . lawful even to divide the plain with landmarks and boundaries: All produce went to a common pool" . . . the reason being that God gave the earth to all in common, that they might live a common life, without insatiable and obsessive greed laying claim to everything, and that no one should go short of what nature produced for all.[34]

Lactantius does not deny the existence of private property, but claims that "people were too generous to enclose the crops that nature gave them or to store them away to keep for themselves, rather than allow the poor a share in what their labor had produced."[35] Equality, as the core virtue, is stressed in other places in Lactantius, too, since *piety* and *equality* are two virtues "inseparably bound up" with justice. Equality means "treating others as one's equal" because God, "who gives being and life to men wished us all to be equal, that is, alike."[36] From this platform, Lactantius approaches the problem of wealth and the inequality that material wealth produces among people, and reaches remarkably similar conclusions to those of Ambrose:

> But someone will say, "Don't you have poor and rich, slaves and masters, in your community? Aren't there distinctions between one member and another?" Not at all! That is precisely the reason that we address one another as "Brother," since we believe we are one another's equals. Since human worth is measured in spiritual not in physical terms, we ignore our various physical situations; slaves are not slaves to us, but we treat them and address them as brothers in the spirit, fellow slaves in devotion to God. Wealth, too, is no ground of distinction, except insofar as it provides the opportunity for preeminence in good works. To be rich is not a matter of *having*, but of

using riches for the tasks of justice; and those whom one would suppose poor are actually no less rich, in that they are short of nothing and hanker after nothing.[37]

One of the most famous defenders of the poor and an outspoken advocate of social justice in the fourth century was John Chrysostom (ca. 349–407). Following the Gospel, Chrysostom takes a radical stance vis-à-vis wealth and its accumulation, and the divisions that it brings among people:

> What goods are these? Money, houses, so many acres of land, crowds of slaves, loads of silver and gold? . . . If these things are goods, it follows that those who possess them must be called good. For is not someone good who possesses what is good? But, tell me, when possessors of these things are greedy and rapacious, are we still to call them good? . . . "But suppose he is not greedy," you say. And how is that possible, since the passion is so all-consuming? "Well, it is possible," you say. No it is not! It is not! Christ proved it himself, when he said: "Make friends for yourselves by means of *unrighteous* mammon" (Luke 16:9). "But what if he inherited from his father?" Then he inherited what had been unjustly accumulated. It does not go back to Adam that his ancestors were rich, but one of the many that came before him must probably have taken and enjoyed the goods of others unjustly.[38]

Chrysostom's "communism" is visible in other places as well, where he advocates equality as something that is in accordance with God's will:

> Because at the beginning God did not make one man rich and another poor. Nor did he introduce the distinction, offering vaults of gold to one and refusing another the right to acquire it. He left the earth free for all alike. But if it is common, why have you so many acres of land, and your neighbor not so much as a spoonful? . . . "The earth is the Lord's and the fullness thereof" (Ps. 24:1)—is it not? If our possessions belong to our common Lord, they belong to our fellow servants too. For all that the Lord owns is common.[39]

Chrysostom sees the source of inequality in alienation, in the unjust and unnatural seizure of the common goods by some, turning them into private property. Wealth, no matter how it has been acquired, is something that, for Chrysostom, just as for the rest of the early Christian thinkers quoted here, makes sense only as a means of support for those in need.

Wealth can be justified only when it is distributed, in other words when it disappears:

> But once someone tries to alienate something to make it his own, contention is introduced; as though nature itself were outraged, that when God would rally us from every quarter, we compete to split off and separate by appropriating things and calling them "mine" and "thine." . . . But, as I said, how can anyone who has wealth be good? It is simply not possible. He is good when he distributes his wealth. . . . Having property, we conclude, is not a good; doing without it is an indication that someone is good.[40]

The similarities between Chrysostom and Ambrose go beyond their critique of private property and wealth. Chrysostom was also ready to criticize imperial polices, and to differentiate clearly between the political sphere ("earthly business" and something that belongs to the "body") and the "spiritual" realm, overseen by the church.[41] However, Chrysostom is also careful not to criticize the imperial power in principle when he explains "how much higher the priesthood is" compared to the "kingship."[42]

The above-discussed authors clearly articulated their opposition to wealth as one of the foremost sources of inequality and the power, domination, exploitation, and injustice built upon it. Additionally, they were also capable of criticizing political power and the misuse of that power, although, as citizens of the Roman Empire (and, from the time of Constantine the Great, even as semistate officials), they rarely questioned the legitimacy of the political power or the oppressiveness of the state. Unlike in Revelation, these critiques do not present an opposition to the imperial power per se, but rather an opposition to concrete policies or concrete personalities and their actions. Nevertheless, individually and as a whole, these authors represent important evidence of a block (no matter how incoherent) of resistance among theologians and church leaders to political authorities, even though this resistance might not have always been based on questioning the legitimacy of the exercise of the political power *in principle*.

At the end of the period usually called "late antiquity," when Christianity had already established itself within the Roman Empire, and when the Western part of the empire was going through dramatic changes that would eventually lead to its collapse—stands the figure of Augustine of Hippo (354–430). His political theology, as elaborated in *The City of God*, bears the mark of both the place and time in which Augustine lived. By contrasting the "city of God" (or "heavenly city") and the "earthly city" ("city of man") Augustine provides a very useful distinction, which left remarkably little trace in later political thought, given his preeminent position as a theological authority (especially in the West). Unlike his "just war" theory, for instance, Augustine's "proto-anarchist" arguments seem to have been much less attractive to the mainstream political thinkers of the medieval and early modern periods. Through the long and complicated text of the *City of God*, one gradually grasps the meaning of these two "cities": The "city of God" and the "city of man" or "city of this world," appear as two different logics of interhuman relationships. In Augustine's words,

> As for the city of this world, it is neither to last forever nor even to be a city, once the final doom of pain is upon it. . . . In fact, the city of man, for the most part, is a city of contention with opinions divided by foreign wars and domestic quarrels and by the demands for victories which either end in death or are merely momentary respites from further war. The reason is that whatever part of the city of the world raises the standard of war, it seeks to be lord of the world, when, in fact, it is enthralled in its own wickedness.[43]

The "city of man" was "first founded by a fratricide," for "Rome began, as Roman history records, when Remus was killed by Romulus," and the same logic of the "city of man" can be seen in the case of Cain and Abel:

> The root of the trouble was that diabolical envy which moves evil men to hate those who are good for no other reason than that they are good. . . . What, then, is revealed in the quarrel between Remus and Romulus is the way in which the city of man is divided against itself, whereas, in the case of Cain and Abel, what we see is enmity between the two cities, the city of man and the City of God.[44]

On the other hand, the "city of God" stands for the eschatological reality of God's Kingdom that cannot (fully) be manifested within the boundaries of this world:

> We all experience as individuals what the Apostle says: "It is not the spiritual that comes first, but the physical, and then the spiritual." The fact is that every individual springs from a condemned stock and, because of Adam, must be first cankered and carnal, only later to become sound and spiritual by the process of rebirth in Christ. . . .

For the true City of the saints is in heaven, though here on earth it produces citizens in whom it wanders as on a pilgrimage through time looking for the Kingdom of eternity. When that day comes it will gather together all those who, rising in their bodies, shall have that Kingdom given to them in which, along with their Prince, the King of Eternity, they shall reign for ever and ever.[45]

In addition to these early Christian authors, another phenomenon from the fourth century has been interpreted as a very radical opposition to "this world" and the existing social and political structures: the rise of monasticism. Monks (from μοναχός—solitary, single) were present in Christianity from the earliest times, although not in an organized or formalized fashion. Monasticism did not represent only the refusal to enter marriage and to procreate. In fact, celibacy can be interpreted as a result of the changed and fundamentally different logic of being upon which monasticism was built—the refusal of the entire social system that was based on the idea of marriage, ownership, family (blood) line, tradition, and the corresponding necessity (as well as power) attached to it. Viewed from this perspective, being a monk is much more about rebelling and rejecting the social institutions and power structures of the ancient world (standing against "this world") than about simply abstaining from sexual intercourse. Monks were (and, if authentic, continue to be), the *punks* of their time.

This radicalism of monasticism, its eschatological orientation and its creative, brave, "rebellious" response to the necessities of "this world" has been obscured in the later tradition. These early "anarchist" monastic tendencies among the early Christians only continued and expanded in the fourth century, when monasticism obtained its classical form with the establishment and growth of monastic "communities" that many perceived as (proto) anarchist types of societies. From this time on, in addition to the *eremitic* (solitary) tradition, we also speak of the *cenobitic* (communal) monastic life—which goes back to St. Pachomius (in the fourth century), and the monastic communities in Egypt.

Monasticism, especially cenobitic monasticism, has long been understood as a reaction against the "Christianization" (i.e., Christian legitimization) of the socio-political sphere, which started in the fourth century.[46] The formation of the organized cenobitic monastic life, which spread in the fourth century, coincides with the rise of symphonic doctrines, and can be interpreted as an opposition to them. This opposition was not an opposition only or primarily in theory, but in actual living practice.

From the very beginning, monasticism has been perceived as a more favorable type of Christian life, one that iconizes human existence in the Kingdom of God. This is clear already from the New Testament, in famous places such as Matthew 19 and 22:

> The disciples said to him, "If this is the situation between a husband and wife, it is better not to marry." Jesus replied, "Not everyone can accept this word, but only those to whom it has been given. For there are eunuchs who were born that way, and there are eunuchs who have been made eunuchs by others—and there are those who choose to live like eunuchs for the sake of the kingdom of heaven. The one who can accept this should accept it." (Matthew 19:10–12)

> Jesus replied, "You are in error because you do not know the Scriptures or the power of God. At the resurrection people will neither marry nor be given in marriage; they will be like the angels in heaven." (Matthew 22:29–30)

Apostle Paul also calls for a monastic life as a better way of Christian life for all those who can endure it:

> Do not deprive each other except perhaps by mutual consent and for a time, so that you may devote yourselves to prayer. Then come together again so that Satan will not tempt you because of your lack of self-control. I say this as a concession, not as a command. I wish that all of you were as I am. But each of you has your own gift from God; one has this gift, another has that.
>
> Now to the unmarried and the widows I say: It is good for them to stay unmarried, as I do. But if they cannot control themselves, they should marry, for it is better to marry than to burn with passion. (1 Corinthians 7:5–9)

Rejecting the logic of "this world," which includes procreation, replication of the social power structures and domination of both natural and socially imposed necessity over human freedom, the logic of monasticism implies a new logic of life, in which other human beings are fellow "sisters" and "brothers" of the heavenly Father. These "sisters" and "brothers" are thus not biological siblings, but those who are "born" again, from "above" (in other words, those baptized into a liturgical communion), for whom the logic and the limitations of this world do not pose the ultimate horizon of meaning, or the criteria of life or goodness.

Monasticism, when practiced properly, can thus be called an icon of the "eschatological" way of life, the one that, within the boundaries of this world, actualizes as closely as possible the logic of the coming Kingdom of God. Living outside "the world" (or the "city," which stands for centers of wealth and power), either as solitary monks or within the organized monastic communities, demonstrates the choice of an alternative way of life, a rejection of the world—not of the "material" (physical) world and the difficulties that characterize human existence in history, but precisely of the world dominated by natural and political logic (i.e., necessity), with the all-penetrating power structures of the state that, in the fourth century, started to assume "Christian" robes. The "explosion" of the monastic life coincides with the blurring of the boundaries between the church and the state. Since the state and power logic started to merge with the church and its organization, monasticism can be perceived as an attempt to preserve the eschatological urge of the Christian faith and its radicalism at the time that official Christianity started making compromises with the "world" on a much larger scale.

Viewed from the outside, living in a monastic community can be understood as living in a "classless" society, in which all members of the community are equal, performing different tasks, participating collectively in the election of their administrators who (for a specified period of time) perform various practical tasks. In this sense, well-functioning monastic communities can be understood as coming very close to what many anarchists would consider "ideal" anarchist communities.[47] Because of their organization (at least in theory) and leading principles, there should be no place for the exercise of power and domination, but rather a joint (communal) life of "sisters" and "brothers" in Christ. All within this community are supposed to decide collectively, elect among themselves those who will perform various duties for a certain period or time, take care of each other, work together and, if necessary, give life for one another (the fact that actual practice is often in a contradiction with this view is a separate issue). In other words, the idea of monastic life is based on Christ's advice on living a Christian life, following logic that is exactly opposite to the logic of "this world":

> You know that the rulers of the Gentiles lord it over them, and their high officials exercise authority over them. Not so with you. Instead,

whoever wants to become great among you must be your servant, and whoever wants to be first must be your slave—just as the Son of Man did not come to be served, but to serve, and to give his life as a ransom for many. (Matthew 20:25–28)

Implicit in this is that the monastic attempt to live a life according to the logic of the Kingdom of God results in the abandonment of the very logic of power structures, including political institutions. As a collective, it can also be understood as an attempt to establish new communities that would, within their local sphere of competence, effectively abolish "worldly" (meaning *coercive*) socio-political orders in order to create a "new society" which would more effectively mirror the reality of the coming Kingdom of God. In this sense, monasticism came to preserve the (ideal of) the (early) Christian way of life, precisely in its "anarchist" dimension.[48]

With time, however, monasteries and monastic orders have gradually been absorbed by the evolving institutional church structures (although the traces of the "anarchist" logic of their communities remain to this day). This has effectively turned the majority of the monastic communities into "world-like" institutions, integrated into the bigger church administration, with its vertical distribution of power. Over the course of the medieval period, monasteries would also become the source of enormous economic power. However, in spite of this, it was precisely the monasteries of this period, both in the East and in the West, that allowed for a significant degree of social mobility, practically unimaginable in other segments of the society (apart from the military formations).[49]

Many conflicts between the ecclesial and political administrations in the post-Constantine time gave rise to a more or less articulated resistance to the political power. In many of these conflicts, monasteries and individual monks were the major source of opposition to the political power. Although the legitimacy of the political power has rarely been explicitly questioned in principle, the church and, specifically, monasticism routinely stood in the way of power, seeking to oppose particular policies and limit the domain of the imperium.[50]

Many episodes from the history of the Eastern Empire are illustrative in this respect. One example is found in the tenth-century disputes between Patriarch Polyeuctus (♟ 956–70) and Emperor John I (♟ 969–76). The patriarch stood up to the emperor's illegitimate rise to power (after the execution of Nikephoros Phokas), and refused to crown him or to allow him to enter the church until he repented.[51] Another strong example is found in the church's (primarily monastic) resistance to imperial aspirations to use the church and faith for political goals, resisting imperial attempts to save the disintegrating empire by forcing a union with Rome, as in the Union of Lyons (1274), imposed by Emperor Michael VIII Palaeologus, and the Union of Ferrara-Florence (1438–43), under Emperor John VIII.[52]

However, the biggest conflict between the church and the state in the history of the Eastern Roman Empire came with the attempts of the emperors to impose iconoclasm, which brought not only a period of tensions but, also, a civil war. The iconoclastic dispute can be viewed as a conflict between the state, via an attempt to spread the political power over the ecclesial/spiritual realm, thus creating a theocratic form of government, and the church (or its factions), resisting those attempts.[53]

The most prominent theologians from this period, who developed the theology of icons, echoed some of the early Christian authors in their attempts to resist the political power and to defend the matters of faith and the church, protecting it from political interference. In the writings of John of Damascus (675/676–749) and Theodore the Studite (759–826), we find an articulated position against the imperial power's involvement in what were strictly church and theological matters. John of Damascus, who had the advantage that he, almost certainly, never entered the Byzantine-controlled territories, famously said:

> We submit to you, O Emperor, in the matters of this life, taxes, revenues, commercial dues, in which our concerns are entrusted to you. For the ecclesiastical constitution we have pastors who speak to us the word and represent the ecclesiastical ordinance. We do not remove the ancient boundaries, set in place by our fathers, but we hold fast to the traditions, as we have received them.[54]

One can also mention, in this context, the phenomenon of *Bogomilstvo* (alternatively also *Bogumilstvo*), a movement whose members resisted both the political and ecclesial power structures. It seems that Bogomilstvo started with the teachings of a priest Bogomil (or Bogumil) in tenth-century Bulgaria. Most of the scholarly work on Bogomilstvo has focused on the heretical elements of their faith, such as the dualistic character of their metaphysics (that seem to have played a more prominent role in the later development of Bogomilstvo). However, more relevant to this context are the *anarchic* tendencies that can be noticed in this movement. It seems that the *Bogomils* were skeptical toward the institutional church, its hierarchy and power. It also seems that it was this aspect of their faith, and not more abstract doctrinal issues, that caused their persecution both in Eastern and Western Europe. Following Ostrogorski, the Bogomils were a movement of protest against the powerful and rich.[55] How much of their belief, in the early period, departed from the mainstream Christian faith is a topic for a separate study.

A particularly important phenomenon in the history of "proto-anarchist" Orthodox political theology is *jurodstvo* (юродство), or "holy foolishness." "Holy foolishness" is most typical of the Slavic world and, specifically, of Russian Orthodoxy in the late medieval and the early modern periods, although the tradition of holy fools, in their various appearances, is much longer. This phenomenon can be traced back to Old Testament figures, such as Prophets Isaiah, Jeremiah, or Elisha, all the way up to the "last prophet of the Old Testament," and the "first prophet" of the New Testament, John the Baptist.

"Holy fools" are "fools for Christ" (1 Corinthians 4:10), those who reject (spontaneously or on purpose) the social conventions, reason, or the logic of "this world" for the sake of freedom. They fight against their own egotism and pride in order to acquire self-emptying, unconditional love. They are the "fools" who defy accepted social codes and common wisdom. They are those chosen by God to "destroy the wisdom of the wise," for "the foolishness of God is wiser than human wisdom, and the weakness of God is stronger than human strength."[56] These often unpleasant characters were capable of telling the ugly truth to those in power but also to the general population, criticizing the hypocrisy and spiritual inertia of the common people. They would challenge the kings and the mighty, reject the authority of the powerful, all on the grounds that all of the former belongs to the vanity of this world, and, as such, is corruptive and deceptive. A holy fool

> must chastise the tsar more often and more severely, since a ruler's crimes are highly visible and more terrible in their consequences. . . . Russian vitae and other sources give special attention to the denunciation of tsars. . . . This stereotype includes the idea that it is not only possible but even inevitable that the holy fool come into direct contact with the tsar.[57]

The connection between holy foolishness and social and political issues has been perceived as a close one, even by contemporary authors. Holy foolishness can even appear as a special type of saintliness, focused on social criticism. Regarding the holy fools of sixteenth- and seventeenth-century Moscow, Giles Fletcher noted,

> These they take as prophets and men of great holiness, giving them a liberty to speak what they list without any controlment, though it be of the very highest himself. . . . Among others at this time they have one at Moscow that walketh naked about the streets and inveigheth commonly against the state and government, especially against the Godunovs that are thought at this time to be great oppressors of that commonwealth.[58]

Holy fools are also more typical of urban contexts. The "patron saint" of the holy fools is St. Andrew (tenth century), whose vita has had a special appeal to later Russian literature and the practice of holy foolishness. According to his hagiography, Andrew was Slavic or Scythian in origin, and was brought to Constantinople as a slave. He acted as if he was insane, and combined this ascetic practice with rigorous fasting.[59]

Another important figure of this tradition is St. Simon of Iurievets (sixteenth century), known for insulting dignitaries, and even for slapping the governor,[60] which eventually led to his death. Other prominent holy fools include Pavel Svedomski, St. Kseniia of St. Petersburg, Fedor the Holy Fool, Nikola of Pskov, and Prokopii of Viatka, who were known for walking naked, insulting people, telling (instructive) jokes, making fun of those who were proud, and defying the well-established social norms and values as well as making scandals, including within the church environment.[61] All of this was part of the regular repertoire of the holy fools. They were believed to be not only prophets of God, able to speak the truth directly, without fear of offending the official church, political authorities, or public morality; they were also actively defying the accepted codes of behavior and social "normality" (including the pride in being a "good" or "pious" Christian)—all of which appear as *insanity* when viewed from the perspective of "this world."

In their prophetic function, holy fools remind Christians that prophecies are there to maintain the tension between the Kingdom of God and "this world."

Parallel to many "symphonic" tendencies in Russia in the post-Mongol times, there were also attempts from church circles to resist the policies of both the church hierarchy and the state that ran counter to some of

Basil the Holy Fool. (Based on a seventieth-century icon of Saint Basil the Holy Fool.)

the basic aspects of Orthodoxy and church life. Such was the activity of Nil Sorsky (or Nilus of Sora, 1433–1508). He became the leader of the "nonpossessors," a group that primarily opposed the vast church land ownership and wealth. As a monk, he argued in favor of simplicity and equality among the monastery brotherhoods and sisterhoods. He was against the practice, which was becoming popular at the time, of introducing various "ranks" among the monks in the monastery, based on their family origin and wealth, as this directly contradicted the very logic of monasticism and liturgy.[62] Nil was on the side of the widespread popular animosity toward church wealth and ecclesiastical power, calling for asceticism of the monks and a hesychastic praying tradition.[63] Nil Sorsky also opposed Joseph Volotsky and his political theology, which affirmed Russian autocracy and close church-state relationships.[64]

The Russian context in the modern period is also very instructive as to the (proto) anarchist ideas. As we have already seen, a strong *anarchist* sentiment—in the sense of its antiwealth and antiprivate property orientation—was present in Narodnichestvo as a more general tendency critical of the upper classes and the Westernization of Russian social life, which was perceived as breaking with the organic (and peasant-communitarian) life of the people.

Among the Slavophiles—who, as we saw, can be seen as the "religious wing" of Narodnichestvo—and Slavophile-inspired authors, one finds very elaborate critiques of the state and church structures (especially in their symbiosis) that were based on the affirmation of authentic Christianity. Ivan S. Aksakov harshly criticized the official ("established") church in Russia, its close alliance with autocracy, and its hypocrisy and formalism, in the name of Christian love, faith, and truth. This illuminating passage we find in Solovyev's *Russia and the Universal Church* is worth of quoting at some length:

> That half the members of the Orthodox Church belong to her only in name; that they are kept within her fold only by the fear of temporal penalties. This is what our Church has come to! It is a dishonorable, depressing and monstrous state of affairs, this riot of sacrilege in the sacred precincts, of hypocrisy ousting truth, of terror in place of love, of corruption under the guise of outward order, of bad faith in violent defense of the true faith! What a denial, within the Church

herself, of her own vital principles, of all that justifies her existence, that falsehood and unbelief should reign where everything should live and move and have its being in truth and faith! And yet the gravest danger is not that the evil has spread among the faithful, but that it has been legalized, that this state of affairs in the Church has been established by statute and that such an anomaly should be the inevitable outcome of the *standard* accepted by the State and by the whole of our society. . . .

Generally speaking, among us in Russia, in Church affairs as in all other matters it is outward decorum that must be preserved at all costs; and with that our love for the Church, our idle love, our indolent faith, is satisfied. We readily shut our eyes and, in our childish fear of scandal, attempt to blind ourselves and everyone else to all that great evil which, under the veil of respectability, is eating like a cancer into the living core of our religious organism. Nowhere else is truth regarded with such horror as in the domain of our Church administration; nowhere else is there greater servility than in our spiritual hierarchy; nowhere is the "salutary falsehood" practiced on a larger scale than in the place where all falsehood should be held in detestation. . . .

Our Church, if we are to take the word of her champions, is a huge but wayward flock, shepherded by the officers of the law who with the lash force the straying sheep into the fold. Does such a picture correspond to the true conception of Christ's Church? If not, she is no longer the Church of Christ. What is she, then? A State institution which can be used in the interests of the State for moral discipline. . . . A Church that is unfaithful to Christ's covenant is the most barren and anomalous phenomenon in the world; she stands condemned already by the word of God. A Church which is a department of State, that is, of a "kingdom of this world," has renounced her mission and will inevitably share the fate of all the kingdoms of this world. She has no intrinsic reason for existence; she has doomed herself to impotence and death.[65]

This is probably the most eloquently expressed critique of the official order and church structures from an Orthodox Christian perspective, which remains very vivid and relevant to this day. A "dishonorable, depressing and monstrous state of affairs," "terror in place of love," and the "outward decorum which must be preserved" are all still reality in many (one is tempted to say most) Christian communities. The concluding remarks, that "a Church which is a department of State, that is, of a 'kingdom of this world,' has renounced her mission and will inevitably share the fate of all the kingdoms of this world" is the starting point for a "theological anarchist" critique of church structures presented later on.

Vladimir Solovyev (also Solovyov, 1853–1900) can also be referred to in this context. He was against the national, or state church, concept, and he advocated Christian universalism based on love. For Solovyev, the church is a perfect social order, established by the Divine Will.[66] In this sense, all other social and political orders are deficient. Solovyev sees the structure of this perfect union and its governance as something that must reflect its very nature: collaborative, council-based administration. Because of his attempts to envision a Christian universalism (which would reunite the officially divided Eastern and Western churches), he also advocated a special role for Peter and Peter's successors (Roman popes) as another element that should be advanced in this Divinely ordered society. In this sense, Solovyev's solution seems to be an attempt to reconcile and merge the synodic principle (typical of the East) with the concept of the "church autocracy" (typical of the West) and harmonize them. He also employs Trinitarian theology in developing his "Trinitarian" social model.[67] Interestingly enough, the liturgical logic, which provides the best illustration of the "unity" or "communal" principles (including those of the Trinitarian theological tradition), does not play a prominent role in Solovyev's arguments on social and political realms.

Anarchism—as a self-conscious political philosophy and practice developed upon that philosophy—is a child of the modern period. It is interesting that three of the main "classical" anarchist authors came from the Russian Orthodox milieu: Michael Bakunin, Leo Tolstoy (1828–1910), and Peter Kropotkin. All three came from an aristocratic/upper-class background, and all three turned against the political system of exploitation and oppression, both in their own country and in general. Bakunin and Tolstoy, however, can be discussed as anarchists who, each in his own way, reacted more explicitly to and against the Orthodox religious and cultural context.

Bakunin rejected the church, Christianity, and religion, and in much of his work he clearly reacted against his own cultural background and the situation both in the Orthodox church in Russia and in nineteenth-century

Russian society. The situation was, for most of the time, one of corruption, of close ties between the institution of the church and the state where theological narratives were often employed in justification of various forms of oppression. However, it was also a place and time in which many intellectual movements flourished. In spite of Bakunin's criticism of religion, one can argue that Bakunin's type of socio-political critique is indebted precisely to the Orthodox Christian tradition. Bakunin's understanding of the value and meaning of freedom resembles to a remarkable degree the role of freedom in later Russian religious philosophy. Bakunin's claims such as "absolute freedom and absolute love—that is our aim; the freeing of humanity and the whole world—that is our purpose,"[68] or "I am a fanatical lover of freedom,"[69] sound remarkably similar to the later Nikolai Berdyaev's claims about freedom and his affirmation of freedom and love as the ontological principles constituting the very core of Christian anthropology and cosmology.

In contrast to Bakunin, Tolstoy embraced Christianity. In his life and work we see an attempt to revitalize the early Christian communitarian life, without church hierarchy.[70] In this sense, and in spite of his "highly unorthodox vision of Christianity,"[71] it is possible to assert that certain elements of Tolstoy's anarchism are based on some of the very basic elements of the *Orthodox* Christian faith (including the prominence of communitarian life, especially related to rural areas).[72] He tried to put his ideas into practice, organizing on his own estate anarchist-like communitarian life.[73] Nevertheless, what one can notice is that Tolstoy's interpretation of Christianity, in its social and political dimension, is remarkably *de-eschatologized*. There is no room there for a sacramental, liturgical communion with the Divine, or an expectation of the coming Kingdom of God. Although formally Christian, these assumed metaphysical positions underpinning Tolstoy's anarchism make his approach to the sphere of the political closer to some of the classical (secular) anarchists, if not so much at the level of strategy as at the level of principles.

The central place in the history of (proto) anarchist Orthodox Christian political theologies belongs to Nikolai Berdyaev. His approach to the socio-political sphere is based on some of the basic premises of his religious philosophy: Freedom and creativity are both the points of departure for Berdyaev's philosophy and its final destination. Freedom and creativity are, for Berdyaev, the central metaphysical concepts that he, then, applies to the socio-political reality. And this is, at the same time, one of the most important distinctions between Berdyaev and anarchists such as Bakunin. While freedom in Bakunin is something that always manifests itself in the social environment, as a property of individuals and societies, for Berdyaev it is primarily an existential concept based on a Christian understanding of the world, which is only secondarily and imperfectly reflected in the socio-political sphere.

Berdyaev's intellectual formation was heavily influenced by Marxism. He departed later from Marxism as a false ontology, and he would turn to Christianity and, in particular, to the Orthodox tradition as the source of his religious-philosophical ideas. Rejecting all types of oppression and slavery, he was able to advocate for "spiritual aristocracy" or an "aristocratic principle." The concepts do not designate political categories, let alone class stratification. "Spiritual aristocrats" are those who are capable of embracing their freedom, those capable of rising to the stature of free persons.[74]

Berdyaev differentiates between the "realm of spirit," which is characterized by freedom and which finds its expression in the human person as a free and creative being, and the "realm of Caesar," which for Berdyaev does not only refer to the political sphere but includes everything that is characterized by necessity (including the natural world):

> Dualism between the realm of spirit and that of Caesar is an absolutely necessary confirmation of man's freedom. But this is not a final dualism: it is dualism in the spiritual and religious life of man. The final monism will be confirmed in the Kingdom of God: it is only revealed eschatologically.[75]

Berdyaev's attitude to the "realm of Caesar" is clear from the following passage, in which he frames the problem of Christianity and politics in a way that remains a cornerstone for every serious Christian approach to the sphere of the political:

> The expression "There is no power but of God" which has been of really fateful significance has all too often meant servility and opportunism in relation to the authority of the state and the sacralization of forms of authority which were anything but Christian. The Apostle Paul's words have no religious meaning whatever: they are purely historical and relative, called forth by the position of Christians in the Roman Empire. St. Paul was afraid that Christianity might turn into an anarchistic, revolutionary sect. He wanted to place Christianity into universal history. We must recall, further, that some

time later, during the reign of Domitian, the state authority was called the beast from the abyss. . . .

And things were worse when the Church seemed to have her own ideal, in the Christian theocracies of history, because these theocracies were Christian only in name, and in reality they denied freedom. . . .

The depth of the problem lies in this, that spirit cannot be dependent upon nature and society, not be determined by them. Spirit is freedom, but in the objectivation of spirit in the course of history, a series of myths were created which were used to confirm the authority of government . . . the myth of monarchy, the sovereign power of the monarch, the myth of democracy—the sovereign power of the people (*Volonté générale*), the myth of communism—the sovereign power of the proletariat. . . . Sovereignty belongs to no one: it is only one of the illusions of objectivation.[76]

He sees a "religious truth" in anarchism, but he objects to the "materialistic" character of most anarchist movements. He realizes that the fundamental intention that we find in anarchism—the love of freedom and the rejection of power or oppression—can only fully be realized in the Kingdom of God:

There is absolute truth in anarchism and it is to be seen in its attitude to the sovereignty of the state and to every form of state absolutism. It is an exposure of the wrongness of despotic centralization. There is religious truth in anarchism; but anarchism is materialistic and as such it has in fact frequently become absurd. . . . The religious truth of anarchism consists in this, that power over man is bound up with sin and evil, that a state of perfection is a state where there is no power of man over man, that is to say, anarchy. The Kingdom of God is freedom and the absence of such power; no categories of the exercise of such power are to be transferred to it. The Kingdom of God is anarchy. This is a truth of apophatic theology; the religious truth of anarchism is a truth of apophatics.[77]

In the end, Berdyaev rejects the label "anarchist" not because his approach to the political sphere had not been skeptical vis-à-vis the power structures (quite the opposite!) but precisely on the grounds that the depth of the issues related to human freedom can only be grasped metaphysically (which ultimately means eschatologically)—not by remaining within the political realm or using it as the ultimate point of reference (as traditional anarchists did). He is aware of the need for the freedom-necessity dualism in the course of history, but he does not consider it to be the final, or satisfactory solution. The point is to arrive at an eschatological monism in which freedom will become the mode of existence:

> It may be said that my view-point is too much under the influence of the anarchist myth, but this is not the case. The idea of a utopia, happy and stateless, is quite foreign to me. Under the conditions of this world, the function of the state will always remain. But the state is of functional and subordinate importance, only. What we must refuse, is the sovereignty of the state. The state has always tended to reach beyond its normal boundaries, and to become an autonomous sphere of life. The state wants to be totalitarian. This applies not only to communism and fascism. . . . One of the classic arguments of Celsius against the Christians is that they are not loyal citizens of the state, that they feel they belong to another kingdom. We have this same conflict today, the eternal conflict between Christ the God-Man, and Caesar the man-god. The inclination to deify Caesar is always present, it is revealed in monarchy, but may also appear in democracy or in communism. Christianity cannot be reconciled to the sovereignty of any kind of earthly authority—not the sovereignty of a monarch, not that of the people or of a class. The only principle reconcilable with Christianity is the assertion of man's inalienable rights. But the state recognizes these unwillingly.[78]

The problem of human freedom in history (and that also means in society) is unsolvable without taking into account the metaphysical roots of the problem and its religious dimension. The path to follow in history is, thus, the path of "religious socialism":

> Socialism's most difficult problem is that of freedom. How can one combine the solution of the problem of bread for everyone, a problem on which human life itself depends, with the problem of freedom, on which human dignity depends? On the basis of materialism, the problem is insoluble, it can be solved only on the basis of religious socialism.[79]

Another crucial figure from the "Silver Age" of Russian thought—Sergei Bulgakov—is relevant for the "proto-anarchist" theological thinking. Bulgakov perceives the immanent injustice and cruelty as being constitutive of the state apparatus, which leads him to the advocacy of an eschatological "theocracy":

> The "legal state" with is guarantees of law and all its worldly prudence and man-related justice, will never do away with the pain caused by the reality of *another* kingdom, one not of cold legality alone, but of love, *another* kind of authority which is "theocratic." But of course this question has meaning only within the Church, where the discourse is not about politics in the usual sense of the word, but rather about the religious triumph over the "political," the *transfiguration* of authority, which is also its manifestation in *New Testament* terms.[80]

This "eschatological theocracy" (or "communism") is in Bulgakov paralleled in the ideal of early Christian communities (such as the community of Jerusalem):

> When all lived together in love and had all in common. This life of the Christian family, which has been called a Christian "communism" or "socialism," remains a guiding star on our horizon.[81]

Bulgakov's critique of economic inequality and exploitation, evidenced in many places,[82] puts him in the tradition of Christian theologians who perceive these social problems as something that does not only call for concrete actions in the socio-political realm, but also for the transformation of one's existence.[83]

Even from this brief reflection upon some of the most important manifestations of the "proto-anarchist" Orthodox political theologies, one can see two main emphases that have historically characterized this trajectory in Christian thought: first, skepticism toward the (illegitimate) exercise of power (which ranges from the condemnation of political power and political leadership as such, to the opposition to power when it begins to interfere with church teachings and liturgical practices); and second, skepticism toward wealth and its accumulation, which is criticized primarily on the grounds of alienation, egotism, lack of consciousness and compassion for others (the poor) as one's fellow sisters and brothers, and the domination that the wealthy segments of the population exercise over the poorer ones.

These two critiques are closely related, as the latter (financial influence) allows for the former—various forms of oppression. Traditionally, financial wealth and political power have been close allies, often virtually indistinguishable. The first can be used for acquiring and expanding the second, and vice versa. Behind both is the quest for power, its preservation and expansion. History has taught us that this has often been the goal in itself. And this is where any serious anarchist critique must begin.

In spite of the fact that one can trace this critical theological approach back to the earliest period of Christianity, anarchism, as a tendency, remained a marginal phenomenon. It will probably remain so. Even if human society established a system bearing the "anarchist" name, power structures would not be eliminated. A total elimination of power structures within history would probably require either a very profound *metanoia* experienced by virtually everyone on this planet, or, which is much more likely, a total *automatization* of the society, a technocratic system in which equality would be artificially imposed, at the expense of human freedom. Such a society might eliminate one evil but would do so at the expense of eliminating the most precious dimension of the human being. The problem of power structures is much deeper; it has to do with the very human existence in this world. Without addressing this dimension, the question of power structures cannot even be posed in a satisfactory way.

BEING AS FREEDOM AND NECESSITY

Ife one aspires to properly understand the place and meaning of the political sphere from an (Orthodox) Christian point of view, and to explore the antagonism between the Orthodox Christian faith and power
structures (in the variety of forms in which they appear), it is necessary to
delve into some of the basic (*metaphysical*) concerns of Orthodox faith. The
problem of power is the problem of the human *being in the world*.

One can safely claim that the freedom-necessity tension occupies a central position in Orthodox Christian theology. This is especially the case in
some of the most fruitful theological discourses within modern and contemporary Orthodox theology—those that are usually labeled as "Orthodox existentialism" or "Orthodox personalism."[1]

Viewed from this perspective, the basic, existential issue that human beings face is their very *createdness*, their existence as created beings and,
ultimately, their mortality. For John Zizioulas (b. 1931):

> The ultimate challenge to the freedom of the person is the "neces-
> sity" of existence. The moral sense of freedom, to which Western phi-
> losophy has accustomed us, is satisfied with the simple power of
> choice: a man is free who is able to choose one of the possibilities set
> before him. But this "freedom" is already bound by the "necessity"
> of these possibilities, and the ultimate and most binding of these
> "necessities" for man is his existence itself: how can a man be con-
> sidered absolutely free when he cannot do other than accept his
> existence?[2]

Being part of the created world, our own being manifests itself as a necessity for us. We are brought into existence, but that existence, and the very act of bringing us into being, is not the result of our freedom. This means that the createdness of our being manifests itself as an existential obstacle.

The mode in which we exist interferes with existence itself. Our existence thus appears as a paradoxical one. On the one hand, our life is the greatest gift given to us, something that allows us to be who we are. At the same time, it is also a challenge to our freedom (which is an expression of our desire to be)—no one asked us if we wanted to be brought into existence or not, how, where, and when, and since no one could have asked nonexistent beings if they wanted to be brought into existence, the very act of bringing us into being (which is a necessity for us) is already the first step forward in making freedom actual. The result is that a created, limited, imperfect existence such as our own is a coercive one; it contradicts freedom on many levels. And yet, at the same time, our existence still allows for more freedom than the absolute necessity of the sterile, inert nothingness—it has the potential for freedom.

Viewed from this perspective, the act of creation manifests itself as a *violent* act, an act of disturbance of the (harmonious) nonbeing. The created being, therefore, rests upon these two opposing forces—the ontic inertia that "remembers" the harmony of nonbeing (the final manifestation of which is death), and the life-giving love, through which the creative act of God brings something into existence, something that has never existed before. This "something" is not just an "objective" presence or biological existence, but existence that manifests itself as a personal presence.

These preliminary observations can be grounded in the narrative that we find in the book of Genesis, as well as in the interpretations of the creation narrative found in the Christian tradition.

God *calls* beings into existence. The declarations "Let it be" and "it was so" (Genesis 1:3–26), as well as later Christian interpretations of the Genesis story, gave birth to the *creatio ex nihilo* doctrine. As I have elaborated elsewhere,[3] the purpose of this doctrine was to stress the absolute freedom of God, as well as His absolute otherness vis-à-vis the world He creates. This means that there is no *natural*, or necessary, connection between the being of God and the existence of the world. The world is not an emanation of God or His harmonious, spontaneous, let alone necessary, *outpour*.

It is a radical act of freedom and love, bringing into existence something that *does not need to exist* by any universal, cosmic laws.

If the actual ("natural") *foundation* of created beings is nothingness, it follows that nothing (ultimately manifested in death) is the primary ontic "stuff" of our being. Consequently, the existence of the created beings— once they are created—is stretched between the primary ontic reality (of nothingness) and the necessary presence of our own, created being. Created beings "naturally" exist between nothingness and necessity. The problem with created beings is that they are not (yet) a fully existing reality, but not a simple nothingness either. They exist *potentially*. This *potential existence* is the possibility given to created beings to fully embrace existence by transforming the compelling (natural) way of being into a *real* existence, based on freedom. The other option is to (paradoxically) reject freedom (and existence as freedom), by affirming the *natural* way of existence (which is necessity), rooted in nothingness.

The story of creation tells us another important thing. The human being was created in "the image and likeness" of God (Genesis 1:26–27). With its distinction between *tselem* and *demuth*, this line has inspired a vast number of theological interpretations. From the very early period, Christian theologians understood this distinction as a sign of the dynamic character of the human being. The difference between the two concepts has been interpreted as an indication that the human being was created as an "open project," supposed to grow from the initial state (or *image*) to the *likeness*, and, in doing so, to develop its potential, in communion with God.[4] Others, however, have interpreted this as a repetition, two ways to say (and to stress) the same.[5]

But what is this "image/likeness"? What makes us *Godlike*? Many answers have been proposed to this question. In my view, the most convincing one, provided already by early Christian literature, is—*freedom*. The human being is Godlike foremost because of his/her capacity for freedom: the possibility not to be (entirely) determined, the possibility to exist as an "open" being. This position can be deduced from the writings of many early Church authors.[6] This Godlike property is the highest dignity given by God to a created being.[7]

For Christians, the dignity of the human being thus rests primarily on this: that human beings are not automatons, that they are not entirely "programmed" entities with the purpose of fulfilling some prearranged "grand design." From the Christian perspective, simply fulfilling the role given to us by a "grand design" would be the humiliation of the human being, even if that "grand design" was the work of God himself. Even the most perfect, harmonious, and most beautiful world would not be worthy of the dignity that God wanted the human being to have—the dignity of a *free being*.

Freedom manifests itself in the capacity to *create* and to *love*. As free beings, humans can determine who they are going to be and how. Their "likeness" is manifested in their capacity to shape this "open project" of their existence. Who they are going to be depends on their freedom and the (creative) way in which they use it, since humans are capable of doing and making things without merely reproducing or following the pregiven patterns. Most importantly, they are capable of creating themselves, of transforming their own existence from potentiality into actuality. This is why creativity should be understood as a metaphysical actualization of freedom.

The obvious consequence of taking this existential freedom seriously is that human beings, in their similarity to God, are capable of transgressing all boundaries, including the boundaries of their createdness. They are capable of rebellion, of saying "no" to any *master*, even if that master is God himself. The capacity to challenge God, to say "no" to Him (or to this world), turns out to be a very essential manifestation of who we are as humans. This is the reason why reducing the human prospect to blind obedience to some higher principle or system, to the fulfillment of legal or ethical norms (which is present in many "Christian" ethical discourses) that make us "good" human beings, represents a radical denial of an authentic Christian anthropology.

As a result, the human capacity of rebellion, of creating alternative worlds and ways of life, appears from the point of view of (Orthodox) Christian theology as an essential feature of our dignity as human beings. This feature is in fact captured with an everlasting vividness in the myth of Prometheus, and also in the Old Testament story of Jacob wrestling with the angel, which is God (Genesis 32:22–31).

Contemporary Orthodox theology operates with the concept of "personhood" as a way of describing those human capacities that constitute the *imago Dei*. Personhood appears as the inclusive term, capable of explaining the image/likeness of God in the human being, which rests (in John

Zizioulas's theology) primarily upon the theological contributions of the Cappadocian fathers and Maximus the Confessor[8] (while he also makes use of modern theological and philosophical approaches, such as those of Maritain, Sartre, and even Heidegger[9]).

In Zizioulas's reading, patristic theology "considers the person to be an 'image and likeness of God.'"[10] "From this standpoint," Zizioulas continues, "patristic theology sees man in the light of two 'modes of existence.' One may be called the *hypostasis of biological existence*, the other the *hypostasis of ecclesial existence*."[11] Following the train of this theological inquiry, to be a person means to exist in a communion, constituted in and through love. This means that one's *existence* as a person is constituted through a communion of love—the communion with other persons in which our own identity is not the result of any pregiven properties of our being (i.e., necessity), but is constituted through the loving relationship. A particular person is thus not the sum of his/her individual properties, but is a relational being, or a "being as communion," who *does not exist* (as a person) outside the loving communion with other persons.

The act of love should be understood here in existential terms, not as a psychological phenomenon, a sentimental feeling of an individual being. The act of love is radical, even "violent" in a certain sense. It possesses the qualities of urgency, immediacy, even *madness*. An act of love is an act of giving a unique and unrepeatable identity to those who are being loved. It is also an act of *creation* in a very fundamental sense. The prototype of this love is the "crazy" love of God,[12] the love with which God loves the world and the human being.

The concept of personhood, following Zizioulas, was first coined to explain who this God, in which Christians believe, is.[13] The Christian answer to this question is that God is love.[14] Not that He *feels* love, or that He (first) *is* and then *loves*, but that God *is* love. Love is the very mode of existence of God (love of the Father, and of the Son, and of the Holy Spirit), it is the *foundationless foundation* of God, the *anatural nature* and the *substanceless substance* of Divinity.

The concept of personhood thus implies that God's being is not based on any necessity. The being (life) itself is the result of freedom, and is identical to it. If there were some "nature" of God, separate from the person(s) of God, God would not exist as freedom but as a necessary realization of some independent or objectivized Divine essence. However, in the Christian understanding of God, God exists as freedom, not for any particular reason or purpose other than that He wants His existence as a communion of love. In Zizioulas's classical formulation, "the goal of person is person itself."[15]

God, moreover, creates (the human being) out of love. He desires a loving relationship with a being who has the capacity of becoming a personal being. This means that the same capacities that characterize the person—communion in/of love and freedom—also become the way of "knowing" God. It is not through a rational inquiry, which looks into particular, individual elements and their properties, that one "knows" God (or, for that matter, human beings as well). On the contrary, *we know* someone or something (in the metaphysically relevant way) through an ecstatic act of freedom and love for another being. "It is only with the heart that one can see rightly," the Little Prince would say. "What is essential is invisible to the eye."[16] We get to know personal (existential) realities only by becoming a person, only through a dynamic and creative movement outside our individual "self" toward the other. Personal realities, freedom, and love are unknowable to an inquiry, which rests on certainty, predictability, applicability, or, ultimately, necessity.

Theosis: From "Image" to "Likeness"

The "likeness" is the goal (*telos*) of this quest for freedom. "Likeness" is the new, personal mode of existence, which is not based on the necessity of our created being. In the Orthodox tradition, this process of acquiring the "likeness" (new mode of existence) is called *theosis* (θέωσις).

Theosis is usually translated into English as "divinization" or "deification." It implies the process of *becoming-like-God*, acquiring a mode of existence that mirrors the existence of God. At the same time, theosis implies the presence of God in those who are becoming Godlike, uniting (without confusion) one's being with God, allowing God to abide in one's person, one's soul as it were. God is present in those who enter a communion with Him in a similar way in which another human being is present in us (through his/her *energies*) when we are in a loving communion with him/her. Through such communion, through the very loving relationship with God, one becomes Godlike and "deified." Theosis is thus the path to salvation, understood as acquiring a new, free existence, becoming divine: "The golden rule of the entire patristic thought says 'God became man [human being] so that man [human being] becomes god'—'Man [human being] becomes by mercy what God is by nature."[17] It thus bridges the gap between the created and the uncreated.

Contrary to this understanding of the existential dynamics of the human being in the world, there have been countless attempts in the history of Christianity to understand the human condition in history and the issue of salvation in terms of debt-paying or in legalistic terms. Even the Incarnation of the Son has all too often been interpreted along these lines, understanding human existence in this world and the purpose of the Incarnation in terms of transgressions (sins, debts) that have to be paid by sacrifice. Christ, following this reasoning, comes to repay for the debt of humanity (original sin), and to "make up" for "breaking the law"—i.e., God's commandment not to eat from the Tree of Knowledge. Christ is sacrificed in order to "make peace" with God.

This naïve, but also potentially very manipulative reading, misses the central point of the Incarnation. The traditional reading of the predominant logic in the Old Testament—just as in many other religious systems of the ancient Mediterranean—does imply a contractual relationship between God and human beings, where there is a system of accountability and where those who do not keep their contractual obligations must (re)pay for their lapses (for obvious reasons, it is always the human beings). "Making things up" with God (or gods) is performed through repentance, renewal of promises (contract) and, crucially, through the offering of sacrifices. This is why, following such a model, Christ had to be sacrificed as an innocent lamb, mirroring the sacrifices offered by the ancient Israeli community to God (primarily through the office of the High Priest of the Temple).[18] The logic of Christianity and the Christian understanding of God cannot be reconciled with this model, or not easily at least. Christianity cannot accept the concept of a god who, out of his or her anger, requires sacrifices to make "peace" with human beings, or a god who chooses to torture people in this or the next world out of his caprice. It is equally unacceptable to have a god who simply must conform to the abstract, metaphysical laws that govern the universe (whether he created them or not)—for example, in the way in which the ancient Greek gods had to accept the Moirai and their decisions. As established before, the Christian God is Love. He is absolutely free. These two things, that He is ontically free and that He exists as Love are, so to speak, the "reasons" why He is God (and not a created being). Attempts to apply any legalistic logic, ethical standards, or vindictiveness to God is a naivety at best, and, more often, a clear denial of the Triune God.

Keeping in mind the previous discussion on necessity, it becomes clear that the Incarnation could not possibly have been something that should be seen in ethical or legal terms (although, formally, viewed from the ancient Israeli perspective, it might appear so). The Incarnation, instead, had something to do with our very existence. The main purpose of the Incarnation of God the Logos, following authentic Orthodox theology, becomes the theosis of the human being, and through the human being, of the entire creation. *God becomes human to enable human beings to become gods.*[19] The serpent from the story of Genesis was right in its articulation of the object of the fulfillment of the dignity of the human being, pronouncing "*You will be like God*" (Genesis 3:5). The target is to become "like" God, to actualize our *likeness* to God. But this process and the acquisition of the real "knowledge" ("opening of eyes"[20]) does not happen through a rational inquiry or through "good" (ethical) behavior ("knowledge of good and evil" in Genesis 3:5), but through the actualization of the human capacities of freedom and love. "Knowing" God (who is a personal being) is possible only for those who aspire to become beings in communion (i.e., persons), those who become capable of wisdom, as knowing *the way God knows*.

The full communion between God and the human being happens in the Incarnation of Christ. In the person of Christ, so to say, the "limitations" of both the Divine and human nature are overcome. God becomes human, which means that the uncircumscribable becomes circumscribable. But this also means that through Divine *kenosis*, the mortal and limited become immortal and unlimited. Thus, the Trinity is not only a communion of Divine persons, but Christ himself is also a communion (of two natures). This implies that the Incarnation of the Son was the purpose of the creation, not strictly related to, or dependent on, the original fall.[21]

As stated before, the Incarnation is a way of bridging the gap between the created and the uncreated, that very separation out of which the threat of the death-bearing nothingness appears. This is what is meant by salvation and the deliverance from sin. Sin, again, should not be understood as a transgression of a law, the breaking of the rule, or a failure to live up to certain (ethical) codes. It means "missing the target of life," an existential failure. The state of the separation from God is *sinful* not because it is *wrong* from an ethical or legal point of view, but because the fullness of existence (life) is impossible in that state. Sin is not about guilt, it is about our willingness and ability (or the lack thereof) to change our way of existence. Sin is about allowing the necessity of our natural life to dominate over our personality, to submit to what we are as pregiven, natural beings. The greatest sin is thus the passive submission to that ontic inertia, to the heavy nothingness in which our created being is rooted. The Incarnation bridges this gap by bringing human nature, in the person of Christ, in the closest possible proximity to God—without separation and without confusion.

This is, in itself, something new and greater than the original state, "before" the Fall. In the Incarnation, God becomes a human being. The communion between God and His creature becomes more perfect than it was in the Garden of Eden. This communion is witnessed then again in the Resurrection, when the death of God (and Christianity actually speaks of the *death of God*) becomes the death of death.

Christ's Incarnation and Resurrection do something else as well; they offer the human being a foretaste of what it means to acquire a Godlike existence. Human beings are given the chance to become Godlike precisely by turning their existence into an existence based on freedom and love. In other words, the Incarnation and Resurrection are not primarily related to the Fall, but to the problem of the necessity of our very createdness. It is a promise of the eschatological existence, a new being, which requires our engagement, a creative effort on the part of the human being.

This new existence is eschatological; it is fulfilled in the Kingdom of God. However, the transformation of our existence begins already here and now, so that it can conform to that eschatological existence that will be(come) fully manifested only at the end of time as we know it, when "this world has passed." This transformation is theosis—a possibility to exist not only *without an end* but also *without beginning.*[22] The one who goes through the transformative experience of theosis (i.e., a saint), thus also becomes a true *anarchos.*[23]

From an Orthodox perspective, it was precisely deification that was the purpose of the Incarnation of God. God becomes human so that the human being can fully become human by becoming divine. This is why it can be reasoned that the Incarnation would have happened even without original sin. The Incarnation of God is intimately linked with the creation of the world and the human being. In the Incarnation and Resurrection of Christ, the created world is affirmed in its potential to exist in a free way. It was given an affirmation that goes way beyond the initial creation. History is given a new meaning; it is a process of theosis, in which the world, through the deification of human beings, is becoming a "new being."[24]

In this process, the natural, necessary, and alienated existence has the opportunity to be transformed into the personal existence. This is where the Church and liturgy appear as the ark taking those who have oriented themselves toward the Kingdom of God to their destination.

An important point here is that, following this tradition, the story of the Incarnation and Resurrection of Christ, and the establishment of the future Kingdom of God, is not a story about finding (and returning to) the paradise lost. With the future Kingdom of God, as a new, personal existence, human beings and the rest of creation acquire more than they were initially granted. In contrast to the Eden (as it is commonly understood), in the eschaton, human beings become (re)created as free beings who, with their very free, creative, and ecstatic movement toward God and each other, overcome all the necessities, including the one of their own (created) being.

Perfection, Imperfection, and Personhood

Many ancient and modern philosophies have been searching for the meaning of human existence in various types of *perfections*, ranging from formal/aesthetic ideals to biological and ethical "perfections." Behind this reasoning is the logic that harmonious immovability is the sign of ultimate reality and perfection, which, when achieved, does not strive toward anything else or anything more since it is already perfect. However, in contrast to this reasoning (so widespread in antiquity), Christianity demonstrates a different approach to the question of the meaning of the world and of the human being, and the question of the "perfection" of both of them.

In the New Testament, Christ preaches, "Be perfect, therefore, as your heavenly Father is perfect" (Matthew 5:48). From the perspective of personalistic theology, this can mean only the *perfection* of self-emptying love. There is not any "grand design," nor any achievement in this world whose perfection (no matter how "perfect") would satisfy Orthodox Christian cosmology and anthropology. The only "grand design" that is worthy of the Christian understanding of both God and the human being is the *openness* of the human being, the possibility of ontic freedom and love.

This freedom and love are dynamic in their character. In order to exist, they also imply the possibility of rejection of one's love or even one's own being. This means that the (formal) *imperfections* of the created world— the possibility that something unpredictable, chaotic, or even evil can happen—allow for the possibility of the most precious capacities of the human being—*freedom*, *love*, and *creativity*—to appear.

This has clear consequences for the issue of morality and ethics. The existence of a "grand design," determining how things are "supposed to be," has traditionally been postulated in many discourses on ethics (and ethics is normally just a formal expression of the corresponding ontological premises). Both in its traditional religious and secular religious versions, the "grand design" idea has served as the ultimate ethical horizon. The presupposition that there is such a metaphysical harmonious order serves as the coordinate system with which one can determine what is "right" (that is, what is in accordance with the structure of the "grand design") and what is "wrong" (that which deviates from the "grand design" and the presupposed harmony of the world and society).

The "grand design" idea, as a metaphysical and ethical point of reference, has the structure of the Greek kosmos. It is the world identified in its essence with a harmonious *order*, which is rational in its structure and which functions as the ultimate *horizon of meaning*. This horizon of meaning codifies the values that are supposed to govern one's actions according to the standards of "good," "reasonable," "desirable," "permitted," "legal," and so forth. In this understanding of the world, what is *permitted* is also *good*, because it is in accordance with the universal order (kosmos). This order produces orders (laws) and demands submission to them. If someone goes against the kosmos, it is reasonable and justifiable to punish him/her, as this is the only logical (as well as ontological) possibility.[25] This logic remains the dominant logic in our societies, and often imposes horrendous suffering unto the people (labeled *criminals* and *offenders* of various types) in the name of the preservation of this "good," "legal," and meaningful order of the world.

The majority of Christian thinkers have not resisted the temptation of understanding the world and Christianity in this way. This is especially visible in the domain of "Christian ethics" as a theological discipline, which rarely escapes the trap of simplistic abstract normativity. What we often find is the adaptation of the "grand design" scheme, in which that traditional kosmos ethics and metaphysics merely appear in new, "Christian" robes. Thus we end up with a God who punishes the villains and criminals in order to preserve the beauty of the cosmos. But such "Christian" ethics makes God obey abstract laws; it turns Him into a metaphysical police officer, a servant of the everlasting abstract impersonal *order*.

However, it can be easily demonstrated that this "grand design" cosmology and the ethics based on it do not have anything to do with *authentic* Christianity. In fact, from an Orthodox Christian perspective, "grand design" ethics appears as fundamentally inhuman and anti-Christian because it does not take seriously human personhood. In this ethics, human freedom is reduced to obeying and accepting what is (predetermined as) "good" and "beautiful." Those who refuse to obey this cosmology and ethics are thus "evil," making it proper and just to punish them, even to eliminate them. This is the point when the "grand design" ethics becomes *evil*; this ethics turns out to be incapable of accepting a human being as a human being, as something/someone that is and has a value beyond and above any particular *right* or *wrongdoing*. Freedom is thus reduced to a purely formal manifestation of the choice between Morpheus's "pills."

Such "Christian" cosmology, naturally then, leads to the question of why we need freedom at all. If one follows the logic of "grand design," freedom becomes more of an obstacle in the existence of the human being than a fundamental property of who we are, or the very essence of human dignity. For "grand design" metaphysicians and moralists, freedom becomes a burden; we would be much better off without freedom since then the "grand design," the harmony and rationality of the world, would be preserved, no suffering would enter the picture, there would be no room for evil to appear, and also no need for *redemption* (which turns out to be quite a messy process).

The Old Testament story of the Fall offers the best illustration of the way in which freedom, as a manifestation of human personhood, can interfere with the beauty and "grand design" of the world. This freedom—which must be understood also as the *possibility of destroying the beauty and harmony of the world and the "grand design"*—is affirmed. Freedom appears more precious than the world itself, or than any "grand design" imaginable.

SOMETHING IS ROTTEN IN THIS
REALITY OF OURS

The Christian understanding of the historical process is paradoxical. On the one hand, Christianity affirms the world we live in, and our existence in history, as something basically "good" (see Genesis 1). Christianity does not reject the material world, history, or our biological body, although many popular discourses and numerous (ill-conceived) theologies routinely say otherwise.

On the other hand, however, Christianity also acknowledges that (to paraphrase Shakespeare) something is rotten in this reality of ours. Christianity acknowledges the limitations of this reality in which we live, and recognizes the distorted and incomplete way in which the reality (we ordinarily experience) exists. The mode of our existence "here" and "now" prevents us—as well as other beings in the universe—from living the fullness of life. It prevents us from being ontically *true*.

The traditional explanation for this *rotten* state of reality has been the story of the Fall and original sin: Because of the Fall, as the transgression against the initial order by God, the human being (deemed "king" of creation), and the rest of the world alongside him/her entered the strange existential condition that we call historical existence. In this most common explanation, we thus live in a fallen world, which departed from its original state as God envisioned it.

However, as we have seen, even the original state was not exactly a state of static perfection. It already was, by the character of its presence, a challenge to our freedom, though it also created the opportunity for an existential movement toward theosis and existence as freedom and love. With the Fall, though, human existence came to face one more necessity—the necessity of a life that manifests itself as a process of disintegration. Death, sickness, suffering, and all other evils become the "stuff" constituting the fallen existence.

Many Christian theologians, following the "grand design" approach, have interpreted the fall primarily in legalistic or ethical terms, holding that the first human beings broke an explicit commandment given by God not to eat from the Tree of Knowledge (Genesis 2:17). Since this rule/order was broken, a punishment logically followed, taking the form of expulsion from paradise and, following expulsion, death and suffering. These would then become *normal* and *natural* properties of the historical existence.

Consequently, as mentioned in the previous chapter, many theologians have traditionally thought of salvation as an essentially legal procedure or transaction, similar to the processes at state courts. One needs to justify oneself before the great (and pretty cruel) master, who has the power to condemn us eternally, and who will torture the condemned ones in ways that reflect a very vivid imagination. (It is not difficult to recognize in this image of original sin, the Fall, salvation, and/or condemnation, the actual practices of the medieval church and state. These practices relied on almost unimaginable cruelties that continue to be utilized by modern states.)

Outside of this legalistic and ethical approach, Orthodox theology has also been interpreting the Biblical verses narrating about the first human beings and their Fall in ontological terms rather than in terms of crime and punishment.[1] A fairly common interpretation, already known from the patristic literature, recognizes in the Fall the first (though, many would argue, unsuccessful) manifestation of human freedom.[2] Human beings departed from the state initially created by God because they actualized their freedom in a way that *missed the* (existential) *target*. One could say that the human being desired an autonomous existence, an existence that would not be a necessity. The Garden of Eden thus stands for the state of communion with God. The Fall, following this interpretation, should not be understood as breaking a commandment, but rather as breaking this communion. Although tragic in its consequences, the Fall thus still signifies human freedom and the capacity to say "no," even to God.

In this way, we find the problem of freedom at the bottom of the whole tragedy of our (fallen) historical existence. Our existence in history is being manifested as a continuous disintegration. Death is the mode of life for those who chose nonexistence to be the building blocks of their (aspired) autonomous existence. This, again, has nothing to do with punishment. It has to do with human freedom manifested as a quest for an autonomous mode of existence, which aspires *to be* independent of God. But the tragedy of this choice is mirrored in the ontic truth that God and the communion with God is *life*. It is the fullness of free existence, and the choice of an autonomous existence means, for created beings, the choice of *disintegrating nothingness* as the foundation of their new autonomous existence.

Created beings—brought into being out of nothing—have no foundation of their existence in anything ontically "stable." The only "stuff," which is *real* (from an eschatological perspective) is free and loving communion with the source of life. The tragedy of this state lies not in the desire to be *nothing* (to reject existence as such), but in the desire for an existence whose building blocks are made out of sterile, yet seductive, nothingness. Historical existence has become, thus, the manifestation of nothingness chosen by humans to be the very foundations of their new existence—an existence that aspires to be something by the means of being nothing.

The existence is thus stretched between two poles of the impossible desire: to be and not to be; to be in the mode of being, and to be in the mode of nonbeing. Historical existence has therefore developed as a certain presence of being without the fullness of life. Put yet another way, it has become the image of hell. (The meaninglessness of this existence has, then, historically been "sweetened" by human aspirations to order such a world, to make the very fallen existence a rational and harmonious whole.)

Therefore the aspiration to break free from the pregiven, necessary existence leads to another necessity. A free existence, characterized by separation and alienation, set apart from the communion of love, remains an ontic impossibility. As a result, the quest for existential freedom, not manifested as love, results in necessity. This "post-Fall" existential logic can be seen in the way in which the natural and, specifically, biological world manifests its historical existence.

Beings in nature do not exist in a harmonious state, which is then only secondarily disturbed by human presence and human activities. The natural state of the world is already, in itself, a state of *madness*. Mutual hostilities, competition between individual beings and species, mutual destruction, and even the constant disintegration of our own bodies (with the cells in our bodies ceaselessly dying, being replaced by new ones, or, worse, forgetting to die, as in the case of cancer) are all manifestations of this alienated, death-bearing existence. Human beings then give their quite substantial contribution to this cosmic tragedy by the enormous destruction and suffering they impose onto the environment, other species, and themselves.

Individual(ized) Mode of Existence

This death-bearing existence in history can be characterized by the concepts of "individuality" or an "individualized mode of existence." These concepts play a prominent role in John Zizioulas's theology. Zizioulas develops the concept of "individuality" in opposition to the concept of "personhood." With a remarkable similarity to Jacques Maritain's distinction between "individuality and personality" (even more so to Christos Yannaras's "individual" vs. "person" dichotomy),[3] Zizioulas traces this distinction between the two different modes (or logics) of being back to patristic theology.[4] The purpose of contrasting the "individual" to "person(hood)" is not, in my view, for the sake of describing our existence within the boundaries of history—since we all exist as "individuals" with the potential to (fully) become "persons"—but rather to point to two different existential logics (based on two different existential foundations) with very different (eschatological) outcomes. In history, we all exist as both individuals (given the reality of the "biological hypostasis") and as persons (given the potential to transform our existence into a God-like existence) simultaneously.

As has been discussed, the personal mode of existence manifests itself through the ecstatic overcoming of one's pregiven being in the communion of love. Individualized existence, on the other hand, is a "substance on its own."[5] Following the individualized existential logic, a concrete being aspires to affirm and solidify its own (particular) identity based on the properties that differentiate that being, as an "objective" datum, from other individuals. One's identity as an individual, in other words, is constituted in opposition to "others," who may pose a threat to who one is as an individual ego.

An individual aspires to find the foundation of its existence in itself, in its own *nature*. Individual, taken in its etymological sense, means the same as "atom," something that cannot be divided anymore, something that is the smallest constituent (whose identity cannot be preserved by further divisions) of the larger whole—in this case, society.

The individualized mode of existence stands for separation as a means of establishing one's own identity. Although this does not necessarily imply *loneliness* (since one is an individual precisely within and vis-à-vis a society), it implies the existence of an "own" identity, and what belongs to "oneself," in opposition to other individuals or society as a whole. An individual first "is," both as a biological and social datum, and, as such, it enters social interactions, becoming a social subject interacting with other individuals in order to do something that benefits individual existences (or particular social groups).

In this logic, individuals need to first have their separate identities, properties, and, very often conflicting, interests (at the beginning only as biological entities), and then these individuals create the larger whole through their actions, which are based on a combination of their individual needs and interests (being, of course, influenced in return by these interactions with other individuals and society as a whole). Society is then the natural space in which individuals exist, but it also includes more specific, delineated social and political collectives (family, political party, interest groups, etc.). In contrast to this, the place where persons are born and where they manifest their identity is the communion of love.

Here we come across the contrast that will be very relevant for the next chapters—the contrast between the "communities of this world" (societies, states, social institutions, interest groups, etc.), which articulate, affirm, and build on the logic of the individualized mode of existence, and the communion that constitutes and affirms the personal mode of existence (the Church, liturgy, and, ultimately, the Kingdom of God). It is critical to avoid (conceptual) confusion between the two, which has been regularly occurring in various political theologies. Confusing the two, one ceases to differentiate between the eschatological communion of love and the social and political structures, and their opposing existential logics. This confusion has been at the very heart of most of the tradition-centered, conservative, and right-wing political ideologies.[6]

If we approach the story of the Fall with the concept of individualized existence in mind, we can say that the Fall stands precisely for the human aspiration to become an individual, as opposed to becoming a person (i.e., *likeness*). The individualized existence is that aspiration to reach an autonomous existence in which "my" identity is a *substance* on its own, and not an ecstatic overcoming of one's individual identity in a communion of love.

The conclusions reached in the previous chapter can be rephrased now. The affirmation of the individualized mode of existence appears at the root of the issue of human separation from God, alienation among human beings and hostility between human beings and the rest of the created world. It is also the source of death, as this individualized existence aspires to ground its identity and its being on the "solid" grounds of its own (individual/natural) "substance," using the building blocks of its own ontic reality—*nothing*.

This is clearly visible in the case of our biological existence or, in Zizioulas's terminology, our "biological hypostasis,"[7] which is the most visible mark of our individual being in history. This biological hypostasis is constituted, for each one of us, through our conception and birth. This existence is tied to the necessity of our (biological) nature and the "natural instinct," and as such it is not a manifestation of freedom.[8] On the other hand, this existence also suffers from individualism as a mode of being, which is manifested as a separation of the (biological) hypostasis at birth— the separation of the (body of the) child from the (body of the) mother, by which an individual biological hypostasis is constituted:

> The body, which is born as a biological hypostasis, behaves like the fortress of an ego, like a new "mask" which hinders the hypostasis from becoming a person, that is, from affirming itself as love and freedom. The body tends towards the person but leads finally to the individual. The result of this situation is that for a man to take the affirmation of his hypostasis further he has no need of a relationship (an ontological relationship, not simply a psychological one) with his parents. On the contrary, the breaking of this relationship constitutes the *precondition* of his self-affirmation.[9]

Following Zizioulas, in order to affirm one's existence as an individual biological being (body), a child "has no need of a relationship with his parents" (except as an individual being that establishes particular relationships from which it benefits). On the contrary, one needs to affirm one's individuality in order to affirm one's existence in this world. "My" body is primarily there where "I" am as an individual, since each body (and "body" here means both the "hardware" of the muscles, bones, skin, and the "software" of our brain activities, consciousness, feelings, or the "soul") has different properties compared to other bodies. Moreover, in order to survive, this individual existence must embrace antagonistic and even hostile environments and act accordingly. In order to survive, one must kill and eat other beings, one must fight for one's place within the social group, one species must fight with others, etc. The physical—not just the symbolic—survival of an individual often depends on this. Our existence in history is thus immersed in the necessity of the fallen, disintegrating being that is characterized by the necessity of separation and hostilities. This is how an individual existence, as an identity on its own, becomes the ultimate value in itself, something that one needs to protect and fight for, in the face of the almost countless threats presented to us by the historical existence.

What seems obviously true from the point of view of this "naturalistic" ontology—that an individual being "possesses" life and existence on its own, as its property, which needs to be protected and affirmed—turns out to be a lie from the point of view of (Orthodox) Christian anthropology and ontology. A self-preservation instinct is the very sign of the state of being that Orthodox theology treats as pathological. This lack of real (eschatological) foundations of our being (as individuals), the lack of freedom (and yet the desire for life), and the fear of other beings in the world that pose a (real or imaginary) threat to the individual being, should be cured. The sickness— and consequently the cure—is not psychological or physiological, and even less so ethical or legal in nature, so none of these medications would help. The cure requires a change in our mode of existence.

The same individualized, fallen logic of existence is manifested in the entire world "out there" that we often call "reality." It is manifested in the time and space categories that to a significant extent determine our existence in this world: The three-dimensional space of "reality" is not there to affirm our presence, or to connect us with others. It rather manifests itself as a means of separation. We are "situated" inside the space, which allows us to approach other beings in the world (which also inevitably means moving away from others). However, this very movement of coming closer to someone (even as close as in the acts of kissing or making love) is an in- dication of separation—no matter how close we come, there's a separation between beings, not a full communion; sooner or later, these individual bodies will distance themselves from one another. Every proximity becomes distance in time; it points to the individual nature of our presence in the world. Even the very fabric of space and time seems to exhibit certain characteristics that can be understood as the torment of being at the very basic level of our grasp of the world that seems to be around us—for example, virtual particles of the quantum fluctuations are neither fully existent nor simply nonexistent; they oscillate between being and nonbeing, providing a nice metaphor for the character of individualized existence in general, which is more a potentiality rather than a fully existent reality.

Time, itself, appears as one of the most paradigmatic manifestations of the individualized mode of existence of the natural world. Time as we know it is the measure of the disintegrating existence spread over the fabric of nonbeing. It is a manifestation of what Nikolai Berdyaev calls "false" or "evil" time, intimately related to the "bad endlessness."[10] It is not the duration (of time) that allows for the growth and preservation of being as an integral existence. On the contrary, a seemingly endless duration is what tears a being apart, what makes the being appear precisely as nonbeing, something as nothing, and nothing as something.[11] Our experience of time merely reveals the ontic fact that beings in their individualized mode of existence are never and nowhere really and fully present. They appear in between the past (which is *not*) and the future (which is *not*), in the immeasurable and, actually, unreal sequence of nonduration called the "present." Since this present is never really "now" or "here," we aspire to transcend every "here" and "now" in order to be (fully) present—that is, to acquire a real existence. However, within the individual mode of being, the fullness of our own existence constantly escapes us.

Liberating the Individual Self (from Itself)

Nevertheless, all of these tragic properties of the historical existence still allow for the manifestation of a different existential logic. Although not without difficulty, space can still be used for connecting the individual existences. Time is a manifestation of the disintegrating character of our existence and, yet, it still allows us to manifest our freedom within the boundaries of this world, although only to a limited degree. In addition to the mutual hostilities between individual beings and entire species, we also find mutual support, cooperation, care, and (nonutilitarian) self-sacrifice, not only among humans but also in the animal world as well.

Even our own, individualized, biological body, which separates us from other human beings and the rest of creatures (and, in separating, secures the survival of the individual), can be used for demonstrating the different existential logic. We are not only capable of doing "illogical" and "unnatural" things that go against the logic of individualized beings, but we also *desire* a different logic of being—the personal mode of existence. This is what is evidenced in love, in the acts of self-sacrifice and selfless help and in the expression of compassion when emptied of any other interests and concerns, other than for the concrete living being we feel love and compassion for, whose tragedy we selflessly embrace and co-share:

> If you love those who love you, what credit is that to you? Even sinners love those who love them. And if you do good to those who are good to you, what credit is that to you? Even sinners do that. And if you lend to those from whom you expect repayment, what credit is that to you? Even sinners lend to sinners, expecting to be repaid in full. But love your enemies, do good to them, and lend to them without expecting to get anything back. Then your reward will be great, and you will be children of the Most High, because he is kind to the ungrateful and wicked. (Luke 6:32–35)

This is also the love of which Paul speaks in 1 Corinthians:

> Love is patient, love is kind. It does not envy, it does not boast, it is not proud. It does not dishonor others, it is not self-seeking, it is not easily angered, it keeps no record of wrongs. Love does not delight in evil but rejoices with the truth. It always protects, always trusts, always hopes, always perseveres. (1 Corinthians 13:4–7)

This love is the "substance" of the *real*, personal, and eschatological existence. By embracing, kissing, giving one's life for another human being, the "elements" of the individualized existence are being used for the affirmation of a different existential logic. The *non-self-affirming* body is thus transformed from being a tragic "mask"[12] to being the instrument of salvation.

The Biblical prophetic descriptions of the (future) paradise point to this logic, which goes beyond the state of individuality. The future mode of existence will be the one in which the logic of the individualized being will be overcome:

> The wolf will live with the lamb, the leopard will lie down with the goat, the calf and the lion and the yearling together; and a little child will lead them.
>
> The cow will feed with the bear, their young will lie down together, and the lion will eat straw like the ox.

The infant will play near the cobra's den, and the young child will put its hand into the viper's nest. (Isaiah 11:6–8)

Up to a point, this can already be seen in particular cases even within the boundaries of this world—for example, when both wild and domestic animals "make friends" and take care of each other even in extreme situations (when that poses a threat to their life), despite belonging to different (and mutually hostile) species. Acts of this type, already found in history, become a prophecy of a different mode of existence. *All beings await salvation*,[13] and their salvation is (in) this future mode of existence, which is based on love.

The exploration of the consequences of the Fall and the different logics of being—one solidifying the necessity that we, as created beings, find ourselves in, and the other, personal, leading to a free mode of existence, based on love—leads to a paradox that can shed additional light on the historical process and the way in which existence, as freedom, becomes operational.

The initial choice that the human being made—to desire existence apart from God—was not only a sign of breaking the communion with God; it was also a manifestation of freedom and, as such, a manifestation of *God-likeness*. In other words, human beings aspired to become "like God" (following the serpent's suggestion), and this aspiration was in itself the affirmation of the dignity of the human being, and the final metaphysical destination of human existence as a Godlike being. This is why, as we have seen, we find already in the patristic literature the appreciation of this intention of human beings (to become "like God") as something not only positive, but something that was envisioned by God from the beginning. What was problematic, and ultimately tragic, was the means that were used to this end—that acquiring Godlikeness was not desired through communion with God, but through separation from Him.

However, human beings did not just choose an ontological impossibility (existence without God, which is equivalent to life without life). This choice was, at the same time, a way to embrace their Godlike humanity, a way to manifest themselves not merely as creatures, but also as "gods." With this choice something new came to be—the impossible existence of an impossible choice, which still manifests freedom as the real "substance" of the (only ontically real) existence.

From this perspective one can read the story of Genesis and the Garden of Eden differently from most of the standard exegeses. The Garden of Eden appears not so much as the paradise lost, but as the image of the (future) Kingdom of God. It becomes the "place" (beyond the limitations of our physical space), and the "time" (outside of the historical, disintegrating time) in which the *creation* of the Godlike beings takes place. In this real (eschatological) reality, the foundations of existence become freedom and love. This liberates the human being from its created and, therefore, compelled existence. This "second creation" (symbolically represented in the Christian tradition with the concept of the "eighth day"), unlike the original creation, does not happen without human engagement. On the contrary, it happens only with a free and creative participation of the human being. The expulsion from the paradise signifies thus the beginning of the historical (potential) existence, through which we actualize our freedom (not to be with God), which results in the individualized existence.

Since our historical existence, viewed from the eschatological perspective, is not yet *real* (complete), it allows for ontically significant freedom to manifest itself. Unlike our biological hypostasis, the Kingdom (and our real "us" in that eschatological Kingdom) is not (yet) "here" and "now," which means that it is not compelled. Moreover, by the actualization of our freedom within the boundaries of this world—by moving away from the individualized to the personal logic of being—we participate in our creation in the Kingdom to come. Thus, literally, our future eschatological (real) hypostasis becomes the product of freedom and love, not of any pregiven set of principles, decisions, or patterns. That is how and why this existence becomes Godlike; our very "being" gets to be made of the "same" *uncreated substance*, that is the personal existence founded on the foundationless, substanceless, and purposeless abyss of freedom and love. A person thus exists without end and without beginning.

That is why the call "let us create" the human being (Gen 1:26) involves human beings, not only God. "Let us create" is the (re)creation that happens beyond the historical time, in the eschaton.[14] The story of Genesis appears thus as the story of both the initiation of creation (out of the historical time) and as the image of its (eschatological) fulfillment. Those who choose communion with God *cocreate* themselves as free beings. They live because they love and are being loved, freely embracing their existence, without any "solid" (pregiven) grounds or reasons.

Eschatology and Liturgy

At this point we can return to the question of how the personal mode of existence can be manifested in history.

As has already been established, this mode of existence follows eschatological logic and as such it can be fully expressed only in the eschaton. However, this eschatological logic is also being manifested already "here" and "now." The beginning of the end of the historical time (or, in other words, the beginning of the fulfilment of the personal mode of existence) started with the Incarnation of God the Logos, who integrated the Divine and the human, uniting two natures in one person. With the Incarnation of Christ, the tension between the Divine and human, between the uncreated and the created was overcome in one concrete person. With the Church, the tension between the necessity of our historical existence and the freedom of the future (eschatological) existence has been offered a solution. Church, as the communion of the faithful, appears as the bridge between history and the eschaton, as the "place" and "time" where the transformation of the individual into a personal mode of existence takes place, where the logic of the new existence is manifested.

In liturgy, already in our individual bodies and already inhabiting concrete places and times in this world, we encounter the Kingdom. In liturgy, the Kingdom comes to us (from the eschaton) and we *iconize* (make present) the eschaton in history.

This is what we find in Zizioulas, where the solution to the individualized existence is both liturgical and eschatological—since the two cannot really be separated.[1] The icon of the eschaton (the Kingdom of God) is the

Church, which here primarily refers to the liturgical gathering, the Eucharistic celebration of the community of the faithful. In this sense, the Church should be differentiated from the institution (church) and its administrative/bureaucratic system.

As such, entering the Church through baptism signifies a "new birth" (birth in the communion of the free and loving ones):

> Jesus replied, "Very truly I tell you, no one can see the kingdom of God unless they are born again." . . . "Very truly I tell you, no one can enter the kingdom of God unless they are born of water and the Spirit. Flesh gives birth to flesh, but the Spirit gives birth to spirit. You should not be surprised at my saying, 'You must be born again.' The wind blows wherever it pleases. You hear its sound, but you cannot tell where it comes from or where it is going. So it is with everyone born of the Spirit." (John 3:3–8)

This "birth from the Spirit," from "above," is linked with the event of the Incarnation: "No one has ever gone into heaven except the one who came from heaven—the Son of Man" (John 3:13).

Entering the Church, through baptism, means changing our compelled, individual existence into the eschatological (free) one. In the Church, our "sisters," "brothers," "fathers," and "mothers" are those who enter the personal relationship with us. Relationships in the Church are supposed to be those established on freedom, not those that are the result of any necessity, be it biological, family, social, political, etc. Entering the Church signifies new relationships (based on love and freedom), and thus new life.

In the liturgy, we are also liberated from the compelling presence of the pregiven physical reality. In the Eucharist, *we offer the world* by bringing to the liturgical celebration some of its ingredients, transformed by our activities (such as bread, wine, and oil). This way, even what we call "physical reality" is brought into a personal presence. Our lives are thus transformed by the Eucharist; they are oriented toward the eschaton. Our *origin* is found in the end (of time and world as we know them). At the end of our lives, we offer then even our body as a Eucharistic offering—the Christian funeral is also supposed to be a liturgical act. We freely offer ourselves to God, we freely *jump* into the abyss of (historical) nonexistence, to be born out of freedom.[2]

The Church thus manifests itself as an eschatological community that is present in history. Its origins are in the Kingdom of God, but it also exists already "here" and "now," as an icon. It announces the new creation: "Therefore, if anyone is in Christ, he is a new creation. The old has passed away; behold, the new has come" (2 Corinthians 5:17). Partaking in the new creation allows us to experience the joy of existence in a very profound way. It is the joy of a creative activity, the joy that is symbolized by the joy of drinking good wine.[3] The liturgy, the joy of free existence, creative work, and loving relationships—these allow for the Glory of God and His Kingdom to shine in this world.

Viewed from this perspective, the Church should not be understood as an elitist society, especially not the club of morally or ethically superior ones. The Church is a "club" of the sick seeking salvation. By "seeking salvation" and by the attempts to change their existence, through the practices of love, they become saints. For Orthodoxy, saints are those very sinners who refuse sin as the defining aspect of their being, who refuse to submit to their (individualized) being. Saints are those who do not accept being the slaves of this world or their own being (as necessity). They are the free and the living ones who have already—and not yet—entered the Kingdom of God. Saints are those who received the Spirit. Saints are not ethically perfect. Saints are, in some sense, necessarily *unethical*—they are those "outlaws" who refuse to submit to the oppressiveness of this world and to be reduced to the limited and derogatory (e.g., petite bourgeois) expectations of what it means to be human. Authentic Christianity launches a "war" against ethical systems, but not in an aggressive or oppressive way through imposing new systems, values, and standards; it does so by freeing the human being from all world ethics, by offering an authentic existence, based on love.

Through the Eucharist, the many come to be One, in communion with one another. The Eucharist thus becomes the icon of the existence of God. The transformation of the individualized existence into a personal, God-like existence is something that takes place in history. It is the process of theosis, which is not a single event, a sudden transformation of iron into gold, but a never-ending process of freeing oneself from necessity as the basis of one's existence, through learning how to love and through manifesting one's personhood through a creative act.

The transformative, *deificatory experience* of the Eucharistic gathering is the focal point and the anchor of the lives of those whose "homeland" has become the Kingdom of God. From this "country," which is outside of history, those who are in search of personal existence go and live in the world, and aspire (always imperfectly) to manifest this new logic of existence—based on freedom and love—and, through them, to transform the world around them.

This is how the tension between the necessity of our individual (historical and biological) existence and our existence as persons (the eschatological existence based on freedom and love) is resolved in the liturgy. The liturgy does not deny historical, biological, and physical existence, but instead aspires to "transfigure" it, putting it into an eschatological perspective in order for that existence to enter the communion with God. It does not negate the paradox, but embraces it and transforms it into a creative, vigilant movement toward the coming Kingdom.

"This World" and the Individualized Mode of Existence

T his brief dive into the realm of Orthodox ontology, eschatology, anthropology, and ecclesiology—which are, in fact, not separate theological "disciplines," but united, inseparable parts of both theological reflection and church life—leads us to the conclusion that there is indeed a tension that Christianity needs to acknowledge. It is not the tension between "material" and "spiritual," but the tension between necessity and freedom.

It has already been said that Christianity does not affirm the spirit-matter or soul-body dualism that characterizes some other religious and philosophical systems. However, when it comes to our existence in history, Christianity does affirm another type of *dualism*—the one between freedom and necessity.[1] This is how the contrast between the Kingdom of God and "this world" (or, just "world"—κόσμος), found in the New Testament, can be understood.

The Gospel of John is much richer in contrasting the Kingdom of God and "this world" than the synoptic Gospels. In John, the Son of God and His Kingdom are contrasted to the "prince of this world" and his dominion:

> Now is the time for judgment on this world; now the prince of this world will be driven out. (John 12:31)

> I will not say much more to you, for the prince of this world is coming. (John 14:30)

> Because the prince of this world now stands condemned. (John 16:11)

In another place, the "world" and the logic of the "world" is contrasted to Christ's Kingdom and the life that his disciples are called to live:

If the world hates you, keep in mind that it hated me first. If you belonged to the world, it would love you as its own. As it is, you do not belong to the world, but I have chosen you out of the world. That is why the world hates you. (John 15:18–19)

Jesus said, "My kingdom is not of this world. If it were, my servants would fight to prevent my arrest by the Jewish leaders. But now my kingdom is from another place." (John 18:36)

A similar logic, when it comes to the contrasting "(this) world" and the Kingdom of God, is also found in some of the Epistles. In the Epistle to Romans (Romans 12:2), we are warned not to "conform to the pattern of this world," and a similar warning is repeated in 2 Corinthians:

I beg you that when I come I may not have to be as bold as I expect to be toward some people who think that we live by the standards of this world. For though we live in the world, we do not wage war as the world does. The weapons we fight with are not the weapons of the world. (2 Corinthians 10:2–4)[2]

1 John is particularly sharp in contrasting "this world" and Christ:

Do not love the world or anything in the world. If anyone loves the world, love for the Father is not in them. For everything in the world—the lust of the flesh, the lust of the eyes, and the pride of life—comes not from the Father but from the world. The world and its desires pass away, but whoever does the will of God lives forever. (1 John 2:15–17)

We know that we are children of God, and that the whole world is under the control of the evil one. (1 John 5:19)

Is it not clear, some might ask, that "the world" here implies the material world (as opposed to the "spiritual" one)? However, many places in the Gospels and in the epistles (including those quoted above) indicate that the "world" should be understood in a different way.

The Gospel of Matthew is abundant in referring to "the world," but this word is often used in a neutral sense, referring to something more like the "reality in which we live":

You are the light of the world. (Matthew 5:14)

The field is the world, and the good seed stands for the people of the kingdom. (Matthew 13:38; see Matthew 13:35)

What good will it be for someone to gain the whole world, yet forfeit their soul? (Matthew 16:26)

In Mark, the "world" is primarily the space for the mission of Christ's disciples:

Truly I tell you, wherever the gospel is preached throughout the world, what she has done will also be told, in memory of her. (Mark 14:9)

He said to them, "Go into all the world and preach the gospel to all creation." (Mark 16:15)

Even in John, the "world" is also used in a more neutral way (parallel to the negative connotations in those places already quoted):

The true light that gives light to everyone was coming into the world. He was in the world, and though the world was made through him, the world did not recognize him. (John 1:9–10)

The next day John saw Jesus coming toward him and said, "Look, the Lamb of God, who takes away the sin of the world!" (John 1:29)

The "world" is affirmed to a great extent in John 3, when God's love of the world is evidenced:

For God so loved the world that he gave his one and only Son, that whoever believes in him shall not perish but have eternal life. For God did not send his Son into the world to condemn the world, but to save the world through him. Whoever believes in him is not condemned, but whoever does not believe stands condemned already because they have not believed in the name of God's one and only Son. This is the verdict: Light has come into the world, but people loved darkness instead of light because their deeds were evil. (John 3:16–19)

Given the plentitude of "materialistic" elements in the Christian faith, which are also affirmed in the Gospels and which include the Incarnation of God, His Resurrection (and the act of eating after the Resurrection[3]), the concepts of "this world" or "the world" (used negatively) do not seem to introduce a spirit-matter, or soul-body dualism in a Manichean or Neo-platonic sense—not even the sphere of "morality" as opposed to "immoral" conduct. Material/physical elements, including our body, are clearly given a positive affirmation in the Christian context. Something else seems to be contrasted here.

The distinction must be made between the two different meanings of the "world" (or "this world"). We can speak of the "world" as God's creation, including the physical/material realm and history. God comes to this "world" and, through the Incarnation, becomes part of it and saves it.[4] On the other hand, the "world" is also a metaphor for the dominion of darkness, evil, of that which rejects God and life with God. "This world in its present form is passing away" (Corinthians 7:31), and "everyone born of God overcomes the world" (1 John 5:4). Here, the "world" is contrasted to the Kingdom of God, history to the eschaton.

It seems that the context of 1 John 2:15–17 further clarifies the difference. The negative connotation of the "world" (or "this world") seems to refer to those aspects of the world (as a whole, as God's creation) that do not follow the path of God, the life that Christ offers. In other words, the negative meaning of "this world" is connected to a particular existential logic, with a way in which we relate to the world, (other) beings in the world, and God and His Kingdom. Paul seems to elaborate on this when he says that all of those who follow "the lust of the flesh, the lust of the eyes, and the pride of life," "will not inherit the kingdom of God" (1 Corinthians 6:9).

In other words, "this world" here implies slavery—the world of necessity, in which one is a slave to passions and pride—and does not do the "will of God." "This world" (understood negatively) thus implies a specific relationship to the world, in which one submits oneself to the logic of the (fallen) world, accepts slavery within the state of necessity in which the world finds itself, and rejects the logic that characterizes a different mode of existence, the one that is affirmed in and by the Kingdom of God. Said differently, "(this) world" can be understood as the individualized mode of existence.

Based on this distinction, I will use the concept of "this world" (as opposed to simply the "world") to point to those aspects of the world that "will not inherit the Kingdom of God," those aspects of the world, and our approach to the world, that demonstrate the logic of necessity as opposed to the logic of freedom.

Thus the tension that Christianity, in my interpretation, affirms is the tension between the individualized mode of existence (based on necessity), and the existence characterized as personhood (based on freedom). The first follows the logic of "this world"; the second is what aspires to change the foundations of the historical (i.e., biological) existence, and transform it into an existence that is based on its eschatological prototype—on freedom and love. The first belongs to the "objectified" world; the second aspires to create unique identities and unique relationships.

To exist in the mode of "this world," it is necessary to follow the logic of the objectified, alienated existence that is not a product of our freedom. It is characteristic of the natural world that particular beings do not relate to other beings and the entire world through freedom and love, but through mutual hostilities. Individual existence is intrinsically linked with the quest for self-preservation and power aspirations. Following the logic of "this world," creatures have a *natural* drive to fight for self-affirmation, to dominate over other beings and even to kill other creatures in order to sustain their own existence. The necessity of existence in the mode of "this world" is not only manifested through self-preservation instincts, domination, clashes, and wars, but also through the necessity of biological reproduction. The logic of "this world" compels individual beings, as well as entire species, to procreate and fight against the (hostile) surroundings in order to sustain and affirm their (individualized) "selves."

How then does this tension between "this world" (as the sphere of necessity) and the Kingdom of God (as the existence based on freedom and love) translate into a theological thinking upon the socio-political sphere? The remaining chapters are dedicated mostly to the exploration of this question.

The Last Temptation of Christ. (Based on the Temptation of Christ scene from St. Mark's Cathedral in Venice.)

THE POLITICS OF NOTHINGNESS

W e saw in the previous chapter that the concept of "this world" can be understood as the sphere of necessity, as those aspects of the (created) world that affirm the logic of individualized existence. Therefore, it is not particular beings that constitute "this world"; "this world," rather, stands for a particular logic of being, which determines one's approach to the world and one's own identity. In that sense, everything that conforms to the logic of necessity and the individualized mode of existence signifies the rejection of freedom and love as the mode of eschatological existence. Consequently, those aspects "will not inherit the Kingdom of God."

The main claim in this chapter is that the political sphere, with its oppressive power structures (institutionalized as well as informal), belongs to "this world," par excellence. The logic of the political sphere with its power dynamics is a paradigmatic expression of the individualized mode of existence.

The perception of the political sphere—understood as the sphere of domination, of exercise of power, and/or of oppression—can be traced back to the New Testament. The political sphere is judged from the point of view of the Incarnation of God, the Logos, and the possibility of a new (eschatological) existence in the Kingdom of God. The tension between the Kingdom of God and "this world" finds its parallel in numerous New Testament stories that narrate about the tension between God (and His dominion) and Caesar (and his kingdom). I use the word "Caesar" here in Berdyaev's sense, as a metaphor for the entire sphere of the political, regardless of the concrete form of government.

The most commonly cited place in the Gospels to illustrate the Christian understanding of politics is the story in which Christ is asked about paying the imperial tax:

> Then the Pharisees went out and laid plans to trap him in his words. They sent their disciples to him along with the Herodians. "Teacher," they said, "we know that you are a man of integrity and that you teach the way of God in accordance with the truth. You aren't swayed by others, because you pay no attention to who they are. Tell us then, what is your opinion? Is it right to pay the imperial tax to Caesar or not?"
>
> But Jesus, knowing their evil intent, said, "You hypocrites, why are you trying to trap me? Show me the coin used for paying the tax." They brought him a denarius, and he asked them, "Whose image is this? And whose inscription?"
>
> "Caesar's," they replied.
>
> Then he said to them, "So give back to Caesar what is Caesar's, and to God what is God's."
>
> When they heard this, they were amazed. So they left him and went away. (Matthew 22:15–22; see Mark 12:13–17)

This episode can be interpreted as making a clear distinction between the political sphere, which belongs to "Caesar," and the realm of God. Jacques Ellul's analysis of "give (back) to Caesar what is Caesar's" remains classical within the Christian anarchist literature. Ellul asks, "But what really belongs to Caesar?"—that is, to the political authority in general—and continues:

> The excellent example used by Jesus makes this plain: Whatever bears his mark! Here is the basis and limit of his power. But where is this mark? On coins, on public monuments, and on certain altars. That is all. Render to Caesar. You can pay the tax. . . . On the other hand, whatever does not bear Caesar's mark does not belong to him. It all belongs to God. This is where the real conscientious objection arises. Caesar has no right whatever to the rest. First we have life. Caesar has no right of life and death. Caesar has no right to plunge people into war. Caesar has no right to devastate and ruin a country. Caesar's domain is very limited.[1]

If by political power ("what belongs to Caesar") we understand the realm of necessity that is attached to the mode of existence of "this world," then Ellul's argument can be read in the following way: Nothing important, nothing essential (from a Christian perspective) belongs to Caesar.

Stephen Moore offers even more radical readings of this passage within the broader context of ancient Israeli political theology:

> "Give to Caesar the things that are Caesar's, and to God the things that are God's" . . . is itself no less enveloped in ambiguity, as its history of reception amply attests. It can be, and has been, read to mean that since, in accordance with Israelite covenantal theology, everything belongs to God, nothing is due to Caesar.[2]

"Giving (back) to Caesar what is Caesar's" can thus be interpreted as a way to delegitimize the Caesar—and *not* to affirm Caesar by affirming the status quo, as is sometimes claimed—at least in all things that *really* matter (from the perspective of the Kingdom of God).

Moore reads the Gospel of Mark in this broader "anti-Imperial," but also anarchist, key. The coming Kingdom of the Messiah is something that delegitimizes the earthly power and the "human basileia," whether in the strictly political or in the religious-institutional context:

> Of course, the Jerusalem temple's destruction is itself but the eschatological prelude to Jesus' parousia, as the ensuing apocalyptic discourse . . . makes plain. And what the parousia will signify, among other things, is the unceremonious cessation of the Roman Empire, as of every other human *basileia*. Jesus will bump Caesar off the throne.[3]

This reading of Mark is in line with the Book of Revelation and its "antiimperial" and "anarchist" understanding of the political realm.[4]

In a more general sense, the Kingdom of God (and of the Messiah) and the kingdom of Caesar are incompatible precisely because they imply two different logics when it comes to answering questions such as "Who is the king (the ruler, the political authority)?," "Who should be the first?," or "Who should we pay respect to?" The Christianity of Jesus of Nazareth seems to approach the issue of power, domination, and self-protection very differently from the logic of "this world" and the corresponding logic of political authority. Christ makes this clear in front of Pilate: "Jesus said, 'My kingdom is not of this world. If it were, my servants would fight to prevent my arrest by the Jewish leaders. But now my kingdom is from another place'" (John 18:36).

Christ's Kingdom does not pose a threat to the political system and political power in the same way in which other kingdoms (other types of power and authority) do. Christ is not another political leader, a protagonist of another political movement or ideology who or which would fight to rule over people. Instead, he poses a threat to the power and authority at a much more fundamental level—by questioning the very logic upon which the political authority, rule, and domination is built, and by refusing to submit to that logic and give it a metaphysical legitimacy. The Kingdom of God is not of "this world"—it cannot be realized within the boundaries and the logic "this world." It overcomes "this world" by offering a different logic of being.

This is also clear from Christ's instructions given to his disciples as to one of the most basic desires that characterize the fallen, individualized existence—the desire to be "the first," the desire to "rule." These desires constitute the core aspect of political power and power structures as such, but Christ's words indicate a very different perspective:

> Jesus called them together and said, "You know that the rulers of the
> Gentiles lord it over them, and their high officials exercise authority
> over them. Not so with you. Instead, whoever wants to become great
> among you must be your servant, and whoever wants to be first must
> be your slave—just as the Son of Man did not come to be served,
> but to serve, and to give his life as a ransom for many." (Matthew
> 20:25–28)

This is one of the most *anarchic* places in the entire New Testament. Here Christ clearly contrasts the logic of His Kingdom and the "rulers of the Gentiles." His logic is the logic of love and the logic of service (out of love), not the one of "rule" and domination. The Christian God and Christian King (Christ) is the God and King who refuses to establish another earthly kingdom that would, necessarily, be governed by the logic of "this world." Moreover, this God and King refuses to rule. He does not exercise power and domination. Instead, He comes as a servant and a healer, someone who does not give orders but who embraces other human beings in a self-emptying love.

In Christ's instructions as to how to relate to other people, the unconditional, free love is taken as the evidence of Christian faith. "Love your neighbor as yourself" (Mark 12:31) is counted as the second greatest commandment, after the love of God, which constitutes the core of Christian faith. Christ's instructions about how to relate to our enemies is even more interesting, since it points to the specifically Christian logic (or the logic of His Kingdom, as a new mode of existence):

> You have heard that it was said, "Love your neighbor and hate your enemy." But I tell you, love your enemies and pray for those who persecute you, that you may be children of your Father in heaven. He causes his sun to rise on the evil and the good, and sends rain on the righteous and the unrighteous. If you love those who love you, what reward will you get? Are not even the tax collectors doing that? And if you greet only your own people, what are you doing more than others? Do not even pagans do that? Be perfect, therefore, as your heavenly Father is perfect. (Matthew 5:43–48)

What is affirmed here is freedom and love as the only real "substance," the only way in which we can meaningfully relate to each other, from an eschatological point of view. Freedom is affirmed because only if one loves unconditionally (even those who hate us or do us evil) is it a completely free love. This love recognizes in the other human being a person, a unique and unrepeatable reality beyond the slavery within the boundaries of "this world," which that person is subjected to. To love means to see someone as a person. *Seeing* someone as a person means forgiving and forgetting one's wrongdoings, one's imperfections, one's ugliness—it means experiencing the joy in someone else's existence, desiring life for that person. It also means readiness to give up all our comforts, all our *interests*, and even our life for that other person. To love is nothing less than to affirm existence, to give *substance* to the things we hope for. Love is thus an expression of faith, in the way in which Paul described it.[5] Love is faith given "flesh and blood." It is, at the same time, the absolute freedom that does not let any obstacles belonging to "this world" (a non–fully existent world), prevent us from seeing the (ontically) "real" content in another human being—the icon of God.

The perfection mentioned in Matthew 5:48 is precisely the perfection of love—the self-emptying and self-sacrificing love, which recognizes the image of God in another human being, no matter what that other being does. Morality and the existential dimension of Christian love are here clearly distinguished. Christian love is the image of Divine love, because it is unconditional, because it "does not envy, it does not boast, it is not

proud. It does not dishonor others, it is not self-seeking, it is not easily an-
gered, it keeps no record of wrongs" (1 Corinthians 13:4–5).

Morality, duties, doing this or that become thus secondary at best. Testimony of this was given not only in the image of Martha and Mary (Luke
10:38–42), but also in the image of the "good" criminal on the cross (Luke
23:39–43). We do not know anything of the deeds of this man, except that
he was a criminal. And, yet, he was the first to enter the Kingdom of God
("Truly I tell you, today you will be with me in paradise"). This was not
because of his deeds (about which we know only that they were *bad*), not
because he followed the law or because of his morality, but because of the
only *deed* that really matters—a free and creative leap of faith, which makes
us capable of love, capable of recognizing God in human beings.

When you love someone, all ethics, internal and external laws, and the
very idea of "good" and "bad" are exposed as false or meaningless. When
you love someone it does not matter if that person is "good" or "bad"; he/
she can be a criminal of the worst kind, or an innocent child. It does not
matter if he/she is beautiful or ugly, rich or poor. Only when you love someone are you able to *see* the *real* him or her, who they are in their eschatological existence, as free persons, as icons of God. When you love you get
to *know* (someone or something) the way God *knows* them, and this is the
reason why you become able to see their real (eschatologically true) face,
their *true nature*. This knowledge is not the corrupt, imperfect knowledge
of "good" and "evil," which objectifies beings in the world and becomes
blind to their true faces, but the wisdom provided by the Tree of Life.

Knowing by the means of loving makes you realize how those who condemn or hate a person for the evil he/she has done are mistaken. They are
blind to the *real reality* of that person. Here the very "subjective" perspective (of those who love) becomes more "objective" (when viewed eschatologically) than the "objective" facts that those who do not love can see.
When you love someone, you *desire* his/her eternal existence, and an eternal communion with that person. This is the icon of God's love and the
icon of salvation. That is why moralistic or legalistic understandings of
Christianity amount to heresies.

Existential Anxiety as the Quest for Power

Here we come to the roots of the logic of "this world," which is reflected
also in the political logic as its chief manifestation. Reading it from the

perspective of the individualized existence, *existential anxiety* is at the bottom of every desire for domination and the exercise of power. The source of all the coercive manifestations of the individualized existence is fear, existential fear. John Zizioulas captures this brilliantly when he says,

> There is a pathology built into the very roots of our existence, inherited through our birth, and that is the *fear of the other*.
>
> This is a result of the rejection of the Other *par excellence*, our Creator, by the first man, Adam. . . . The essence of sin is fear of the other, which is part of this rejection. Once the affirmation of the "self" is realized through the rejection and not the acceptance of the Other— this is what Adam chose in his freedom to do—it is only natural and inevitable for the other to become an enemy and a threat.[6]

We are (given the properties of the individualized mode of existence discussed above) at some level *aware* that the "substance" of the individualized being is *nothing*. It is the fear of the void that constitutes our natural, individualized existence (as well as "this world" in general) and that compels individual beings to try to protect, affirm, and "expand" their presence as individuals, in the hope that they will "forget" that, as individual beings belonging to "this world," they are *nothing*. The quest for power, self-affirmation, and domination over other beings is at the very core of our individualized existence. Procreation is part of the same desire; it is the quest of an individual being, the being that is existentially (although not necessarily rationally) *aware* of one's *real* substance as an individual(ized) being, to spread and multiply one's biological hypostasis (through one's genetic material) over the course of time. Instead of "giving life," giving birth becomes an act of "giving death" (infecting that new being with the "virus" of individualized, natural existence). Merely affirming an individual existence—both in the case of domination over others and in the case of affirmation of the "biological hypostasis"—without changing the existential logic, does not result in giving this existence a real (eschatological) *substance*. Without the change of the existential logic, an individualized existence is turned into a malign kind of overgrowth. It results in the multiplication of nothingness, an impossible existence that aspires to be(come) something.

This is the tragedy of the individual existence, which aspires to become something by seeking power as a means of self-affirmation. As individual beings, faced with the existential fear of disintegration and nothingness (which is the only "natural substance" of our individualized, biological, and historical existence), we aspire to convince ourselves and others that we exist. This fear is the source of all aspirations to manifest our individual power, to dominate, to be the "first," to harm others, but also, as mentioned above, to procreate (which intimately relates politics and sex). Through all of these attempts, rooted in the most fundamental existential fear, we aspire to affirm our individual being. This appears as logical and, moreover, as the only possible way to act for an individual seeking to affirm his/her (individual) existence within the boundaries of "this world," and following the logic of that world. Egotism is the logical consequence of the applied philosophy of the individualized existence taken to its logical end.

Thus, the very acts of the exercise of power, domination, oppression, expansion, aggression, and violence reveal the tragic impotence, fear, and weakness that characterize the individual existence. The more those in power exercise and expend their power, the more unfree they become. The supreme ruler becomes the biggest slave, who is trapped not only within the oppressiveness of his/her own individualized being (which relies on the logic of ontic slavery), but also within the very power structures of which he/she became part.[7] Those in power, the oppressors, become thus grotesque caricatures of what the human being could (have) be(en)—the *king* of creation (in the image of the Divine King). Beings of "this world" act out of existential fear. The ultimate manifestation of necessity, which is built into the very fabric of individual existence and which drives "this world," is death.

Viewed from this perspective, the words of Christ about love and service turn out to be not a sentimental call to "be nice" or "polite" to each other. On the contrary, in His affirmation of unconditional, self-emptying love, Christ is offering an antidote for the very fundamental illness that troubles our being. We either love—and we liberate through that love ourselves from our (individualized) "self," offering all we have (including our lives) for others—or we die. In Matthew, we read: "For whoever wants to save their life will lose it, but whoever loses their life for me will find it" (Matthew 16:25).

Contrary to the instincts of self-preservation and self-affirmation dominating the individualized existence, Christ calls for the application of an inverse logic: to empty the emptiness of an individual existence, to stop the growth of an (eschatologically insubstantial) individual being, and to grow instead with self-emptying love as one's existential principle. This is the way "trampling down death by death," which entered the Paschal liturgical hymnography, works in practice.

We need to lose ourselves to reach ourselves. Personal existence becomes the new logic that contradicts the logic of political power at the most fundamental level. Addressing this existential issue, thus, leads to the annihilation of the main source of both the quest for power and the logic of "this world."

Good as Evil

We have already seen that ethical behavior, or doing "good," in an abstract way, is not one of the central concerns in Christianity. The central task is the change of the mode of existence, in which love becomes the basis of our being. Doing *good* actively, and not being able to do any harm, comes then as a result (not the cause) of the changed existential logic. Just following ethical norms, without the existential change, becomes not only insufficient but also, potentially, dangerous. Without grounding our being in love, any ethical principle can be turned into an abstract dogma, which is then applied at the expense of concrete, living human beings, who are often sacrificed or tortured in order for some ethical or legal principles to be sustained and (re)affirmed. Christians should always remember that their God suffered and was killed as a criminal, legally, within the established order and prevalent morality of that time. This is what Christians should always bear in mind when they condemn criminals—they may easily condemn (again) their God. Morality and legality are, frequently, those "horizons of meaning" that typically produce more evil than good by dehumanizing concrete human beings and/or imposing suffering and death in the name of noble causes. Historically speaking, legality has often been nothing more than institutionalized oppression and injustice. Moralism and legalism (even when they pretend to be "Christian") appear thus as one of the worst enemies of authentic Christianity.[8]

This result can be seen in the ethical or political program of the Grand Inquisitor, which remains a paradigmatic image of a very profound rejection of God and His Kingdom in the name of "good," and in the name of "responsible" policies and ethics, to borrow from today's political jargon. The program of the Grand Inquisitor can be characterized as an attempt to deal with the socio-political issues and the imperfections of this world based on the principles that are, formally speaking, *good*, *ethical*, and *just*, and can even be understood as, formally, "Christian." The logic of that program, however, does not depart from the logic and aspirations of "this world." On the contrary, it operates within "this world," trying to perfect it.[9] The Grand Inquisitor aspires to create a "perfect world," to make people *happy*, to feed them, to watch over them and to take care of them, since they are innocent, "little children." The price for this "care," for the creation of a "perfect world," is human freedom:[10]

> Know, then, that now, precisely now, these people are more certain
> than ever before that they are completely free, and at the same time
> they themselves have brought us their freedom and obediently laid it
> at our feet.[11]

The sacrifice of freedom is the price for the happiness within "this world":

> For only now . . . has it become possible to think for the first time
> about human happiness. Man was made a rebel; can rebels be
> happy? . . . [Y]ou rejected the only way of arranging for human hap-
> piness, but fortunately, on your departure, you handed the work
> over to us.[12]

The Grand Inquisitor wants to make the Kingdom of God on earth, to create a perfect society within the boundaries of this world. However, human freedom is an obstacle in such a plan; it has to be sacrificed in order to achieve *happiness* within a "perfect" society. In such a world, there is no need for Christ. In fact, his presence is disruptive: "Why, then, have You come to hinder us?" asks the Inquisitor.

The challenge that the Grand Inquisitor presents to Christ is the same one Christ was presented with in the desert and is the same challenge that every human being is presented with: Give up your freedom and faith and you will obtain *bread* (that is, you will satisfy your basic biological needs), *miracle* (i.e., spectacles, attraction, phantasms, entertainment), and *the rule over the world* (i.e., political/financial power and security).[13] Security, safety, happiness, and conformity, as the *blessings* of "this world," are contrasted here to freedom and a new mode of existence. That is the conflict between "this world" and the Kingdom of God. Within the boundaries of "this world," Christians remain *rebels*, which means they reject the happiness that this world promises, they refuse all the "perfections" that this world can provide. In other words, they refuse to buy into any ideological narrative that "this world" has to offer.

The logic of "this world" does not only manifest itself in the will for power and domination; submission to those who exercise power and domination is the other side of the same coin, another manifestation of the logic of "this world." This is why domination and slavery, the exercise of power and submission, remain the constants within the boundaries of "this world." Both are signs of the individualized mode of existence, of the slavery rooted in nonbeing. The Grand Inquisitor addresses this point as well:

> In the end they will lay their freedom at our feet and say to us: "Better that you enslave us, but feed us." . . . They will marvel at us, and look upon us as gods, because we, standing at their head, have agreed to suffer freedom and to rule over them—so terrible will it become for them in the end to be free! . . .
>
> With us everyone will be happy, and they will no longer rebel or destroy each other, as in your freedom, everywhere. Oh, we shall convince them that they will only become free when they resign their freedom to us, and submit to us. Will we be right, do you think, or will we be lying? They themselves will be convinced that we are right, for they will remember to what horrors of slavery and confusion your freedom led them.[14]

An important lesson from the Grand Inquisitor is that those common, "good," even God-fearing people are more often than not those who contribute to the oppression, who can be blamed for the (unnecessary) horrors in which the world finds itself. Through their consent to be manipulated, through their passivity, their vanity that makes them an easy target of the manipulation (marketing) strategies, they contribute to the violence, oppression, and disasters produced by those who are "in charge."

It may seem, following the logic of the main argument, that we are faced here with a dualism—in other words, with an irreconcilable difference between "this world" and its powers and the Kingdom of God, which can only be resolved through an essentially monistic creation of the "new heaven and new earth."[15] However, this would leave us with little or nothing that could help us deal with more practical social and political issues.

As we have seen in previous chapters, the dominant impulse in Christian theology has been one of trying to justify the aspirations of those in power and conform to the dominant political-ideological narratives, giving political institutions a kind of metaphysical meaning. This design made many people look at political institutions as the "image" of the eschato-logical Kingdom.

We have seen how every time that state structures have been acknowl-edged as "icons" of the Kingdom of God, they have also turned out to be *false icons*—i.e., idols. Nations, states, corporations, clans, families, even institutional churches function as idols every time they claim (or are per-ceived as having) a metaphysical character. We have seen that the power structures of "this world" are not in an iconic relationship with the King-dom of God because they manifest the individualized logic of existence, which requires the affirmation of self-interest, and the quest for power. We have also seen that the only *true icon* of the Kingdom of God is the Church, which means the Eucharistic gathering of the faithful. Only there does the future (eschatological) mode of existence become present already in the "here" and "now"; only there are the many gathered around Christ, in the communion of love. That means that only the Church, which manifests itself as a communion of love, is capable of iconizing the King-dom in history. All other "kingdoms" (i.e., institutions) of "this world" that aspire to be icons of the Kingdom of God, or to establish the Kingdom of God within the boundaries of "this world," are nothing but idols—false images of false gods. They cannot be accepted and legitimized as icons of the Kingdom of God if one aspires to remain loyal to Christ and His Kingdom.

Any attempt to offer a justification of power structures based on Christian faith contradicts what can be called the *Christian eschatological theocracy.* A theocracy—yes, but an eschatological one, in which Christ is the "king" (that is, a *servant* and a *friend*[16]). This means that Christian loyalty to the "eschatological theocracy" of Christ results in an anarchist position when it comes to any system of power and rule in history—because these sys-tems of power tend to replace this future Kingdom of God with the vari-ous types of secular "kingdoms of God" on earth and because they affirm some of the features of the individualized logic of existence, which is in opposition to the eschatological mode of existence.

On the other hand, since the sphere of the political, as a sphere of power struggle and, thus, as a manifestation of the necessity of "this world," "will not inherit the Kingdom of God," the accusation of what is sometimes called "political Nestorianism" is also avoided.[17] Yes, there are *things* in the world that do not have their place (their "prototype") in the Kingdom of God or that do not have their hypostasis rooted in the eschatological "stuff" making up all eschatological beings—freedom and love. All those relation-ships, actions, and logics that are rooted in necessity and individualized existence are idolatrous; they are uprooting themselves from the real existence.

A similar problem occurs in many Christian anarchist theories that as-pire to offer certain models for building "Christian societies" (on a large scale) within the boundaries of this world that would be "just." The prob-lem here is not that such an approach often ignores the problem of plural-ism, that the global society, as well as many local ones, is composed of many different religious groups, which makes it very difficult to imagine how a "Christian society" (which was not a reality even in the Middle Ages when many societies exhibited a much higher degree of social cohesion—especially in terms of confessional belonging—than is the case nowadays) could be formed without requiring every member of the polity to be (a cer-tain type of) a practicing Christian.

There is also another issue with such conceptualizations and actualiza-tions of large-scale "Christian societies." Let us try to imagine a society in which most or virtually all of its members aspired to practice, freely, the Christian way of relating to other human beings (even only at the level of visible practices), by giving up wealth, treating everyone with love and com-passion, offering unreserved help and self-sacrifice for others. That would undeniably lead to a more humane type of social organization and to some kind of classless, anarchist society. If this, by some unrestrained stretch of imagination, is established on a more general level (e.g., a province or a region), it might be a solution to the majority of issues related to "power over" (both in formal and informal power structures).[18] However, even then such a community would still be lacking the most important thing from the Christian perspective—the fullness of "new creation," of new existence in full communion with God. Moreover, such a society would probably be so highly inefficient and incapable of dealing with so many practical is-sues (apart from practicing Christian love and patience) that it would likely collapse in the end, leading to the formation of new (formal and informal) power structures.

The remaining chapters will deal with the question of the possibility, applicability, and limitations of an "Orthodox Christian anarchism" in the social, political, and ecclesial environments. This issue is a difficult one because, although the logic of "this world" is in sharp contrast to Christian existential logic, the question of how to deal with the many manifestations of the individualized mode of existence in history remains. Christians live in the world, so they are, just like everyone else, part of the historical process, with all of its proximities and distances from the eschaton. Christians still need to interact with a variety of manifestations of the individualized mode of existence such as hatred, physical oppression, hunger, illness, and death. Far from offering conclusive answers, let alone prescriptions, the following chapters will try to approach the issue of "Orthodox Christian anarchism" with an awareness of the manifold challenges presented to us by contemporary (global) society.

THEOLOGY AS A CRITICAL DISCOURSE?

T he previous chapters showed how and why the sphere of the political, with its power dynamics, is in collision with the Christian faith,
which puts its hope in Christ and His Kingdom. The problem has to do
with our individualized existence, and therefore it cannot be completely
resolved within the historical process. Consequently, there is only one "ideal
society"—the Kingdom of God—which is not a new model for organizing
a society and/or state, but, instead, a new mode of existence. As long as we
exist in the individualized mode of existence (in history), every attempt to
build the Kingdom of God on earth necessarily results in various types of
oppression and even totalitarianism. All "earthly kingdoms" that aspire to
be the Heavenly one become false icons (idols). The only icon of the eschatological Kingdom of God remains the Church as liturgy, not any social
or political institution or ideology. The logic of political institutions and
power structures can never mirror the eschatological mode of existence
because their very logic is rooted in the individualized being and its needs.
This is why giving these institutions a sacred character (through the concepts of "holy state," "holy nation" or "holy war," for instance) means rejecting the Kingdom of God.

This poses some important questions such as: What do we do in the
present context? Since Christianity is primarily concerned with *changing
the mode of existence*, rather than with ordering human societies, does this
mean that Christians should essentially stay passive in the socio-political
sphere? If yes, is this not an implicit affirmation of the status quo? Are
Christians going only to criticize every exercise of power, without offering

any concrete solutions, without engaging with the reality of human life and the socio-political structures that, in so many ways, influence life on this planet? On the other hand, if Christians should engage with the manifold issues that the socio-political reality presents, what should this engagement look like?

As we have seen, the sphere of necessity (including the socio-political sphere) cannot artificially be separated from the Christian aspiration to live a life according to the logic of the eschatological reality. We live in history both as individuals and as persons. We all manifest, on a daily basis, in various ways and to various degrees, the existential logic of the new (eschatological) creation, as well as the logic of "this world." To orient one's life toward the eschaton does not mean that one, miraculously, becomes someone else, someone who is not an individual anymore, someone who is free from the constraints of "this world" or someone who no longer needs to cope with his/her own egotism, or various exercises of power. To practice one's personhood takes askesis, a life-long fight with one's own limitations in order to train oneself to love, to empty one's self from one's ego. Christians (that is, the members of the liturgical community) still live in the socio-political sphere, together with non-Christians. They are still influenced by it, and they influence it. This is why Christians need to articulate (anew) their position vis-à-vis the social and political realities of each given period of time.

From the point of view of Orthodox ontology and anthropology, domination over other people and oppression of any kind is a priori *illegitimate*. However, the paradox of our existence in history is that, sometimes, it is necessary to exercise domination and authority in order to protect others or society as a whole. For instance, if there is a mass murderer who is killing people all around, we need to stop that person from harming others, disarm and isolate him/her in order to protect others. This is, no doubt, an act of power and authority, but it can be justified on the grounds of protection of others and society as a whole from something that is obviously harmful. Does it mean that because this exercise of power and authority is justifiable on pragmatic grounds, it is also something that Christians should consider as immanently good? A short answer would be—*no*.

Exercise of power, even if its purpose is prevention of another harmful exercise of power, still belongs to the realm of "this world," which Christianity rejects in principle, as another manifestation of the tragedy of our individualized existence. Although in many cases necessary, because we live in the individualized state of being, and not in the Kingdom of God, acts of violence cannot be called "good" or "just" from a Christian perspective, even when they are necessary, and committed in response to violence. This is even more dramatic in the case of killing other people as a protective measure, which Christians must never affirm or praise if they want to remain faithful to Christ. As St. Athenagoras said, in the second century:

> We cannot endure to see someone be put to death, even justly . . . because for us even watching a man being slain is next to killing him, we have forbidden watching such spectacles. How, then, can we, who do not even look on, lest guilt and pollution rubs off on us, put people to death?[1]

This is why most of the so-called "Christian" doctrines of "just war" (not to mention monstrosities such as the "Christian" advocacy of capital punishment or torture) are "Christian" only in name. From an authentic Christian perspective, there can never be a "just" war, a "just" exercise of violence. Even when we kill others in order to respond to an aggressive attack (and not in our self-protection, but because without reacting to that attack we would participate in the death of those who cannot defend themselves), this is not "okay." It can be justified, sometimes on pragmatic, political, or ethical grounds, but it cannot be justified from a Christian eschatological perspective.[2] The act of killing or torturing another human being is an act equivalent to the destruction of the universe, even if that human being is the worst criminal. It remains an act against God, an act of the destruction of His image and a cosmic tragedy. This is a paradox that Christians need to embrace in their historical journey if they do not want to falsify Christianity in order to have instant, ready-made solutions to every situation.

More to the point, Christian logic is not manifested in the attempts to punish those who have committed injustice, or to go after the villains who are harming one's individual well-being. The Christian logic is manifested primarily in our dedicated attempt to forgive those villains and to recognize in them the icon of God, which has been brought to such a miserable, hyperindividualized state that it cannot but seek self-affirmation and impose oppression and pain unto others. Praying for the aggressors, for their salvation, loving those who commit crimes against us, *not* seeking revenge and *not* rejoicing in their pain or punishment—that is the Christian way. This way is illogical and, probably, even completely *insane* when viewed from the point of view of "this world" and its logic. However, that is the Christian way, which does not lose sight of the eschaton. Christians know that real *justice* exists only in the eschatological realm. Justice for Christians does not consist of punishing a crime, or in "making up" for the broken commandments, but of an all-forgiving, all-embracing love. Punishment, doing evil in response to evil, never does justice according to the eschatological logic; it does not heal, but instead only multiplies the sickness in this world.

This is clearly very different from what is advocated by the various ethical and (in)justice systems of "this world." In the "kosmos" logic, every crime must be punished in order to reestablish the world and its *harmony*. In contrast to the eschatological community, the political communities of "this world" are governed by authorities that exercise their power over those they govern, either legally and legitimately or, as is more often the case, illegally and illegitimately. This is quite different from the Christian idea of authority and subordination, expressed in Christ's words, "For who is greater, he who sits at the table, or he who serves? Is it not he who sits at the table? Yet I am among you as the one who serves" (Luke 22:27).

In the eschatological logic, service and love replace the power of "this world," which belongs to the kingdom of Caesar. But to achieve the fullness of existence, which is based on love, we need to be "born again." As a result, the tension between the Kingdom of God and kingdom of Caesar remains, and it must remain during the entire course of history. Maintaining this tension helps us not to de-eschatologize eschatology by confusing two different existential logics. Those not ready to embrace the tension and the paradox—who want instant solutions and "user friendly" manuals always telling them what to do and how so that they can feel like they are "good" Christians, "righteous" and "blameless"—those have completely misunderstood Christianity.

We have seen, historically, many attempts to develop laws based on Christian values and virtues, or to give these values and virtues a formal, legal codification, which serves then as the basis for their institutional application. We also know that this ends in creating new oppressive systems that are "Christian" only in name. We have also seen many unfortunate examples of institutional churches producing documents, "teachings," and "doctrines" that aspire to codify a certain approach to a variety of social and political issues, and turn it into the "official" "Orthodox," "Church," or "Christian" approach. Such documents, in my view, produce more harm than help to the Church. The problem is that what Christianity affirms and preaches can never be expressed through laws, formally codified and implemented as an ethical or legal system. There is a simple reason for that: All regulations, norms, and systems have a compelling character. Something that has a compelling character cannot give birth to freedom.[3]

This puts Christians, making an effort to live *eschatological anarchism*, in the position of "anarchists" vis-à-vis the political sphere. This means that Christians are always and in principle skeptical toward any power structure and any (especially illegitimate) exercise of power because these affirm the individualized mode of existence and thus contradict the logic of love. However, Christians also recognize the necessary "evil" that comes with "this world," precisely because this is not the Kingdom of God, and, because of this, history is not a context in which the personal mode of existence can be fully materialized. This, furthermore, means that Christians should be supportive of all attempts aimed at deconstructing illegitimate power structures and reducing the oppression and power exercise to its absolute minimum (as in the above given case of preventing an act of murder, for instance). They should never forget that even the greatest villains are human beings and, potentially, saints as well. Because of this, they should be treated as humanly as possible, since the acts of oppression and violence represent that very individualized state of being that contradicts the Christian faith.

At the same time, nothing should prevent Christians from participating in all institutions and projects that lead toward the well-being of all people, regardless of their nationality, race, gender, religion, wealth, class, or any other preexisting properties that belong to "this world." Christians should know that these categories do not define who we are as human beings, in the eschatological sense.

Christians should also not remain silent when it comes to environmental destruction, the extinction of entire species, economic models that lead to slavery, enormous suffering, and the death of human beings and animal life. Christian anthropology can help here in showing how self-imposed constraints (through, for instancing, fasting practices), out of love for the entire natural environment, can be beneficial in reducing the amount of suffering and waste, which has today reached a cataclysmic scale.

In doing so, however, in improving the living conditions on this planet, Christians should always be careful never to canonize, idealize, or sanctify particular political and economic models, institutions, or ideologies, no matter how good they may appear. They can always be improved or adjusted to better serve human needs in this world, as well as the needs of other living creatures. We can always be more human and humane than we are. However, no matter how good or efficient socio-political constructs might appear in a given context, political institutions and ideologies will never be a manifestation of the Kingdom of God on earth; they will always remain the institutions of "this world," something that cannot, in principle, give us a new being. Although one should be sensitive to various social issues out of love for God, for other human beings, and for the rest of creation, one should not be too preoccupied with this world. Enthusiastic Christian activists, who dedicate their energies to addressing many concrete social and political issues, should always keep in mind Christ's words, "Martha, Martha . . . you are worried and upset about many things, but one thing is needed. Mary has chosen what is better, and it will not be taken away from her" (Luke 10:41–41). This does not mean that one should give up the practical work that improves people's living conditions, but rather that one should keep in mind the priorities. Christians should have faith in God, trust Him and not our human abilities to create perfect societies.[4] Until the historical Eucharists merge with the eschatological one.

Anarchists have historically been mostly focused on critiquing and deconstructing the state as the source of oppression. This is quite understandable given the position of state power as, historically, the preeminent source of political, financial, military, and other types of domination.[5] In many ways, states continue to hold this position, and the threat to freedom and democracy still comes from the old-fashioned state structures. It is not only in oriental despotic states, but also in what is usually (not without cynicism) called the "free" and "democratic world" that governments use police brutality, surveillance (conducted with or without substantial corporate help), torture, and executions. Accusations of "terrorism," spreading fear about the existence of all kinds of threats to "national security," are regularly used in order to exercise almost unlimited power over individuals and groups, revoking their human and civil rights.[6] Advanced industrial societies are rapidly sinking into new forms of (spectacle-flavored, high-tech) totalitarianism, in which people prefer to close their eyes and rely on empty ideological narratives about the "free" and "democratic" societies in which we supposedly live rather than confront the ugly reality. The remains of the old-fashioned democratic institutions and the rule of law seem to be incapable of dealing with these problems, partly because the new totalitarianism is not evolving in confrontation with these institutions, but rather in collaboration with them.[7]

However, focusing exclusively on the oppression coming from the old-fashioned state apparatus can also be very misleading. In addition to the state, we have witnessed the rise of other power agents that can often be even more oppressive and authoritarian than the traditional state apparatus. Simply dismantling state structures, while relying blindly on a "spontaneous" organization of people, does not necessarily or automatically lead to a more just or democratic society. On the contrary, it can result in various other kinds of oppressiveness that are even worse than the state structures that have some degree of legitimacy and accountability. Without a sufficient level of socio-political awareness, democratic culture, and responsibility among the people, the elimination of state structures can easily result in a state of chaos, without any functioning or meaningful social infrastructure. This state of chaos (or "anarchy" as this concept is commonly understood) can quickly turn into rule by local gangsters, terrorists, mafia bosses, and similar undesirable powerholders.[8]

There is also another much more organized and influential type of power structure that can "run the show" in the absence of efficient state structures—large international corporations. The phenomenon of the *corporatization* of almost all segments of today's social, political, and even private lives seriously interferes with a meaningful exercise of democracy in many countries. Under the pretexts of *efficiency, marketability*, and *competitiveness*, the (neoliberal) business logic tends to dismantle, absorb, or replace many of the traditional competences of the state. In this ideology, making a profit becomes the ultimate political, epistemological, and even ontological value and criterion, to which all particular practices and social institutions must serve. Even traditional institutions, such as universities, which were meant to be places of free inquiry, joint decision-making, and creativity, are becoming more and more corporatized, reducing the freedoms of thought and speech and limiting the possibility of creative inquiry.[9] The logic of free inquiry and personal growth, of creativity, solidarity, and shared decision-making, is being replaced by a corporate-like, dictatorial managerial class, restricting or completely abolishing some of the freedoms and good practices that were typical of serious academic work. Freedom of speech or thought, which, once upon a time, used to be a litmus test for the presence of both civil and academic freedoms, is under attack. Instead of focusing on solving real issues, the focus of the mainstream media as well as of the system of education is often on "trigger words" and the affirmation of a culture of extreme individualism and hostilities. At the root of this is the same consumerist logic that is employed in the advertising industry. The public sphere becomes thus dominated by self-censorship and aggressive impositions of the ideology of "political correctness," as well as by the contemporary versions of witch-hunts, which are, under the pretext of morality, launched every time individuals or groups want to destroy a person's credibility, reputation, and even life. This significantly restricts the space for free thinking, free speech, and meaningful discussion within the public sphere.

This is just one example of the negative impact corporatization can have, yet it is an important one given the role education plays both politically and economically. The corporate logic, however, corrupts society as a whole. It has become "normal"—through decades-long propaganda efforts to create this kind of "normality"—for medical institutions to exist not primarily to heal but to make profits. Factories are there not to produce quality goods or contribute to the real needs of the society, but to make profits as quickly and easily as possible, disregarding the effects on society, people, and the environment as a whole.

While the dominant ideology of marketability and profits is precisely that—an ideology, and a very oppressive one—it is normally propagated as an "objective" and "ideology-free" mechanism, which allows for the maximization of freedom. This way, the spectacular, highly concentrated, and privately owned wealth (and the political power that accompanies it) becomes a self-explanatory authority, a sign of undisputed success.

In such a world, there can be no meaningful concept of justice or freedom, even from a purely secular perspective. Private dictatorships are effectively replacing (more-or-less functioning) democratic institutions in the West, whose purpose was to prevent the concentration of power in private hands, nontransparent procedures, and unaccountability. Under the pretexts that everything is business and that private businesses function most efficiently, we have reached an unprecedented level of privatization, up to the point that now even that which by definition is a *public* sphere—the political sphere and political institutions—has been privatized. It is not only that in many "democracies" the elections are essentially bought, that legislation is passed based on the legal corruption known as "lobbying," or that the media sphere is dominated by private corporations, promoting private interests—the point has been reached where (in the US, for instance) there are even privately owned prisons, which means that slavery has now been even formally reinstalled.

This already murky picture can be much worse if we consider some poor "third world" countries, where the political sphere is often controlled by the local mafia-style oligarchy in symbiosis with their international sponsors.

One should not forget in this context the negative effects of the many technological innovations that were perceived as providing more democracy and transparency. Without questioning the enormous positive aspects of the technological advancements, the way the new technologies are often used is more than alarming. Some of the private corporate dictatorships have already become a contemporary (just much more advanced) version of "Big Brother," constantly "watching" over their users, collecting data about them and using them regularly for private profit or for nontransparent government purposes. It is not just the privacy issue that is alarming here, but also the systemic collection of private data, of people's habits and social interactions, with the goal of turning people into perfect consumers, influencing, as much as possible, their opinions and emotions.[10] Virtual "social networks" have started structuring social interactions in a specific way, which is what former Facebook executives now openly talk about, trying to raise consciousness of the hazardous effects of the genie they let out of the bottle.[11]

Digital technologies, in their symbiosis with nondemocratic and unaccountable power structures, are paving the road to new forms of totalitarianism.[12] We are already in a new "dark" age. The darkness of this age does not come from the lack of information, or from the difficulty of accessing it. In a certain sense it comes from its abundance, from the information pollution to which we are all exposed on a daily base. Information technologies have made enormous quantities of information readily available, and yet (to paraphrase Jean Baudrillard) there is less and less meaning and understanding. The enormous proliferation of (mostly useless and superficial) information leads to the problem of absorption. The attention span is becoming increasingly short, so even noticing particular information, let alone memorizing or examining it, becomes extremely difficult for the general population. Scattered attention, little or no reading (beyond the length of the average comments on social media), fragmented pieces of information that lack a broader context—that is the environment in which the "posttruth" society and the culture of "fake news" grow naturally. To filter this information (to get to "what is relevant to you"), we rely more and more on the same technology: The search engines and advertisements that websites show you (using complex tracking instruments) filter the information for you, based on your interests, previous browsing history, demonstrated "habits" in the virtual (or real) world, etc. In other words, to deal with the information pollution, most people end up in their individual virtual bubbles, without the time, energy, or critical thinking skills to analyze them, to form a solid and critical knowledge about the world and society in which they live.

The result is that we mostly deal in the public sphere (including here virtual "social media") with superficial opinions that can (and do) change the next day, even the next hour. What people think and argue, in favor of or against something, depends largely on what is the latest fashion on the (classical) mainstream media as well on social networks (among certain populations of their users). The possibilities to manipulate people's feelings and thoughts, from subjects such as fashion to food, ecology, and politics, are enormous; they range from the possibility of paying the "networks" and news distributors to advertise certain opinions, events, or products, to the "bots"—real people or "artificial intelligence"—who (anonymously or hidden behind fake profiles) post comments and "share" news in order to create a certain perception of what the "public opinion" on the subject is. The problem is thus not only one of online data collecting and data manipulations; the problem today is also an epistemological one.

The overwhelming presence of digital technologies in practically all spheres of our private and public lives seems to be shaping a new epistemology in which interhuman relationships and society, its functioning and organization, are understood in analogy to digital systems (computer programs).[13] In the name of efficiency, based on statistic models, algorithms are being used not only to address practical social needs, but also as a paradigm of a successful, even "perfect" (automated) social organization. It is clear how easy it is, in such situations, to manipulate people's desires, opinions, or value judgments, and present them as "popular" or "democratic."

The internet was expected to be the big "democratizing" tool, where everyone (theoretically at least) could participate and express their views. However, it has also become a new tool of surveillance and manipulation (only far more sophisticated). The digital information collecting (bigdata) surpasses by far the scale of surveillance prophesied by Yevgeny Zamyatin and George Orwell. All the collected data can be used for the purposes of profit-making, but also for the purposes of influencing what people think and how they behave, and, when necessary, for the purposes of targeting individuals and social groups, their denunciation, and, in more extreme cases, for putting them into jail or into torture chambers.[14] While, as pointed out above, the public sphere, traditionally understood, is becoming increasingly privatized; digital technologies are also being used to turn what used to be the private sphere (what people do in the comfort of their private spaces) into a public thing. Many "observers" (companies and governments) have instant access to people's private life through the very fact that you own one of their most recently produced "smart" devices that are capable of recording both audio and video materials, for commercial as well as for political/ideological purposes. What once characterized totalitarian regimes is now practiced to a much larger degree on a daily basis, across the globe, including in our advanced "liberal" and "democratic" societies.

Bigdata thus function as a self-fulfilling prophecy. Complex "all-knowing" and "all-seeing" algorithms and databases (constantly expanding, becoming more and more sophisticated) resemble the god of the Deists. Computer technologies are effectively creating such a god, but that is not the Christian God, whose primary attribute is not to be all-knowing but to be all-loving.

This new god of bigdata and complex algorithms is, however, different from the Deist god insofar as it does interfere with the world in which we live. We already have economic theories pretending to be "objective" by (supposedly) eliminating the political from their equations, relying purely on mathematical approximations. We already have digital currencies that aspire to create money that will have "objective," apolitical value by relying on computer algorithms. It is not difficult to imagine a political platform in the near future that will advocate a complete submission of the political system and political processes to a computer program—in the form of artificial intelligence, for instance—under the pretext that this is the way social and political issues will and should be dealt with in an efficient, impersonal, neutral, and ideologically free way. The decision-making process can thus be transferred to an algorithm, under the (mistaken) expectation that the algorithm can find the "best" solution to "fix" the (broken) political system or particular problems that traditional politics could not. Such a society would be more totalitarian than anything we have seen so far.[15]

All of this highlights the immanent dangers we are presented with when it comes to the functioning of (something that could meaningfully be called) democracy. It also highlights the importance of education, not as a system of indoctrination (which helps the power structures to remain and expand) but as a way of acquiring critical thinking skills. Part of education needs to be the critical use of technology and media literacy that can help the general population to gain a better understanding of the manipulation strategies.

The above mentioned realities, far from being a comprehensive list of all the power-related challenges that the world is facing today, seem to be sufficient to justify the need for reviving an anarchist approach to the socio-political sphere. If viewed from this perspective, it becomes clear that anarchist ideas and values are neither just an expression of fancy intellectual concepts nor an immature, naïve, or idealistic political philosophy but, instead, a very basic need that can help us deal with the manifold problems of contemporary (global) society.

Power structures have historically taken many different forms, with each carrying various degrees of influence and oppressiveness, from patriarchal families or street gangs, to terrorist groups, states, international organizations, church administration, or the corporate sector. No one knows what the new forms of power structures will be in the future, but whatever they are, it is likely that they, too, will exercise power and opportunism in the name of efficiency and of noble ideas such as security, democracy, freedom, or justice (although the "age of cynicism" might give rise to the power structures that will not even need a noble narrative as a pretext for their exercise of power; "rule over us" and "oppress us" might easily be the future motto that the masses will happily adopt).

The Oppressiveness of the (Individualized) Self

In their practice of anarchism in the socio-political sphere, Christians should always be on the side of those oppressed and suffering, and always skeptical and critical of the ideological mainstream, never accepting any narratives that are used against concrete human beings, even when these narratives claim to be most noble, ethical, and progressive. Christians should never turn against concrete people; they should never reject them (no matter how good or evil they are). They should, however, condemn and reject harmful policies, actions, and values. Christians should always keep in mind that not only the oppressed, but also the oppressors need salvation. We can condemn their actions, but never reject concrete human beings. No matter how vicious they might be, they are also tragic figures in search of true life and meaning that will fill the void within their being from which the evil they do comes.

In criticizing power structures and arguing in favor of freedom, both in the ontic and in the socio-political realms, I am aware of the complexity of the situation in which we find ourselves. If there is a lesson to be learned from Christian anthropology, it is that our historical existence is tragic. However, it is precisely this imperfect and tragic existence that has the opportunity to be transformed into its own eschatological prototype—a true existence that manifests itself as love and freedom.

It is true that we are faced with many oppressive mechanisms in history, and it is also true that, from an anarchist perspective, we should aim at exposing them and, if they are proven illegitimate, dismantling them. However, this is only one side of the coin. The other side is that we are not only oppressed from the outside but also—and primarily so—from the inside, from within our own individualized being. The tragedy of our historical existence is not only that our individual existence suffers from so many challenges presented by our surroundings (natural and social), but also that our very existence (our individual being) oppresses us. We live in the state of necessity; our own (mortal) being is limited and poses a threat to our existence.

When we elevate this tragedy of our historical existence from an individual to the social level, we find that it is not only that there are oppressors out there ("them") that individuals and groups ("us") should fight against. This "us" is problematic as well, and is a vital factor within the whole power dynamics equation.

One of the biggest problems in our socio-political lives is that people mostly prefer to be oppressed, prefer to be guided (even in the wrong direction), and prefer to be deceived rather than to embrace their freedom and the responsibility that comes with it. This is the old problem so brilliantly captured by Dostoyevsky's "The Grand Inquisitor." Most people will choose to be led, to be deceived, and to continue to be deceived rather than to realize their mistake and respond to the problem of their individual existence in an authentic and creative way. For the sense of security and comfort ("happiness"), most people will gladly sacrifice truth, their own freedom, their dignity, other human beings, even their friends. For just a

THEOLOGY AS A CRITICAL DISCOURSE?

little more, for maintaining a (false) sense of entitlement and obtaining a piece of power, they will already be ready to impose enormous suffering on other fellow human beings.

Political, ideological, and media elites live and replicate because of this feature of the individualized existence, which is in a constant, desperate search for meaning. The elites, of course, readily provide various narratives (meanings), ranging from reality shows to more elaborate ideological constructs and interpretations such as economic or political theories. All types of narratives are used in order to rationalize the current state of affairs, and make us feel good within a certain "horizon of meaning," which must be protected so that the institutions of "this world" do not lose their power. People find comfort in the belief that there is a meaning "out there" (although it may not be accessible to them), that there is someone "in charge," who provides (or will provide) stability and security (if not now, then in the future). The list of those "in charge," who are supposed to deliver this stability, security, and meaning is a long one; it can include state authorities, CEOs, intellectuals, scientists, priests. . . . Both those in power and, even more, those who sacrifice their freedom on the altar of (imaginary) security find themselves in a position in which they need to defend the dominant (ideological) narratives—the "horizon of meaning" which must be sustained.

As a result, whenever there is a crisis (or when a crisis is needed), various scapegoats will be identified and sacrificed in our modern-day versions of circuses—the mass media, "social networks," and the like—for the pleasure of the masses. The same masses (*populus*) will readily greet the various types of abuses of power in the name of the preservation of the prevailing "morality," "national interests," "national security," "democracy," etc. Through the exploitation of such (real or fabricated) scandals, through the public executions of the scapegoats, but also through the offering of less mobilizing but all the more superficial media products (such as soap operas or talk shows/reality programs), the media/entertainment industry will make sure that the general population is "properly" directed in what and how they are supposed to feel and think, turning them effectively into passivized individuals, whose potential for real social initiative and protest is reduced to sitting in front of their (TV, computer, cellphone, or other) screens, and consuming . . . consuming evermore. This "lifestyle" will, naturally, be depicted as a desirable one, fancy and "cool," which seductively calls the masses to immerse themselves in it as much as possible.

The modern propaganda industry—as if it followed a *manual* written by the Grand Inquisitor himself—will also make the masses feel that they are "in charge," that they are those who are making the decisions and that they enjoy great, if not unlimited, freedom. Contemporary versions of "participatory" culture, convenient (online or shopping mall) purchasing, interactive software, personalized online "experiences," and various technological devices (from cellphones to Alexa), all produce an illusion of the universe orbiting around "me."

The effect is that individuals are getting more and more isolated from each other. Making authentic contact with another human being becomes unnecessary, even deeply frustrating. Every personal, human contact becomes a potential source of distress and harassment that should be avoided. In such a universe, rebellion and self-assurance is expressed by "blocking" all the online content that we do not like, posting comments or customer reviews or joining in defamatory media campaigns against individuals or groups that are targeted as "bad guys," and then sentenced to execution in the public (media) arena, so that the real issues are successfully kept outside the public gaze. This brings pleasure to the masses, making them feel good and righteous. After the public executions of all the scapegoats and the defamed "bad guys," the "little children" will return to their screens, happily and self-righteously consuming another pack of their favorite (extra large) meal and soda. It is difficult to think of a more telling sign of corruption and impotence. In this anthropology, the human being is reduced to a happy slave. This happy slave individual is the ideal citizen-consumer that the neoliberal world demands, profiting on the affirmation of the individualized mode of existence.

This is why the anarchist approaches that focus exclusively on the oppressors and that believe that once we get rid of those in power, we will reach an "ideal" form of society, are, in my view, both naïve and mistaken. It is certainly important to fight oppression and identify and deconstruct the power structures. However, the reason why those power structures exist in the first place is not only that we are not strong enough to get rid of them. It is, very often, because we are not strong enough to live without them. People need power structures to tell them what to do and how, to assure them that they are good and to take away from them the responsibility for the heavy burden of freedom. In this way, average citizens—being similar to those "little children" the Grand Inquisitor talked about—are also participants in the oppression and crimes of those in power. They legitimize those crimes and oppression. As previously noted, through their acceptance of being manipulated, through their passivity, through their vanity that makes them easy targets of marketing/manipulation tactics, they contribute to the evil, violence, and oppression in this world.

Only by taking this aspect into account can a critique of authority and oppression be complete or meaningful. Christian anthropology teaches us that we are primarily oppressed by our own individualized being, and by the mode of existence in which the world finds itself.

The above-described approach differs from most anarchist and Christian anarchist theories in that it does not presuppose some immanently "good" human nature (in "this world") that, when allowed to freely express itself, leads to a free, equal, and just social organization.[16] While a more free, equal, and just social organization is not only very much needed but is also a real possibility, the question of the power dynamics (which is, as we have seen, "built into the system" of "this world," so to speak) remains a stumbling block for many anarchist discourses.

Setting aside for a moment the theological perspective, many practical questions also remain to be explored more in depth if we want to arrive at a more humane local or global society. If, for instance, small communities that are based on equality and solidarity are offered as a model, it is not clear how these communities would resist powerful (e.g., international) organizations. Should small communities (that do not exceed the size of a medium-size village) as a model be applied universally? Is that realistic? One could claim that larger conglomerates (tribes, states . . .) have historically appeared not only because of the quest for more power and domination (which is true), but also because they, in a certain sense, provided individuals and groups (from their perspective at least) more freedom, more opportunities, and better living conditions. In order to provide those *better* living conditions (which has always, historically, meant providing better living conditions for *some*), those conglomerates needed an ideology that would inspire, articulate, and direct the development toward the desired socio-political goal. And this can easily turn into the creation of a Kingdom of God on Earth. This is a paradoxical dynamic that poses a threat for each anarchist theory that seeks to achieve justice, freedom, equality, and material prosperity within the boundaries of "this world"—that it would turn into a more or less coherent and prescriptive theory/ideology, which is needed in order to be (more) effective in achieving the envisioned goals.

We find a similar challenge in most Christian anarchist theories that advance morality, an optimistic view of the human being (in "this world"), and a possibility of creating a society that would be based on "Christian values."[17]

What seems to me to be an authentic (Orthodox) Christian "anarchist" position is a skepticism toward the formation of a "good," "just," "free," let alone "perfect" social model. A certain "indifference" toward socio-political structures is also needed in this context since "the present form of this world is passing away."[18] This "indifference" does not mean that one should be indifferent to human suffering or to opportunities to help someone. What it implies is that Christians should not be obsessed by, or despair about, socio-political (or any other) issues in light of their faith and hope that the Kingdom of God, the full communion in Christ, which is the most important thing, is approaching.

This clearly differentiates Christian theological "anarchism" from most of the leftist or anarchist approaches to the socio-political sphere: It is not only its "negative" (both apophatic and critical) approach to political (power) structures, and its refusal to formulate overarching, coherent, and prescriptive theories as the ideal socio-political whole (that turn out to be *blinding* ideological narratives about that socio-political whole); it is also its highlighting of the existential roots of power aspirations. At the same time, the recognition that we deal with something much more complex than the "good" human nature waiting to spontaneously manifest itself once external power structures are dismantled, prevents an Orthodox theological reflection upon the political from falling into an individualistic solution (à la Max Stirner), which seems to be the only logical (secular) anarchist alternative to the naïve (anthropological) anarchist optimism. Both the affirmation of individualistic freedom (anthropo-anarchist pessimism) and the creation of a collective/communal paradise on earth (anthropo-anarchist optimism) are avoided if one keeps sight of the Kingdom of God, and affirms, on that basis, freedom, justice, and human dignity.

Excurse III

"LEFT," "RIGHT," AND CHRISTIAN

From an anarchist perspective, autocratic, oppressive regimes are clearly illegitimate and should be dismantled, preferably in a peaceful way.[19] However, a much
more interesting case, in this context, is the case of so-called "democratic"
systems[20] where, supposedly, the citizens, or at least the majority of them, exercise some influence over policy and decision-making. In these societies, political parties (normally more than two), with different programs and ideological
orientations (theoretically speaking, at least), participate and compete for the
support of the voters. The concepts of the "left" and the "right" are, thus, still
used to characterize the opposing poles of the "democratic" political spectrum,
even though, in reality, the differences between major political parties often
tend to be so minimal that one can speak more of factions within the one predominant (business) party or business (profit)-driven ideological system.

The question that is, then, usually asked, is: Which option should Christians
support? How should they act within the pluralistic political system (even when
this pluralism is only nominally there)? Are there some political orientations
("left" or "right") that are, by definition, closer to the Christian worldview and
the political philosophy that stems from it?[21]

Traditionally, religion (and the church) tended to be an ally of the political
right. As Pantelis Kalaitzidis put it: "What one realizes... is that there is a nearly
universal tendency among religious intellectuals to lean toward the far right and
authoritarian ideologies in general."[22] As we have seen in the previous chapters,
religious institutions and religious narratives have traditionally supported the
dominant power structures and the dominant socio-political narratives (regardless of the political system, unless the state power becomes openly hostile
toward the church). In the modern period, alliances between (modern) nations
and Christianity, or the (nation) state and the church, became very common.
On the other hand, however, the relationship between the political "left" and
the church has traditionally been antagonistic, if not openly hostile. How can
this ideological divide between the "left" and the "right," then, be understood
from the perspective of Orthodox political theology?

Although the "(Orthodox) Christian anarchist" approach to the sphere of
the political does not imply a particular political program, or a coherent (secular) vision of the political sphere, the very inclination toward the affirmation of

the freedom of human beings and a critical stance toward power structures would make it, when transferred to the political realm, a natural ally of the "left" end of the political spectrum (even what is today called the "radical left"). The situation is, however, more complicated and requires a bit of unpacking since the vocabulary used in the political realm (including the realm of political science) is not exactly a model of clarity. So, let me first address the very concept of the political "left" and "right."

More than two decades ago, Norberto Bobbio noticed that, "never has so much been written against the traditional distinction between left and right, which is now thought to have run its course and to be completely without meaning, always supposing it had one in the past."[23]

There are many objections raised against the (traditional) "left/right" divide. Some claim that thinking in terms of "left" and "right" belongs essentially to modernist ideological narratives, and so cannot be applied to the "postmodern" age or, especially, to the so-called "postideological" age. Others would claim that this divide is simply useless in the contemporary context, when the issues that we are facing today (such as ecological problems, with their many social and economic implications) simply do not fall into the traditional categories of the "left" or "right."

Although it is true that the context has changed quite significantly compared to, say, nineteenth-century parliamentary multiparty systems, one can, without much effort, demonstrate that we still live in highly ideologically charged times,[24] in which ideology is by no means absent but simply takes different forms that, indeed, do go beyond the boundaries of the traditional "grand" modernist ideological narratives. Ideologies range nowadays from "free market" ideology and the ideology of "humanitarian interventionism" to more subtle ideological narratives such as hyperindividualism and (hyper)consumerism, techno-fundamentalism, etc., which have direct political and economic implications. The question is, thus: Can contemporary ideologies be related to the more traditional ideological (left/right) discourse and, if so, to what extent?

Over the past decades, the political spectrum has been both significantly broadened when it comes to the type of issues that various political options address, and, at the same time, significantly narrowed in the sense that most of the relevant and dominant political options essentially buy into the same business- and market-driven ideological narrative. This often makes it difficult to say, in contemporary "democracies," what is an authentically "leftist" as opposed to a "right-wing" position vis-à-vis many social issues, or if the positions and issues on a political map can be associated with the (traditional) "left" and "right" wing poles at all.

In spite of the validity of these remarks, it seems to me that it remains useful to try to conceptually differentiate between the "left" and "right" ideological options (although they can hardly ever be found in a "pure" form in any concrete context), since this can illuminate the sources and consequences of concrete policies and actions.

Who's Right and Who's Left?

The difficulty, however, remains when it comes to defining these concepts. Should we define them based on their positions vis-à-vis economic polices? Although this seems to be logical, since it is the "left" that has traditionally advocated economic justice and economic equality, to take this as the sole criterion could be very misleading. In the US, for instance, the common, popular way of distinguishing between the "right" and the "left" is to use the criterion of "small" vs. "big" government advocacy. Following this criterion, arguments in favor of a "small government," more economic freedoms (for the corporate sector, of course), and deregulation are indicative of an orientation to the "right," while arguing in favor of a "big government" and/or stronger government regulations of the market forces, universal healthcare, etc., would indicate a "leftist" approach. The problem with both of these approaches is that neither "option" dares to question the very premises of the political and economic system that is based on exploitation and extreme inequality, advocating instead for only minor adjustments within the currently existing system.

The economic criterion, however, would not be the only indicator for differentiating the traditional "right" and the "left" in most European countries. In Europe, the "right" still primarily refers to nationalistic ideologies and, in more extreme cases, to chauvinism and racism, while the "left" signifies a more internationalist, even universalist, platform, with, to be sure, both economic equality and the welfare state at its core. This is all-too-easily (and wrongly) translated in Europe nowadays into a simple, binary set of opposing positions: the pro-EU one (which, in practice, often means support for the nontransparent Brussels administration that is under the predominant influence of big businesses as well as German political elites) is often identified as a "leftist" perspective, and the anti-EU one (which often means pronational, nationalistic, or even fascist positions, as well as support for corrupt and unaccountable national leaderships that are often in symbiosis with big businesses and similar political options outside their state) is identified as the "right."

An additional problem when analyzing the "right" and the "left" is that these labels are often used by the party's political opponents, meaning that the terms do not necessarily describe how a particular political option perceives itself, but rather how its policies are perceived in a broader political discourse or by their political rivals. When "right" and "left" labels are used by the opposite or, supposedly, "neutral" ideological perspective, to identify the ideological "others," they usually reflect negative presuppositions, and their usage can even have openly hostile intentions.

On top of this, since "far right" (identified with national socialism and fascism) and "extreme left" (identified with Marxism and Stalinism) became the widespread labels for some of the most dangerous ideological projects of the twentieth century that had disastrous consequences, many feel uneasy accepting those labels and, therefore, argue in favor of abandoning them completely.

My own reservation as to the left/right divide has to do with its binary character. "Left" and "right" often seem a reductionist attempt to simplify very complex (economic, ideological, and political) systems into merely two poles, or two "pills," to employ again the terminology from The Matrix. The choice of "either this or that" is not only restrictive but, if taken dogmatically, can actually be understood as an ideological blackmail that reduces complex socio-political realities to an extremely simplified picture.

Keeping all these reservations in mind, I do think that thinking about the concepts of the "right" and the "left" can still be useful in our attempt to understand the genesis and the operational logic behind many of the contemporary political options. Moreover, I think that one can affirm the political *left*, with its ideas of social justice, for instance, even if there is no corresponding (traditional) political right on the other side of the political spectrum.

The models I am going to develop and dwell upon here are primarily theoretical ones—meaning that they would rarely appear in a pure form in political reality. Reality is (almost always) too complex to mirror relatively simple theoretical models. And yet, as I said before, these models can be helpful in making sense of the various narratives that tend to describe the socio-political sphere, as well as their origins and their objectives. This means that my reclamation of the concepts of "left" and "right" should not be understood as an attempt to construct a conceptual cage into which the variety of ideas that we find in the political arena must necessarily fit, but rather as potentially useful orientation signs that guide us when importing some foundational ideas into a particular ideological position.

The "Right"

Based on the history of the "right" wing political options (such as nationalism), one can see the "right" as those ideologies that understand society as basically an organic, harmonious whole. This is considered to be true even if the idea that there are very many roles in the society is accepted, along with the reality that many people do not live a harmonious life within the assumed overall social (and cosmic) harmony. This fact is usually explained by invoking the sense of a basic underlying unity: There are different roles that we must all fulfill to contribute to the well-being of the state/society/nation as a whole. This well-being of the state/society/nation always requires some sacrifice (usually, to be sure, from those at the bottom of the social and political pyramid).

If a disruptive element appears (as it always does) and social tensions and conflicting interests start to question the narrative about this "harmonious" state or endanger its very functioning (as they do), right-wingers will come up with a plausible explanation. They will elucidate that this harmonious and organic social entity is not in a harmonious state because of the intrusion of "others," of those who do not *really* and *organically* belong to "our" (harmonious) social whole. These "others"—and *not* some fundamental, structural properties of our societies—are responsible for disturbing the organic social whole in the right-wing discourse. The list of "others" (as internal or external threats) can include virtually any social group; it can include national, ethnic, or racial others (e.g., Chinese, Arabs, Russians), religious others (e.g., Christians, Muslims, or even "others" within one religion such as Catholics and Protestants, Shia and Sunni Muslims, etc.), cultural or gender others (e.g., immigrants, women, homosexuals), and so forth.

In other words, from the perspective of the "right," society should be in its "natural" and primordial balance. In this harmonious society, everyone assumes one's own, God- or nature-given place. This is why, in the right-wing discourse, all the manifestations of social conflicts and problems can never be traced back to "us." Some basic social imbalances, which have to do with the way "we" are, are invisible from this ideological perspective. The collective "us" (whose existence is presupposed) can never be the source of the problem—it is always the fault of the "others." Those "others" do not really belong "here," either because they lack the "authenticity" necessary for the preservation of the harmonious socio-political whole (the "right" way of behavior, skin color, language, culture, etc.), or because they are "traitors," "foreign spies," or "heretics," who choose not to conform to the immanently good and harmonious social whole to which "we" belong.

In more extreme forms of the right-wing ideology, the anthropology that is derived from these basic (often implicit and subconscious) ontological and political-philosophical premises is a fundamentally anti-Christian anthropology. We very often find various appropriations of social Darwinism, exceptionalism, or what I have called elsewhere the "ideology of youth" that, quite similarly to its fascist predecessors, celebrates youth, strength, and other biologically determined characteristics as key anthropological values.[25]

Based on the above given description of the underlying logic of the "right," the traditional "right" places the nation, or other types of collective identity above the person and tends to limit freedom every time the activities or positions of individual people or social groups are perceived as an "intrusion" or a potential danger to the supposed social harmony, the presumed "natural state" of "how things are supposed to be." The exclusion of others who are perceived as "intruders" very often leads to their dehumanization, deprivation of equal treatment, and, in more extreme cases, segregation or even physical elimination. To see how this mechanism functions, it is not necessary to go to what are widely considered the darkest chapters of Western history—it is enough to take a look at the recent "refugee crisis" in Europe, or at the culture of fear and hatred (against Muslims, Mexicans, Russians, etc.) in the US, turning most of the (mainstream) political sphere to the moderate or extreme right.[26]

When right-wing logic is merged with particular religious ideas, it can result not only in strengthening the internal social cohesion—which can even lead to totalitarian political systems—but also in "just" and "holy war" theories and actions, which are then often merged with imperial aspirations. When the protection of the national, ethnic, cultural or religious identity becomes the ultimate point of reference, all actions against "others" become justifiable.

Advocating, openly or implicitly, the supposed harmony of the socio-political sphere, the right-wing options also have the potential of becoming on-tologies on their own, and a substitution for the Kingdom of God. In such a situation, political or church leaders can easily become national prophets, and the nation or the state can become a god. This alliance between churches and states—between the specific interpretations of Christianity and the political ideologies that we have seen so many times in history—very often leads to a profound rejection of the very need for the Kingdom of God.

Viewed from this perspective, the right can be seen as advocating a pseudo-ecclesial character of the society-state (organic whole) as well as sacrifices to be made for the nation and the state. The "Christian" right turns out to be espe-cially anti-Christian precisely in its attempt to de-eschatologize Christianity and to turn the church into yet another institution of "this world," which is supposed to contribute to this world's socio-political order (and, of course, to the interests of those in power).

The idea that one can achieve an organic stability and harmony within the socio-political whole is, both theologically and practically, dubious. As we have seen, Christianity understands the sphere of "this world" as fundamentally im-balanced, disruptive, and, indeed, tragic. This is because reality (the entirety of creation) does not exist in a way that would be in accordance with its own (eschatological) telos. Although love is the way to transform the historical (indi-vidualized) existence in such a way that it becomes an existence according to its telos, this process cannot be completed and universally accomplished within the boundaries of "this world." This is how and why the right-wing solution, which relies on some imagined primordial "harmony" of the socio-political sphere ("this world") that "others" disturb, appears as fundamentally confused. The way the political right relates to "others" is also something that is in a direct contradiction with Orthodox Christian anthropology. This anthropology sees in the neighbor—precisely in that "other" who is the target of right-wing fears—the source of one's own (personal) identity. Those "others," who are the "threat" in the right-wing discourse, are those who become the source of our salvation.

In spite of this, there is one element that we can, sometimes, identify in the traditional right that can be appreciated from a Christian perspective. It is the call for mutual support, care for other members of the community, self-sacrifice for the common good. Even though political leaderships often (mis)use these ideas as empty phrases to homogenize society or to profit from the sacrifices made by others, one cannot deny that the values of mutual support, active and voluntary contributions to the well-being of the community (including phenomena such as "ecological patriotism"), or care for those in need do characterize social life in many conservative and tradition-oriented communities throughout the world, and that this element alone can reflect the Christian understanding of self-emptying, sacrificial love (as long as it is not for the sake of targeting some adversarial "others").

The "Left"

The traditional "left," on the other hand, seems to approach the socio-political sphere with a very different idea of what the basic structure of the socio-political reality looks like. From the point of view of the "left," social conflicts (between different classes) is the basic point of departure. Conflicts are based on discrepancies between various interests within society, which then translate into power structures. In its traditional form, it is a conflict over economic interests, but this conflict can also be generalized and applied to all sorts of conflicting interests that must be factored in when thinking about the social sphere. This is why the ideals of social justice and economic equality—which then translate into claims for just wages, social security, universal accessibility to healthcare and education, etc.—characterize the traditional leftist perspective in a very fundamental way.

Of course, this perspective raises the question as to whether there is any basic difference between the "right" and the "left," since from the "leftist" perspective, described this way, the "class others" may appear to be performing, structurally, the same function that ethnic, national, or any other "others" perform for the "right." In other words, the question is: Is there a structural difference between the characteristics and roles that the "bourgeois others" perform within the social space (from a leftist perspective), compared to the role that ethnic "others," for instance, perform in a "right" wing perspective, both "curving" the harmonious social space?

An interesting phenomenon is noticeable in the way we are able to think about the socio-political reality from a particular ideological perspective. The class conflict, as the very fundamental characteristic of our social reality (and a problem that should be addressed), can only really be thought about from a "leftist" perspective. The right wing can think of other types of (undesirable)

THEOLOGY AS A CRITICAL DISCOURSE? 229

"othernesses" that curve the social space, but not of class, and, consequently, not of the power structures that stem from the underlying class struggle. If, in populist right-wing discourse, the upper class also becomes the target of attacks, it is always merged with some other "otherness" mentioned above (the typical example here would be the figure of the "rich Jew" in Nazi Germany). The "pure" class enemy, so to speak, can be targeted only from a leftist perspective.

The ideology of big business, in its neoliberal form, is quite an intreresting case in this sense. It is "right" wing (in the sense in which this concept is used nowadays in the US), but, at the same time, it also exploits a "leftist" understanding of the basic structure of the social fabric, in terms of economic inequality and, even, class struggle. However, unlike in the traditional "left," class conflict and economic inequality are positively (one could also claim cynically) evaluated in this case, and even promoted as something "good." More inequality and poorer citizens mean a higher concentration of wealth in fewer pockets. This means that economic imbalance and different social classes are not denied, but are instead praised as a positive fact about social reality, both in economic and ethical terms. In this sense, the "age of cynicism" allowed for the contemporary "big-business right" to be more straightforward about its agendas than the traditional capitalists or aristocrats, many of which used to have the old-fashioned perception of inequality as something immanently unjust—which is why there was a need to compensate for this "primordial sin" through endowments, charity work, etc., or, alternatively, to rationalize this gap through (pseudo)religious narratives about "God's will" or God's "calling." In the neoliberal discourse, greed becomes a self-explanatory value, rooted in social Darwinism.

The "left," thus, seems to be able to think of social conflict as the primordial state of (social) affairs, which becomes the point of departure in thinking about and changing society. This social conflict translates into power structures that, supposedly, "keep society together," which makes the left's assessment of these power structures so different from those of other ideological perspectives. Viewed from a "leftist" perspective, the "left" targets the *real* problem in the (imbalanced) social space—the power structures that manifest themselves as concrete social classes. This is why, from the leftist perspective, the "class other" cannot be replaced by any other type of "otherness."[27] In right-wing discourse (again, viewed from a "leftist" perspective) the "other" appears as a formal (mis) perception of the curvature of the social space, effectively masking the underlying social conflicts. This makes the figure of the "other," for the right, replaceable—if it is not the "Jews" or "Arabs," it can be "refugees" or domestic "traitors." Ultimately, this means that for the left, the position of the "class other" (if, and only if it is intrinsically linked with the existing power structures) is structurally different from right-wing "otherness."

Of course, this does not mean that the temptation to treat the "class other" in a similar way in which the right-wing treats other "others" is absent on the "left." In fact, based on the historical experience, this is quite a real danger. The "left" leans toward right-wing logic every time the figure of the "class other" becomes the point of fixation, divorced from the issues of power structures and exploitation. This was precisely the case in most of the (officially) communist regimes after the communist parties took over. The logic of the "class other" that targeted the "old bourgeoisie" in Bolshevism was emptied of its substance, since it ceased to target the new "red bourgeoisie" that was assuming power, replacing the ancien régime. Thus, the fixation on the (precommunist) "bourgeois exploitation" made many of those communists blind to the new reality of power structures, turning many of the disempowered into the victims of the new exploitation.[28] This is why the "left" effectively turns into the "right" every time it assumes the narrative of a social harmony as a way of masking the (new) power structures, and the narrative about the disturbance of that harmony as a way of masking the interests of those in power.

Viewed from this perspective, it becomes easier to understand how and why the concepts of "conservative," on the one hand, and "revolutionary/progressive" on the other, have come to signify the "right" and the "left." The "right" tends to justify the existing social order (often by referring to "tradition")—i.e., it tends also to eliminate those who disturb its harmony, just as it tends to affirm the harmony of the socio-political whole when defending the existing power structures (economic elites, a hierarchically organized society, etc.). On the other hand, the "left" wants to change what is perceived as the basic injustice built into the very fabric of the (imbalanced) social sphere, and to articulate, on that basis, various interests in order to create a more harmonious (and more horizontally organized) social sphere. This means that, in a certain sense, the "right" and the "left" start from opposing premises, but tend to "borrow" some elements from the premise of the other in their movement toward their own desired goal—while the "right" starts from the idea of harmony, trying to eliminate the disturbing factors, the "left" starts from the recognition of primal disturbance, but tends to reach a more or less just and harmonious social space. Of course, actual political practice, being the practice of various power agents, virtually always presents these (ideal) models in a more or less confused form.

From what has been said so far, it could appear that vis-à-vis the socio-political sphere, the "left" represents the closer ideological pole of the political spectrum to some of the basic elements of Orthodox Christian political theology. The (conceptual) advantage of the "left," when viewed from the perspective of "Orthodox Christian anarchism," lies in its acknowledgment of the antagonistic and imbalanced nature of the socio-political reality as the point of departure in our understanding of that reality and its recognition that this reality can, and should, be changed. This position can be reconciled with the broader Orthodox understanding of the character of our reality, which is important both as a metaphysical statement and as a political program. If understood properly, this expectation of change keeps (potentially, at least) the socio-political institutions as well as citizens in a state of vigilance, ready to change the political realm when needed, in order to deal with the manifold (often conflicting) interests and challenges. This can be beneficial as it helps our thinking of the socio-political sphere primarily in practical terms and in terms of how to organize the political sphere to best respond to the manifold interests and needs of the individuals and social groups. The "left" should, thus, resist attempts aimed at establishing a "perfect" human community, a kind of "Kingdom of God" on Earth, based on an abstract set of principles (whether they be the traditional "organic" societies or "liberal democracies").

Another advantage of the "left" is that it tends to overcome both national and other kinds of boundaries that separate people from each other. In this way, the dignity of the human being is affirmed as a universal value, something that overcomes all racial, national, ethnic, religious, gender, or other categories. In this aspect, the "left" appropriates (although in secular terms) the Christian anthropological universalism in which there is "neither Jew nor Greek, slave nor free, male nor female" (Galatians 3:28). Advancing claims for economic justice, universal healthcare, social security, education accessible to all, etc., the left becomes compatible with the Christian understanding that the ultimate value is the human person him/herself, who, as such, should never be a means to any (other) end, even if that end appears as the most noble one.

However, it is also possible to see where potential misunderstandings and conflicts between the "left" and Orthodoxy may appear. The problem with what is perceived as the radical variation of the "left" is that it can easily end up in the exclusion of the "class others." "Class enemies" can be "demonized" to the point of their dehumanization, which is precisely what happened in Stalinism or in other "communist" regimes. In this case, as I pointed out earlier, the logic of such a "left" effectively turns into the logic of the "right." The elimination of the "class enemy" then becomes just another ideological narrative to mask the fact that the new ("communist") ruling class has taken over, perpetuating the existence of power structures that now need a new narrative to legitimize themselves.

The secular eschatologies, such as that of orthodox Marxism, also represent another challenge, another temptation to look for the Kingdom of God on earth. The communitarian egalitarianism and internationalism that we find on the left, although in itself very valuable, can often be interpreted as the pseudo-ecclesial dimension. This is why the promise of an "ideal society" within history cannot be meaningfully reconciled with Orthodox Christian political theology.

This also means that a certain form of a (secular) "kingdom of God" on earth, which would be administered by the secular (pseudo-ecclesial) structures (e.g., states, corporations, experts), is, potentially at least, sought on both sides— "left" and "right." The solution to the existential problem is thus sought in the political realm, which is the reason why such political solutions and projects often acquire a metaphysical (and pseudo-ecclesial) significance and character.

What Do We Do?

Since political structures are governed by many, often conflicting interests and forces, one meaningful and justifiable way to organize these voices would be to provide mechanisms that maximize the freedom and opportunities of all members of society, provided this freedom would not interfere with the freedom and opportunities of other people. This means that, starting from some basic presuppositions of the Christian anthropology, such as the freedom and dignity of each human person, Christians can, in principle and especially in Western cultural contexts, support various types of secular, pluralistic, and democratic society, not as a God-given form of the social organization but as a *lesser evil*, in which the manifold issues stemming from our individualized existence can be addressed in a less oppressive way that affirms the values of human freedom and dignity. Although there can be no ideal system of government in this world, there can be better ones that, to a point, allow for a higher degree of manifestation of human freedom and well-being. Although there is nothing necessarily Christian in this claim, such a vision of society can be related to the Christian faith in personal freedom and in the human capacity to say "no" to all oppressive institutions, including religious ones.

There is, however, another reason why certain forms of *secular* society—those refusing to give a privileged position to any religious teaching or institution (including some of the dominant forms of *civil religions*)—can be beneficial for Christians and the institutional church, which suffers from many of the same weaknesses found in other social and political institutions. History shows us how the institutional church can mirror (other) social and political institutions by imitating the political models of a hierarchically organized society and instituting and/or affirming a vertical distribution of power. In this sense, a dialogue with a more "horizontally" organized society can be beneficial for the church. This would be particularly useful in societies with a strong Orthodox presence as the dominant and traditional faith: Secularizing the political sphere can prevent the secularization of the church by limiting the dangerous alliance between the church and state.[29]

The church and other religious communities should have the freedom to do their missionary work, but they should not need or wish to have the state behind them—advocating their goals and obtaining an ideological support in return—or to be linked to state instruments of oppression to "encourage" the people to move in the "right" direction. Democratic institutions and procedures—at least in theory if less common in practice—can help Christians rethink church structures from the point of view of Christian anthropology and eschatology. The democratic process can, in fact, remind Christians that some modern secular ideas and values have Christian roots, and that some distinctly modern phenomena, such as political pluralism, can remind the institution of the church to become more communitarian in its functioning, and, ultimately, more Christian.

One should also avoid being dogmatic about any particular sociopolitical models. What may work in one context is not necessarily applicable in another. If one aspires to forcibly impose, say, the idea of a Western type of political institutions onto societies with a very different set of institutions, values, and traditions, without understanding that complexity, one can easily produce more harm than good. Advocating, abstractly, the idea of (Western-type) democracy and imposing the (Western) understanding of this concept onto what seem to be (or are) autocratic systems can, instead, result in making those societies even less free. If one cares about real people, their freedom and well-being, it is crucial to understand local contexts and help people there (if they need and ask for help) develop what would best work for them under their given circumstances, rather than aggressively impose what seems to *us* to be good and just.

One should also be careful not to confuse the concepts that we use (such as "democracy") with realities, which are always much more complex than the overly simplified political science vocabulary can encompass. These concepts, although sometimes even useful, have only a relative and not an absolute value, and the content of what they refer to changes depending on the context in which they are used.

In conclusion, it is necessary to stress that Christian thinkers, and especially theologians, should be careful not to repeat mistakes from the past. Christian thinkers should refrain from constructing theological narratives that glorify and justify contemporary social orders (especially those in which they live) as ideal or "Christian" per se, no matter how great they may seem under the given circumstances. The "perfect society" from the Christian point of view can only be the eschatological reality of the Kingdom of God. Only there will interpersonal relationships, and the very existence of each human being, be based on freedom and love. In such a "society," the external and authoritative exercise of power will be neither possible nor needed.

When we look at the socio-political sphere from the point of view of Orthodox ("anarchist") political theology, we realize that we should refrain from constructing universally applicable, overarching, coherent "theories" of the socio-political that would be prescriptive. Such theories/theologies (if they aspire to be consistent with Christian faith) are neither possible nor desirable; they would necessarily end up in being another conceptual cage, another simplistic "horizon of meaning" whose purpose would be to give us simple prescriptions/guidelines to navigate through an extremely complex world, and to make us, ultimately, feel happy about ourselves. Another prescriptive, well-rounded political theory/ideology has the potential to become another civil religion (one can even claim that that is the precondition for their success) with an oppressive potential. That way it would affirm the very thing that Orthodox Christian "anarchism" seeks to deconstruct—various types of oppression—in order to affirm human freedom.

Even if we managed to create an all-encompassing theory that would affirm universal values, principles, and procedures (the "good") upon which a polity can be established and function in a harmonious way, such a theory (and such practice) would still not be able to change the mode of human existence, which Orthodox theology points to as the very source of oppression and which has metaphysical roots. Since the Orthodox political theology that I advocate here sees the oppressiveness manifested in the political sphere as part of a larger issue, which has its existential dimension, political instruments and theories are in principle incapable of resolving it. The tension and the paradox of every Christian engagement with the political (or the "world" for that matter) need to be preserved and embraced as such.

The tension, and even dualism, between the kingdom of necessity, domination, and power ("this world") and the Kingdom of God can help Christians and the church understand political institutions and ideas as functional and, to a limited degree, maybe even necessary categories that, however, do not have metaphysical significance per se. With such awareness, Christians can play a constructive role in contemporary society, always being an opposition to all power structures, oppressive mechanisms, and official ideologies (whether they are called "left" or "right," "atheist," or "Christian")—especially those that require obedience and submission. Their criticism and corrective role within society can be grounded not only in secular affirmations of human freedoms and rights, but also in Christian anthropology, which affirms human dignity, freedom, and love as metaphysical categories that will "inherit the Kingdom of God."

What Do We (Really) Do When We (Don't) Do (Something)?

If one aspires to understand, let alone to change, the contemporary social, political, and economic systems, and to do so from the perspective of "Orthodox Christian anarchism," one cannot overlook the issue of labor. Human labor is not only the central economic issue, but one of the central issues of any anthropology, including the Christian one.

Labor is today generally perceived as a coerced activity, something that people are forced to do in order to survive. This is typical of slave labor, but the logic and the kind of labor that we find in most capitalist systems is not fundamentally different. Wage labor has been perceived already in "classical" capitalist times as a new type of slavery,[30] and slave labor and capitalism are intrinsically linked. The contemporary version of slavery is precarious labor, in which human labor is reduced to a dehumanized resource, whose only purpose is to contribute to the replication and expansion of the global oligarchy. This new type of slavery, in which the workers are basically stripped of any rights or claims, is justified under the pretext of "efficiency," "competitiveness," and "rationalization." The result is that labor is perceived also by the workers as a coerced thing, and—because it is compelled—as something alienated from them, from who they are as human beings. The neoliberal system also addresses this issue: It commodifies this very alienation by offering, as a solution, the "consumerist paradise," in which buying "happiness" in shopping malls and through efficient online purchasing is advertised as the ideal, a way for people to just passively consume as long as they can afford it, and even if they cannot afford it, a loan will be waiting for them to keep them trapped in this "paradise" of the (alienated) production-consumption cycle.

From a Christian perspective, human labor is something that characterizes the human being in a very fundamental way. To work is to manifest ourselves as free and creative beings. That is why labor, if it is to be worthy of the dignity of the human being, must be free, and it must be creative. This way it acquires a very personal meaning and *communitarian* significance. Our work should be there to help us develop as human beings, to develop our talents. The products of our work, however, should not serve an individual, egotistic purpose; they should be there for others, for the entire community. Free labor is thus oriented toward others, not toward individual profits whose accumulation can actually harm others. Free work means that I work not because I *have to* (i.e., because somebody forces me, as in the labor camps, or because I will die of hunger if I don't work), but I work because I manifest my creative potentials through what I do: I manifest who I am, I grow as a human being. This *materialization* of human creativity is not individualistic. The products of my work, my talents, and my skills—whether they be medical services, scientific inventions, engineer's constructions, teaching, or art—are there for the sake of others and the entire community. Free and creative work becomes a manifestation of personhood; it helps both the producers and those who use the products of such work to grow as persons.

This dimension of human labor is well understood by Bulgakov. For him, human labor bears metaphysical significance, as the way of making the human being present outside the boundaries of one's individual self:

Labour, which is the actuality of human existence, objectivising human being beyond its own limits and making the world "objective" to us, is a living link between subject and object, the bridge by which the ego may go out into the world of [other] realities and which connects that world indivisibly with itself.[31]

Bulgakov further insists that human labor and the economic activities attached to it should never be ends in themselves:

Economic activity should never be allowed to become autonomous, making itself an end in itself, as economism would like to have it—growth in wealth for the sake of growth in wealth.[32]

The question, then, is: How can the current global system be changed? We witness internationalized global capital, but without the internationalization of the labor force, without their global initiative. Workers all over the earth are affected by the global economic system and the changes within it, and yet their initiatives have only very limited outreach: At best they can acquire a national significance. This is why the question of mobilization of workers and their global "class consciousness" needs to be addressed.

The conception of labor as a creative activity and something that should not be a matter of profits is probably the realm in which the authentically Christian perspective and an authentically leftist perspective can most easily understand each other. Linking work and profit-making diminishes the dignity of human labor, and human labor always reflects the dignity of the human being and the dignity of interhuman relations. Transforming the real *substance* of any human work—which includes creativity, knowledge, innovations, skills—into profit-oriented activity, with its market(ing) and business-driven logic, is the primordial sin of capitalism.

What is needed in many industrially developed societies is a culture of solidarity, compassion, and the acceptance of other human beings as human beings (sister or brother co-sufferers), instead of simply focusing on formal procedures, legal frameworks, and institutions (of power). Through the public discourse as well as through the system of education, a more communitarian culture can be developed against the culture of egotism, of hyperindividual self-indulgence that creates and sustains oppressive economic and political systems. On the other hand, in those societies in which people need to rely on tradition in their daily functioning to a much greater extent, where the role of the local community (family, tribe, village . . .) is much stronger in determining how one should behave, what one should hold as right or wrong, what one can think, etc., a meaningful anarchist intervention would be to expose the coercive potential of such collectivism. In such a context, bringing a sense of individualism as a possibility of someone to think, express him/herself, and act in the ways that differ from those preferred by the traditional or dominant culture would be a way of deconstructing the coercive elements of those local (formal and informal) power dynamics. In both of these cases, using not only different but to some extent opposite strategies (given the difference in social/cultural environments), a genuine anarchist intervention can bring more freedom and lead to a redefinition of the rules and procedures that a certain community is based on, to allow for more authentic, meaningful, and free interhuman relationships.

Excurse IV

CHRISTIAN "ANARCHISM" AND THE INSTITUTIONAL CHURCH

If "Orthodox Christian anarchism" is based on the affirmation of human dignity and freedom, and on the critique of all power structures and the illegitimate exercise of power—whether this exercise of power is practiced by individuals or institutions—and if this critique aspires to be consequential, then it should also be applied to the internal functioning of the institutional church and its power structures. In fact, Christians should be the first ones to criticize the negative phenomena within the church, in order to correct them, not from an abstract, secular, moralistic perspective, but as co-sufferers, as those who take upon themselves the responsibility for the church and desire to improve things. They should never instinctively defend everything that happens within the church. However, their position should be different from the positions of those (often secular and even openly antichurch circles) who assume the position of moral superiority, whose critique is aimed at harming the church.

The extent of the power and wealth of the institutional church within particular societies has varied throughout history. As we have seen from the previous chapters, there were times when the political structures were very unfavorable toward the church. This was the case during the persecutions in the Roman Empire, or under the totalitarian regimes in the twentieth century, or, more recently, under the fundamentalist Islamist regimes. In contrast to this, there were also times when the church was extremely favored by the political structures, which was the case in the Eastern Roman Empire, and which is still the case in most of the countries where Orthodoxy has been the dominant and traditional faith. There were also times when the church assumed a political role, similar to the church of Rome. All of this made an impact on the scale of power, wealth, and influence that the church was able to exercise within the given socio-political context. These different social and political contexts, each one in its own way, influenced both the way the ecclesial power structures work internally and how the exercise of power affects the institution of the church.

The organization of the ecclesial power structures has traditionally mirrored those of the state, which is not that surprising if we keep in mind some variations of the symphonic doctrine. Systems, institutions, regulations, "rules," and "law" were designed to secure the correct *traditio* of truth and true (correct) faith. This, at least up to a point, has been the case. However, what these systems and institutions have also been doing—and some could cynically remark that this has been, historically, their primary job—is the traditio of power structures, their strengthening and expansion. Many of those institutions, regulations, and laws ignored, in part or completely, a simple existential truth of Christianity: that *faith is an act of freedom*, and that true faith can only exist as a manifestation of human freedom and creativity that can never be petrified, scrutinized, and utilized by turning it into an (abstract) ethical or legal framework.

In spite of their pretense to be something else, something "not of this world," ecclesial power structures function in a similar way to other types of institutions of "this world." The institutional church—as a set of bureaucratic procedures, hierarchical organizations, financial transactions, and the like—suffers from the same expressions of the individualized existence such as greed, oppression, or self-affirmation. These illnesses of individualized existence do not miraculously disappear simply because we call it "church." Simply calling someone "Christian," or a "priest," does not transform them from individuals into being God's angels. They remain imperfect people who build imperfect institutions. Although one could expect the institutional church to follow, as much as possible, the logic of liturgy, it must be recognized that this is not often the case. Because priests are greedy and the church is dysfunctional, many become disappointed, up to the point that they become atheists. They should, however, understand that the reasons for that have to do with the individualized mode of existence, and that there is no reason why the institution of the church should, in a supernatural fashion, be spared from the illnesses that the people who make up the institutional church suffer from (as does the rest of the world). Such a "perfect" church would, moreover, have little to say to the very imperfect human beings we all are.

The Church, which is professed in the symbol of faith ("One Holy, Catholic and Apostolic"), is a fundamental aspect of Christianity, and Orthodoxy has traditionally insisted on the Catholicity as a vital feature of Christianity. The Church, in this sense, implies a *community*; it is the image of God's existence. As a liturgical gathering, the Church is the "place" and "time" (iconizing the eschatological beyond place and time) where our personhood is constituted. The Church is, thus, an eschatological reality; it refers to the communion of God with His creation in freedom and love. This is the meaning of the often-misunderstood idea, advanced in respect to Zizioulas's theology, that the

"Eucharist makes the Church."[33] This means that the eschatological identity of the Church in history does not exist first as an organization or an institution (with its hierarchy, administrative procedures, etc.), which then "performs" the liturgy (just as it performs many other rituals and functions). On the contrary, the act of performing the liturgy is the act of the constitution of the Church (in history). If this is the case, a distinction needs to be made between the liturgical gathering as making the Kingdom of God manifested "here" and "now" and the institutional organization of the church, with its bureaucracy, procedures, and bank accounts.

The first sharp difference between the logic of liturgy and the logic of institutional church structures is that the former is based on the logic of the new existence in which there is mutual service, affirmation of freedom, and love throughout the liturgical gathering. Liturgical gatherings should follow Christ's advice about rejecting the logic that prevails among the "rulers" and "high officials" (who "exercise authority" over Gentiles): In Matthew, we read, "it shall not be so among you" (Matthew 20:25–27). The logic of the liturgy (and, consequently, of the Church as liturgy) is remarkably "anarchic." In this collective work of the faithful, there is no externally imposed subordination of some to the others, but rather various services that the faithful perform, iconizing the logic of the eschatological Kingdom; the one who is the *first* is there to serve everyone (as the icon of Christ). All the members of the community are "sisters" and "brothers." This is a sign of the new identity that the baptized acquire, their new birth "from above" (John 3:3), and it means that the limitations of the biological hypostasis, individual(ized) existence, or our social class and material standing (which all belong to "this world") have been "washed away" (Hebrews 10:10) as that "sin" from which the individual is liberated through baptism. Everyone participates in the Eucharist as a "citizen" of the Kingdom of God, where biological and family roles (those of the father, mother, children, etc.), social and political functions, national identities, and so on, are overcome. Liturgy as the icon of the Kingdom can be called a manifestation of the *eschatological communism* or, put differently, *eschatological theocracy*.

On the other hand, however, the logic of the institutional church very often manifests itself in greed, corruption, power games, financial and political manipulation, the egotism of those performing ecclesial roles, and so forth. This exercise of power and domination within the institutional church is often defended under the pretext of mirroring the "Divine order," which is (mistakenly) envisioned as an organization with a pyramidal distribution of power and a vertical chain of command. This type of rationalization is quite comparable to similar rationalizations of political institutions claiming to be established or "blessed" by God.

Many ecclesiastical institutions continue to exploit the medieval under-standing of the *taxis* of the world, and the medieval *aura* that surrounds these institutions and their history. With its clear hierarchical order (often claimed to be based on the liturgical roles), vertical distribution of power, and the "episco-pocentric" organization, the institutional church resembles to a much higher degree medieval society than the liturgical logic. The role of the laity ("simple believers") in this system is equivalent to those of the feudal serfs—to be obe-dient and provide material security for the higher social classes. However, it would be misleading and wrong to think of the ecclesial power structures as just an archaic relic of the past, inefficient in the present-day context. On the con-trary, church power structures have proven to be very flexible and adaptable when it comes to embracing various modalities of their replication and survival. The way in which they often work today follows to quite a significant degree the functioning of the corporate sector.[34] The contrast between the church institu-tions organized this way and the Church as liturgy can hardly be clearer.

The usual way in which the dominant ecclesiastical order is theologically ar-ticulated is that it is based on the liturgical roles that derive their identity and meaning from their eschatological prototypes. Thus, the bishop, as the one pre-siding over the liturgical gathering, becomes the image of Christ in His Kingdom. Presbyters, in such imagery, stand for the apostles, deacons for angels, and the laity represents all the "citizens" of the Kingdom of God. The complicated li-turgical decorum that has evolved over the centuries often obscures the es-sential elements of the *iconicity* of the liturgical gathering, coming together *epi to auto*, offering the thanksgiving prayer, and sharing the common meal. Sometimes the elaborate formalism of the liturgical performance obscures the eschatologi-cal orientation and movement of the liturgical service, becoming more of a staged performance than the place where the faithful encounter God.

The problem, however, begins when the liturgical roles (of the bishops or presbyters) are mirrored in the institutional organization of the church and translated into the power structures. The mistake, in my view, that is often made lies in the translation of the liturgical roles (that stand in the relationship of iconicity to their eschatological prototypes, with the Eucharist and Christ, in his

Eucharistic presence-absence, at its center) into the institutional exercise of power (outside of the liturgy). And this is the crucial disconnect that makes this method of justification of the rigid, hierarchically organized institutional church problematic. In other words, iconizing Christ at the liturgical gathering—which is the role of the one who presides over the liturgy—is by no means *naturally* or *necessarily* linked with the administrative duties and the exercise of power that occur within the church administration outside of the liturgy. In still other words, there is no theological (icon-based) reason why someone who presides over the liturgical gathering should also be a full-time manager of the (institutional) church property or bank accounts, be the "boss" of his "subordinates," in charge of virtually all aspects of their lives. The purpose of particular liturgical roles is to iconize the existence of those who love and are being loved in a "class-less society," where there is not any exercise of power whatsoever. Church as the community of those who love and who aspire to transcend the limitations of the individualized existence mirrors this by offering a common Eucharistic meal, at which God Himself serves, and we serve each other. These roles cannot be mirrored in the administrative and institutional contexts because the premise is false: Power or hierarchy cannot be assumed within "this world" on the basis of a person's liturgical role because the liturgical logic recognizes neither power nor hierarchy. Applying the liturgical logic of the function and meaning of the "first" (bishop) to the nonliturgical context (e.g., of the institutional church, state, corporation) does not result in spreading this logic outside the liturgical context, but rather in obscuring the meaning of the liturgical roles. What in the liturgical context means to be the "first" (i.e., to be the icon of Christ, and to serve everyone) often turns out to be the despotic "first" outside the liturgical context, where the personal relationships of love are replaced by institutional power, in which everyone serves the "first."

The historical justification for this *taxis* can be found in the Apostolic Canons (28, 29, and 31) that specify the primacy of bishops in governing the church, and especially church property. This can be understood as an attempt to preserve the strictly church business within the church structures, limiting, in this way, the possibility of excessive interference of other (e.g., political) factors in the governance of the church. Rethinking the power structures within the church does not exclude the bishops or priests from the management of the church and its property, but the extent and character of their power in these matters should be revisited, especially in traditional Orthodox contexts.

There are many practical, not strictly liturgical issues that Christians need to take care of in between the liturgical gatherings to enable those very gatherings to take place. Some degree of institutional church organization is very probably inevitable, even if it is only reflected in performing certain practical services for the benefit of the whole community. The point is that this institutional infrastructure should try to serve the Church as liturgy, and not vice versa. It should not confuse the administrative element—which often completely obscures the liturgical/eschatological identity of the Church—with the liturgical one. The institutional church infrastructure should not be simply or primarily a professional (business) entity, largely or completely divorced from the liturgical logic.

As Christians aspire to change their mode of existence—which is the purpose of the liturgical gathering—this changing of the mode of existence is clearly not something that they can forget about in between these liturgical gatherings. This shift in the logic of existence requires a constant effort; the new logic of existence draws its identity and strength from the liturgy and the Kingdom of God, but it is a transformative experience in all aspects of Christian lives. To make the institutional church better serve the Church as the eschatological community, the institutional infrastructure should not be *oppressive*. The exercise of power should be kept to its absolute minimum, always trying to affirm our love for other human beings and forgiveness. The church should aspire to mirror the logic of liturgy to a greater extent in all aspects of its functioning, from the decision-making process and church governance to missionary and charity work, and—yes—the conceptual tools that are used to articulate all of these.[35]

Just as with the political sphere, I do not think that one should be prescriptive here and formulate certain *models* that should be adopted and practiced in each local church worldwide. All local contexts are different, and local traditions, cultures, and customs vary to a significant extent, so the type of organization that makes sense to a local church in a South American city might not necessarily be applicable or useful in a central Siberian village, and vice versa. However, Christians should always try to advance love as the mode through which they relate to others and themselves, as much as it is possible and no matter how difficult or imperfect this may be in its concrete application. It should never be about formal perfection, but about attempts (and failures) to acquire the perfection of love.

One way toward a more meaningful institutional organization of the church could be the *deprofessionalization* of the priestly service. By this I certainly do not mean that those performing liturgical services should be less competent, educated, or dedicated to what they do but rather that, whenever possible, they should not perform these services as a full-time job. This step, although almost unthinkable under the present rigidity of the ecclesial power structures, would be the most logical from the point of view of the Eucharistic theology. The professional clergy obscures the basic identity of the Church as the icon of the (future) Kingdom, which means an icon of the new mode of existence, by merging the professional, institutional, and other concerns that primarily belong to the logic of "this world" with the iconic function of the liturgical service.[36] All of the baptized are *priests* of God's creation, and all of the so-called "laity" ("people of God") have many different jobs they do for a living, but then they assume their roles in liturgy as the icon of the Kingdom at the liturgical gathering. Would it not be logical then to apply the same logic to the clergy (bishops and priests)? If priests and bishops practiced the same kind of life—if they were doctors, artists, engineers, taxi drivers, or bakers and then performed their specific priestly roles when the Church gathered together for a liturgical celebration—this would, arguably, significantly change the power (im)balance and would allow for Christians, including many priests, to witness the Kingdom of God much more convincingly. The only exception here to the above list of professions would be those occupations that compel individuals to act, on a daily basis, in a way that is in direct contradiction with the personal mode of existence (for instance, participation in the police and military forces or higher echelons of bank or state management).

However, this proposal probably belongs to a very distant future, and it might not work in every social and cultural context. In some cases, the argument can be made, the amount of work and attention needed from the bishop to keep his diocese in order or to advance it is such that it does require a full-time position. It is, nevertheless, important to work on this "re-evangelization" of the church, making the faithful more aware of the important ecclesial and theological issues and providing a space for a more articulate and meaningful participation of the laity in the church life. Even though this proposal for a *reliturgization* (or *re-eschatologization*) of the church may seem radical, I do not advocate here any revolutionary methods. I advocate practices of love, mutual support, working together, and education as a path to long-term change for the better. Simply abandoning the present structures or reforming the church in a manner in which many Protestant communities function, would not help our salvation and would threaten the ethos of the Orthodox church that, in spite of the many problems attached to it, is worthy of preservation and affirmation. We also witness to the fact that there are bishops who are primarily spiritual *fathers* to their priests and all the faithful people, and who, with admirable devotion, energy, and love serve their local churches, transforming them into real icons of the Kingdom of God. This means that manifesting the transformative power of the Kingdom of God in this world can be done even under the current organization of the church.

That means that simply making the church "laity-dominated" (or governed) instead of "clergy-dominated" would not necessarily be very helpful either, and would not affirm the liturgical identity of the church. Experiments in this vein have been practiced in the US, for instance (probably under the impact of Protestant denominations), and some have, as a result, wound up with laity-dominated church boards (icons of the corporate CEOs) that often terrorize local priests and even bishops. The opposite is the reality in most of the traditional Orthodox countries where, more often than not, bishops and priests mirror the roles of the CEOs in the way they exercise a strictly vertical distribution of power, demanding absolute obedience. None of these modes of managing the church reflects the logic of liturgy.

One should also note that present church structures, although themselves immersed in the deep waters of the world that "lies in evil," could still play a positive role if the will was found. They are among very few islands in the contemporary world that still have the resources to resist the all-penetrating business and marketing logic and the consumer mentality. They could be witnesses to and a haven for a different, non-business or -profit-driven work ethic, and for interpersonal relationships that are not based on alienation, domination, fear, or submissiveness. Present church structures could affirm the human creativity and dignity that global capitalism ruthlessly attacks. They could offer a model of cooperative work that would be very different from the tragic vision of the human being and the world that the current capitalist system is presenting to us.

The End and the Beginning

In conclusion, I would like to summarize the main ideas presented in this text.

Christianity should not be understood as a particular teaching, system of rules, or codified practices. It should also not be understood as a political or social program, an ethical or legal system, or ideology. The main purpose of (Orthodox) Christianity is not to offer a description of "what the world looks like," but to proclaim a new mode of existence. The Church is there to offer the *means* for acquiring this new existence, to facilitate this existential change.

The very act of aspiring to be in the mode of the Kingdom of God becomes the way to give testimony to this new (eschatological) existence, to proclaim the Kingdom. The Kingdom is being manifested in history through the very attempt to change one's existence. In offering/practicing this new mode of existence, Christians, of course, also interpret the meaning of the world around them, and offer various accounts vis-à-vis "what, why, and how" questions. However, all these accounts or interpretations are limited, imperfect, subject to our partial knowledge and/or experience, and dependent on the means we use to give these accounts (i.e., words, images). They are also informed by the *Zeitgeist* of the time we live in. This is the reason why a text—even that of the Holy Scripture—cannot "contain" the Truth in principle, but only point to it. Focusing solely on the text, expecting the Truth to be buried in the "original" meaning of the text, is not only a sign of bad epistemology; this method always bears an imminent danger of turning that text (i.e., a particular interpretation of the text) into another idol/ideology that requires reverence.

This is the reason why Orthodox Christians do not approach the New Testament as the Truth incarnate. If a text, a book, or a system of rules or teachings were a sufficient (or even appropriate) means of salvation, God could have sent us those texts, books, and laws, saving us all (not least Himself!) a lot of trouble. This is how the absence of any writings from Christ and the inconsistences (also *deficiencies*) found in the Biblical text can be interpreted: The accounts are imperfect (and yet important!) testimonies to what "we have heard, which we have seen with our eyes, which we have looked at and our hands have touched" (1 John 1:1), fully acknowledging their limited nature and scope since "Jesus did many other things as well. If every one of them were written down, I suppose that even the whole world would not have room for the books that would be written" (John 21:25). They are there, in all their limitations and *imperfections,* not to diminish the importance of the living (and loving) encounter with the living (and loving) God. The *event* of Christ is crucial: his making the Kingdom present through His Incarnation, Death, and Resurrection. Thus, Christian truth—although it needs to be interpreted and "made sense of" in each and every historical period—is not reducible to any (theological) concepts or texts. Christian Truth is Christ. This Truth can only be grasped through an effort to make an existential change, allowing Christ to live in us.

The same holds true for Christian theologians and Christian attempts to offer an answer to the many issues and challenges that history presents. Sometimes it is important to formulate theological perspectives vis-à-vis particular issues (including socio-political ones). However, in spite of the importance of these issues and particular views, the eschatological perspective remains the only normative one. In this case (following the apophatic tradition), the normative is open-ended. Paradoxically enough, freedom becomes the only relevant *nomos*. We can and we should give our best to come up with *authentic theologies*, but we should never turn any particular account into an all-encompassing, systematic, and fully consistent system of ideas (i.e., ideology) that is supposed to provide answers to all questions, replacing a personal encounter and the eschatological (open-ended) "normativity" with a discursive normativity and texts.

Theology needs to keep the (theological) discourse open, without ready-made, instant solutions that become abstract dogmas. Those abstract dogmas are, then, very often automatically applied to all of the contexts, ignoring their differences and complexities. This often ends up in totalitarianisms of various kinds. Theology (especially "critical theology"), should have a certain level (and a certain type) of *inconsistency*, as a corrective factor.[1]

When it comes to the social and political realm, Christians should always keep in mind that all political structures and social models are necessarily deficient; they all exhibit ecclesial longing, in which they manifest themselves as deficient communities in a fallen state, composed of individuals governed by (more or less oppressive) laws and interests instead of love. The fundamental problem of social and political communities is not social or political, but existential. The solution is in the restored communitarian sense (of love), the one with an ontic significance. This, however, transgresses the boundaries of history.

In addressing the manifold challenges that the present-day power structures present us with, Christian thinkers should be very careful not to repeat the mistakes of the past. They should never construct theological narratives that glorify or justify any social order or ideology as ideal or "Christian." The *perfect society*, from a Christian point of view, can only be the Kingdom of God. Only there the interhuman relations and the very existence of each human being is based on freedom and love. In such a "society," an external and authoritative exercise of power is neither possible nor needed.

The tension between the kingdom of necessity, domination, and power ("this world") and the Kingdom of God can help Christians and the Church understand concrete political institutions and procedures in functional rather than in metaphysical terms. With such awareness, the Church and Christians can play a very constructive role in contemporary society, being always in opposition to all of the orders of power and to all oppressive mechanisms and official ideologies, regardless of the form in which they might appear (even if that form is "Christian"). Their criticism and corrective role within the society can be grounded not only in secular affirmations of human freedoms and rights, but in Christian anthropology, which affirms human dignity, freedom, and love as metaphysical categories that will "inherit the Kingdom of God."

Viewed from this perspective, Christianity appears as being against all systems and ideological constructs (including those formally "Christian") that are understood as more valuable than the human being him/herself, in the concreteness and uniqueness of human personal identity. Christianity must be against all the systems, rules, or orders that are imposed (internally or externally) as a necessity. Authentic Christianity advocates—and indeed participates in—the creation of the world that is the result of our freedom, not independent of it. From the perspective of Christian faith, if something is "necessary," or if there is compelling "evidence" for it, it is not (ontically) true.[2]

Absolute power is absolute slavery. The quest for power is a diabolic expression of the quest for freedom, a caricature of freedom that manifests itself in the existential sickness—the desire to dominate over other human beings, to be "first," to have control over the world. Although it is rooted in the desire to be (absolutely) free—which, then, translates into the desire to be on "top," to dictate rather than to be dictated to—it, in fact, leads into the opposite direction, resulting in the complete submission, slavery, and impotence that characterize the "kings."

Focusing on love as a mode of existence renders ethical or legal systems irrelevant and unworthy of the dignity of the human being. To love is not only more, but also something different from merely "good," "desirable," or "allowed" behavior. When you love someone or something, you are compassionate; you desire the life (existence) of those you love to continue and to expand until it reaches the fullness of the everlasting free and loving existence.[3] From this perspective, both ethical and legal systems appear as the signs of the fallen existence, something that stands for the very nature of the fallen world rather than any "ideal" to which the human being should strive for.

Only through freedom and love can the human being become what they can and should be: Godlike beings who respond, freely and creatively, to God's love, to the call to partake in the Divine life and the communion of the Divine persons.

To make the leap of faith, to be truly free, requires courage. Christianity, when authentic, takes the human being outside his/her comfort zone, and faces him/her with his/her own being, with the horrors of the individualized self. Christianity is an existential risk, something that requires an existential change. Looking from this perspective, science, religion, morality and rationality, but also, one could claim, all facets of culture, although positive in their own domains, function as those comfort zones in which certain *meanings* are constructed and kept, protecting the human being from the meaninglessness (in the most profound sense) of the reality around us. Eschatologically oriented Christianity seems to pose the existential questions of the human being—the questions of freedom, life, and death—in the most radical way. Rejection of faith (as freedom) in the name of the absolutization of reason or logic, looks from this existential perspective as a naïve epistemology, which reflects even more naïve ontology. It turns out to be quite similar to the naïve religious narratives that advocate obedience to authority or simple "follow-the-rules" ethics, stubbornly ignoring other aspects of historical existence for the sake of their own comfort and the sense of security that they receive from the (illusionary) meaning they construct.

Freedom, creativity, and love, as the eschatological foundations of human existence, constitute the basis for "Orthodox Christian anarchism." It is not primarily a political philosophy (except in a very general sense), but an approach to "this world" and its power structures based on an eschatologically rooted ontology and anthropology. It is a radical intervention into the entire fabric of the constructs and comfort zones we make (some of which are conditioned biologically, others culturally, yet others psychologically and so on) in order to protect ourselves from confronting the unpleasant world we live in, and the unpleasant reality of our own individualized being. This confrontation, however, seems to be necessary for salvation, for a creative act of entering a new existence.

Dealing with the issues of this world involves embracing the paradox that very often we cannot simply do the "right" or "good" thing (from a Christian perspective), and that often doing a good thing (from one perspective) means doing another evil as well (as in the case of "just wars" for instance). Although there are certain principles and values that can be affirmed, and upon which Christians can act in the world, Christian enterprise goes beyond "right" and "wrong" into the realm of love, freedom, and creativity, as existential categories, something that cannot fully be manifested except as "new creation."

Authentic Christianity and Christians are, and will always remain, a marginal voice in this world. There has never been and there will be no "Christian states" or "Christian societies" (except for the liturgical communities) within history. Christians are the "salt of the world" (Matthew 5:13). That is why they have never formed, and can never form, a dominant cultural view: One cannot ground a state or a culture based on existential freedom and love. This is where, when it comes to the socio-political sphere, the position of Christians is similar to the position of critically engaged intellectuals and dissidents. Being on the margins, swimming against the current, as it were, is the natural state of those who are "in the world," but are not "of the world."

In this understanding of anarchism as skepticism toward every exercise of power, the focus on the human being and human freedom should never be replaced by abstract dogmas, coherent political theories, or ideologies (including the traditional anarchist ones). We should always remember that sometimes we gain more freedom by establishing a system (social, political, administrative), and at other times, under different circumstances, more freedom is gained by destroying a system. When one "regime of freedom" is established within the boundaries of this world (e.g., when "free" nation states are established against imperial oppression), it becomes another regime of unfreedom. When the prophets of freedom become the defenders of the established, dominant (positive) values, they often turn into tyrants who terrorize others in the name of those ideals, ideas, and theories that brought them into the position of power, where they can be "official" spokespersons for that "regime of (un)freedom."

Since Christianity is primarily focused on existential issues, Christian theology is both transcendental (focused on eschatological things) and very practical in its focus on the ways in which the human experience of the "here" and "now" relates to this new, eschatological existence.[4] This means that other issues that are related to our historical existence (for example, social, ethical, aesthetical, or, say, agricultural concerns) are secondary. One should not be too preoccupied with this world (which is "passing away") and its concerns. That said, one should not understand this (as Orthodox theology and Church practice have often been [mis]understood) as a withdrawal from the world or indifference to "worldly" affairs. *Faith without works is dead* (James 2:20), which is another way of saying that actualized faith and the existential change it generates are elements of the same process—the former leads to the latter; the latter makes the former actual. There cannot be a simple withdrawal from the world, nor can there be the acquisition of this new existence without historical existence. The point is to start from this existence, and to practice the new being (that is eschatological in nature) already "here" and "now," making the eschatology present and active in history. Christians should practice the new being diligently (even though that practicing will always be imperfect), trying to creatively transgress the boundaries of the individualized being. Above all, they should love. This is the way to *do* theology and to make the glory of God shine in this world.

Rome, 2018

ACKNOWLEDGMENTS

One needs to give credit where credit is due.

I am grateful to my dear friends and colleagues Nadieszda Kizenko, Vlada Stanković, Frederick Lauritzen, and Valentina B. Izmirlieva. Their extensive knowledge and kindness helped me significantly to improve the manuscript.

My gratitude extends to Carla Tumbas, who invested a lot of time and energy in addressing the manifold formal aspects of the production of this text. Without her help, this wouldn't be the same book.

I also want to thank many other dear friends and colleagues who helped me form and improve my theological and philosophical views. Through endless discussions over many years (not to forget many memorable parties as well), I sharpened some of the ideas presented here. More importantly yet, they allowed me to *experience* what a Christian theological enterprise is ultimately about, and how it can be practiced.

Thank you and cheers!

NOTES

Introduction

1. Throughout the text, the difference between the concept of "Church" (capital "C") and the concept of "church" (lowercase "c") is maintained. "Church" refers here to the "One Holy, Catholic, and Apostolic Church," which is identical to the "mystical" or "eschatological" Church. This Church stands for the communion between God, human beings, and the rest of creation. That means that the "Church" ultimately signifies the reality of the Kingdom of God, which is manifested in history in its "iconic" form in the liturgy. The other concept, the "church," refers to the institutional aspect of the Christian community, to the ecclesial administration that normally functions similarly to the rest of the institutions of "this world." The intention in making this distinction is to say that although these terms do not refer to two completely separate and disconnected spheres, they cannot be simply merged either. The distinction—although not necessarily a sharp contrast—must be preserved.

Anarchism and (Orthodox) Christianity: An (Un)Natural Alliance?

1. "Anarchy is terror, the creed of bomb-throwing desperadoes wishing to pull down civilization. Anarchy is chaos, when law and order collapse and the destructive passions of man run riot. Anarchy is nihilism, the abandonment of all moral values and the twilight of reason. . . . In the popular imagination, in our everyday language, anarchy is associated with destruction and disobedience but also with relaxation and freedom." Marshall 2008, ix.

2. "Politics is the science of liberty. The government of man by man (under whatever name it be disguised) is oppression. Society finds its highest perfection in the union of order with anarchy." Proudhon 1876, 286.

3. See Michael Bakunin, "Marx, the Bismarck of Socialism":

> The State has always been the patrimony of some privileged class or other; a priestly class, an aristocratic class, a bourgeois class, and finally a bureaucratic class. . . . But in the People's State of Marx, there will be, we are told, no privileged class at all. . . . There will . . . be no longer any privileged class, but there will be a government, and note this well, an extremely complex government. . . . It will be the reign of *scientific intelligence*, the most aristocratic, despotic, arrogant and contemptuous of all regimes. There will be a new class, a new hierarchy of real and pretended scientists and scholars, and the world will be divided into a minority ruling in the name of knowledge and an immense ignorant majority. (In Krimerman and Perry 1966, 87)

4. One of the most famous examples of this is the Haymarket incident of 1886 in Chicago. A bomb explosion, which happened during the workers' protests, was used by the police and the legal system as a pretext to execute and jail several workers/anarchists, without even a semblance of a fair trial (their guilt, *nota bene*, was never established). Repressive measures against anarchists (or those labeled as such) were also regular in Czarist Russia. They continued during the revolutionary time and in the time of civil war (following the October Revolution). It seems that Lenin considered Russian anarchists the most dangerous enemy of the Bolsheviks during the civil war. See Goldman 1923.

5. Quoted in Chomsky 2014, 1.

6. Noam Chomsky, "The Kind of Anarchism I Believe in, and What's Wrong with Libertarians." Noam Chomsky interviewed by Michael S. Wilson (May 28, 2013), available at: http://chomsky.info/interviews/20130528.htm.

7. Chomsky 2014, 2. See also Rudolf Rocker's understanding of anarchism quoted therein.

8. Francis Dupuis-Déri, "Anarchy in Political Philosophy," in Jun and Wahl, eds. 2010, 13.

9. See Daniel Guérin 1980, 11.

10. See Stirner 2000:

> What is left when I have been freed from everything that is not I? Only I, and nothing but I. But freedom has nothing to offer to this I himself. As to what is now to happen further after I have become free, freedom is silent. . . . Now why, if freedom is striven after for love of the I after all, why not choose the I himself as beginning, middle, and end? . . . My freedom becomes complete only when it is my—might. (148, 151)

11. See Uri Gordon, "Power and Anarchy: In/equality + In/visibility in Autonomous Politics":

The vacuum created by the lack of formal communication structures is filled by the existing friendship-networks among part of the group's participants. This creates a friendship-elite—a class of leaders who form an in-group, while those who are not part of it remain disempowered. . . . The lack of formal structure 'becomes a smokescreen for the strong or the lucky to establish unquestioned hegemony over others. . . . The rules of how decisions are made are known only to a few and awareness of power is curtailed by those who know the rules, as long as the structure of the group is informal.' (In Jun and Wahl, eds. 2010, 52)

12. This is an old temptation that goes back to the very early days of Christianity. Not only the mainstream Christianity, which often promoted its official political theologies by confusing the eschatological Kingdom of God with the "kingdom of this world," but also many alternative (sometimes also perceived as "anarchist" or "proto-anarchist") political theologies, that were against oppression or vertical organization of church/society, did not resist this temptation. One can, for instance, understand Pelagianism as one such attempt to create a "perfect" society—the Church—within the boundaries of history:

> Peter Brown . . . reminds us that what is essentially at stake in the Pelagian dispute is the idea of the Church as the community of all Christians. The Church is the institutional name for the being-together of those who are Christians. ". . . . For Pelagius and the Pelagian the aim remained not to produce the perfect individual, but, above all, the perfect religious group. . . . Thus the most marked feature of the Pelagian movement is far from being its individualism: it is its insistence that the full code of Christian behaviors, the *Christian Lex*, should be imposed, in all its rigours, on every baptized member of the Catholic Church." (Richard Fitch, "The Pelagian Mentality: Radical Political Thought in Fifth Century Christianity," in Christoyannopoulos, ed. 2011b, 23–24)

This approach (which Fitch perceives as *anarchist*), when viewed from an Orthodox Christian perspective, lacks an eschatological orientation. It forgets that the goal for Christians is not any kind of perfection (including moral) within the boundaries of this world, but a communion with God and the new mode of existence. It is, therefore, not surprising that a certain Pelagian mentality underpins many Christian anarchist discourses. Sometimes it is not any formal perfection, of either an individual or a group, that is advanced as the foundation of Christian anarchism, but *love*, which, by all means, does represent the very core of Christian faith. As Christoyannopoulos notes, "Christian anarchists believe that a just social order can only be secured through the persistent enactment of brotherly love, not through any system of rewards and punishments policed by a scolding father. The ordering principle of society would thus be love, not the threat of violence" (Alexandre J. M. E. Christoyannopoulos, "Christian Anarchism: A Revolutionary Reading of the Bible," in Jun and Wahl, eds. 2010, 150). What one could question in these cases is not the affirmation of love (against violence or rewards), which is certainly correct, but rather the implicit expectation that a "just" social order can be achieved in history, and that it can be based on love. An even more radical case can be found in some Protestant theological approaches that saw the importance of the church being inversely proportional to the rise and development of the Christian state—the more the Christian state is manifested in history, the less important and prominent the church becomes. See Tihomirov 2008, 145–46.

13. See Stiglitz 2012, 2015.

14. See Dawes 2010.

15. According to *Forbes*, as of May 2017, the estimated market capital of Apple was $752 billion (https://www.forbes.com/companies/apple/); Google's brand value was $101.8 bn. (https://www.forbes.com/companies/google/); Microsoft's market cap was $507.5 bn. (https://www.forbes.com/companies /microsoft/). For the purposes of comparison, according to the World Bank, the GDPs of the following world countries in 2016 were Bulgaria: $53.2 billion, South Sudan: $9 bn, Congo: $7.8 bn, Somalia: $6.2 bn. See https://data .worldbank.org/data-catalog/GDP-ranking-table/.

16. "For the anarchist, freedom is not an abstract philosophical concept, but the vital concrete possibility for every human being to bring to full development all the powers, capacities, and talents with which nature has endowed him, and turn them to social account." Daniel Guérin, in Chomsky 2014, 2.

17. See Pierre-Joseph Proudhon, *God Is Evil, Man Is Free*, 1849.

18. "It is evident that this terrible mystery is inexplicable—that is, absurd, because only the absurd admits of no explanation. It is evident that whoever finds it essential to his happiness and life must renounce his reason, and return, if he can, to naive, blind, stupid faith. . . . Then all discussion ceases, and nothing remains but the triumphant stupidity of faith." Bakunin, "God and State," in Bakunin 1973, 117.

19. "Man has felt like a slave and rejected the yoke of God. Atheism sprang out of the very heart of the Church and the notion of freedom became prominent again." Zizioulas 1975, 433.

The Symphonia Doctrine: Introduction

1. As Cyril Hovorun notices, the term "symphonia" as a descriptor of church-state relations did not play a relevant role in the "Byzantine" empire.

> First of all, the Byzantines did not call the relationship between their church and the state a symphony. In the more than 3,800 occurrences of the word

συμφωνία and its variations in the *Thesaurus Linguae Graecae*, there are almost no references to the relationship between the church and the state. During the entire period of the supposed symphony between the church and the state, their *modus vivendi* was not called symphony. Symphony meant other things, such as agreement, a pact or concord, as well as consent within the churches or within the polity, but not between them. (Hovorun 2016, 282)

2. "Even when the ideals of a *symphonia* approach cannot be realized because its basic presuppositions do not exist in the body politic, the values *symphonia* supports and encourages can find some partial realization. The *symphonia* approach can point to values and procedures that will help the state realize, at least in measure, some of its goals and purposes in a moral and ethical context." Harakas 1992, 260. See also Harakas 1976.

3. Although more than half a century old, Francis Dvornik's monumental study, *Early Christian and Byzantine Political Philosophy: Origins and Background*, volume I, is still relevant in this respect. See Dvornik 1966.

Early Christianity: Who's Conducting "Symphonia"?

1. All quotations from the Old and the New Testaments follow the New International Version, except where the NIV significantly diverges from other standard versions in English, or from the meaning expressed in the Greek text, in which case the (New) King James version, and other translations, are used in order to render the Biblical quotations more precise.

2. The question of "authorship" of many of the early Christian documents, including the "pastoral epistles" has long been debated (for a summary of the main arguments, see Arland J. Hultgren, "The Pastoral Epistles," in Dunn 2003, 142–44). In my view, the quest for the "original authorship" of these texts (just as the quest of their "original" meaning) reflects a (secular) modern approach, which applies typically modern (Protestant) ideas about what constitutes the text, its meaning and its origin, that are often projected and imposed unto the past. Since the epistles have been treated as authoritative from the very early period, since the question of authorship is not crucial for the present analysis, and, finally, for the sake of clarity, I will simply refer to the epistles using their traditionally accepted names, and to their "author" as "Paul," even though it is clear that the authorship in many cases might easily be collective.

3. The enthusiasm that can be read from these early documents about the political rule and appreciation of authority and even institutions of the ancient Roman Empire becomes more intelligible if we keep in mind the extremely unfavorable historical context in which the early Christian community was trying to consolidate itself. In this sense, this political theology can be read as an attempt of the early Christian leaders to "make peace" between this Jewish sect

and the Roman authorities, and to brand Christianity as something that was not subversive to the dominant political order (at least not as subversive as some of the other radical, prophetic Jewish movements). For the dynamics of the constructions of the image of "otherness" in the earliest period of Christianity, see Pagels 1996.

4. Theophilus of Antioch, *To Autolycus*, Book 1, in O'Donovan and O'Donovan, eds. 1999, 14.

5. For a more developed argument in this respect, see Džalto 2013b.

6. *First Letter of Clement to the Corinthians*, in Ehrman 2003, 1:145.

7. See Clement of Alexandria, *Stromateis*, Book 1:

> We can divide kingship as follows: One kind is divine; that is the rule of God and of his holy Son, by whom the earthly and external goods are supplied as well as perfect happiness. . . . The second kind, inferior to purely rational (*logikon*) divine administration, brings to the task of kingly rule only the active part of the soul (*thumoeides*); which is how Heracles ruled the Argives and Alexander the Macedonians. The third kind aims at only one thing, to conquer and overthrow. . . . The fourth kind of kingship, and the worst, is that which operates at the promptings of passion; Sardanapalus is an example, and there are others who have made their aim complete gratification of the passions. (In O'Donovan and O'Donovan, eds. 1999, 32–33)

8. This theory (which, after all, may not entirely be a figment of imagination) can also be found in non-Christian sources such as Numenius of Apamea. See Guthrie 1917, 2, 101, 106, and 146.

9. Clement of Alexandria, *Stromateis*, Book 1, in O'Donovan and O'Donovan, eds. 1999, 35.

10. Origen, *Against Celsus*, Book 8, in O'Donovan and O'Donovan, eds. 1999, 41. See also Homer, *Iliad*, Book 2.

11. See Origen, *Against Celsus*, Book 8:

> Indeed, the more pious a man is, the more effective he is in helping the emperors—more so than the soldiers who go out into the lines and kill all the enemy troops that they can. . . . [H]ow much more reasonable is it that, while others fight, Christians also should be fighting as priests and worshipers of God, keeping their right hands pure and by their prayers to God striving for those who fight in a righteous cause and for the emperor who reigns righteously, in order that everything which is opposed and hostile to those who act righteously may be destroyed? (In O'Donovan and O'Donovan, eds. 1999, 44)

12. Tertullian, *To Scapula*, in *Latin Christianity: Its Founder, Tertullian*, http://www.documentacatholicaomnia.eu/03d/0160-0220,_Tertullianus,_Ad _Scapulam_[Schaff],_EN.pdf, 160.

13. Tertullian, *Apology*, in Bettenson and Maunder, eds. 2011, 8.

Divus Constantinus and Court Theology in the Eastern Empire

1. Digeser 2012, 12.

2. Digeser 2012, 12.

3. Digeser 2012, 34.

4. Lactantius, *Divine Institutes*, Book 5, in O'Donovan and O'Donovan, eds. 1999, 49.

5. Digeser 2012, 45.

6. Early Christian sources (Eusebius and Orosius) mention Philip the Arab (ca. 204–49) as an earlier precedent. However, the legend depicts his Christianity more as a matter of personal devotion than a matter of institutional and broader political significance. One way to understand this legend is to see it as an attempt to construct a narrative about the widely spread existence of (crypto) Christians in the pre-Constantine period, not only among the general population, but also among the highest echelons of Roman society, including the emperors. This reflects the desire, as Dagron puts it, "to show that imperial Rome had been virtually Christian from the start and that the conversion of Constantine was not an absolute beginning but the moment when the schema of a temporal order planned from time immemorial and under way since Augustus emerged into the light of day," and "to make the Christian age coincide with the beginning of the empire, and not with its Christianisation." Dagron 2007, 128.

7. Charanis 1974, 31.

8. Among the numerous studies dedicated to the subject, see Elliot 1996 and Leithart 2010.

9. As Peter Brown points out, "As the fourth century progressed, it became increasingly plain that the Christian bishops, by conquering the cities from the bottom up, were in a position to determine the policies of the emperor." Brown 2005, 78.

10. For a detailed examination of the use of the title of pontifex maximus, especially in the fourth century and after, see Cameron 2016.

11. See Dijkstra and Espelo 2017.

12. Eusebius, "Speech on the Dedication of the Holy Sepulcher Church," in O'Donovan and O'Donovan, eds. 1999, 58.

13. Eusebius, "A Speech for the Thirtieth Anniversary of Constantine's Accession," in O'Donovan and O'Donovan, eds. 1999, 60.

14. Eusebius, *Ecclesiastical History*, X:9 (in Eusebius 2018, 381–82). The original account had been written before Crispus fell from mercy and was killed by Constantine, resulting in his *damnatio memoriae*.

15. See Eusebius, "A Speech for the Thirtieth Anniversary of Constantine's Accession":

Let, then, our emperor, on the testimony of truth itself, be declared alone worthy of the title; who is dear to the supreme Sovereign himself, who alone is free, nay, who is truly lord, above the thirst of wealth, superior to sexual desire, victorious even over natural pleasures, controlling, not controlled by, anger and passion. He is indeed an emperor and bears a title corresponding to his deeds, a Victor in truth, who has gained the victory over those passions which overmaster the rest of men, whose character is formed after the divine original of the supreme sovereign and whose mind reflects as in a mirror the radiance of his virtues, Hence is our emperor perfect in discretion, in goodness, in justice, in courage, in piety, in devotion to God; he truly and only is a philosopher, since he knows himself, and is fully aware that supplies of every blessing are showered on him from a source quite external to himself, even from heaven itself. (In O'Donovan and O'Donovan, eds. 1999, 62)

16. See again Eusebius, "A Speech for the Thirtieth Anniversary of Constantine's Accession":

And then with thanksgiving and praise, the tokens of a grateful spirit, to the author of his victory, he proclaimed this triumphant sign by monuments as well as words to all mankind, erecting it as a mighty trophy against every enemy in the midst of the imperial city and expressly enjoining on all to acknowledge this imperishable symbol of salvation as the safeguard of the power of Rome and of the empire of the world. (In O'Donovan and O'Donovan, eds. 1999, 63–64)

17. "But to the Church of God he paid particular personal attention. When some were at variance with each other in various places, like a universal bishop appointed by God he convoked councils of the ministers of God." Eusebius, *Life of Constantine*, I:44 (in Eusebius 1999, 87).

18. Eusebius, *Life of Constantine*, IV:24 (in Eusebius 1999, 161).

19. In this "ideal" unity, one can also see the prototype of what would later become the papal ideology, which combined the classical Roman heritage, imperial ambitions, and the ecclesiastical role of the bishop.

20. "Admittedly, Eusebius presented Constantine as the emperor chosen by God to reveal to the world the power of the cross, but within a 'divine economy' in which the empire was already the providential instrument of salvation." Dagron 2007, 132.

21. See Eusebius, *Ecclesiastical History,* IV:26 (in Eusebius 2018).

22. Dagron 2007, 130.

23. Compare to the elaborate account of the age of Saturn in Lactantius's fifth book of *Institutes*, where he quotes many of the ancient authors, including Ovid, Virgil, and Cicero.

24. Ostrogorski 1998, 80.

25. In this sense, Anthony Kaldellis is right when he ascribes to the Eastern Roman Empire the "Republican" Roman elements (see Kaldellis 2015, especially Chapters 4 and 5). It is true that state and church rhetoric can obscure the role of the people (or, at least, the citizens of the capital) in monarchies and autocracies, which, at times, could have been decisive. Even Ostrogorski points out the changing role of the Senate during the history of the Eastern Empire. A typically Roman republican element is certainly the concept that the legitimate emperor does not need to be from the dynastic bloodline, which does not mean that there were no dynasties (similar to the Roman, post-Augustus times). There were times when the imperial office was weakened, and then regained its importance. The thing seems to be that the very "republican" element contains, actually, two opposing elements. The stronger role of the senate/aristocracy has traditionally been ascribed to the typically "republican" form of government vs. the stronger role of the "chief" (king, emperor) that characterizes the autocracy (monarchy). However, one should be careful not to artificially impose a sharp contrast or a clear demarcation line between the *autocratic* imperial concept and the concept of "republic." A strong imperial office is often established with popular support (and this is also, arguably, a typically "republican" element) against the strong or decisive role of aristocracy. This tension continues to be one of the governing elements of domestic policies even in modern "democracies" and "republics."

26. See Ostrogorski 1998, 151.

27. See Dionysius (Pseudo) Areopagite, *Celestial* and *Ecclesiastical Hierarchy*, . One should add that the Dionysian concept of hierarchy, both ecclesiastical and heavenly, can also be interpreted in a more favorable way to imply that the purpose of the various "ranks" is only to "iconize" the one (Christ), leading the church community for instance toward God. The moment there's another one (of a "higher" rank), the lower "ranks" dissolve, thus again turning the many into some kind of egalitarian community, always only with the "one" who is performing the iconic role, until everything is subsumed into one community with Christ as its "first." Approaching *Corpus Areopagiticum* this way, it suddenly exposes itself as, potentially, a much more *anarchist* text than traditionally read.

28. Quoted in Scott 1932, 30.

29. Quoted in Scott 1932, 43.

30. Quoted in Desmond 2011, 156.

31. Desmond 2011, 156.

32. Nikolaishvili 2011, 348n8, 351. Compare to Oliver and Joan O'Donovan's description of the kingly prerogatives in the early Middle Ages in the West:

The theocratic king-priest (*rex et sacerdos*), endowed with episcopal powers, was responsible for the temporal and eternal welfare of his subjects. Regenerated by baptism, supernaturally equipped by royal anointing, the new Moses (or David, or Solomon, or Melchizedek), vicar of God or of Christ, superintended his imperial church, mediating the divine will by teaching and enforcing Christian doctrine and morality. His ecclesiastical administration and jurisdiction was Byzantine in scope, including nomination of bishops, convening of church councils and promulgating of canons. (O'Donovan and O'Donovan, eds. 1999, 174)

33. *Euchologion*, quoted in Dagron 2007, 58.

34. For more on the critique of the (Old Testament–based) arguments in favor of "Orthodox monarchy" or "Orthodox autocracy," see Džalto 2009.

35. This, among other reasons, caused a lot of tension and even open conflicts between the supreme ecclesial and political authorities in medieval (Western) Europe. As Friedrich Heer put it: "Pope and Emperor sat enthroned in brotherly amity, both of them watching over Christendom, which meant mankind; the spiritual sword belonged to the Pope, the secular sword to the Emperor," but, at the same time, "the Emperor was the foundation of the state, just as Christ was the foundation of the Church. . . . [T]he Emperor as head of the hierarchy dispensed the high mysteries of his high-priestly office." Heer 1998, 267–69.

36. In 1166, John Hagiophlorites compared the emperor "implicitly to Moses and explicitly to Solomon." See Dagron 2007, 253.

37. Ostrogorski 1998, 95–96.

38. That the same logic would have prevailed in the West, had the empire survived there, is clear from the way the emperors tried to deal with the popes in Rome every time they would find themselves on opposite sides. It is also visible from the development of the papacy, which, as already noted, implemented the same basic logic in articulating the relationship between the ecclesial and the political.

39. Hovorun writes:

It seems that Maximus was not against symphony as such. But he certainly stood for some distinctiveness and self-sufficiency of the church in its relationship with the state. . . . Maximus rebuked interference of the state to the sacrosanct domains of the church, including doctrine and liturgy. Remarkable in this regard was an episode during his trial, when he was asked about the role of the emperor in the church. Maximus, first, denied the emperors the right to interfere in the matters of doctrine: "No emperor was able to persuade the Fathers who speak of God to be reconciled with the heretics of their times by means of equivocal expressions." This is because it was not the business of civil authorities "to make an inquiry and to define on the subject of the saving teachings of the catholic church," but an exclusive responsibility and "the mark of priests." (2015b, 61)

40. This is quite similar to the attempts of the popes to affirm the principle that they have the final say in church matters. In this time, popes were still not rejecting the supreme authority of the emperor as a political leader. The papacy was, however, growing in its independence from the emperor and the (usually obedient) patriarchs after the fifth century. The conflict would only grow in the subsequent period.

41. It is interesting to note that this position is essentially not very different from some modern variations of secular models, in which different segments of the society (such as state and religious institutions) still participate in one universal (one is tempted to say *secular religious*) "whole." This is the model of "cooperation" between the state and the church/religious institutions instead of their radical separation, which one finds in most European states (without one official state religion/church).

42. "The Church and the state, that is, *sacerdotium* (religious power) and *imperium* (imperial power) were meant to form a sole body based on agreed reciprocity in which none intends to take over the other's role but on the contrary, both redefine their content and purpose in a complementary way." Brînzea 2014, 142.

43. See Dagron 2007, 159–66. What is interesting about this phrase is the somewhat paradoxical way in which it was used—in the first letter, the pope denounces this title used by the emperor, while, in the second letter, the pope uses the same title, calling the emperor to be(come) the (true?) *emperor* and *bishop* ("We beg you, become bishop and emperor as you have written!" in Dagron 2007, 162).

44. Ostrogorski 1998, 177, 189, 191, 202.

45. Gregory wrote:

Hearken to us, emperor: abandon your present course and accept the holy church as you found her, for matters of faith and practice concern not the emperor, but the pope, since we have the mind of Christ [1 Cor. 2:16]. The making of laws for the church is one thing and the governing of the empire another; the ordinary intelligence which is used in administering worldly affairs is not adequate to the settlement of spiritual matters. Behold, I will show you now the difference between the palace and the church, between the emperor and the pope; learn and be saved; be no longer contentious. If anyone should take from you the adornments of royalty, your purple robes, diadem, scepter, and your ranks of servants, you would be regarded by men as base, hateful and abject; but to this condition you have reduced the churches, for you have deprived them of their ornaments and made them unsightly. Just as the pope has not the right to interfere in the palace or to infringe upon the royal prerogatives, so the emperor has not the right to interfere in the churches, or to conduct elections among the clergy, or to consecrate, or to administer the sacraments or even to participate in the sacraments without the aid of a priest; let each one of us abide in the same calling wherein he is called of God [1 Cor. 7:20]. Do you see, emperor, the difference between popes and emperors? . . . Do you see now, emperor, the difference between the church and the empire? Those emperors who have lived piously in Christ have obeyed the popes, and not vexed them. But you, emperor, since you have transgressed and gone astray, and since you have written with your own hand and confessed that he who attacks the father is to be execrated, have hereby condemned yourself by your own sentence and have driven from you the Holy Spirit. You persecute us and vex us tyrannically with violent and carnal hand. We, unarmed and defenseless, possessing no earthly armies, call now upon the prince of all the armies of creation, Christ seated in the heavens, commanding all the hosts of celestial beings, to send a demon upon you; as the apostle says: "to deliver such a one unto Satan for the destruction of the flesh, that the spirit may be saved" [1 Cor. 5:5]. (*Letter of Pope Gregory II to the Emperor, Leo III, 726 or 727*, in Thatcher and McNeal, eds. 1905, 97–99)

46. See Runciman 2003, 72.

47. St John of Damascus, *On Divine Images*, Treatise II, 12, quoted in Damascus 2003, 69.

48. Ostrogorski 1998, 237.

49. Ostrogorski 1998, 241. *Epanagoge/Eisagoge* was, however, short-lived. Leo VI revoked it in the first year of his rule, and replaced it with the *Procheiros Nomos*, which elevated the role of the emperor. See Stanković 2012.

50. One can see the influence of typically Western political theologies—that affirmed the power of the highest church offices even in the political realm (such as the influence of the *Donatio Constantini*)—on the political theological thinking in Constantinople in this period. See Dagron 2007, 240–47. Also Stanković 2013.

51. See Ostrogorski 1998, 322.

52. Dagron 2007, 253.

53. Dagron 2007, 254.

54. Job Iasites, in the name of Patriarch Joseph, quoted in Dagron 2007, 255.

55. See Ostrogorski 1998, 361–62.

56. See Gierke 1922; Canning 2003.

57. Ostrogorski 1998, 417.

58. Meyendorff 1989, 113.

59. Meyendorff 1989, 116.

60. Patriarch Philotheos, quoted in Meyendorff 1989, 116.

61. Quoted in Meyendorff 1989, 116. That the ("papist") claims for a universal power of the bishop/patriarch of Constantinople do not belong only to the distant past can be seen from the recent developments in Ukraine, where the "ecumenical" patriarch clearly demonstrated his aspirations to act as a universal souverain, who alone decides in church matters across the Orthodox world, and irrespectively of the position and opinion of other (local) bishops and patriarchs.

62. Ostrogorski 1998, 512.

63. Patriarch Anthony, quoted in Charanis 1974a, 90.

64. Patriarch Anthony, quoted in Ostrogorski 1998, 513.

65. "The theory was clear and simple. The practice was more complicated." Runciman 2003, 3.

Conducting "Symphonia" in Russian Lands

1. See, for example, Meyendorff 1989.

2. Alternatively also Русь (Rhos; Gr. Ῥῶς). These terms are mentioned in medieval Russian, Byzantine, and Arabic sources (see Thulin 1978). Although the terms "Russia" and "Russian" are of a later date (and there is much debate whether they can be used to cover the earlier periods or not), for the sake of simplicity, the term "Russia" will be used here to address both the Kievan state and the later states of Muscovite Russia and the modern Russian Empire.

3. See Obolensky 1971.

4. "The pagan religion and the legal concepts and customs associated with it in no way fostered the development of feudalism; if anything, they even hindered it" (Boris Rauschenbach, "The Development of Kievan Rus' in the Wake of Christianization," in Hamant 1992, 44). Nikolai Todorov agrees with this and even more explicitly stresses the significance of religion in the creation of the ideological as well as socio-political structures of the medieval Russian state:

> Slavonic paganism had shown that it was incapable of forming a new kind of stable society. This is borne out as much by the failure of the Eastern and some of the Western Slavs to form durable states as by their fruitless attempts to erect a mythological pantheon to serve as an ideological standard and institutional basis for the state as a more advanced type of organization than clan alliances. (Nikolai Todorov, "The Conversion of Rus' to Christianity," in Hamant 1992, 37)

5. Rauschenbach, "The Development of Kievan Rus'," in Hamant 1992, 45. See also Shchapov:

The great medieval empire of Byzantium, guardian of the classical and Near Eastern heritage, which had spread Christian culture in all directions, with its brilliant capital Constantinople, attracted the Russians by its political authority and wealth. . . . The leaning towards Constantinople rather than Rome and the choice of Eastern rather than Western Christianity was determined by a number of circumstances. Perhaps one of the most important of these was the recognition in the East of the right to liturgy in local languages and the translation of the Holy Scripture into these languages with the use of its own system of writing for each of them. . . . In the Western world, where there were many feudal states, the power of the Church was marked by greater stability than that of the king. Desiring to establish a Church organization in Rus' that was not insubordinate to the secular power, the Prince of Kiev . . . turned to the Byzantine rather than the Roman model. (Yaroslav Shchapov, "The Assimilation by Kievan Rus' of the Classical and Byzantine Heritage," in Hamant 1992, 57–58)

We also find essentially the same arguments in Iannis Karayannopoulos's "Christianization: A Turning-Point in the History of Rus'," in Hamant 1992, 65–67.

6. Rauschenbach, "The Development of Kievan Rus'," in Hamant 1992, 48.

7. Rauschenbach, "The Development of Kievan Rus'," in Hamant 1992, 46.

8. See Shchapov, "The Assimilation by Kievan Rus'," in Hamant 1992, 58.

9. It should be understood that the church-state relationships (and, consequently, the character of political theologies) would change more than once during the later history of Russia, and only the most important aspects of those changes will be addressed here, in the context of the further developments of the classical expressions of symphonia.

10. Quoted in Bercken 1999, 63–62.

11. Karayannopoulos, "Christianization," in Hamant 1992, 68.

12. Jean-Pierre Arrignon, "The Religious Achievements of Yaroslav the Wise," in Hamant 1992, 101.

13. This seems to hold true, even if the hypothesis about the existence of a previous church dedicated also to St. Sophia on the same site is correct. See Arrignon, "The Religious Achievements," in Hamant 1992, 94–104.

14. See Bercken 1999, 148–49.

15. Rauschenbach, "The Development of Kievan Rus'," in Hamant 1992, 53.

16. Quoted in Bercken 1999, 146. This was, however, not the first occurrence of the idea. It appeared already in the "Russian Chronograph" in 1512. See Laats 2009, 104.

17. Examples of them can be found in the papal claims of the source of their political authority, as well as in the attempts to legitimize Western medieval

kingdoms by relating them to Rome and Roman tradition (e.g., the Holy Roman Empire). Similar (and contemporary) tendencies to those in Russia can also be found in England, when Queen Elizabeth was compared with Constantine the Great, and England with "new Israel" (see Bercken 1999, 148–49). In the East, Moscow was also not a novelty. Already, the Bulgarian capital of Veliko Tarnovo was referred to as the new "czar-grad" (Czar's City—which is also the Slavonic name for Constantinople).

18. Bercken 1999, 142.

19. See Bercken 1999, 142.

20. The church in Moscovite Russia would, occasionally, refer to the stories developed in the West when it needed to defend its authority or property. A characteristic case we find at the moment of the confiscation of Novgorod's church treasury by Ivan III, which led Archbishop Genadii to commission the "Short Sermon," in which a variation of the Donation of Constantine legend was used. Constantine supposedly issued a decree that not only granted the pope—that is, the church—the lands, but also made church possessions sacrosanct. The "Other Sermon" explicitly accused Ivan of attempting to make the church dependent on state finances, which met with the strong opposition of charismatic characters such as Nil Sorskii (see David B. Miller, "The Orthodox Church," in Perrie 2006, 351).

21. Laats 2009, 102.

22. Laats 2009, 104.

23. Bogatyrev 2007, 276.

24. See Bercken 1999, 151.

25. Bogatyrev 2007, 257.

26. See Perrie 2006, 245.

27. David B. Miller, "The Orthodox Church," in Perrie 2006, 358.

28. Laats 2009, 110.

29. See Berdyaev 2004.

30. Bercken 1999, 147.

31. See Poe 1997, 7–15.

32. Rowland 1996, 592.

33. Rowland 1996, 596–97.

34. See, for example, Rowland 1996:

> In other tales about the Time of Troubles we find Muscovy referred to as "the New Zion," "the New Israel," "the remnant of the Christian tribe," and the Muscovites as the "People of the Lord," "Your [God's] People," or "the Sheep of the Word." "In truth," exclaimed Prince Ivan Khvorostinin, "we are called the newly enlightened Israelites." Conrad Bussow even reported that the second False Dmitrii included a reference to Muscovy as a "second Israel" in his formal title. (605)

35. Rowland 1996, 608.

36. Perrie 2014.

37. Bercken 1999, 166.

38. See Fedotov 1966 (chapter 5).

39. Beazley 1914, xii, xiv.

40. See Petro 2009.

41. Beazley 1914, xi–xii, xiv.

42. Beazley 1914, xviii.

43. "Matters of religion and morality are an important part of the work of the *Veche*, which banned pagan superstitions, punished the black art, designated the favoured few from whom a new archbishop might be chosen, or deposed an unpopular prelate." Beazley 1914, xv.

44. See 1 Peter 2:9.

45. This has, then, direct implications as to the church autocephaly issue, which resulted in the unfortunate (and theologically completely unacceptable) concept of "national churches," which is rivaled only by (equally unacceptable) imperial universalism of the "ecumenical" patriarchate.

46. See Džalto 2009.

47. Incidentally, this logic is comparable to modern "Christian" nationalisms and exceptionalisms, across various Christian denominations.

48. This is comparable to the Germanic idea of the "people" (*das Volk*), as in the sense of a more primordial reality out of which the state emerges as its natural and organic expression.

49. Freeze 1985, 90.

50. Freeze 1985, 91.

51. See Bercken 1999, 170.

52. See Bercken 1999, 174.

53. Bercken 1999, 179.

54. Bercken, 1999, 179. However, Paul, being raised German, was arguably repeating in this instance more contemporary Lutheran models, rather than the Byzantine one.

55. See Walicki 1979, 111.

56. Bulgakov's name has various transliterations in English. In addition to "Sergei" (Russian: Сергей), we also find "Sergius," "Sergej," and "Sergii." For the purposes of this text, as well as for the consistency of the references, I will use in the text only "Sergei," while the other versions are listed in the bibliography following the form in which his name was used in the individual publications.

57. Rowan Williams, introduction to "Heroism and the Spiritual Struggle," in Bulgakov 1999, 60–61.

The Modern Nation, Ethnicity, and State-Based Political Theologies

1. For the logic of the "secular sacred" and, more specifically, the logic of the "civic (political) religious," see Gentile 2006.

2. Already, Rousseau recognized the need for a "civil religion" for the preservation of the modern political community once the traditional religion has been marginalized or expelled from the public sphere:

> There, is therefore a purely civil profession of faith of which the Sovereign should fix the articles, not exactly as religious dogmas, but as social sentiments without which a man cannot be a good citizen or a faithful subject. While it can compel no one to believe them, it can banish from the State whoever does not believe them—it can banish him, not for impiety, but as an anti-social being, incapable of truly loving the laws and justice, and of sacrificing, at need, his life to his duty. If any one, after publicly recognising these dogmas, behaves as if he does not believe them, let him be punished by death: he has committed the worst of all crimes, that of lying before the law. . . . [T]olerance should be given to all religions that tolerate others, so long as their dogmas contain nothing contrary to the duties of citizenship. But whoever dares to say: Outside the Church is no salvation ought to be driven from the State, unless the State is the Church, and the prince the pontiff. (Jean-Jacques Rousseau, *The Social Contract*, 1762, quoted in Rousseau 1923, 121–22)

This "civil" religion (i.e., national/political ideology, with some of the traditionally religious "flavors," such as the feeling of "urgency" or the "mystical" unity of individuals with a collective) was supposed to provide national cohesion and stability. However, the result in most of the countries (including those with a majority of Orthodox population) was that the modern "civil" or "secular" religions absorbed the traditional expressions of religiosity, turning the Protestant, Roman Catholic, or Orthodox faith and the corresponding church institutions into a component of the secular "civil" and national-religious program.

3. The latest examples in this respect are the attempts to create autocephalous "Macedonian," "Montenegrin," and "Ukrainian" Orthodox Churches, as political projects of the governments of these countries (that only recently became independent), aimed at solidifying national identities and homogenizing the national body.

4. Berdyaev 2004, 58.

5. Berdyaev 2004, 60.

6. See Berdyaev 2004, 58.

7. Bercken identifies four main streams of the Slavophiles: "Classic Slavophiles," "State Nationalism," "Pan-Slavism," and Konstantin Leontiev's "Byzantinophile" Slavism (see Bercken 1999, 205).

8. Also spelled Aleksej Chomjakov, Michail Pogodin, Nikolaj Danilevskij, and Konstantin Leont'ev, as in Bercken.

9. See Walicki 1979, 94–95.

10. See Bercken 1999, 206–14.

11. See Noble 2015, 147.

12. Popović 1993, 3.

13. Popović 1993, 30.

14. Popović 1993, 31.

15. Popović 1993, 34.

16. Popović 1993, 32.

17. Popović 1993, 35. Occasionally however, Popović was also very critical of the misuse of the church for political goals. We find one of the strongest of such critical remarks in the text "Unutrašnja misija naše crkve" (The Inner Mission of Our Church), where he claims:

> The Church is a Divinehuman eternity, incarnated within the boundaries of time and space. She is in this world, but is not of this world (John 18:36). She is in this world to lift this world up to that other world, from which she herself comes from. She is universal, catholic, Divinehuman, eternal; therefore, it is a blasphemy, an unforgivable blasphemy against Christ and the Holy Spirit to turn her into a national institution, to narrow her down to small, transient, ephemeral national goals and methods. Her goal is above-national, it is universal, all-human—to unite all people in Christ, all people, irrespectively of their nationality, race, class. There is neither Jew nor Gentile, neither slave nor free, nor is there male and female, for you are all one in Christ Jesus (Galatians 3:28), because Christ is all, and is in all (Colossians 3:11). (Popović 2012)

18. Jevtić 2009, 371.

19. "We can see this fact even more clearly in the 'political theology' or 'christology' of Christian Rome where the monarchy and the empire imitate the Incarnation. Thus, as Jesus Christ was both God and man, so Orthodox monarchical society likewise possessed two dimensions, one earthly and one heavenly, united as the two Natures in Christ." Azkoul 1979. See also Azkoul 1984.

20. See Moss 2014, 2016, 2018a, 2018b. More of his works are available from his website: http://www.orthodoxchristianbooks.com/.

21. See Vorobievsky:

> День отречения Николая II стал поистине мистическим. Сама преисподня поспешила вздохнуть с облегчением. . . . Да, кульминацией атак на Третий Рим стало убийство Православного Императора. . . . Так почему же не пришел антихрист, когда пал

'удерживающий'? Еще в день отречения Николая II от трона, когда
в храмах пели покаянный канон Андрея Критского, в церкви села
Коломенского под Москвой произошло чудо. Была обретена
старинная икона Божьей Матери—Державная. В руках Богородицы—
знаки монаршьей власти. Но держава не увенчана крестом—символ
обезглавленной России. Что увидели в этом духовные очи
православных людей? Матерь Божья явилась со скорбным ликом,
одетая в царственный пурпур. И возвестила таким образом, что
берет роль 'удерживающего' на себя. ("От Кремля до Града
Небесного," in Vorobievsky 1999)

22. The previous three "theories," following Dugin, are liberalism,
communism, and fascism. See "The Fourth Political Theory: Beyond Left and
Right but Against the Center" at http://www.4pt.su/en.

23. In an interview with *The Economist*, Dugin explains some of his ideas
regarding the meaning and the role of the "czar" and "czardom":

> *The Economist*: You must be quite disappointed with Mr. Putin, because the
> Russian Empire has still not returned besides very small little pieces of
> small republics.
>
> Dugin: Yes, I am very disappointed. For me, Putin is only an actor who
> plays the role of Tsar. I believe not in Putin, but in the eternal tsar that has
> many names and many forms. He could be called President, leader, tsar, king,
> emperor, but it is a function to be tsar. Putin has fulfilled this function much
> better than Yeltsin and Gorbachev. But he still makes too many delays. He
> thinks that this is realist. I think that this is cowardice.
>
> *The Economist*: So he's not a real tsar?
>
> Dugin: Nobody is the real tsar. Everybody only plays the role of the tsar.
> The real tsar for us is Christ. Everybody else is a kind of representative of
> the tsar.
>
> *The Economist*: How do you recognize the Tsar?
>
> Dugin: By will. By the space. The tsar is innerly linked with the space.
> What is this space? For us Russians, the space is difference. He who can
> manage to make unity out of differences, is the real tsar. He who collects
> and does not lose. That is very important. It is an integration process. It is a
> kind of sign of the tsar. He who destroys is a bad tsar. He who constructs is
> a good tsar. Putin has frozen the split and the fall of the Russian Federa-
> tion. He began to reconstruct step by step. He is much more of a real tsar
> than Yeltsin and Gorbachev because of that and many other things. But
> first of all, that is the first sign—if something begins to grow. At the same
> time, the tsar should defend our identity and defend the tsardom. If the
> tsar defends the tsardom, he's a good tsar. If the tsar weakens the tsardom,

and the concept, he is a bad tsar. What is interesting is that most of you consider our church to be servile, following the orders of the tsar, but one of the theorists of the tsardom, Joseph Volotsky, affirmed that if the tsar denies or weakens the tsardom, he should be killed. That was from one of the saints of the Russian Church—the most pro-tsardom. The tsardom is much more important than the tsar. (https://www.geopolitica.ru/en/article /russian-identity-and-putin)

24. Quoted in Webster 2003, 5.
25. See Webster 2003, 2004.

Newer Approaches

1. Sergeev 2003, no pagination.
2. Fedotov 1950.
3. Fedotov 1950. See also Fedotov 1966 (chapter 5).
4. See Papanikolaou 2012, 36–43.
5. Bulgakov 1999, 78.
6. Bulgakov 1999, 256–57.
7. Papanikolaou 2012, 5.
8. See Kalaitzidis 2012.
9. See Kalaitzidis 2012, 121–33.
10. See Hovorun 2008, 2015a, 2015b, 2017.
11. See Hovorun 2016, 2018a, 2018b.
12. See Athanasios N. Papathanasiou, "The Politics of a 'Weak Force'" in Stoeckl, et al. 2017, 97–110 (and his works cited therein).
13. See Bigović 2010; Krstić 2012, 2014.
14. Krstić 2006, 241.
15. "When a nation, civil or ethnic, represents fully or predominantly a monoconfessional Orthodox community, it can in a certain sense be regarded as the one community of faith—an Orthodox nation." *The Bases*, II. 3.
16. "The weakness of the human rights institution lies in the fact that . . . while defending the freedom (αὐτεξουσίον) of choice, it tends to increasingly ignore the moral dimension of life and the freedom from sin (ἐλευθερία)." *The Russian Orthodox Church's Basic Teaching* II. 2.
17. *Social Ethos*, II §10.
18. *Social Ethos*, II §10.
19. See Hobsbawm 2007, 7.
20. See Yannaras 2002:

> The horror of inhuman behavior, the complete destruction of any sense of individual rights, reached its culmination during the 20th century. Even today, when the global hegemony of the West is hailed as the triumph of

the defense of human rights, practices of genocide, ethnic cleansing, slaughter of innocent people, torture, policing and censorship, even slavery, lie on the everyday agenda of the international arena. It suffices to recall the tragedy of the Palestinians, Kurds, Serbs, or northern Cyprus to realize that the West usually decides which people have human rights and to which people these should by definition be denied.

21. Yannaras 2002.

Political Theology as Ideology: A Deconstruction

1. Of course, similar models that searched for a unity between the religious/heavenly/spiritual realm and the political sphere can be found in earlier civilizations as well. In spite of many more recent studies that are much more elaborate and correct in some aspects, Francis Dvornik's classic work, *Early Christian and Byzantine Political Philosophy*, vol. 1 (Dvornik 1966), remains, in my view, an extremely insightful account of the religious-political ideas from ancient Egypt and Mesopotamia to the Hellenistic kingdoms and ancient Judaism that constitute the background against Christian political philosophy, both *historical* and *prophetic*, should be seen.

2. In the words of Theophylact of Ohrid, "every emperor is an image of God." Quoted in Speros Vryonis Jr., "The Patriarchate of Constantinople and the State," in Hotchkiss and Henry 2005, 112.

3. The same logic applies to those variations of symphonia in which the ecclesial leader (patriarch, pope) assumes the regal/imperial prerogatives.

Alternative and "Proto-Anarchist" Political Theologies

1. Illustrative in this sense is the case of Petr Chaadayev (1794–1856), whose harsh critique of Russian society (in *Philosophical Letters*), its history, and the Byzantine heritage earned him the qualification of a "mentally ill" person. See Bercken 1999, 182–90.

2. In particular, the New Testament books have often been cited in the context of Christian anarchist literature. See Ellul 1989, 2011a, 2011b, 2012; Christoyannopoulos 2011 (especially 73–106).

3. Some interpret early Christian theology primarily in terms of the Christian confrontations with the Roman Empire and their protest against the imperial cult. See Taubes 2004, 16.

4. Moore 2006, 99. Later on, in the same book, Moore examines this thesis by employing "catachresis" as a conceptual tool in understanding the appropriation of the imperial (Roman) imagery and turning it against the Roman rule.

5. Moore 2006, 112. He also noted that "the book's representation of the Roman imperial order is essentially parodic . . . and parody is a species of

mimicry: it mimics in order to mock," the result being that "the 'heavenly' order in Revelation is busily engaged in imitating or mimicking the 'earthly' order, notwithstanding the book's own implicit charge that the earthly is merely a counterfeit copy of the heavenly." Moore 2006, 112.

6. This is paralleled in the early Christian prayer, which we find in *Didache*: "May grace come and this world pass away . . . Maranatha!" *Didache* 10:6.

7. For the topic of the Essenes and their political positions, see Osborn 2010, 25–29; Kohler 1920.

8. I am putting aside at this point the Gospels and the portrayal of political power there, as I will analyze them more closely in the next chapter.

9. Justin, *First Apology*, in O'Donovan and O'Donovan, eds. 1999, 11.

10. Pagels 1989, 39.

11. Clement of Alexandria, *Exhortation to the Heathen* X, in Clement of Alexandria 1867, 87. However, in *The Miscellanies* (or *Stromata* I, XXIV), Clement offers a somewhat different argument, differentiating between various types of rule ("royalty"), starting from the Divine as the perfect one, descending to the fourth and the "worst" kind of rule, the one "which acts according to the promptings of the passions." See Clement of Alexandria 1867, 455–56.

12. The popular form of *credo quia absurdum* represents an appropriation of Tertullian's original argument on the crucifixion of Christ, which reads "Et mortuus est dei filius; credibile prorsus est, quia ineptum est." *De Carne Christi* V.4.

13. Tertullian, *Apology*, in O'Donovan and O'Donovan, eds. 1999, 26.

14. *Epistle to Diognetus*, in Ehrman 2005, II:139–41. See "If you are a Christian, no earthly city is yours. . . . Though we may gain possession of the whole world, we are withal but strangers and sojourners in it all!" John Chrysostom, *Homilies on the Statues*, 17.12. https://www.newadvent.org/fathers/190117.htm.

15. Irenaeus of Lyons, *Against Heresies*, in O'Donovan and O'Donovan, eds. 1999, 17.

16. Irenaeus of Lyons, *Against Heresies*, in O'Donovan and O'Donovan, eds. 1999, 17.

17. "If, therefore, the great God showed future things by Daniel, and confirmed them by his Son, and if Christ is the stone which is cut out without hands, who shall destroy temporal kingdoms and introduce an eternal one, which is the resurrection of the just; as he declares, 'the God of heaven shall raise up a kingdom which shall never be destroyed,' let them accept their defeat and come to their senses, who reject the Creator and do not agree that the prophets were sent beforehand from the same Father from whom also the Lord came, but who assert that prophecies originated from diverse powers." Irenaeus of Lyons, *Against Heresies*, in O'Donovan and O'Donovan, eds. 1999, 21.

18. "Kings are not appointed by the son of Kronos . . . but by God who governs all things and knows what he is doing in the matter of the appointment of kings." Origen, *Against Celsus*, Book 8, in O'Donovan and O'Donovan, eds. 1999, 41; "Indeed, the more pious a man is, the more effective he is in helping the emperors—more so than the soldiers who go out into the lines and kill all the enemy troops that they can." Irenaeus of Lyons, *Against Heresies*, in O'Donovan and O'Donovan, eds. 1999, 44.

19. "Christians do more good to their countries than the rest of mankind, since they educate the citizens and teach them to be devoted to God, the guardian of their city; and they take those who have lived good lives in the most insignificant cities up to a divine and heavenly city." Origen, *Against Celsus*, Book 8, in O'Donovan and O'Donovan, eds. 1999, 45.

20. Origen, *Against Celsus*, Book 8, in O'Donovan and O'Donovan, eds. 1999, 45.

21. "He is even more bitter than Pilate. For Pilate, when he perceived the injustice of the deed, washed his hands; but this man, while he banishes the saints, gnashes his teeth against them more and more." Athanasius, *History of the Arians*, VIII:68.

22. "Godless, unholy, without natural affection, he feared not God . . . this modern Ahab, this second Belshazzar of our times." Athanasius, *History of the Arians*, V:45.

23. "And yet one ought not to wonder that after so many letters and so many oaths Constantius had altered his mind, when we remember that Pharaoh of old, the tyrant of Egypt, after frequently promising and by that means obtaining a remission of his punishments, likewise changed, until he at last perished together with his associates." Athanasius, *History of the Arians*, IV:30.

24. "Constantius, as it were Antichrist himself, to be its leader in impiety? He for its sake has earnestly endeavoured to emulate Saul in savage cruelty." Athanasius, *History of the Arians*, VIII:67. "Now what other person besides Constantius has ever attempted to do these things? He is surely such a one as Antichrist would be." VIII:74.

25. "I urge, I beg, I exhort, I warn, for it is a grief to me, that you who were an example of unusual piety, who were conspicuous for clemency, who would not suffer single offenders to be put in peril, should not mourn that so many have perished. Though you have waged battle most successfully, though in other matters, too, you are worthy of praise, yet piety was ever the crown of your actions. The devil envied that which was your most excellent possession. Conquer him whilst you still possess that wherewith you may conquer. Do not add another sin to your sin by a course of action which has injured many [. . .] I dare not offer the sacrifice if you intend to be present." Ambrose, *Letter* 51, quoted in https://sourcebooks.fordham.edu/source/ambrose-let51.asp.

26. "For I would not that your law should be set above the law of God. The law of God has taught us what to follow; human laws cannot teach us this. They usually extort a change from the fearful, but they cannot inspire faith." Ambrose, *Letter* 21, quoted in https://sourcebooks.fordham.edu/source/ambrose-let21.asp.

27. Ambrose, *Sermon against Auxentius*, 31–36, quoted in O'Donovan and O'Donovan, eds. 1999, 74–75.

28. This mindset informed entire cultures. An illustration of that we find already at the level of language. For instance, the Slavic word for "poor" is *ubog*, and it denotes both those who are without material means, as well as those who suffer, are oppressed, marginalized or "unfortunate." This word literally translates as the one who is "with God" or the one "close to God."

29. Ambrose, *The Story of Naboth*, 31–36, quoted in O'Donovan and O'Donovan, eds. 1999, 75.

30. Ambrose, *The Story of Naboth*, 31–36, quoted in O'Donovan and O'Donovan, eds. 1999, 77.

31. See Ambrose, *Letter* 7, quoted in https://sourcebooks.fordham.edu/source/ambrose-let21.asp.

32. Ambrose, *The Story of Naboth*, in O'Donovan and O'Donovan, eds. 1999, 76.

33. See Comaroff and Comaroff 2000; Cox 2016; Kirby 2019. All, of course, in reference to Weber's *The Protestant Ethic* (1930).

34. Lactantius, *Divine Institutes*, V, in O'Donovan and O'Donovan, eds. 1999, 49–50.

35. Lactantius, *Institutes*, V, in O'Donovan and O'Donovan, eds. 1999, 50.

36. Lactantius, *Institutes*, V, in O'Donovan and O'Donovan, eds. 1999, 52.

37. Lactantius, *Institutes*, V, in O'Donovan and O'Donovan, eds. 1999, 53.

38. John Chrysostom, *Twelfth Homily on 1 Timothy*, in O'Donovan and O'Donovan, eds. 1999, 101.

39. John Chrysostom, *Twelfth Homily on 1 Timothy*, in O'Donovan and O'Donovan, eds. 1999, 102.

40. John Chrysostom, *Twelfth Homily on 1 Timothy*, in O'Donovan and O'Donovan, eds. 1999, 103.

41. See John Chrysostom, *Fourth Homily on the Text "I Saw the Lord . . . ,"* in O'Donovan and O'Donovan, eds. 1999, 98–99.

42. "I say this not to criticize royalty as such, only those infatuated with lunatic obsessions; and that you may learn how much higher the priesthood is than kingship." John Chrysostom, *Fourth Homily on the Text "I Saw the Lord . . . ,"* in O'Donovan and O'Donovan, eds. 1999, 100.

43. Augustine 1958, 327.

44. Augustine 1958, 328–29.

45. Augustine 1958, 324–25.

46. "Older rationalizations of the rise of monasticism have included the suggestion that it was a response to the imperial adoption of Christianity in the fourth century, a call to return to the values of Christian martyrdom or a result of a widespread and deep-seated anxiety." Marilyn Dunn 2003, 1.

47. Communal monastic life as a form (prototype) of an anarchist community is a largely underdeveloped area of (Christian) anarchist studies. One of the reasons for this can be the absence of the tradition of cenobitic monastic life in most Protestant areas, where much of the Christian anarchist thinking initially took place.

48. See "And thus they brought division into the society of the time, shattering its fabric, while forming active social nuclei rendered fruitful by the greatness of their sacrifices. In the face of the Empire as a politico-religious unity, they might be said to represent a kind of *social anarchism*." Sturzo 1962, 26.

49. It is important to mention in this context one of the most famous monks from the sixth/seventh centuries—Maximus the Confessor. His opposition to the imperial power in church/theological matters was already mentioned. Here, however, one should also keep in mind the possibility of an "anarchist" reading of Maximus and his social ethics. See Brown Dewhurst 2018.

50. Some of the "heresies" can, arguably, be also read along the lines of their opposition to the power and exercise of violence by the state and/or the institutional church. For instance, Richard Fitch makes an attempt to first deconstruct the traditional interpretations of Pelagianism and then to offer an *anarchist* reading of Pelagius's teachings. See Richard Fitch, "The Pelagian Mentality: Radical Political Thought in Fifth Century Christianity," in Christoyannopoulos 2011, 2–29; Bradstock and Rowland 2002, 12–33.

51. See Ostrogorski 1998, 279. On the contrary, and paradoxically enough, sometimes the emperors were those who were defending the church and faith against the church hierarchy and the monasteries, as in the attempts of Nikephoros Phokas (⚜ 963–69) to restrict the growth of church and monastery real estates. This policy seems to have been motivated not only by economic reasons, but primarily by the emperor's piety, given his criticism of the greed of the monks who forget their religious duties and turn the monastic life into an "empty comedy" that insults the name of Christ. See Ostrogorski 1998, 275.

52. See Ostrogorski 1998, 432, 521–22.

53. See John A. McGuckin, "The Theology of Images and the Legitimation of Power in Eighth Century Byzantium," *St. Vladimir's Theological Quarterly* 37, no. 1 (1993): 39–58.

54. John of Damascus, *Apology* II:12, quoted in Damascus 2003, 69.

55. Ostrogorski 1998, 259–60. See Lape 1982.

56. "For the message of the cross is foolishness to those who are perishing, but to us who are being saved it is the power of God. For it is written: 'I will destroy

the wisdom of the wise; the intelligence of the intelligent I will frustrate.' Where is the wise person? Where is the teacher of the law? Where is the philosopher of this age? Has not God made foolish the wisdom of the world? For since in the wisdom of God the world through its wisdom did not know him, God was pleased through the foolishness of what was preached to save those who believe. Jews demand signs and Greeks look for wisdom, but we preach Christ crucified: a stumbling block to Jews and foolishness to Gentiles, but to those whom God has called, both Jews and Greeks, Christ the power of God and the wisdom of God. For the foolishness of God is wiser than human wisdom, and the weakness of God is stronger than human strength." 1 Corinthians 1:18–25.

57. A. M. Panchenko, "Holy Foolishness as Social Protest," in Hunt and Kobets, eds. 2011, 121.

58. Giles Fletcher, quoted in A. M. Panchenko, "Holy Foolishness as Social Protest," in Hunt and Kobets, eds. 2011, 99.

59. See Hunt and Kobets, eds. 2011, 149–224, 305–36.

60. Sergey A. Ivanov "Simon of Iurievets and the Hagiography of Old Russian Holy Fools" in Hunt and Kobets, eds. 2011, 269–80.

61. As Rowan Williams noted:

> Some holy fools are described as throwing stones at churches or at the houses of the devout, praying in taverns, laughing at funerals, weeping at weddings or baptisms and so on: the story of the angel who takes human shape and causes scandal by his incomprehensible activities is found in various forms from seventh-century Byzantium onward, ultimately being recycled as a Russian folktale about an angel who takes service with a parish priest. (Williams 2018, 5)

62. In 1515, contrary to the very spirit of traditional monasticism, the rule of the Simonovsky and Kirillo-Belozersky monasteries divided the monks into three classes, with corresponding privileges for each class.

63. See Perrie 2006, 347–48.

64. See Bercken 1999, 151.

65. Ivan S. Aksakov, quoted in Solovyev 1948, 63–65.

66. Solovyev 1948, 99.

67. See Solovyev 1948, 186.

68. Michael Bakunin, "From a Letter of Bakunin to His Sisters," in Bakunin 1973, 35.

69. Michael Bakunin, "The Paris Commune and the Idea of the State," in Bakunin 1973, 196.

70. "Of all godless ideas and words there is none more godless than that of a Church. There is no idea that has produced more evil, none more inimical to Christ's teaching, than the idea of a Church. [. . .] But in the early times of

Christianity the conception of a Church was only employed to refer to all those who shared beliefs which I considered true. That conception of the Church is quite correct if it does not include those who make a verbal expression of religion, instead of its expression in the whole of life—for religion cannot be expressed in words." "Church and State" in Tolstoy 1934, 334, 336–37.

71. "Tolstoy's politics were inextricably connected with his moral views which in turn were based on a highly unorthodox version of Christianity." Marshall 2008, 362.

72. "According to Tolstoy, the essence of this Christian alternative is best expressed in Jesus' Sermon on the Mount. . . . Tolstoy thus understands Jesus as spelling out a revolutionary and indeed wiser method for human beings to deal with evil, with fear, violence and insecurity: when treated unjustly, do not use force or retaliate, but respond with love, forgiveness and generosity." Alexandre J. M. E. Christoyannopoulos, "Christian Anarchism: A Revolutionary Reading of the Bible," in Jun and Wahl, eds. 2010, 150–51.

73. For more on Tolstoy's anarchism, see Christoyannopoulos 2008, as well as Marshall 2008, 362–83.

74. See Berdyaev:

I ought to say a word or two about [J. F.] Hecker's false interpretation of my own views. The terminology I use, the words "aristocratic principle," "the new Middle Ages," etc. clearly lead him astray. He regards me as a supporter of feudal aristocracy, which is almost laughable. A supporter of feudal aristocracy in our day would have to be regarded as mad. In actual fact, I am a supporter of the classless society, that is to say, in that respect I am very near to communism. But for all that, I am a supporter of the aristocratic principle as a qualitative principle in human society, but a personal qualitative principle, not one which depends upon class or property; that is to say, I am a supporter of spiritual aristocracy. (2004, 178–79)

75. Berdyaev 1952, 42.
76. Berdyaev 1952, 70–71.
77. Berdyaev 1944, 147–48.
78. Berdyaev 1952, 72.
79. Berdyaev 1952, 65.
80. Bulgakov 1999, 160.
81. Bulgakov 1999, 283.
82. See "Economic Activity and 'Theurgy,'" "The Soul of Socialism," in Bulgakov 1999.
83. For a thorough, and yet concise overview of Bulgakov's "Sophic economy," see Payne and Marsh 2009. See also Dunn 2011.

Being as Freedom and Necessity

1. Here I keep in mind primarily the work of Nikolai Berdyaev, Vladimir Lossky, and John Zizioulas, to whom my own theological and philosophical approach is mostly indebted. However, their approaches reflect some of the much earlier Christian ideas that we find in the works of the Cappadocian fathers and St. Maximus the Confessor, up to St. Symeon the New Theologian and Gregory Palamas.

2. Zizioulas 1984, 42.

3. Džalto 2014.

4. Lossky 1976, 114–34; see also Lossky 1974.

5. See Džalto 2014, 27–29.

6. For a short overview of the treatment of the *imago Dei* issue in the patristic literature and in the later Orthodox tradition, see Lossky 1997 (chapter six).

7. As we will see later, the rest of the created world is not completely discharged of freedom; animals and even plants and the mineral world do reflect various degrees of freedom and are also capable of participating (to various degrees) in love as the *materialization* of freedom.

8. It is important to note that Zizioulas's approach to the patristic theology—especially his attempts to develop the individual-person tension based on the Cappadocian Fathers—has been questioned and critically examined. See Turcescu 2002.

9. See Knight 2007 (especially 35–78 and 109–23); Papanikolaou 2004. See also Yannaras 2007.

10. Zizioulas 1985, 50.

11. Zizioulas 1985, 50.

12. See Evdokimov 1973.

13. "The concept of the person with its absolute and ontological content was born historically from the endeavor of the Church to give ontological expression to its faith in the Triune God." Zizioulas 1985, 36.

14. "Dear friends, let us love one another, for love comes from God. Everyone who loves has been born of God and knows God. Whoever does not love does not know God, because God is love." 1 John 4:7–8.

15. Zizioulas 1985, 47.

16. Antoine de Saint-Exupéry, *The Little Prince* (original edition 1943), chapter 21.

17. Evdokimov 1973, 49.

18. However, such a reductionist reading does not do justice to the concept of sacrifice, not only in the Old Testament tradition but also in the ancient Oriental sacrificial practices more generally. Offering sacrifices does not necessarily imply the existence of angry gods who require satisfaction through some kind of punishment. Sacrifices can also be understood as rituals that are aimed at *making us better*, by using the taboo of death. An interesting understanding of ancient

sacrificial rituals, that were up to a point applicable to the Temple offerings, is found in George Hersey's reading of the ancient Greek tropes. See Hersey 1988, 11–45.

19. See Athanasius of Alexandria: "For he was incarnate that we might be made god; and he manifested himself through a body that we might receive an idea of the invisible Father." Athanasius of Alexandria 2011, 107.

20. Genesis 3:5 and 3:7 can (and I think should) be read in connection to Luke 24:31, John 9, Acts 26:18, and Ephesians 1:18.

21. This is what can be derived from several places in the patristic texts. To my knowledge, the earliest clear indication of this (setting aside many Old and New Testament places that allow for multiple interpretations) is found in Irenaeus:

> Hence also was Adam himself termed by Paul the figure of Him that was to come [. . .] because the Word, the Maker of all things, had formed beforehand for Himself the future dispensation of the human race, connected with the Son of God; God having predestined that the first man should be of an animal nature, with this view, that he might be saved by the spiritual One. For inasmuch as He had a pre-existence as a saving Being, it was necessary that what might be saved should also be called into existence, in order that the Being who saves should not exist in vain. (*Against Heresies*, III:22.3)

Maximus the Confessor is much clearer in this regard. In *Ad Thalassium* 60, Maximus says:

> This is the great and hidden mystery, at once the blessed end for which all things are ordained. It is the divine purpose conceived before the beginning of created beings. In defining it we would say that this mystery is the preconceived goal for which everything exists, but which itself exists on account of nothing. . . . It is the mystery which circumscribes all the ages, and which reveals the grand plan of God (cf. Eph 1:10–11), a super-infinite plan infinitely preexisting the ages. The Logos, by essence God, became a messenger of this plan (cf Isa 9:5, LXX) when he became a man and, if I may rightly say so, established himself as the innermost depth of the Father's goodness while also displaying in himself the very goal for which his creatures manifestly received the beginning of their existence. . . . For the union between a limit of the ages and limitlessness, between measure and immeasurability, between finitude and infinity, between Creator and creation, between rest and motion, was conceived before the ages. This union has been manifested in Christ at the end of time, and in itself brings God's foreknowledge to fulfillment, in order that naturally mobile creatures might secure themselves around God's total and essential immobility. (Maximus the Confessor 2003, 124–25)

22. "Those who share in the energies and act in conformity with them are by God made gods without beginning or end through grace." St. Gregory Palamas, *Against Akindynos*, 5.24, quoted in Thomas 2008, 25. See St. Gregory Palamas: "If grace were not unoriginate, how would one become through participation in this grace 'unoriginate like Melchisedec, of whom it is said that his days had no beginning and his life no end'? Or how, 'like Paul, could a man live the divine and eternal life of the Word dwelling in him?" Gregory Palamas, *Triads* III.3.8 (quoted in Palamas 1983). See also Hebrews 7:3. Something similar is implied by Maximus the Confessor in *Ad Thalassium* 22.

23. See ἄναρχος (III.) in Liddell, Scott 1996, 120.

24. This is the reason why there is often a lot of confusion between the Orthodox understanding of what it means to be a *saint* and various popular (as well as non-Orthodox) understandings of this concept. To be a saint is to go through the transformative experience of theosis. To be a saint is to acquire the Holy Spirit. This is very different from linking holiness with moral perfection or the fulfillment of ethical standards.

25. This has been the essential structure of Greek tragedies. We find a similar structure in mainstream Hollywood movies when, in an entirely predictable, schematic, and some would say *kitschy* way, "good guys" triumph over "evil" and (re)establish the disturbed order and the meaning of the world.

Something Is Rotten in This Reality of Ours

1. Although the delight of describing the way in which eternal condemnation and suffering will happen is not absent from the Orthodox tradition, by any means. In contrast to the vivid imagery that understands hell as the place of everlasting fire, pain, and/or darkness, a remarkably different image of the eternal infernal suffering is attributed to St. Macarius the Great. The story tells about Macarius, who found the skull of a former pagan priest. The skull told him of the core of their eternal suffering: "It is not possible to see anyone face to face, but the face of one is fixed to the back of another. Yet when you pray for us, each of us can see the other's face a little." Ward 1975, 137.

2. See Dumitru Stăniloae's account on the Fall (and the Fathers cited therein), in Stăniloae 2000, 163–89.

3. See Maritain 2015, 31–46; Yannaras 2007.

4. Zizioulas's approach has been criticized as one-sided and as lacking solid foundations in patristic theology. See Knight 2007 (especially relevant are Chapters 2, 5, and 6); Torrance 2011.

5. See Zizioulas 1985, 27–33.

6. We find similar confusion on the opposite side of the political spectrum in the pseudo-ecclesial, secular religious ideologies and projects that aspire to

forcibly turn the entire society into "communes," pretending that the (secularized) eschatology has arrived, or is about to arrive.

7. See Zizioulas 1985, 50–53.

8. See Zizioulas 1985, 50.

9. Zizioulas 1985, 51.

10. See Berdyaev 2001, especially 27–96.

11. See Berdyaev 2001, 69–70.

12. "All this means that man as a biological hypostasis is intrinsically a tragic figure . . . at the same time it [body] is the 'mask' of hypocrisy, the fortress of individualism, the vehicle of the final separation, death." Zizioulas 1985, 52.

13. See Romans 8:19–21: "For the creation waits in eager expectation for the children of God to be revealed. For the creation was subjected to frustration, not by its own choice, but by the will of the one who subjected it, in hope that the creation itself will be liberated from its bondage to decay and brought into the freedom and glory of the children of God."

14. This is also how the symbolic meaning of the Jerusalem Temple can be interpreted. Following Margaret Barker's interpretations of the First Temple tradition, the Holy of Holies can be seen as an image of the Kingdom of God (the eschaton). See Barker 2010, 17, 37, and 215. The high priest was the image of God, and the entering of the high priest from the Holy of Holies (Heaven) into the Holy Place (with his priestly garments) symbolized the Incarnation (see Barker 2010, 193–216). This can, further, be interpreted as "dressing" the human beings into the garments of glory (i.e., *becoming* human, and by becoming [fully] human becoming also *divine*); these are the same garments that the priests, kings, prophets, and, ultimately, *gods* (children of God) eschatologically acquire, as those who join God in their own creation. See Psalm 82:6, "I said, 'You are gods; you are all children of the Most High.'"

Eschatology and Liturgy

1. See Zizioulas 1985; Zizioulas 2008, 105–60.

2. See Gondikakis 1998, 84–90, 97–99.

3. See Psalm 75:8, 104:15.

"This World" and the Individualized Mode of Existence

1. The concept of "spirit" has been, occasionally, used in the context of Christianity to designate the realm of freedom as opposed to the realm of necessity (see Berdyaev 1952). Traditionally, in Orthodox theology the concepts of "Spirit" or "spiritual," when properly used, always imply the Holy Spirit. Something or someone is "spiritual" when the Holy Spirit is present there. And where the Spirit is, there is freedom.

2. See Ephesians 2:2; Colossians 2:8, 2:20.

3. See Luke 24:40–43.

4. See John 4:42.

The Politics of Nothingness

1. Ellul 2011a, 60–61.

2. Moore 2006, 33.

3. Moore 2006, 31.

4. See also Klaus Wengst's classical analysis of the conflicting logics of the Pax Romana and the Christian understanding of the social-political reality and interhuman relations, in Wengst 1987.

5. "Now faith is the substance of things hoped for, the evidence of things not seen." Hebrews 11:1.

6. Zizioulas 2009, 1–2.

7. We find a similar idea expressed in a lapidary way by Milovan Đilas: "No one can take freedom from another without losing his own." Đilas 2014, 93.

8. The lesson we can learn from the Orthodox Christian tradition, which goes back to the New Testament, is that it is easier for any criminal or any morally "corrupt" person to become a saint than it is for those moralistic, pious, self-righteous people who do everything "right" but have no desire for another human being, who do not have compassion, who do not wrestle with God and themselves, exposing in that way the rottenness of their individual existence to the healing love of God. Morally "good" behavior and legally "right" acts still remain within the boundary of this world, and therefore by themselves do not necessarily indicate one's *saintliness*—i.e., one's openness to the presence of the Holy Spirit. On the other hand, those who do *evil*, but still aspire to change their mode of existence, who repent and seek forgiveness, demonstrate that they are on the path of liberation.

9. Solovyev sees the contrast between the logic of the state and other institutions of "this world" and Church logic as something that reflects the Divine realm. For him, "The purpose of legal justice is not to transform the world which lies in evil into the kingdom of God, but only to prevent it from changing *too soon* into hell." Solovyev (Solovyof) 1918, 376.

10. The same motif is echoed, with an everlasting vividness, in Kubrick's *A Clockwork Orange*.

11. Dostoyevsky 1990, 251.

12. Dostoyevsky 1990, 251.

13. See Matthew 4:1–11.

14. Dostoyevsky 1990, 258.

15. See Isaiah 65:17; Revelation 21:1.

16. See Matthew 20:28; John 13:1–17; John 15:15.

17. See Papanikolaou 2017.

18. Uri Gordon (following Starhawk) elaborates the concept of "power over" as "power through domination" (distinct from "power-to" [do something] and "power with/among" that are both perceived as nonoppressive). See Uri Gordon, "Power and Anarchy: In/equality + In/visibility in Autonomous Politics," in Jun and Wahl, eds., 2010, 41. "Power over," manifested through force, coercion, manipulation, and authority (see Gordon, ibid., 42) is the most visible and most problematic aspect of power; however, from an Orthodox Christian perspective, "power to" and "power with/among" can also exhibit signs of the individualized existence.

Theology as a Critical Discourse?

1. Athenagoras, *Plea on Behalf of the Christians* 35, quoted in Kalantzidis 2012, 91.

2. I have discussed the issue of "just(ifiable) war" theories and Orthodoxy in more depth in Džalto 2017.

3. See Berdyaev:

> Freedom cannot have any sort of roots within being. . . . In being there is as it were no place for freedom. . . . The problem of freedom is a problem of spirit, and it is not resolvable in any naturalistic metaphysics of being. If freedom cannot be rooted in any sort of being, nor in any sort of nature, nor in any sort of substance, then there remains only one path for the affirmation of freedom—the acknowledgement, that the well-spring of freedom is the nothing, from out of which God created the world. Freedom is manifest prior to being and it determines for itself the path of being. (1928)

4. See Richard A. Davis's exploration of the concept of (political) "indifference," in Christoyannopoulos, ed. 2009, 82–105.

5. See Kropotkin:

> Anarchists recognize the justice of both the just-mentioned tendencies towards economic and political freedom, and see in them two different manifestations of the very same need of equality which constitutes the very essence of all struggles mentioned by history. Therefore, in common with all socialists, the anarchist says to the political reformer: "No substantial reform in the sense of political equality and no limitation of the powers of government can be made as long as society is divided into two hostile camps, and the laborer remains, economically speaking, a slave to his employer." But to the state socialist we say also: "You cannot modify the existing conditions of property without deeply modifying the powers of government and renounce parliamentary rule. To each new economic phase of life

corresponds a new political phase. Absolute monarchy corresponded to the system of serfdom. Representative government corresponds to capital-rule. Both, however, are class-rule. But in a society where the distinction between capitalist and laborer has disappeared, there is no need of such a government; it would be an anachronism, a nuisance. Free workers would require a free organization, and this cannot have any other basis than free agreement and free cooperation, without sacrificing the autonomy of the individual to the all-pervading interference of the State. The no-capitalist system implies the no-government system." (Peter Kropotkin, "Revolutionary Pamphlets," in Krimerman and Perry, eds. 1966, 225–26)

6. The discoveries made by Julian Assange (and Wikileaks) and Edward Snowden and the treatment to which these individuals were subjected to by "democratic" governments of the "free" world are classic examples in this regard.

7. See Wolin 2017.

8. Some contemporary anarchist authors recognized this problem and focused on secular freedom and equality as the most important things for anarchist theory and practice. Thus, Colin Ward proposes four principles behind the anarchist theory of social organization: Anarchist communities should be voluntary, functional, temporary, and small (see Colin Ward, "Anarchism as a Theory of Organization," in Krimerman and Perry, eds. 1966, 387). All these principles (especially the proposal that any organization of anarchist communities should be temporary and small) seem to be very compatible with the (Orthodox) Christian approach to the socio-political sphere, as long as they remain practical/functional guidelines that are situated in a concrete social, cultural, and historical reality, with the purpose of providing more freedom, justice, and better living conditions for all members of society (without confusing it with the Kingdom of God, or replacing liturgical gatherings with social-political works).

9. See Džalto 2018b (and Nikki Johnson-Huston's article cited therein).

10. See Zuboff 2019.

11. The most outspoken individuals in this respect are Sean Parker, former Facebook president, and Chamath Palihapitiya, former Facebook senior executive—see their interviews at https://www.youtube.com/watch?v =J54k7WrbfMg. For the theological and anthropological implications of this, see Džalto 2012.

12. See: "Instead of being a force of democratization and emancipation, the digital revolution may turn out being the opposite and contribute to undermine democracy and political self-determination." Hendricks and Vestergaard 2019, 119. See also Wolf 2012; Motupalli 2018.

13. See Kitchin 2018.

14. See Feldstein 2019.

15. First steps in this direction can be seen in the "social credit system" (or "social credit scores") introduced in China. See "China's social-credit scoring is best understood not as a single system but as an overarching ideology: encompassing punishments and rewards, to improve governance and stamp out disorder and fraud. Commercial schemes mostly handle the perks, state schemes the punishments. Both work in concert to encourage socially responsible behavior." Campbell 2019.

16. This problem is present also in Ward. He recognizes that the problem is not only in the oppression from "above" but also people's participation in oppressive systems:

> I said that it is governments which make wars and prepare for wars, but obviously it is not governments alone—the power of a government, even the most absolute dictatorship, depends on the tacit assent of the governed. Why do people consent to be governed? It isn't only fear: what have millions of people to fear from a small group of politicians? It is because they subscribe to the same values as their governors. Rulers and ruled alike believe in the principle of authority, of hierarchy, of power. (Colin Ward, "Anarchism as a Theory of Organization," in Krimerman and Perry, eds. 1966, 387)

It seems that in Ward's understanding of power dynamics there is no room for an existential dimension of power issues. This may be the reason why, in the end, he seems to subscribe to Kropotkin's vision of anarchy, the "theory of spontaneous order," which holds that "a collection of people will, by trial and error, by improvisation and experiment, evolve order out of chaos—this order being more durable and more closely related to their needs than any kind of externally imposed order." Ward, "Anarchism as a Theory of Organization," in Krimerman and Perry, eds. 1966, 389.

17. The goals of certain Christian anarchist groups—such as the Catholic Worker Movement—are sometimes understood along these lines. See: "The anarchism of the Catholic Worker Movement is a 'romanticized and nostalgic notion of a medieval free commune. Their model amounts to a variation of an authoritarian corporate one: the church becomes the state.'" Harold Barclay, "Anarchist Confrontations with Religion," in Jun and Wahl, eds. 2010, 177.

18. See 1 Corinthians 7:31; 1 John 2:17.

19. This section is a slightly revised version of an earlier article—"What's Wrong with the 'Left' and the 'Right'? An Orthodox Christian Perspective"— that first appeared in a Russian volume on political theology (see Džalto 2019), then in English (see Džalto 2020).

20. I put "democratic" in quotation marks because the concept of "democracy" is used today mostly as an honorific, not a descriptive term. That is to say that "democracy" is mostly used to differentiate "us" (the "good guys")

from "them" (the nondemocratic "bad guys"). Apart from this problem, many societies that we commonly call "democracies" are, in reality, *plutocracies*, where there is little or no correspondence between the interests and attitudes of the majority of the population and the character of the policies that the ruling class formulates and implements.

21. These questions bear a special importance in the context of contemporary Europe and the US, where we witness the rise of (far) right-wing (even neofascist) political options that use Christianity as an ideological pretext for their racist, anti-immigration or antirefugee policies. They often advance concepts such as "Christian Europe" (against, for instance, the perceived threat from the "Muslims"), "Christian politics" (by which they often mean traditional and more authoritarian styles of government and/or nationalistic ideologies), and "Christian family" (against, primarily, the perceived threat of changing the traditional gender roles within the patriarchal system).

22. Kalaitzidis 2012, 25.

23. Bobbio 1996, xxii.

24. Moreover, it is hard to imagine what an "ideology-free" society would look like—as long as it is composed of living human beings.

25. Džalto 2013a, 67–73.

26. The same logic is also at work in the case of what is sometimes perceived as "liberal" or "left" (primarily in the US), as in the case of what is, broadly speaking, called "political correctness." In this ideological discourse, if someone dares to say or even think anything that this ideological position has a priori proclaimed problematic or unacceptable, that becomes a sufficient reason to dehumanize a person or a group by launching defamatory media campaigns, dehumanizing the ideological "enemy," excluding them, and even executing them. There is no dialogue and no recognition of the other human being's humanity. The "horizon of meaning" must be preserved, and so the sacrifices must be offered on its altar.

27. See Žižek:

> There is much talk today about the obsolescence of the difference between Right and Left; in order not to be deceived it is useful to remember the asymmetry of these notions: a leftist is somebody who can say "I am a left-winger"—that is, recognize the split, the Left/Right distinction; whereas a right-winger can invariably be recognized by the way he positions himself in the centre and condemns all "extremism" as "old-fashioned." In other words, the Right/Left distinction is perceived as such (in Hegelese: posited) only from a Left perspective, whereas the Right perceives itself as being in the "centre"; it speaks in the name of the "Whole"; it rejects the split. The articulation of the political space is thus a paradox well exempli-

fied by the deadlocks of sexuation: it is not simply the articulation into two poles of the Whole, but one pole (the Left) represents the split as such; the other (the Right) denies it, so that the political split Left/Right necessarily assumes the form of the opposition between "Left" and "centre," with the place of the "Right" remaining empty. (Žižek 2008, 139n22)

28. It is interesting to note in this context an observation by a Yugoslav dissident, Milovan Đilas, who in his youth used to profess the Stalinist-type of communist faith:

> It was in the Red Army, from an army commander, that I first heard a thought that was strange to me then, but bold: When Communism triumphs in the whole world, he concluded, wars would then acquire their final bitter character. According to Marxist theories, which the Soviet commanders knew as well as I, wars are exclusively the product of class struggle, and because Communism would abolish classes, the necessity for men to wage war would also vanish. But this general, many Russian soldiers, as well as I in the worst battle in which I ever took part came to realize some further truths in the horrors of war: that human struggles would acquire the aspect of ultimate bitterness only when all men came to be subject to the same social system, for the system would be untenable as such and various sects would undertake the reckless destruction of the human race for the sake of its greater "happiness." (Đilas 2014, 36)

29. Secularization can also turn into another abstract dogma that, when applied aggressively and automatically, can also produce negative effects. A classic example of this is the rise of religious fundamentalism.

30. See:

> Wage labor is now entirely respectable, as is self-employment, whereas slavery has been stigmatized throughout the world. . . . For most of human history, wage labor has been perceived as something akin to slavery and American democratic thought up to and including the Jacksonian era was heir to this pre-capitalist perception. . . . It was the Republicans themselves who made the dramatic break with the past in assimilating wage labor to "freedom." This ideological shift had momentous consequences. (Ashworth 1995, 114)

31. Bulgakov 1999, 121.
32. Bulgakov 1999, 150.
33. See McPartlan 1993.
34. For more on this issue, see Džalto 2018.
35. One of the most elaborate investigations of the possibilities and challenges of a "reliturgization" of the church (with an attempt at developing theological

tools for a constructive criticism of the conceptual theological apparatus we use, as well as institutional practices) has been presented in Michael Hjälm's 2011 dissertation, *Liberation of the Ecclesia* (see Hjälm 2011).

36. The *professional* clergy has its foundations in Canon 5 of the Apostolic Canons, which specifies that a "bishop or an elder or a deacon shall not mix in with the doings of this world. But if they do this, let them be deposed." Quoted in Schodde 1885, 63. It is, of course, clear that there have been many "doings of this world" that bishops have been historically undertaking (often out of necessity), even in the pre-Constantine times as well as after (performing administrative/judicial roles for instance).

The End and the Beginning

1. Compare to "In Praise of Inconsistency" by Leszek Kołakowski; see Kołakowski 1964.

2. This was, to an extent, captured in Herman Hesse's *Steppenwolf*; his words can be paraphrased and interpreted in a Christian key: "And I knew that my dreams had been right. . . . It was life and reality that were wrong." See Herman Hesse, *Steppenwolf*, translated by Basil Creighton, updated by Joseph Mileck (New York: Holt, Rinehart and Winston, 1963), 50.

3. The contrast between love (together with the freedom and authenticity of existence that go with it), and "good" or "proper" behavior is very well captured in *One Flew over the Cuckoo's Nest* (directed by Miloš Forman), and in the more recent movie *Philomena* (directed by Stephen Frears). In both of them, those who are, formally speaking, on the side of the law, rules, procedures, or even Christianity (the management of the mental hospital in the first case, and the convent nuns in the second one) are actually portrayed as the exponents of a much more horrifying and systematic *madness*, a deep inhumanity and (in the second case) anti-Christianity, in contrast to those who formally appear as the villains, who broke some rules or exhibited what is considered immoral or illegal behavior.

4. Vladimir Lossky makes a similar point when discussing theology and mysticism in the Orthodox tradition, in the introduction to his *The Mystical Theology of the Eastern Church*: "Thus, we are . . . led to a conclusion which may seem paradoxical enough: that Christian theory should have an eminently practical significance; and that the more mystical it is, the more directly it aspires to the supreme end of union with God." Lossky 1976, 9.

BIBLIOGRAPHY

Afanasiev, Nicholas. 2012. *The Church of the Holy Spirit*. Notre Dame, Ind.: University of Notre Dame Press.

Alexis-Baker, Nekeisha. 2006. "Embracing God and Rejecting Masters: On Christianity, Anarchism and the State." *The Utopian* 5 (October 1, 2006): 76–83. http://www.utopianmag.com/files/in/1000000044/embracing.pdf.

Andrews, Dave. 1999. *Christi-Anarchy: Discovering a Radical Spirituality of Compassion*. Eugene, Oreg.: Wipf & Stock.

Angelov, Dimiter. 2007. *Imperial Ideology and Political Thought in Byzantium, 1204–1330*. Cambridge: Cambridge University Press.

Ashworth, John. 1995. *Slavery, Capitalism, and Politics in the Antebellum Republic*, vol. 1. Cambridge: Cambridge University Press.

Athanasius. 1892. *History of the Arians*. Translated by M. Atkinson and Archibald Robertson. https://www.newadvent.org/fathers/2815.htm.

Athanasius (the Great) of Alexandria, St. 2011. *On the Incarnation*. Translated by John Behr. Yonkers, N.Y.: SVS Press.

Augustine, Saint. 1958. *The City of God: An Abridged Version*. Translated by Gerald G. Walsh et al. New York: Image Books Doubleday.

Avrich, Paul. 1971. *The Russian Anarchists*. Princeton: Princeton University Press.

Azkoul, Michael. 1979. "Sacred Monarchy and the Modern Secular State." *Centar za istraživanje pravoslavnog monarhizma*. http://www.czipm.org/azkoul.html.

———. 1984. *Sacred Monarchy and the Modern Secular State*. Montreal: Monastery Press.

Baird, Catherine. 1995. "Religious Communism? Nicolai Berdyaev's Contribution to Esprit's Interpretation of Communism." *Canadian Journal of History* (April 1995): 29–47.

Bakunin, Michael. 1973. *Selected Writings*, ed. Arthur Lehning. London: Jonathan Cape.

Barker, Margaret. 2010. *Creation: A Biblical Vision for the Environment*. London: T&T Clark.

Barnes, Timothy D. 1993. *Athanasius and Constantius: Theology and Politics in the Constantinian Empire*. Cambridge, Mass.: Harvard University Press.

The Bases of the Social Concept of the Russian Orthodox Church. 2000. http://orthodoxrights.org/documents/russian-church-freedom-and-rights.

Beach, Lee. 2015. *The Church in Exile: Living in Hope after Christendom*. Downers Grove, Ill.: IVP Academic.

Beazley, Raymond C. 1914. Introduction to *The Chronicle of Novgorod, 1016–1471*, translated by Robert Michell, vii–xxxvi. London: Royal Historical Society.

Belle, Gilbert Van, and Joseph Verheyden, eds. 2014. *Christ and the Emperor: The Gospel Evidence*. Leuven: Peeters.

Berdyaev, Nikolai. 1928. "The Metaphysical Problem of Freedom." Translated by S. Janos. http://www.berdyaev.com/berdiaev/berd_lib/1928_329.html#1.

———. 1944. *Slavery and Freedom*. New York: Charles Scribner's Sons.

——— (Berđajev, Nikolaj). 2001. *Smisao istorije: ogled filozofije čovečje sudbine*. Belgrade, Serbia: Dereta.

Berdyaev, Nicolas. 2004. *The Origin of Russian Communism*. Ann Arbor: University of Michigan Press.

———. 2009. *The End of Our Time*. Translated by Donald Attwater. San Rafael, Calif.: Semantron Press.

———. 2015. *The Philosophy of Inequality: Letters to My Contemners, Concerning Social Philosophy*. Translated by Stephen Janos. Mohrsville, Pa.: FRSJ Publications.

Bercken, Will van den. 1999. *Holy Russia and Christian Europe*. London: SCM Press.

Bettenson, Henry, and Chris Maunder, eds. 2011. *Documents of the Christian Church*. Oxford: Oxford University Press.

Bigović, Radovan. 2010. *Crkva u savremenom svetu*. Belgrade, Serbia: Službeni glasnik.

Bobbio, Norberto. 1996. *Left and Right: The Significance of a Political Distinction*. Chicago: The University of Chicago Press.

Bogatyrev, Sergei. 2007. "Reinventing the Russian Monarchy in the 1550s: Ivan the Terrible, the Dynasty, and the Church." *SEER* 85, no. 2 (April 1997): 271–93.

Bradstock, Andrew, and Christopher Rowland, eds. 2002. *Radical Christian Writings: A Reader*. Malden, Mass.: Blackwell.

Brînzea, Nicolae. 2014. "Evolutions and Involutions in the Church-State Relationship." *European Journal of Science and Theology* 10, no. 2 (April 2014): 139–47.

Brown Dewhurst, Emma. 2018. "To Each According to Their Needs: Anarchist Praxis as a Resource for Byzantine Theological Ethics." In *Essays in Anarchism and Religion,* vol. 2, edited by Alexandre Christoyannopoulos, 58–93. Stockholm: Stockholm University Press.

Brown, Peter. 2005. *The Rise of Western Christianity.* Malden, Mass.: Blackwell.

Bulgakov, Sergii. 1999. *Towards a Russian Political Theology.* Edited and with an introduction by Rowan Williams. Edinburgh: T&T Clark.

———. 2000. *Philosophy of Economy: The World as a Household.* Translated and edited by Catherine Evtuhov. New Haven: Yale University Press.

Cameron, Alan. 2016. "*Pontifex Maximus*: from Augustus to Gratian—and Beyond." In *Emperors and the Divine—Rome and Its Influence,* edited by Maijastina Kahlos, 139–59. Helsinki: Helsinski Collegium for Advanced Studies.

Cameron, Averil. 2006. *The Byzantines.* Malden, Mass.: Blackwell.

Campbell, Charlie. 2019. "How China Is Using 'Social Credit Scores' to Reward and Punish Its Citizens." https://time.com/collection-post/5502592 /chinasocial-credit-score/ (January 16, 2019).

Canning, Joseph. 2003. *A History of Medieval Political Thought: 300–1450.* London: Routledge (electronic edition).

Charanis, Peter. 1974a. "Church-State Relations in the Byzantine Empire as Reflected in the Role of the Patriarch in the Coronation of the Byzantine Emperor." In *The Ecumenical World of Orthodox Civilization: Russia and Orthodoxy,* vol. 3, edited by Andrew Blane, 77–90. The Hague: Mouton.

———. 1974b. *Church and State in the Later Roman Empire.* Thessaloniki: Kentron byzantinon ereunon.

———. 1982. "On the Question of the Evolution of the Byzantine Church into a National Greek Church." *Byzantina* 2 (1982): 97–109.

Chomsky, Noam. 2014. *On Anarchism.* London: Penguin Books.

Christoyannopoulos, Alexandre. 2008. "Leo Tolstoy on the State: A Detailed Picture of Tolstoy's Denunciation of State Violence and Deception." *Anarchist Studies* 16, no. 1: 20–47.

———. 2011. *Christian Anarchism: A Political Commentary on the Gospel.* Exeter, U.K.: Imprint Academic.

———, ed. 2011. *Religious Anarchism: New Perspectives.* Newcastle upon Tyne, U.K.: Cambridge Scholars.

Clement of Alexandria. 1867. *Works of Clement of Alexandria.* Translated by William Wilson. Edinburgh: T&T Clark.

Coleman, Heather J., ed. 2014. *Orthodox Christianity in Imperial Russia: A Source Book on Lived Religion.* Bloomington: Indiana University Press.

Comaroff, Jean and John. 2000. "Privatizing the Millennium: New Protestant Ethics and the Spirits of Capitalism in Africa and Elsewhere." *Africa Spectrum* 35, no. 3: 293–312.

Cox, Harvey. 2016. *Market as God*. Cambridge, Mass.: Harvard University Press.

Curtiss, John Shelton. 1940. *Church and State in Russia—The Last Years of the Empire—1900–1917*. New York: Columbia University Press.

Dagron, Gilbert. 2007. *Emperor and Priest: The Imperial Office in Byzantium*. Cambridge: Cambridge University Press.

Damascus, St. John. 2003. *Three Treatises On the Divine Imaged*. Translated and with an introduction by Andrew Louth. Crestwood, N.Y.: SVS Press.

Damico, Linda H. 1987. *The Anarchist Dimension of Liberation Theology*. New York: Peter Lang.

Dawes, Milton. 2010. "Corporate Dictatorship?" *ETC.: A Review of General Semantics* 63, no 3: 294–99.

Demacopoulos, George, and Aristotle Papanikolaou , eds. 2017. *Christianity, Democracy, and the Shadow of Constantine*. New York: Fordham University Press.

Desmond, William. 2011. *Philosopher-Kings of Antiquity*. London: Continuum.

Dewhurst Brown, Emma. 2018. "To Each According to Their Needs: Anarchist Praxis as a Resource for Byzantine Theological Ethics." In *Essays in Anarchism and Religion*, vol. 2, edited by A. Christoyannopoulos and M. S. Adams, 58–93. Stockholm: Stockholm University Press.

Digeser, Elizabeth DePalma. 2012. *The Making of a Christian Empire: Lactantius and Rome*. Ithaca: Cornell University Press.

Dijkstra, Roald, and Dorine van, Espelo. 2017. "Anchoring Pontifical Authority: A Reconsideration of the Papal Employment of the Title *Pontifex Maximus*." *Journal of Religious History* 41, no. 3: 312–25.

Đilas, Milovan. 2014. *Conversations with Stalin*. London: Penguin.

Dostoyevsky, Fyodor. 1990. "The Grand Inquisitor." In *The Brothers Karamazov*. Translated by Richard Pevear and Larissa Volokhonsky. New York: Farrar, Straus and Giroux.

Drake, H. A. 1976. *In Praise of Constantine: A Historical Study and New Translation of Eusebius' Tricennial Orations*. Berkeley: University of California Press.

Duer, Hans Peter, ed. 1974. *Unter dem Pflaster liegt der Strand. Anarchismus Heute*, vol. 1. Berlin: Karin Kramer Verlag.

———, ed. 1975. *Unter dem Pflaster liegt der Strand. Anarchismus Heute*, vol. 2. Berlin: Karin Kramer Verlag.

Dunn, D. G. James, ed. 2003a. *The Cambridge Companion to St Paul*. Cambridge: Cambridge University Press.

Dunn, David James. 2011. "*Symphonia* in the Secular or How to Be Orthodox When You Lose Your Empire." In *Power and Authority in Eastern Christian*

Experience. The Sophia Institute Studies in Orthodox Theology, vol. 3, edited by Fevronia K. Soumakis, 209–18. New York: Theotokos Press, Sophia Institute.

Dunn, Marilyn. 2003b. *The Emergence of Monasticism: From the Desert Fathers to the Early Middle Ages*. Malden, Mass.: Blackwell.

Dvornik, Francis. 1966. *Early Christian and Byzantine Political Philosophy: Origins and Background*. Washington, D.C.: The Dumbarton Oaks Center for Byzantine Studies.

Džalto, Davor. 2009. "Fides et Regnvm." In *Crkva u pluralističkom društvu*. Belgrade: Christian Cultural Center—Konrad Adenauer Stiftung.

———. 2012. "Beauty Will Destroy the World? An Aesthetics of the Cross." In *Beauty and the Beautiful in Eastern Christian Culture* (Sophia Studies in Orthodox Theology), vol. 6, edited by Natalia Ermolaev, 279–91. New York: Theotokos Press.

———. 2013a. *Res Publica*. Požarevac, Serbia: Odbor za prosvetu i kulturu eparhije požarevačko-braničevske, Otačnik.

———. 2013b. "Nationalism, Statism, and Orthodoxy." *St Vladimir's Theological Quarterly* 57, no. 3–4: 503–23.

———. 2014. *The Human Work of Art: A Theological Appraisal of Creativity and the Death of the Artist*. Crestwood, N.Y.: SVS Press.

———. 2017. "Da li je moguć 'pravedni' rat? (Ne)pravoslavne teologije rata." In *Pravoslavlje i rat*, edited by Borislav Grozdić, 179–203. Belgrade: IFDT, Odbrana.

———. 2018a. "Our Neoliberal Orthodoxy." *Public Orthodoxy*. https://publicorthodoxy.org/2018/03/12/neoliberal-orthodoxy/.

———. 2018b. "How Much Is . . . Stupid? Neo-Liberal Academia and the Death of Education." *Dissident Voice*. https://dissidentvoice.org/2018/05/neo-liberal-academia-and-the-death-of-education/.

———. 2019. "Что не так с 'левым' и 'правыми'? Точка зрения православного христианина." In *Политическое богословие,* edited by Aleksei Bodrov and Mikhail Tolstoluženko, 280–304. Moscow: St Andrew's Biblical Theological Institute.

———. 2020. "What's Wrong with the 'Left' and the 'Right'? An Orthodox Christian Perspective." In *Theology and the Political: Theo-political Reflections on Contemporary Politics in Ecumenical Conversation*, edited by Alexei Bodrov and Stephen M. Garrett, 163–84. Leiden: Brill.

Edwards, Douglas R. 1996. *Religion and Power: Pagans, Jews, and Christians in the Greek East*. Oxford: Oxford University Press.

Ehrman, Bart D., ed. 2005. *The Apostolic Fathers*, vol. 1–2. Cambridge, Mass.: Harvard University Press.

Eller, Vernard. 1987. *Christian Anarchy: Jesus' Primacy over the Powers*. Grand Rapids, Mich.: Wm. B. Eerdmans.

Elliot, Thomas G. 1996. *Christianity of Constantine the Great*. Scranton, Pa.: University of Scranton Press.

Ellul, Jacques. 1989. *The Presence of the Kingdom*. Colorado Springs: Helmers & Howard.

———. 2011a. *Anarchy and Christianity*. Eugene, Oreg.: Wipf and Stock.

———. 2011b. *The Subversion of Christianity*. Eugene, Oreg.: Wipf and Stock.

———. 2012. *The Politics of God and the Politics of Man*. Eugene, Oreg.: Wipf and Stock.

Eusebius. 1999. *Life of Constantine*. Translated and with an introduction and commentary by Averil Cameron and Stuart G. Hall. Oxford: Clarendon Press.

———. 2018. *Ecclesiastical History: Complete and Unabridged*. Translated by C. F. Cruse. Peabody, Mass.: Hendrickson Publishers.

Evdokimov, Paul. 1973. *L'amour fou de Dieu*. Paris: Éditions du Seuil.

Fedotov, Georgy P. (Георгий Петрович Федотов). 1950. "Республика Святой Софии." https://www.yabloko.ru/Themes/History/Fedot/fedot-8.html.

———. 1966. *The Russian Religious Mind, vol. 2: The Middle Ages: The Thirteenth to the Fifteenth Centuries*. Cambridge, Mass.: Harvard University Press.

Feldstein, Steven. 2019. "The Road to Digital Unfreedom: How Artificial Intelligence Is Reshaping Repression." *Journal of Democracy* 30, no. 1: 40–52.

Freeze, G. L. 1985. "Handmaiden of the State? The Church in Imperial Russia Reconsidered." *Journal of Ecclesiastical History* 36, no. 1: 82–102.

Gentile, Emilio. 2006. *Politics as Religion*. Princeton: Princeton University Press.

Gierke, Otto. 1922. *Political Theories of the Middle Ages*. Cambridge: The Syndics of the Cambridge University Press.

Goldman, Emma. 1923. *My Disillusionment in Russia*. New York: Doubleday.

Golitzin, Alexander. 1994. "Hierarchy versus Anarchy? Dionysius Areopagita, Symeon the New Theologian, Nicetas Stethatos, and Their Common Roots in Ascetical Tradition." *St Vladimir's Theological Quarterly* 38: 131–79.

Gondikakis, Vasilije. 1998. *Sveta liturgija otkrivenje nove tvari*. Novi Sad, Serbia: Beseda.

Graham, Robert. 2015. *We Do Not Fear Anarchy: We Invoke It. The First International and the Origins of the Anarchist Movement*. Oakland, Calif.: AK Press.

Gramsci, Antonio. 1999. *The Antonio Gramsci Reader: Selected Writings 1916–1935*. Edited by David Forgacs. London: Lawrence and Wishart.

Guérin, Daniel. 1980. *Anarhizam*. Zagreb: Naprijed.

Guthrie, Kenneth Sylvan. 1917. *Numenius of Apamea, the Father of Neo-Platonism: Works, Biography, Message, Sources, and Influence*. London: George Bell & Sons.

Gvosdev, Nikolas K. 2000. *Emperors and Elections: Reconciling the Orthodox Tradition with Modern Politics*. Huntington, N.Y.: Troitsa Books.

———. 2001. *An Examination of Church-State Relations in the Byzantine and Russian Empires with an Emphasis on Ideology and Models of Interaction.* Lewiston, N.Y.: The Edwin Mellen Press.

Hamant, Yves, ed. 1992. *The Christianization of Ancient Russia: A Millennium: 988–1988.* Paris: UNESCO.

Harakas, Stanley Samuel. 1976. "Orthodox Church-State Theory and American Democracy." *Greek Orthodox Theological Review* 21, no. 4: 58–62.

———. 1992. *Living the Faith: The Praxis of Eastern Orthodox Ethics.* Minneapolis: Light and Life Pub.

Harris, Jonathan, ed. 2005. *Palgrave Advances in Byzantine History.* New York: Palgrave Macmillan.

Harrison, Carol, et al., eds. 2014. *Being Christian in Late Antiquity.* Oxford: Oxford University Press.

Hatlie, Peter. 2007. *The Monks and Monasteries of Constantinople, ca. 350–850.* Cambridge: Cambridge University Press.

Heer, Friedrich. 1998. *The Medieval World: Europe 1100–1350.* London: Phoenix.

Hendricks, Vincent F., and Mads Vestergaard. 2019. *Reality Lost: Markets of Attention, Misinformation and Manipulation.* Cham, Switzerland: Springer.

Hersey, George. 1988. *The Lost Meaning of Classical Architecture.* Cambridge, Mass.: MIT Press.

Hjälm, Michael. 2011. *Liberation of the Ecclesia: The Unfinished Project of Liturgical Theology.* Södertälje, Sweden: Anastasis Media.

Hobsbawm, Eric. 2007. *Globalisation, Democracy and Terrorism.* London: Little Brown.

Hotchkiss, Valerie, and Patrick Henry, eds. 2005. *Orthodoxy and Western Culture: A Collection of Essays Honoring Jaroslav Pelikan on His Eightieth Birthday.* Crestwood, N.Y.: SVS Press.

Hovey, Craig, and Elizabeth Phillips, eds. 2015. *The Cambridge Companion to Christian Political Theology.* New York: Cambridge University Press.

Hovorun, Cyril. 2008. *Will, Action and Freedom: Christological Controversies in the Seventh Century.* Leiden: Brill.

———. 2015a. *Meta-Ecclesiology: Chronicles on Church Awareness.* London: Palgrave Macmillan.

———. 2015b. "Maximus the Confessor—the Father of the Eastern and Western Churches." *International Journal of Orthodox Theology* 6, no. 3: 54–62.

———. 2016. "Is the Byzantine 'Symphony' Possible in Our Days?" *Journal of Church and State* 59, no 2: 280–96.

———. 2017. *Scaffolds of the Church: Towards Poststructural Ecclesiology.* Eugene, Oreg.: Cascade Books.

———. 2018a. *Political Orthodoxies: The Unorthodoxies of the Church Coerced.* Minneapolis: Fortress Press.

———. 2018b. "From Christology to Political Theology." *Religious Theory: E-Supplement to the Journal for Cultural and Religious Theory* (February 26, 2018): http://jcrt.org/religioustheory/2018/02/26/from-christology-to-political-theology-cyril-hovorun/.

Hunt, Priscilla, and Svitlana Kobets, eds. 2011. *Holy Foolishness in Russia: New Perspectives.* Bloomington, Ind.: Slavica.

Hussey, J. M. 2010. *The Orthodox Church in the Byzantine Empire.* Oxford: Clarendon.

Jevtić, Atanasije. 2009. *Bog otaca naših.* Mount Athos, Greece: Hilandar Monastery.

Joireman, Sandra F., ed. 2009. *Church, State, and Citizen: Christian Approaches to Political Engagement.* Oxford: Oxford University Press.

Jun, Nathan J., and Shane Wahl, eds. 2010. *New Perspectives on Anarchism.* Lanham: Lexington Books/Rowman & Littlefield.

Kalaitzidis, Pantelis. 2012. *Orthodoxy and Political Theology.* Geneva: World Council of Churches.

———. 2014. "Church and State in the Orthodox World: From the Byzantine 'Symphonia' and Nationalized Orthodoxy, to the Need of Witnessing the Word of God in a Pluralistic Society." In *Religioni, Libertà, Potere*, edited by Emanuela Fogliadini, 39–74. Milan: Vita e Pensiero.

Kalantzidis, George. 2012. *Caesar and the Lamb: Early Christian Attitudes on War and Military Service.* Eugene, Oreg.: Cascade Books.

Kaldellis, Anthony. 2015. *The Byzantine Republic: People and Power in New Rome.* Cambridge, Mass.: Harvard University Press.

Kirby, Benjamin. 2019. "Pentecostalism, Economics, Capitalism: Putting the *Protestant Ethic* to Work." *Religion* (May 24, 2019): https://www.tandfonline.com/doi/abs/10.1080/0048721X.2019.1573767?journalCode=rrel20.

Kitchin, Rob. 2018. "Big Data, New Epistemologies and Paradigm Shifts." *Big Data & Society* (April–June 2014): 1–12.

Knight, Douglas H., ed. 2007. *The Theology of John Zizioulas: Personhood and the Church.* Burlington: Ashgate.

Knox, Zoe. 2003. "The Symphonic Ideal: The Moscow Patriarchate's Post-Soviet Leadership." *Europe-Asia Studies* 55, no. 4: 575–96.

Kohler, K. 1920. "The Essenes and the Apocalyptic Literature." *The Jewish Quarterly Review* (New Series) 11, no. 2: 145–68.

Kołakowski, Leszek. 1964. "In Praise of Inconsistency." *Dissent* 11, no. 2: 201–9.

Krimerman, Leonard I., and Lewis Perry, eds. 1966. *Patterns of Anarchy: A Collection of Writings on the Anarchist Tradition.* Garden City, N.Y.: Anchor Books, Doubleday & Co.

Krstić, Zoran. 2006. "Socijalno učenje u pravoslavnoj teologiji." *Bogoslovlje* 65, no. 1: 240–46.

———. 2012. *Pravoslavlje i modernist: teme praktične teologije*. Belgrade, Serbia: Službeni glasnik.

———. 2014. *Crkva u društvu: u prošlosti i sadašnjosti*. Požarevac: Eparhija Braničevska, Odbor za prosvetu i kulturu.

Laats, Alar. 2009. "The Concept of the Third Rome and Its Political Implications." In *Religion and Politics in Multicultural Europe: Perspectives and Challenges*, vol. 1, edited by Alar Kilp and Andres Saumets, 98–113. Tartu: Tartu University Press.

Lampert, Evgeny. 1945. *Nicolas Berdyaev and the New Middle Ages*. London: James Clarke.

Legalisse, Erica. 2019. *Occult Features of Anarchism*. Oakland: PMP.

Leithart, Peter J. 2010. *Defending Constantine: The Twilight of an Empire and the Dawn of Christendom*. Downers Grove, Ill.: IVP Academic.

Lenin, V. I. 1970. *Krieg und Revolution*. Berlin: Deutscher Militärverlag.

Lenski, Noel, ed. 2006. *The Cambridge Companion to the Age of Constantine*. Cambridge: Cambridge University Press.

Lerner, Ralph, and Muhsin Mahdi, eds. 1972. *Medieval Political Philosophy: A Sourcebook*. Ithaca: Cornell University Press.

Lewis, Ewart. 1954. *Medieval Political Ideas*, vol. 1 and 2. London: Routledge & Kegan Paul.

Liddell, Henry George, and Robert Scott. 1996. *A Greek-English Lexicon*. Oxford: Clarendon Press.

Ljuben, Lape, ed. 1982. *Bogomilism in the Balkans in the Light of the Latest Research*. Skopje: Macedonian Academy of Sciences and Arts—Serbian Academy of Sciences and Arts—Academy of Sciences and Arts of Bosnia and Herzegovina.

Lossky, Vladimir. 1974. *In the Image and Likeness of God*. Crestwood, N.Y.: SVS Press.

———. 1976. *The Mystical Theology of the Eastern Church*. Crestwood, N.Y.: SVS Press.

———. 1997. *The Mystical Theology of the Eastern Church*. Crestwood, NY: SVS Press.

Maritain, Jacques. 2015. *The Person and the Common Good*. Notre Dame, Ind.: University of Notre Dame Press.

Marshall, Peter. 2008. *Demanding the Impossible: A History of Anarchism*. London: Harper Perennial.

Maximus the Confessor, St. 2003. *On the Cosmic Mystery of Jesus Christ*. Translated by Paul M. Blowers and Robert Louis Wilken. Crestwood, N.Y.: SVS Press.

Mayendorf, John. 1989. *Byzantium and the Rise of Russia.* Crestwood, N.Y.: SVS Press.

McGowan, Andrew B. 2014. *Ancient Christian Worship: Early Church Practices in Social, Historical, and Theological Perspective.* Grand Rapids, Mich.: Baker Academic.

McPartlan, Paul. 1993. *The Eucharist Makes the Church: Henri de Lubac and John Zizioulas in Dialogue.* Edinburgh: T&T Clark.

Medlin, William K. 1952. *Moscow and East Rome: A Political Study of the Relations of Church and State in Muscovite Russia.* Geneva: Librairie E. Droz.

Meyendorff, John. 1989. *Byzantium and the Rise of Russia: A Study of Byzantino-Russian Relations in the Fourteenth Century.* Crestwood, N.Y.: SVS Press.

Moore, Stephen D. 2006. *Empire and Apocalypse: Postcolonialism and the New Testament.* Sheffield, U.K.: Sheffield Phoenix Press.

Moss, Vladimir. 2014. *The Rise and Fall of Christian Rome.* http://www.orthodoxchristianbooks.com/downloads/529_THE_RISE_AND_FALL_OF_CHRISTIAN_ROME.pdf.

———. 2016. *The Rise and Fall of the Russian Autocracy.* http://www.orthodoxchristianbooks.com/downloads/591_THE_RISE_AND_FALL_OF_THE_RUSSIAN_AUTOCRACY.pdf.

———. 2018a. *A Monarchist Theology of Politics.* http://www.orthodoxchristianbooks.com/downloads/740_A_MONARCHIST_THEOLOGY_OF_POLITICS.pdf.

———. 2018b. *The Mystery of Christian Power.* http://www.orthodoxchristianbooks.com/downloads/739_THE_MYSTERY_OF_CHRISTIAN_POWER.pdf.

Motupalli, Venkat. 2018. "How Big Data Is Changing Democracy." *Journal of International Affairs*: https://jia.sipa.columbia.edu/how-big-datachanging-democracy.

Nikolaishvili, Sandro. 2011. "Byzantine Imperial Ideology and Political Thinking: Model for the 12th-Century Georgian Kingship." *Phasis* 14, no. 26: 346–47.

Noble, Ivana, et al. 2015. *Wrestling with the Mind of the Fathers.* Yonkers, N.Y.: SVS Press.

Novak, Ralph Martin, Jr. 2001. *Christianity and the Roman Empire: Background Texts.* Harrisburg, Pa.: Trinity Press.

Nucho, Fuad. 1966. *Berdyaev's Philosophy: The Existential Paradox of Freedom and Necessity: A Critical Study.* Garden City, N.Y.: Anchor Books.

Obolensky, Dimitri. 1971. *The Byzantine Commonwealth: Eastern Europe, 500–1453.* London: Weidenfeld & Nicolson.

———. 1994. *Byzantium and the Slavs.* Crestwood, N.Y.: SVS Press.

O'Donovan, Oliver, and Joan Lockwood O'Donovan, eds. 1999. *From Irenaeus to Grotius: A Sourcebook in Christian Political Thought.* Grand Rapids, Mich.: William B. Eerdmans.

Oravecz, Johannes Miroslav. 2014. *God as Love. The Concept and Spiritual Aspects of Agape in Modern Russian Religious Thought*. Grand Rapids, Mich.: William B. Eerdmans.

Osborn, Ronald E. 2010. *Anarchy and Apocalypse: Faith, Violence, and Theodicy*. Eugene, Oreg.: Cascade Books.

Ostrogorski, Georgije. 1998. *Istorija Vizantije*. Belgrade, Serbia: Narodna knjiga-Alfa.

Pagels, Elaine. 1989. *Adam, Eve, and the Serpent*. New York: Vintage Books.

———. 1996. *The Origin of Satan*. New York: Vintage Books.

Palamas, Gregory. 1983. *The Triads*. Translated by Nicholas Gendle. Mahwah, N.J.: Paulist Press.

Papanikolaou, Aristotle. 2004. "Is John Zizioulas an Existentialist in Disguise? Response to Lucian Turcescu." *Modern Theology* 20, no. 4 (October 2004): 587–93.

———. 2006. *Being with God: Trinity, Apophaticism, and Divine-Human Communion*. Notre Dame, Ind.: University of Notre Dame Press.

———. 2012. *The Mystical as Political: Democracy and Non-Radical Orthodoxy*. Notre Dame, Ind.: University of Notre Dame Press.

———. 2017. "Overcoming Political Nestorianism: Towards a Caledonian Politics." In *Grace, Governance and Globalization*, edited by Stephan van Erp, Martin G. Poulson, and Lieven Boeve, 114–24. London: Bloomsbury.

Parenti, Michael. 2011. *The Face of Imperialism*. Boulder, Colo.: Paradigm Pub.

Payne, Daniel P., and Christopher Marsh. 2009. "Sergei Bulgakov's 'Sophic' Economy: An Eastern Orthodox Perspective on Christian Economics." *Faith & Economics* 53 (Spring): 35–51.

Perrie, Maureen, ed. 2006. *The Cambridge History of Russia: From Early Rus' to. 1689*. Cambridge: Cambridge University Press.

———. 2014. "Moscow in 1666: New Jerusalem, Third Rome, Third Apostasy." *Quaestio Rossica* 3 (2014): 75–85.

Petro, Nicolai N. 2009. "The Novgorod Model: Creating a European Past in Russia." In *Cities after the Fall of Communism: Reshaping Cultural Landscapes and European Identity*, edited by John J. Czaplicka et al., 53–74. Baltimore: Johns Hopkins University Press.

Plechanow, G. W. 1946. *Über materialistische Geschichtsauffassung*. Moscow: Verlag für fremdsprachige Literatur.

Poe, Marshall T. 1997. "'Moscow, the Third Rome': The Origins and Transformations of a Pivotal Moment." Report. https://www.ucis.pitt.edu /nceeer/1997-811-25-Poe.pdf.

Popović, Justin. 1993. *Svetosavlje kao filosofija života*. Valjevo, Serbia: Manastir Ćelije.

———. 2012. "Unutrašnja misija naše crkve." https://svetosavlje.org/unutrasnja
-misija-nase-crkve/.

Pott, Thomas. 2010. *Byzantine Liturgical Reform: A Study of Liturgical Change in the Byzantine Tradition*. Crestwood, N.Y.: SVS Press.

Proudhon, P. J. 1876. *What Is Property? An Inquiry into the Principle of Right and of Government*. Vol. 1 in *The Works of P. J. Proudhon*. Princeton: Benj. R. Tucker.

Purpura, Ashley M. 2017. *God, Hierarchy, and Power: Orthodox Theologies of Authority from Byzantium*. New York: Fordham University Press.

Ramet, Pedro, ed. 1988. *Eastern Christianity and Politics in the Twentieth Century*. Durham, N.C.: Duke University Press.

Rousseau, Jean-Jacques. 1923. *The Social Contract and Discourses by Jean-Jacques Rousseau*. Translated by G. D. H. Cole. London: J.M. Dent and Sons.

Rowland, Daniel B. 1996. "Moscow—The Third Rome or the New Israel?" *Russian Review* 55, no. 4 (October): 591–614.

Runciman, Steven. 2003. *The Byzantine Theocracy*. Cambridge: Cambridge University Press.

The Russian Orthodox Church's Basic Teaching on Human Dignity, Freedom and Rights. 2008. http://orthodoxeurope.org/page/3/14.aspx.

Saltman, Richard B. 1983. *The Social and Political Thought of Michael Bakunin*. Westport, Conn.: Greenwood Press.

Scheibert, Peter. 1956. *Von Bakunin zu Lenin: Geschichte der russischen revolutionären Ideologien 1840–1895*. Leiden: Brill.

Schodde, George H. 1885. "The Apostolic Canons, Translated from the Ethiopic." *Journal of the Society of Biblical Literature and Exegesis* 5, no. 1–2: 61–72.

Scott, S. P. 1932. *The Civil Law*, vol. 16. Cincinnati: The Central Trust Company. http://www.constitution.org/sps/sps16.htm.

Sergeev, Mikhail. 2003. "Liberal Orthodoxy: From Vladimir Solov'ev to Fr. Alexander Men." *Occasional Papers on Religion in Eastern Europe* 23, no. 4, article 2. https://digitalcommons.georgefox.edu/ree/vol23/iss4/2/.

Shchapov, Yaroslav N. 1993. *State and Church in Early Russia: 10th– 13th Centuries*. Translated by Vic Schneierson. New Rochelle, N.Y.: Aristide D. Caratzas.

Shiffrin, Steven H. 2009. *The Religious Left and Church-State Relations*. Princeton: Princeton University Press.

Simonsen, Sven Gunnar. 1996. "Raising 'The Russian Question': Ethnicity and Statehood—*Russkie* and *Rossiya*." *Nationalism & Ethnic Politics* 2, no.1 (Spring 1996): 91–110.

Smither, Edward L. 2014. "Did the Rise of Constantine Mean the End of Christian Mission?" In *Rethinking Constantine: History, Theology, and Legacy*, edited by Edward L. Smither, 130–45. Eugene, Oreg.: Pickwick Pub.

Social Ethos. 2020. *For the Life of the World: Toward a Social Ethos of the Orthodox Church.* https://www.goarch.org/social-ethos#.

Sohn-Rethel, Alfred. 1987. *The Economy and Class Struggle of German Fascism.* Translated by Martin Sohn-Rethel. London: Free Association Books.

Solovyev, Vladimir. 1948. *Russia and the Universal Church.* London: Geoffrey Bles—The Centenary Press.

——— (Solovyof). 1918. *The Justification of the Good: An Essay on Moral Philosophy.* London: Constable and Company.

Soumakis, Fevronia K., ed. 2011. *Power and Authority in Eastern Christian Experience.* New York: Theotokos Press, The Sophia Institute.

Staniloae, Dumitru. 2000. *The Experience of God: Orthodox Dogmatic Theology,* vol. 2. Brookline, Mass.: Holy Cross Orthodox Press.

Stanković, Vlada. 2012. *"Living Icon of Christ*: Photios' Characterization of the Patriarch in the Introduction of the *Eisagoge* and Its Significance." In *ΣYMMEIKTA: Collection of Papers Dedicated to the 40th Anniversary of the Institute for Art History, Faculty of Philosophy, University of Belgrade,* edited by Ivan Stevović, 39–43. Belgrade: Faculty of Philosophy.

———. 2013. "The Path toward Michael Keroularios: The Power, Self-Presentation and Propaganda of the Patriarchs of Constantinople in the Late 10th and Early 11th Century." In *Zwei Sonnen am Goldenen Horn? Kaiserliche und patriarchale Macht im byzantinischen Mittelalter,* edited by Michael Grünbart, Lutz Rickelt, and Martin Marko Vučetić, 137–54. Münster: Lit Verlag.

Steenwyk, Mark van. 2012. *That Holy Anarchist: Reflections on Christianity & Anarchism.* Minneapolis: Missio Dei.

Stiglitz, Joseph. 2012. *The Price of Inequality: How Today's Divided Societies Endangers Our Future.* New York: W.W. Norton & Company.

———. 2015. *The Great Divide: Unequal Societies and What We Can Do about Them.* New York: W.W. Norton & Company.

Stirner, Max. 2000. *The Ego and Its Own,* edited by David Leopold). Cambridge: Cambridge University Press.

Stoeckl, Kristina, et al., eds. 2017. *Political Theologies in Orthodox Christianity.* London: Bloomsbury T&T Clark.

Sturzo, Luigi. 1962. *Church and State.* Notre Dame, Ind.: University of Notre Dame Press.

Tabbernee, William, ed. 2014. *Early Christianity in Contexts: An Exploration across Cultures and Continents.* Grand Rapids, Mich.: Baker Academic.

Taubes, Jacob. 2004. *The Political Theology of Paul.* Translated by Dana Hollander. Stanford, Calif.: Stanford University Press.

Temple, William. 1943. *Christianity and Social Order.* New York: Penguin.

Thatcher, Oliver J., and Edgar Holmes McNeal, eds. 1905. *Source Book for Mediæval History*. New York: Scribners.

Thomas, Stephen. 2008. *Deification in the Eastern Orthodox Tradition: A Biblical Perspective*. Piscataway, N.J.: Gorgias Press.

Tihomirov, Lav. 2008. *Monarhija*. Belgrade, Serbia: Ukronija, Logos.

Tolstoy, Leo. 1934. *On Life and Essays on Religion*. Translated by Aylmer Maude. Oxford: Oxford University Press.

Torrance, Alexis. 2011. "Personhood and Patristics in Orthodox Theology: Reassessing the Debate." *The Heythrop Journal* 52: 700–707.

Thulin, Alf. 1978. "'The Third Tribe' of the Rus." *Slavia Antiqua 25* (1978): 99–139.

Treadgold, Warren. 1997. *A History of the Byzantine State and Society*. Stanford: Stanford University Press.

Turcescu, Lucian. 2002. "'Person' versus 'Individual,' and Other Modern Misreadings of Gregory of Nyssa." *Modern Theology* 18, no. 4 (2002): 527–39.

Vermes, Geza. 2013. *Christian Beginnings: From Nazareth to Nicaea, AD 30–325*. London: Penguin Books.

Vorobievsky, Yuri (Воробьёвский, Юрий Ю.). 1999. *Путь к Апокалипсису: стук в золотые врата*. Свято-Троицкой Сергиевой Лавры: Патриарший издательско-полиграфический центр. https:// royallib.com/read/vorobevskiy_yuriy/put_k_apokalipsisu_stuk_v_zolotie _vrata.html#1038378.

Vysheslavtsev, B. P. 2002. *The Eternal in Russian Philosophy*. Translated by Penelope V. Burt. Grand Rapids, Mich.: William B. Eerdmans Publishing.

Wainwright, Geoffrey, and Karen B. Westerfield Tucker, eds. 2006. *The Oxford History of Christian Worship*. Oxford: Oxford University Press.

Walicki, Andrzej. 1979. *A History of Russian Thought: From the Enlightenment to Marxism*. Stanford, Calif.: Stanford University Press.

Ward, Benedicta, ed. 1975. *The Sayings of the Desert Fathers: The Alphabetical Collection*. Kalamazoo, Mich.: Cistercian Publications.

Webster, Alexander F. C. 2003. "Justifiable War as a 'Lesser Good' in Eastern Orthodox Moral Tradition." *St Vladimir's Theological Quarterly* 47, no. 1: 3–57.

———, and Darrell Cole. 2004. *The Virtue of War: Reclaiming the Classic Christian Traditions East and West*. Salisbury, Mass.: Regina Orthodox Press.

Wengst, Klaus. 1987. *Pax Romana and the Peace of Jesus Christ*. London: SCM Press.

Wickham, Chris. 2006. *Framing the Early Middle Ages: Europe and the Mediterranean 400–800*. Oxford: Oxford University Press.

Williams, Rowan. 2018. "Holy Folly and the Problem of Representing Holiness: Some Literary Perspectives." *Journal of Eastern Christian Studies* 1, no. 1: 3–15.

Wogaman, Phillip, J. 2000. *Christian Perspectives on Politics*. Louisville, Ky.: Westminster John Knox.

Wolf, Naomi. 2012. "The New Totalitarianism of Surveillance Technology." (August 15, 2012): https://www.theguardian.com/commentisfree/2012/aug/15/new-totalitarianismsurveillance-technology.

Wollin, Sheldon S. 2016. *Politics and Vision: Continuity and Innovation in Western Political Thought*. Princeton: Princeton University Press.

———. 2017. *Democracy Incorporated: Managed Democracy and the Specter of Inverted Totalitarianism*. Princeton: Princeton University Press.

Yannaras, Christos. 2002. "Human Rights and the Orthodox Church." Paper presented at the Holy Cross Greek Orthodox School of Theology (October 4, 2002). http://jbburnett.com/resources/yannaras/yannaras_rights&orth.pdf.

———. 2006. *Orthodoxy and the West: Hellenic Self-Identity in the Modern Age*. Translated by P. Chambers and N. Russell. Brookline, Mass.: Holy Cross Orthodox Press.

———. 2007. *Person and Eros*. Translated by Norman Russell. Brookline, Mass.: Holy Cross Orthodox Press.

Yoder, John Howard. 1994. *The Politics of Jesus: Vicit Agnus Noster*. Grand Rapids, Mich.: William B. Eerdmans.

Young, Frances, et al., eds. 2006. *The Cambridge History of Early Christian Literature*. Cambridge: Cambridge University Press.

Žižek, Slavoj. 2008. *For They Know Not What They Do: Enjoyment as a Political Factor*. London: Verso.

Zizioulas, John D. 1975. "Human Capacity and Human Incapacity: A Theological Exploration of Personhood." *Scottish Journal of Theology* 28: 401–48.

———. 1985. *Being as Communion: Studies in Personhood and the Church*. Crestwood, N.Y.: SVS Press.

———. 2008. *Lectures in Christian Dogmatics*. Edited by Douglas Knight. London: T&T Clark.

———. 2009. *Communion and Otherness: Further Studies in Personhood and the Church*. Edited by Paul McPartlan. London: T&T Clark.

Zuboff, Shoshana. 2019. *The Age of Surveillance Capitalism: The Fight for a Human Future at the New Frontier of Power*. London: Profile Books.

INDEX

Page numbers in italics denote an illustration. Scare quotes have been omitted from the index.

national identities, modern, 89–91, 94
nationalism, 90, 93, 105
nationalisms, Christian, 270n47
nation, chosen, 57, 78, 81–82, 117–18
nation states. *See* nations
nations, 82–83, 88–100, 107, 271n1, 274n15.
    See also state
necessity, 152, 157–68, 170, 171, 187, 190, 192,
    197, 205, 250. *See also* freedom-necessity
    dualism
negative anarchism, 9–11
neighbors, 134, 137, 194, 227
Nemanjić dynasty, 95
Neo-Eurasianism, 97
neoliberalism, 229, 236
Nestorianism, political, 105, 201
networks, social, 212, 213
new birth, 181, 207
new chosen nation, 81–82
new chosen people, 82
new creation, 13, 182, 202, 251
new existence, 162–66, 180–82, 202, 204, 241,
    244, 247, 252
New Israel, 57, 78–79, 81–82, 115, 269n17,
    269n34
New Jerusalem, 77–79
New Jerusalem monastery, Russia, 79
New Roman Empire. *See* Eastern Empire
New Rome, 73, 269n17
New Testament, 124–26, 141, 190–95, 248,
    275n2 ("Alternative . . . Political Theologies").
    *See also names of specific New Testament
    texts*
New Zion, 79, 269n34
Nicaea, Council of, 46
Nicholas I (czar, Russia), 85, 93
Nicholas II Romanov (czar, Russia), 87, 96, 97
Nikephoros Phokas, 143, 279n51
Nikon (patriarch, Moscow), 79
Nil Sorsky (Nilus of Sora), 148
nonbeing, 158, 171, 176
nonpossessors, 148
normalities, 16–17, 146, 211
normativity, 167, 248
nothingness, 159, 171, 174, 196–97
Novellae (Justinian), 55, 75
Novgorod Republic, 73–74, 79–81, 103

O'Donovan, Joan, 263n32
O'Donovan, Oliver, 263n32
Old Testament: Christian political theology
    and, 56–57, 117; democracy and, 102–3; on
    Israel, 115; political powers and, 56–57, 69–71,
    73, 77, 78, 85, 117–18, 264n32, 264n36;

state and, 78–79, 81–82. *See also* Genesis,
    Book of
Olga (great princess, Russia), 67
One Flew over the Cuckoo's Nest (Forman; film),
    292n3
ontology, Christian, 1, 170, 282n13
openness, 159, 160, 166–67
oppression, 4–5, 10–11, 15, 190, 205, 210,
    216–19, 235, 289n16
oppressiveness of individualized existence,
    215–19
order, 8, 39–40, 171, 255n2, 289n16
order, socio-political. *See* society
organization, social. *See* society
Origen of Alexandria, 130–31; *Against Celsus
    (Contra Celsum)*, 40, 260n11
Orthodox autocracy, 57, 96–97
Orthodox Christian anarchism, 1, 11–12, 21,
    105, 128, 202–3, 220–22, 231–35, 251
Orthodox Christian anthropology, 5, 208, 227
Orthodox Christianity, 5, 7–24, 104, 105, 123,
    205–6. *See also* Christianity
Orthodox democracy, 83
Orthodox diaspora, 101
Orthodox monarchy, 57, 83, 96–97, 272n19
Orthodox nations, 82–83, 89, 107, 274n15
Orthodox people, 89
Orthodox political theology. *See* political
    theology, Orthodox
Orthodox theology. *See* theology, Orthodox
Ostrogorski, Georgije, 30, 58, 145, 263n25
others, 22, 132–38, 172, 196, 225–32, 290n26
Ottoman Empire, 89

Pagels, Elaine, 127
Palihapitiya, Chamath, 288n11
Pan-Slavists, 93
papacy, 52, 60, 99, 264n35, 264n38, 265n40,
    265n45
papal ideology, 77, 113, 262n19
Papanikolaou, Aristotle, 104, 105
Papathanasiou, Athanasios, 106
Parker, Sean, 288n11
parousia, 192
Path to the Apocalypse, The (Vorobievsky), 97,
    272n21
patriarchate, 72, 75, 84, 107, 267n61, 270n45.
    See also power structures, ecclesial
patriarchs, 33, 52, 56, 57, 61, 63–65, 83–84,
    267n61. *See also* powers, ecclesial
patriotism, 107, 130, 277n19
patristic theology, 161, 172, 282n8, 284n4
Paul (apostle), 35–36, 141, 152, 177, 187, 194–95
Paul (czar, Russia), 85, 270n54

DAVOR DŽALTO is Professor of Religion and Democracy in the Department of Eastern Christian Studies at Stockholm School of Theology, and president of The Institute for the Study of Culture and Christianity. He is the author and editor of numerous books, including *The Human Work of Art, Religion and Realism*, and *Yugoslavia: Peace, War, and Dissolution* (by Noam Chomsky).

ORTHODOX CHRISTIANITY AND CONTEMPORARY THOUGHT

Aristotle Papanikolaou and Ashley M. Purpura, series editors

Christina M. Gschwandtner, *Welcoming Finitude: Toward a Phenomenology of Orthodox Liturgy*

Pia Sophia Chaudhari, *Dynamis of Healing: Patristic Theology and the Psyche*

Brian A. Butcher, *Liturgical Theology after Schmemann: An Orthodox Reading of Paul Ricoeur*. Foreword by Andrew Louth.

Ashley M. Purpura, *God, Hierarchy, and Power: Orthodox Theologies of Authority from Byzantium*.

George E. Demacopoulos, *Colonizing Christianity: Greek and Latin Religious Identity in the Era of the Fourth Crusade*.

George E. Demacopoulos and Aristotle Papanikolaou (eds.), *Orthodox Constructions of the West*.

John Chryssavgis and Bruce V. Foltz (eds.), *Toward an Ecology of Transfiguration: Orthodox Christian Perspectives on Environment, Nature, and Creation*. Foreword by Bill McKibben. Prefatory Letter by Ecumenical Patriarch Bartholomew.

Aristotle Papanikolaou and George E. Demacopoulos (eds.), *Orthodox Readings of Augustine*.

Lucian N. Leustean (ed.), *Orthodox Christianity and Nationalism in Nineteenth-Century Southeastern Europe.*

John Chryssavgis (ed.), *Dialogue of Love: Breaking the Silence of Centuries.* Contributions by Brian E. Daley, S.J., and Georges Florovsky.

George E. Demacopoulos and Aristotle Papanikolaou (eds.), *Christianity, Democracy, and the Shadow of Constantine.*

Aristotle Papanikolaou and George E. Demacopoulos (eds.), *Fundamentalism or Tradition: Christianity after Secularism*

Georgia Frank, Susan R. Holman, and Andrew S. Jacobs (eds.), *The Garb of Being: Embodiment and the Pursuit of Holiness in Late Ancient Christianity*

Ecumenical Patriarch Bartholomew, *In the World, Yet Not of the World: Social and Global Initiatives of Ecumenical Patriarch Bartholomew.* Edited by John Chryssavgis. Foreword by Jose Manuel Barroso.

Ecumenical Patriarch Bartholomew, *Speaking the Truth in Love: Theological and Spiritual Exhortations of Ecumenical Patriarch Bartholomew.* Edited by John Chryssavgis. Foreword by Dr. Rowan Williams, Archbishop of Canterbury.

Ecumenical Patriarch Bartholomew, *On Earth as in Heaven: Ecological Vision and Initiatives of Ecumenical Patriarch Bartholomew.* Edited by John Chryssavgis. Foreword by His Royal Highness, the Duke of Edinburgh.

Davor Džalto, *Anarchy and the Kingdom of God: From Eschatology to Orthodox Political Theology and Back.*

www.ingramcontent.com/pod-product-compliance
Lightning Source LLC
Chambersburg PA
CBHW022136020426
42334CB00015B/921